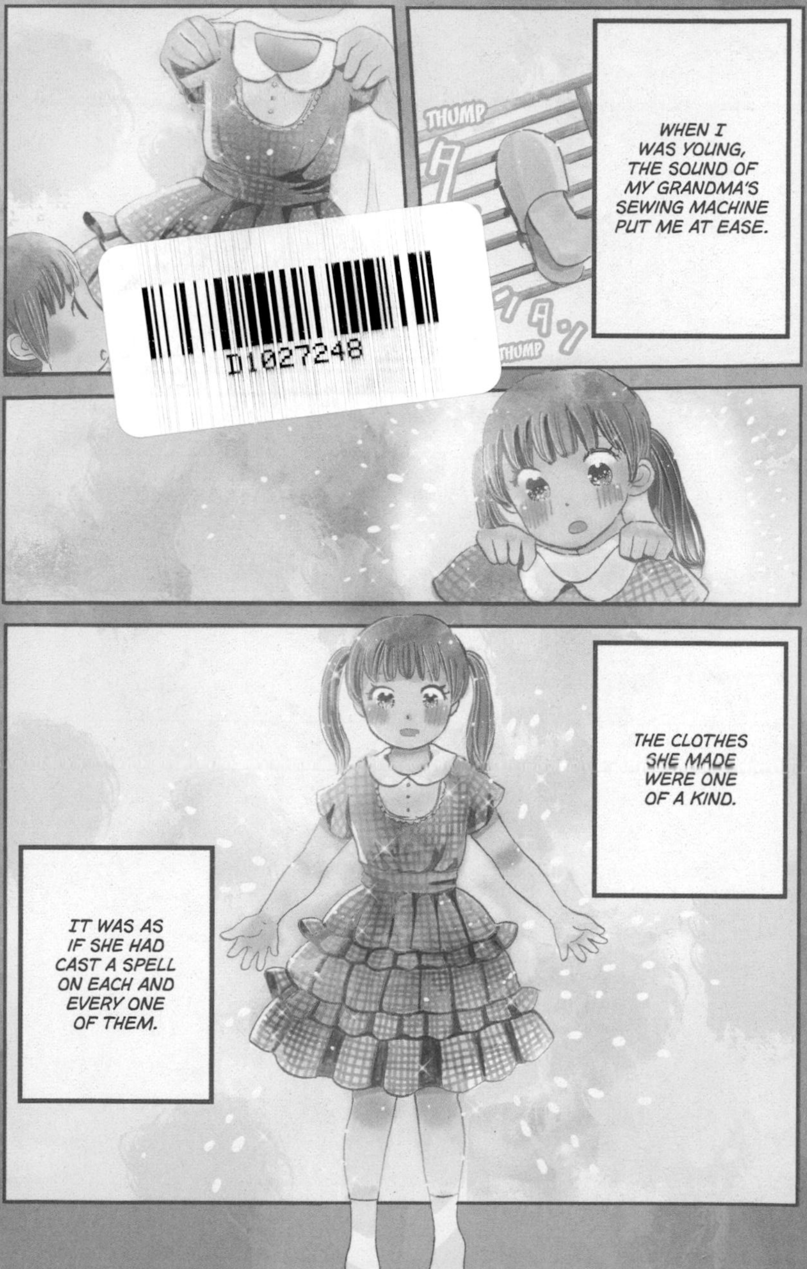
THUMP
WHEN I WAS YOUNG, THE SOUND OF MY GRANDMA'S SEWING MACHINE PUT ME AT EASE.
THUMP
THE CLOTHES SHE MADE WERE ONE OF A KIND.
IT WAS AS IF SHE HAD CAST A SPELL ON EACH AND EVERY ONE OF THEM.

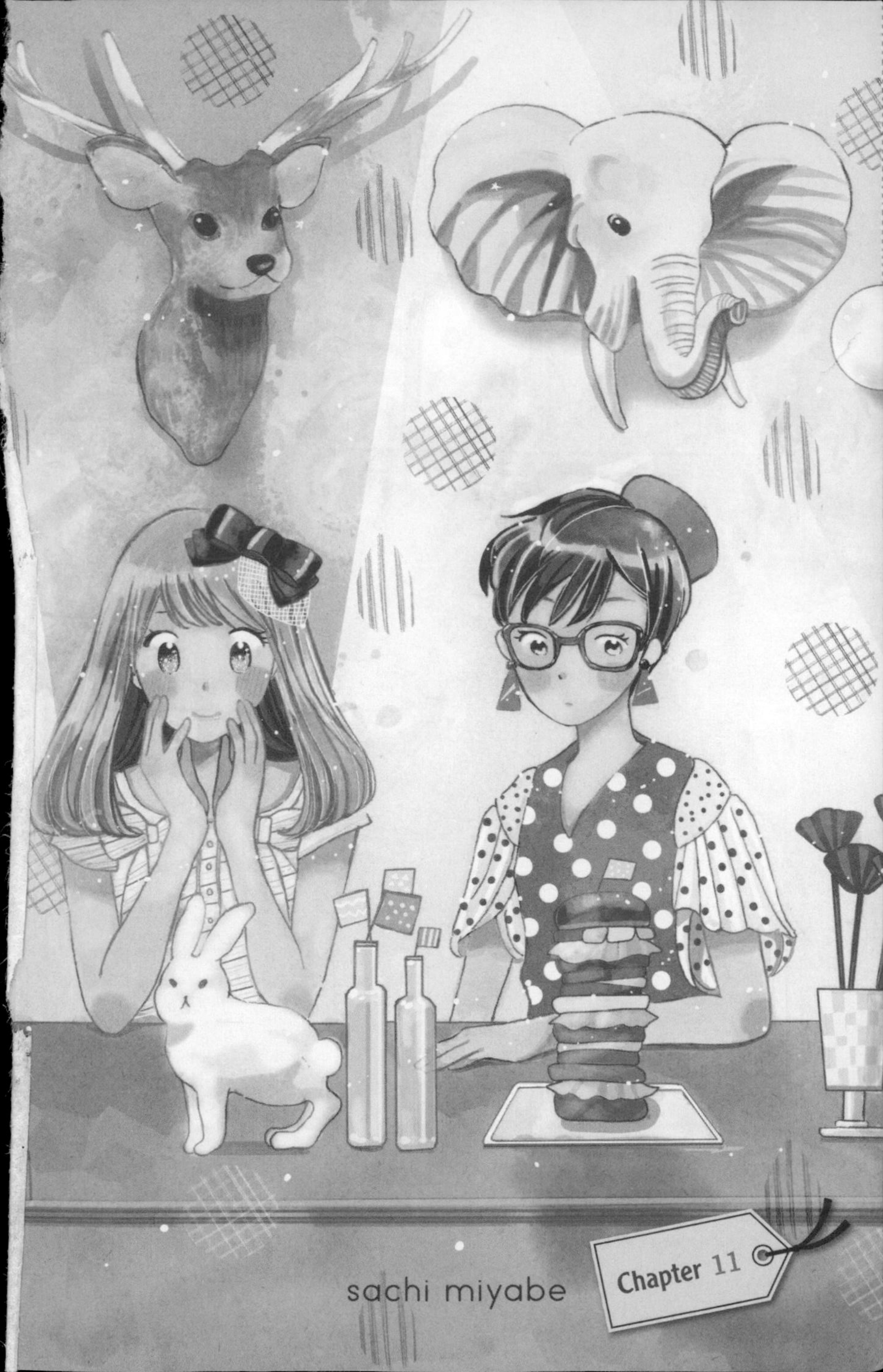
Chapter 11
sachi miyabe

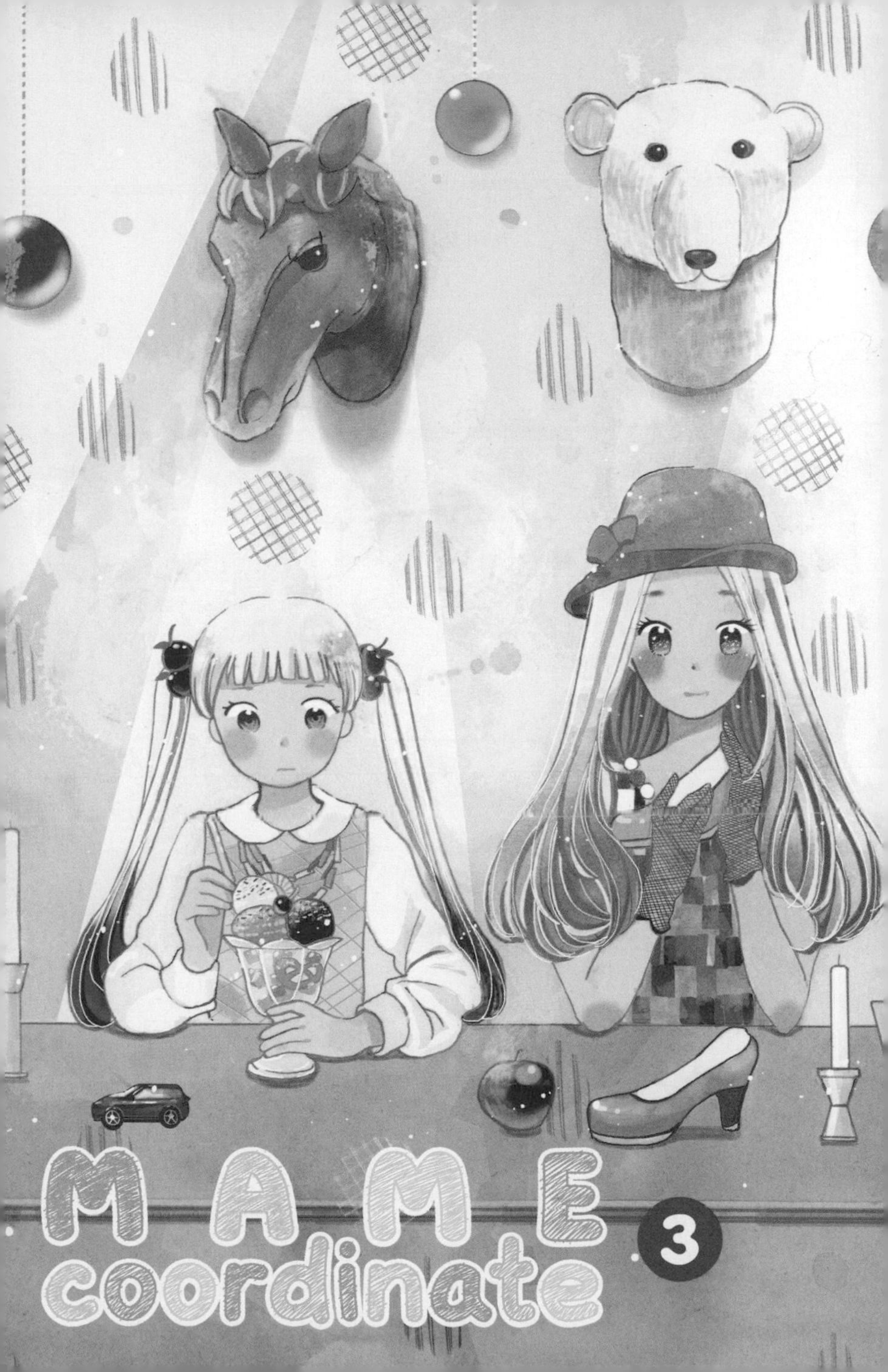
MAME
coordinate
3

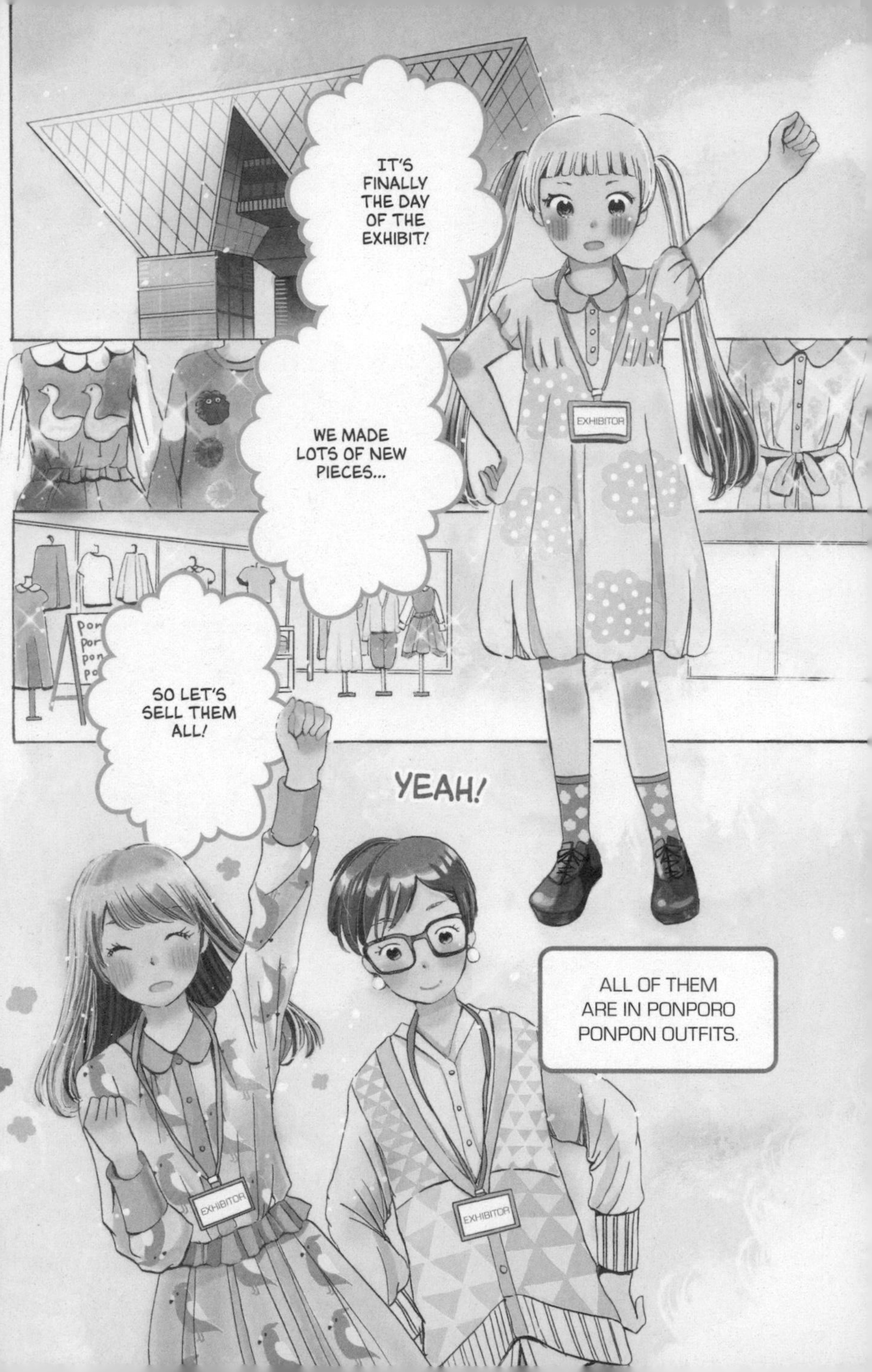
IT'S FINALLY THE DAY OF THE EXHIBIT!
WE MADE LOTS OF NEW PIECES...
SO LET'S SELL THEM ALL!
EXHIBITOR
YEAH!
ALL OF THEM ARE IN PONPORO PONPON OUTFITS.
EXHIBITOR
EXHIBITOR

Contents

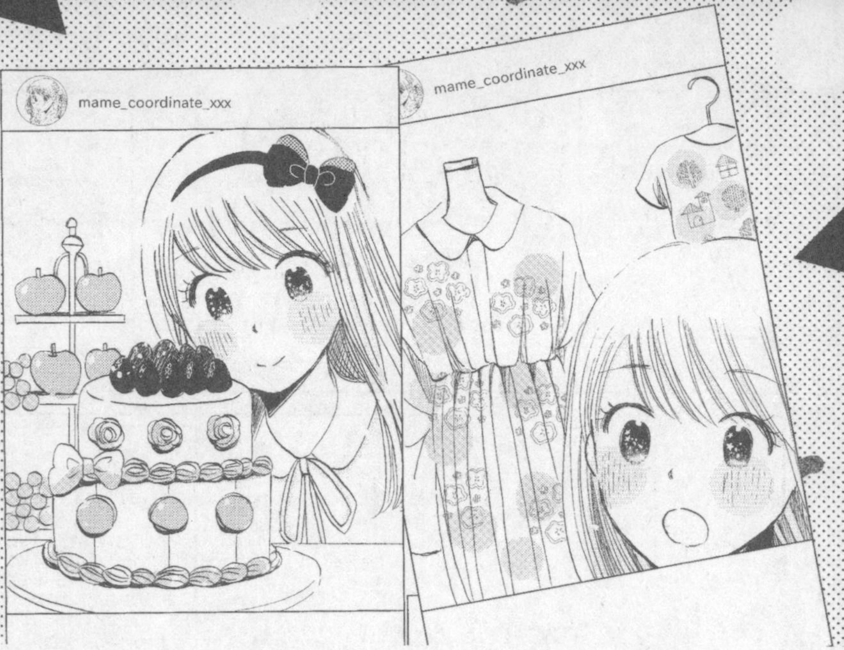
mame_coordinate_xxx
mame_coordinate_xxx

MAME coordinate 3

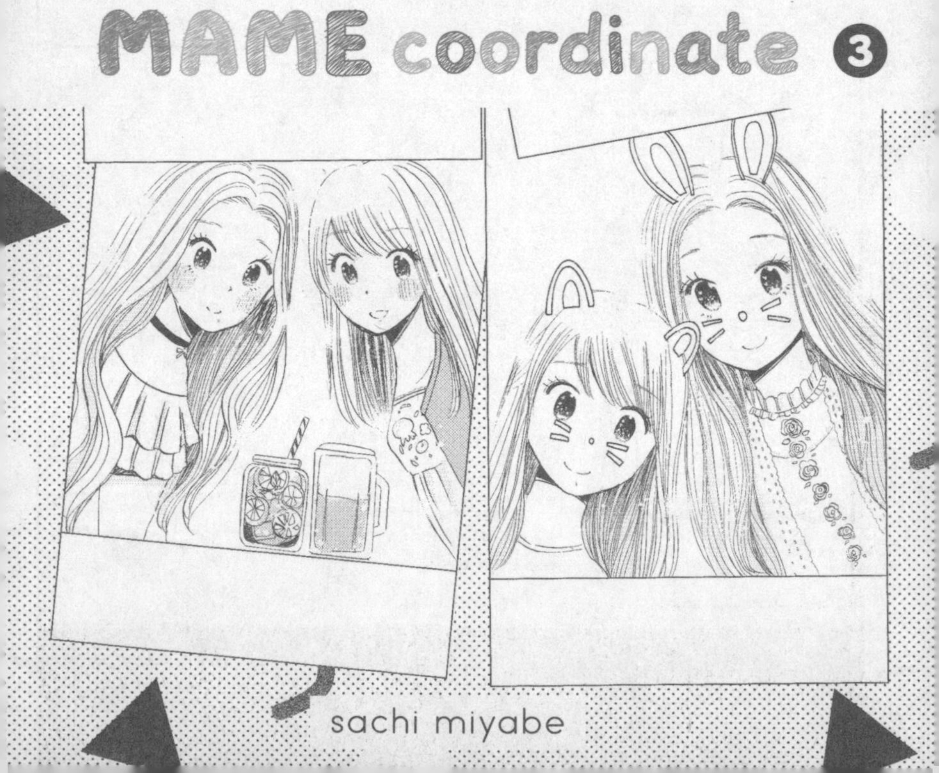

sachi miyabe

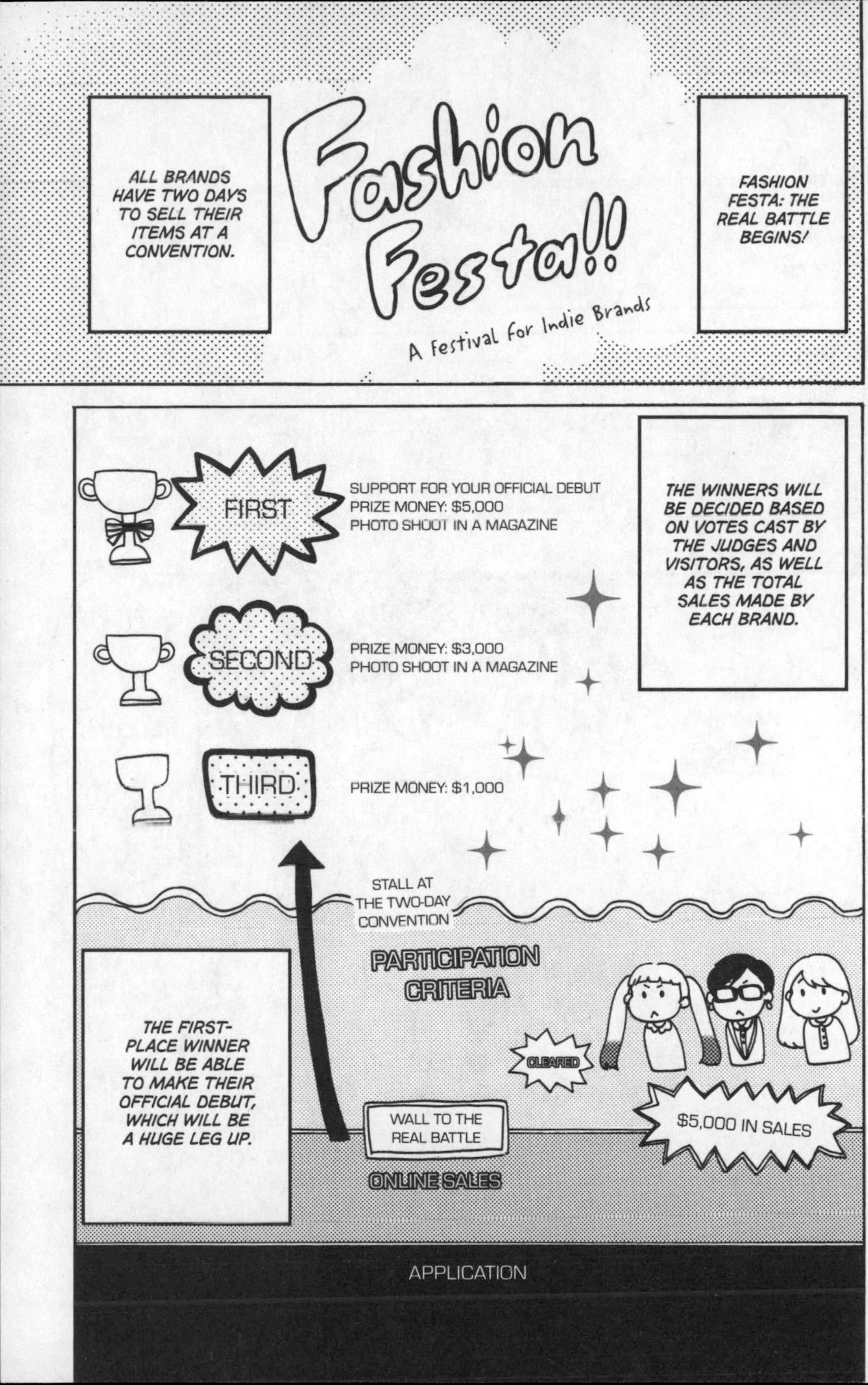

FASHION FESTA: THE REAL BATTLE BEGINS!
Fashion Festa!!
A Festival for Indie Brands
ALL BRANDS HAVE TWO DAYS TO SELL THEIR ITEMS AT A CONVENTION.
THE WINNERS WILL BE DECIDED BASED ON VOTES CAST BY THE JUDGES AND VISITORS, AS WELL AS THE TOTAL SALES MADE BY EACH BRAND.
SUPPORT FOR YOUR OFFICIAL DEBUT
PRIZE MONEY: $5,000
PHOTO SHOOT IN A MAGAZINE
FIRST
PRIZE MONEY: $3,000
PHOTO SHOOT IN A MAGAZINE
SECOND
PRIZE MONEY: $1,000
THIRD
STALL AT THE TWO-DAY CONVENTION
PARTICIPATION CRITERIA
CLEARED
$5,000 IN SALES
WALL TO THE REAL BATTLE
ONLINE SALES
APPLICATION
THE FIRST-PLACE WINNER WILL BE ABLE TO MAKE THEIR OFFICIAL DEBUT, WHICH WILL BE A HUGE LEG UP.

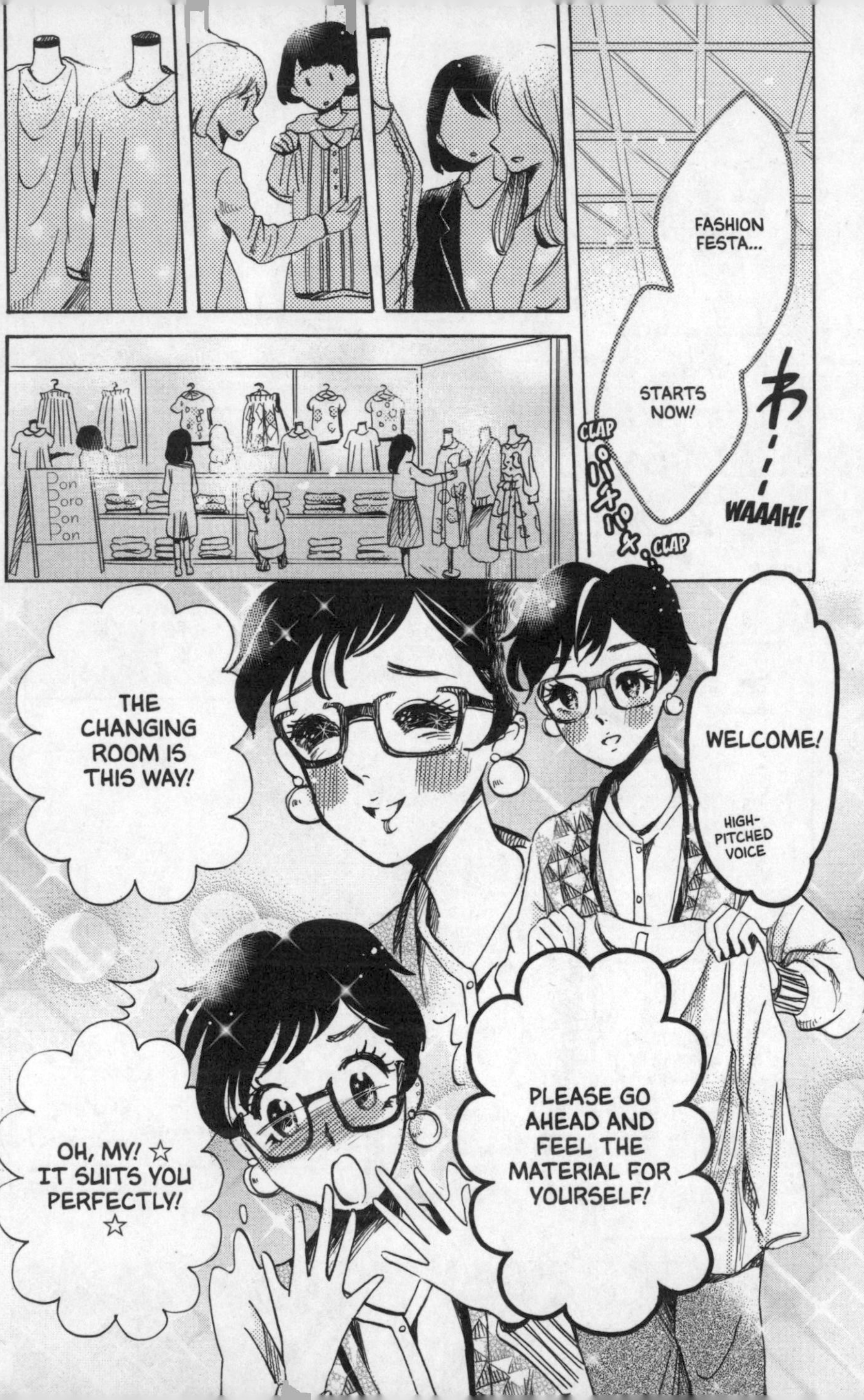
FASHION FESTA...
STARTS NOW!
WAAAH!
CLAP
CLAP
WELCOME!
HIGH-PITCHED VOICE
THE CHANGING ROOM IS THIS WAY!
PLEASE GO AHEAD AND FEEL THE MATERIAL FOR YOURSELF!
OH, MY! ☆ IT SUITS YOU PERFECTLY! ☆

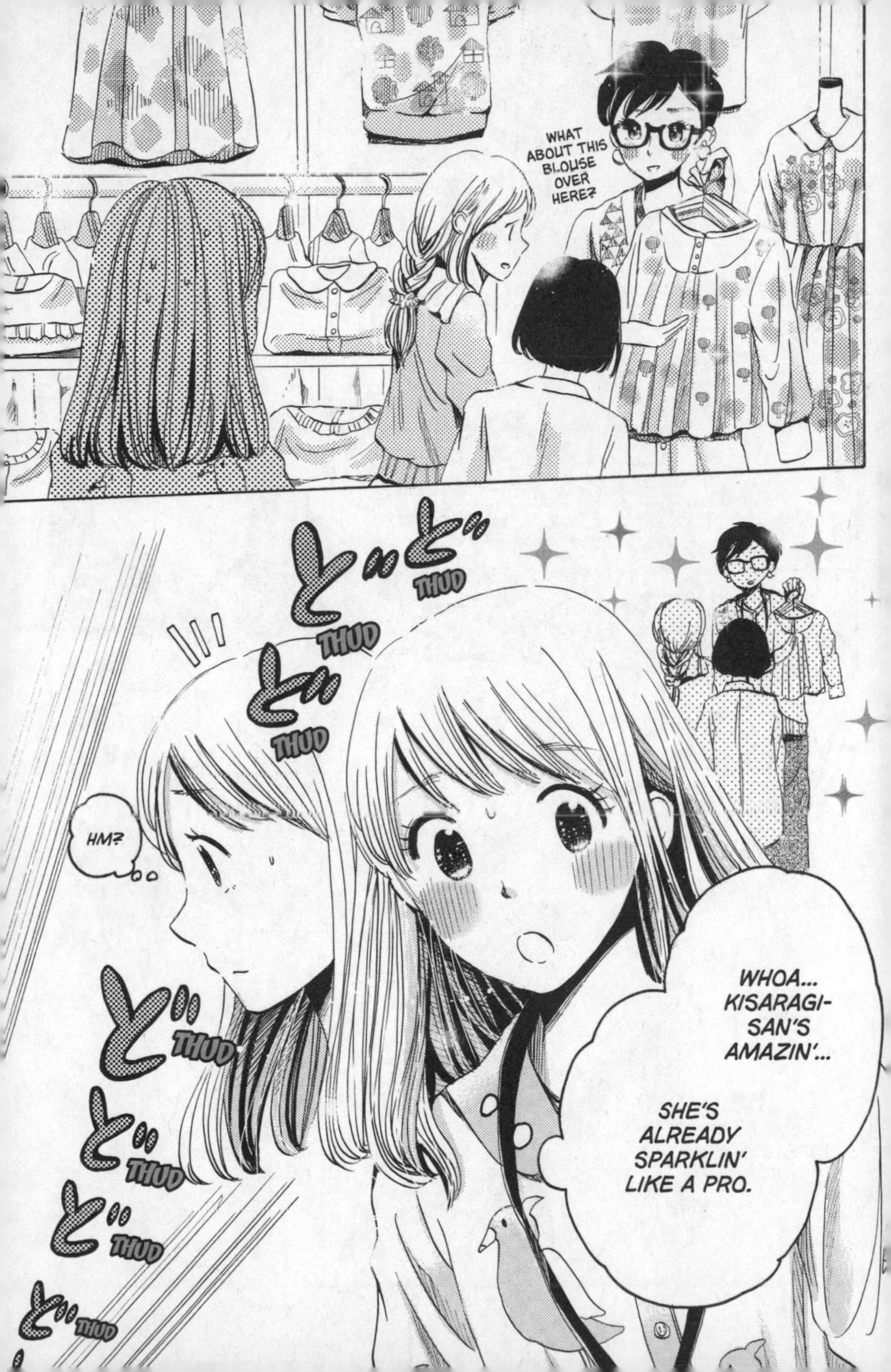
WHAT ABOUT THIS BLOUSE OVER HERE?
どっど THUD
どっ THUD
HM?
WHOA... KISARAGI-SAN'S AMAZIN'...
SHE'S ALREADY SPARKLIN' LIKE A PRO.
ど THUD
ど THUD
ど THUD
ど THUD

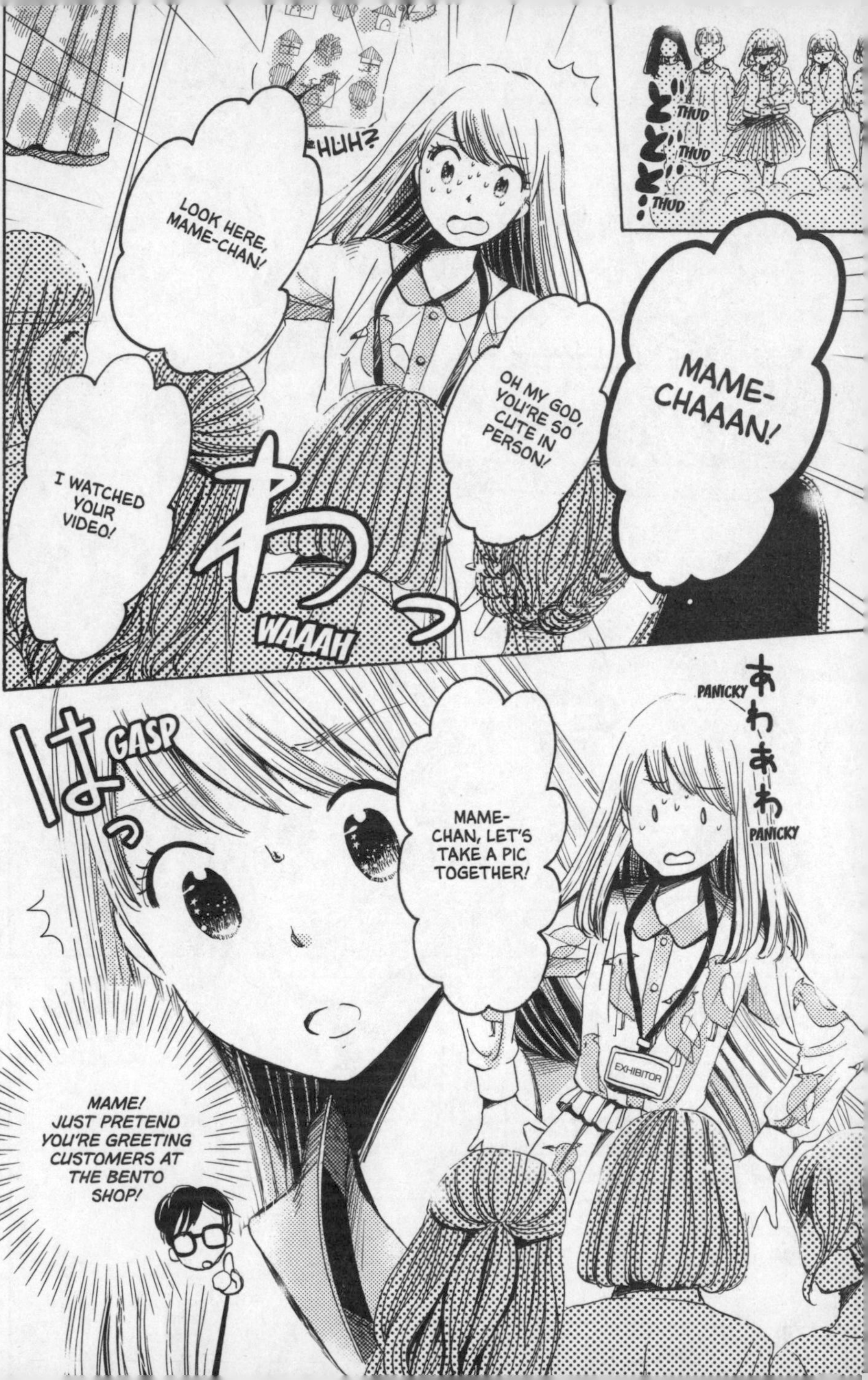
どどど
THUD
THUD
THUD
MAME-CHAAAN!
OH MY GOD, YOU'RE SO CUTE IN PERSON!
HUH?
LOOK HERE, MAME-CHAN!
I WATCHED YOUR VIDEO!
わっ
WAAAH
あわあわ
PANICKY
PANICKY
MAME-CHAN, LET'S TAKE A PIC TOGETHER!
はっ
GASP
EXHIBITOR
MAME! JUST PRETEND YOU'RE GREETING CUSTOMERS AT THE BENTO SHOP!

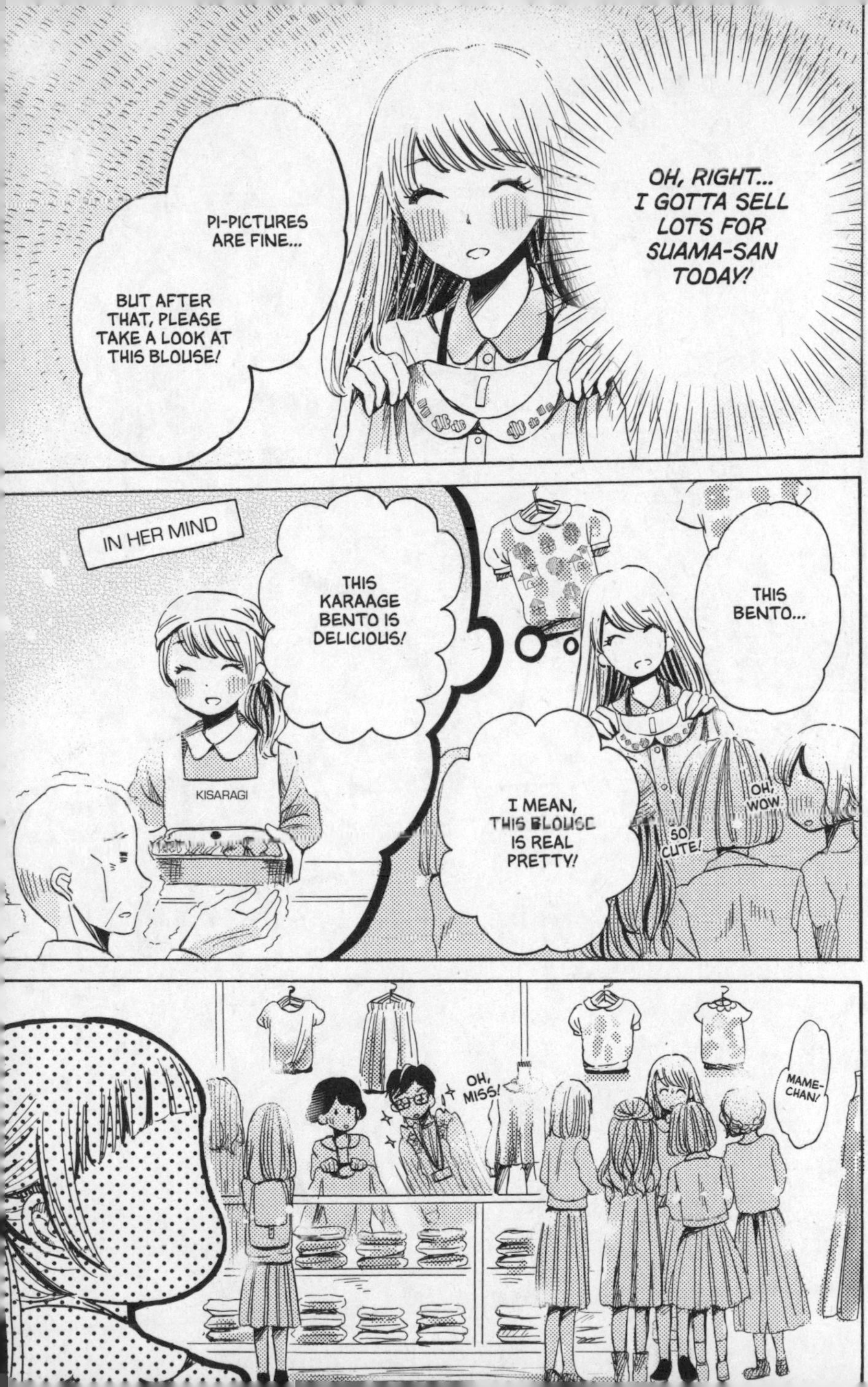
OH, RIGHT... I GOTTA SELL LOTS FOR SUAMA-SAN TODAY!
PI-PICTURES ARE FINE...
BUT AFTER THAT, PLEASE TAKE A LOOK AT THIS BLOUSE!
THIS BENTO...
OH, WOW
SO CUTE!
I MEAN, THIS BLOUSE IS REAL PRETTY!
IN HER MIND
THIS KARAAGE BENTO IS DELICIOUS!
KISARAGI
MAME-CHAN!
OH, MISS!

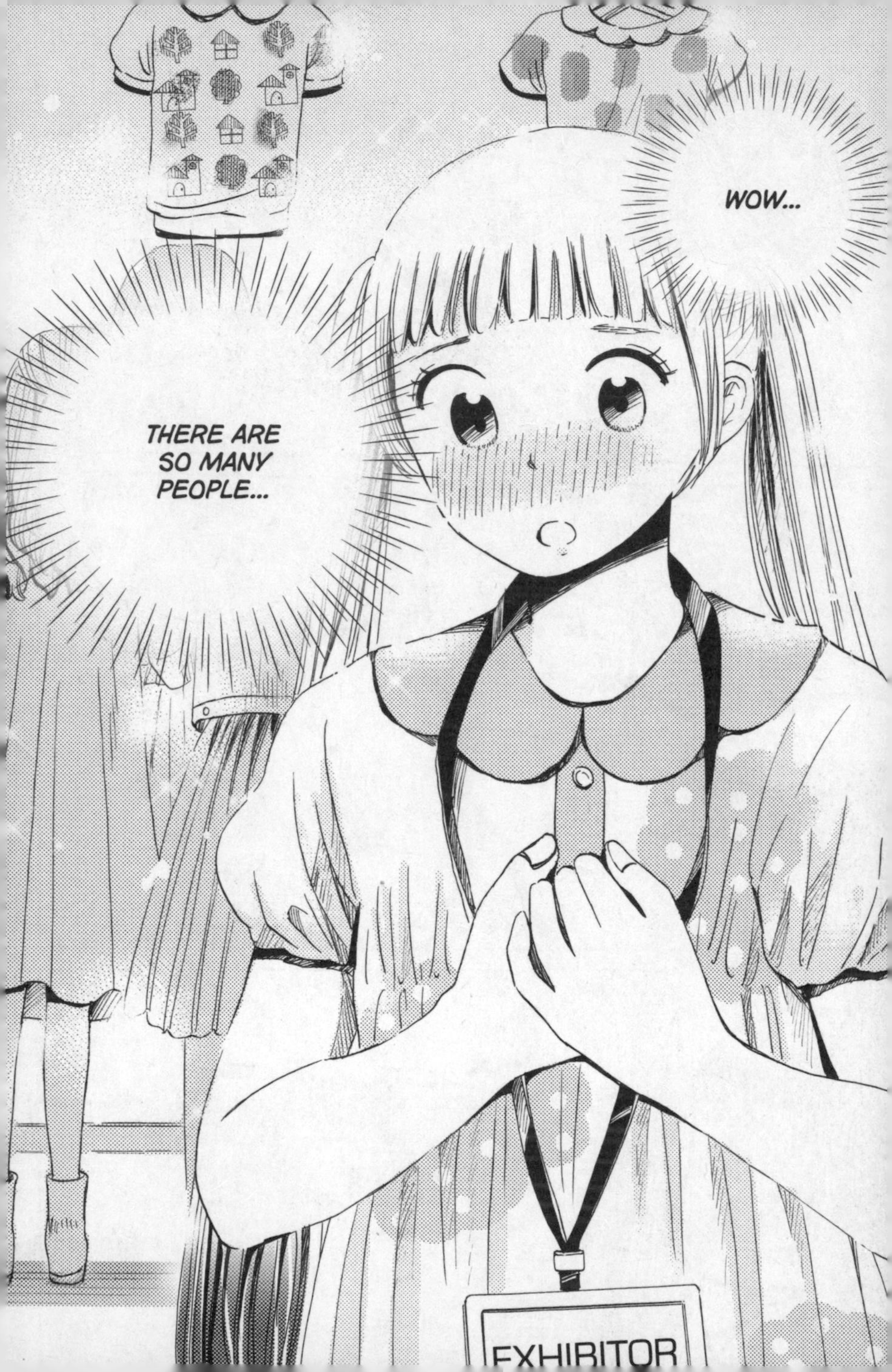
WOW...
THERE ARE SO MANY PEOPLE...
EXHIBITOR

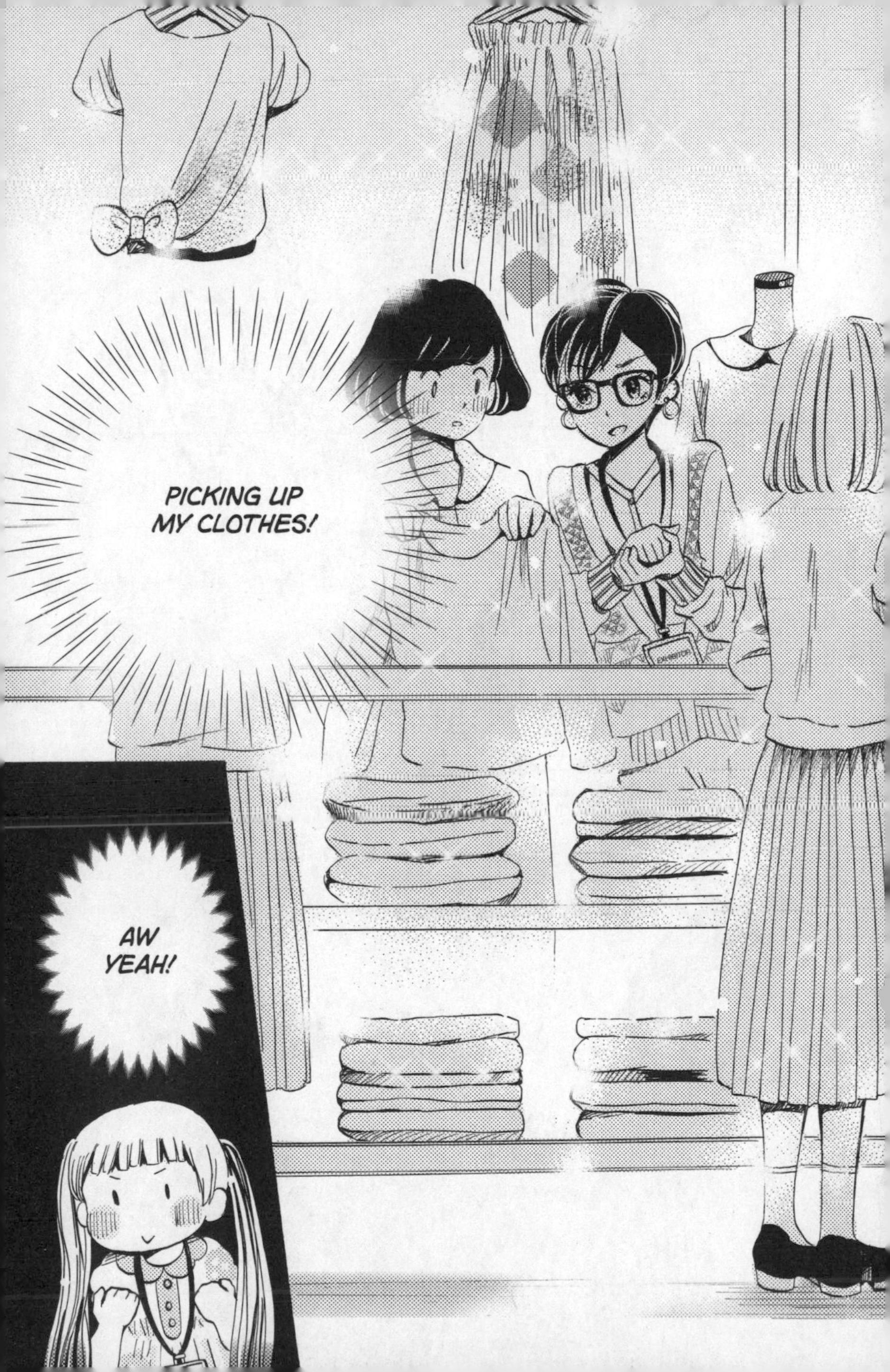
PICKING UP MY CLOTHES!
AW YEAH!

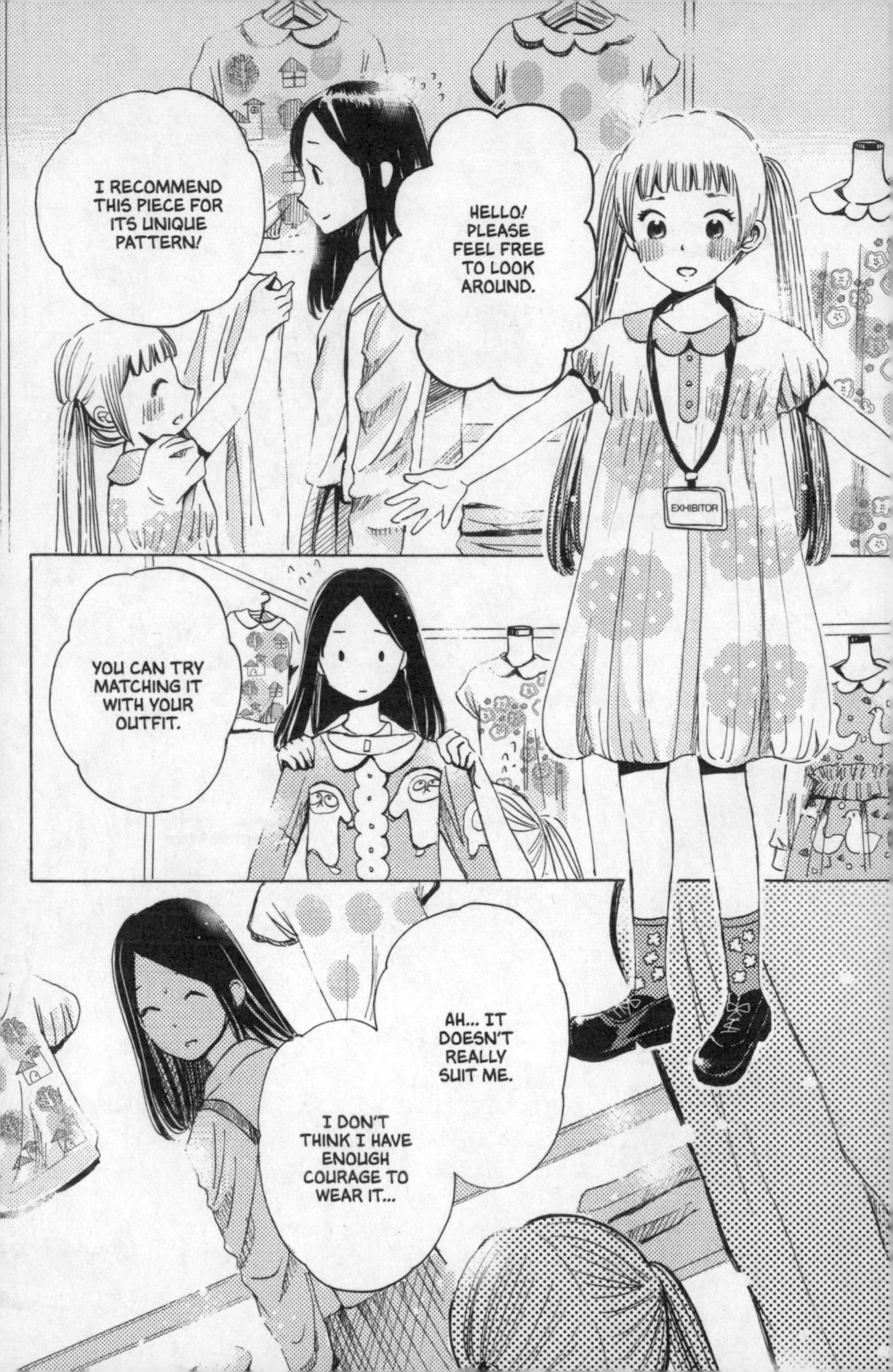
HELLO! PLEASE FEEL FREE TO LOOK AROUND.
EXHIBITOR
I RECOMMEND THIS PIECE FOR ITS UNIQUE PATTERN!
YOU CAN TRY MATCHING IT WITH YOUR OUTFIT.
AH... IT DOESN'T REALLY SUIT ME.
I DON'T THINK I HAVE ENOUGH COURAGE TO WEAR IT...

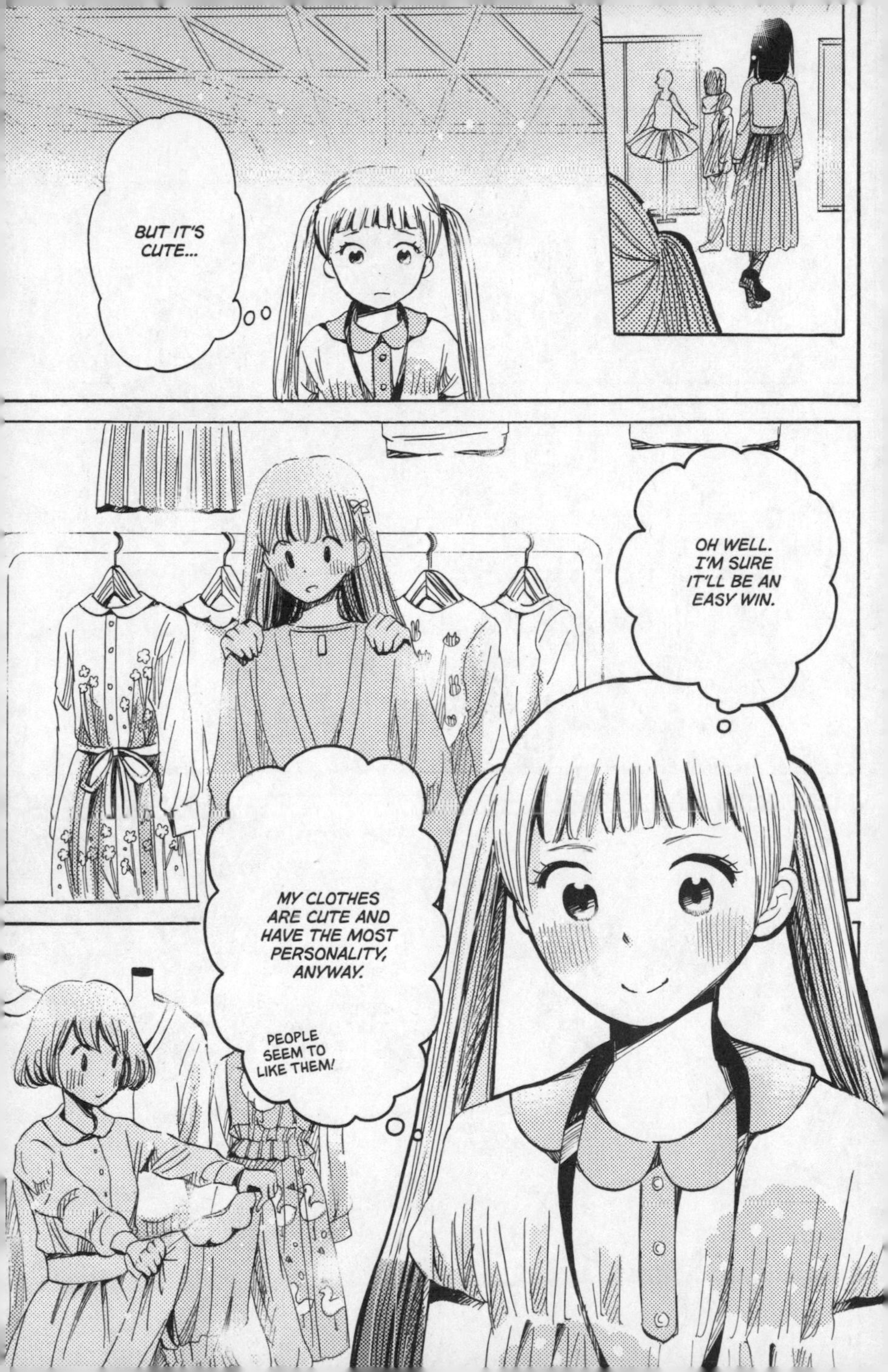
BUT IT'S CUTE...
OH WELL. I'M SURE IT'LL BE AN EASY WIN.
MY CLOTHES ARE CUTE AND HAVE THE MOST PERSONALITY, ANYWAY.
PEOPLE SEEM TO LIKE THEM!

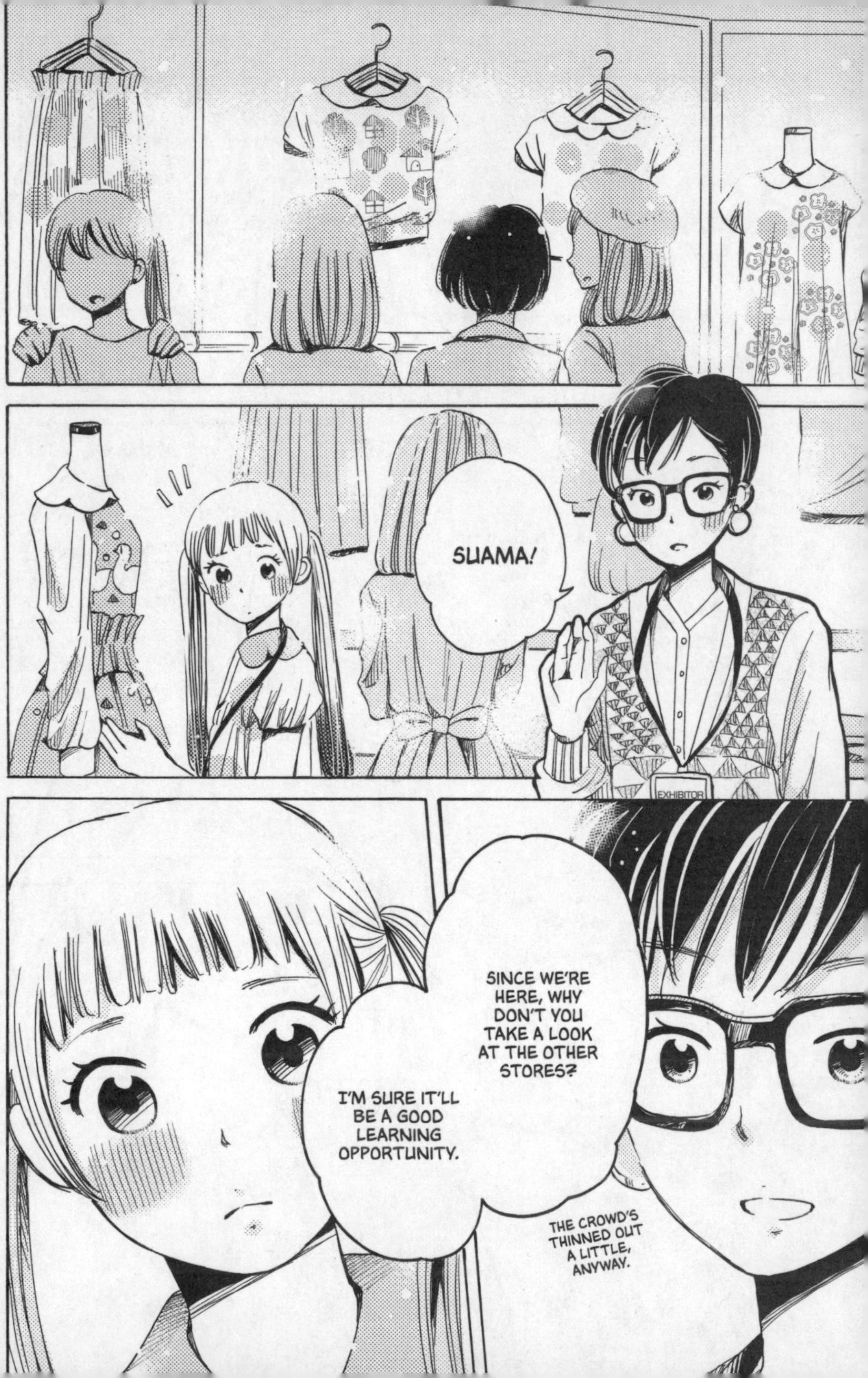
SUAMA!
EXHIBITOR
SINCE WE'RE HERE, WHY DON'T YOU TAKE A LOOK AT THE OTHER STORES?
I'M SURE IT'LL BE A GOOD LEARNING OPPORTUNITY.
THE CROWD'S THINNED OUT A LITTLE, ANYWAY.

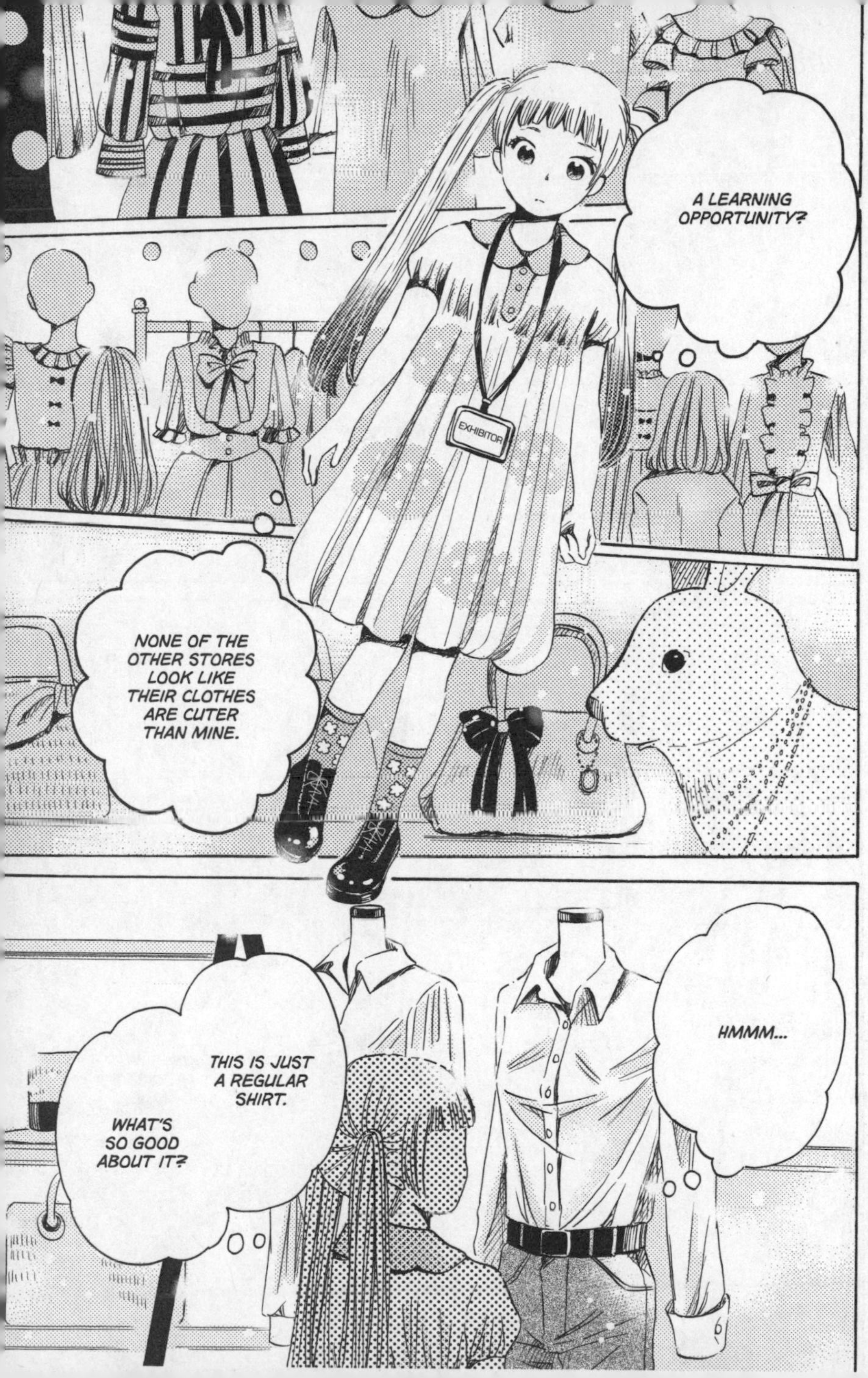
A LEARNING OPPORTUNITY?
EXHIBITOR
NONE OF THE OTHER STORES LOOK LIKE THEIR CLOTHES ARE CUTER THAN MINE.
HMMM...
THIS IS JUST A REGULAR SHIRT.
WHAT'S SO GOOD ABOUT IT?

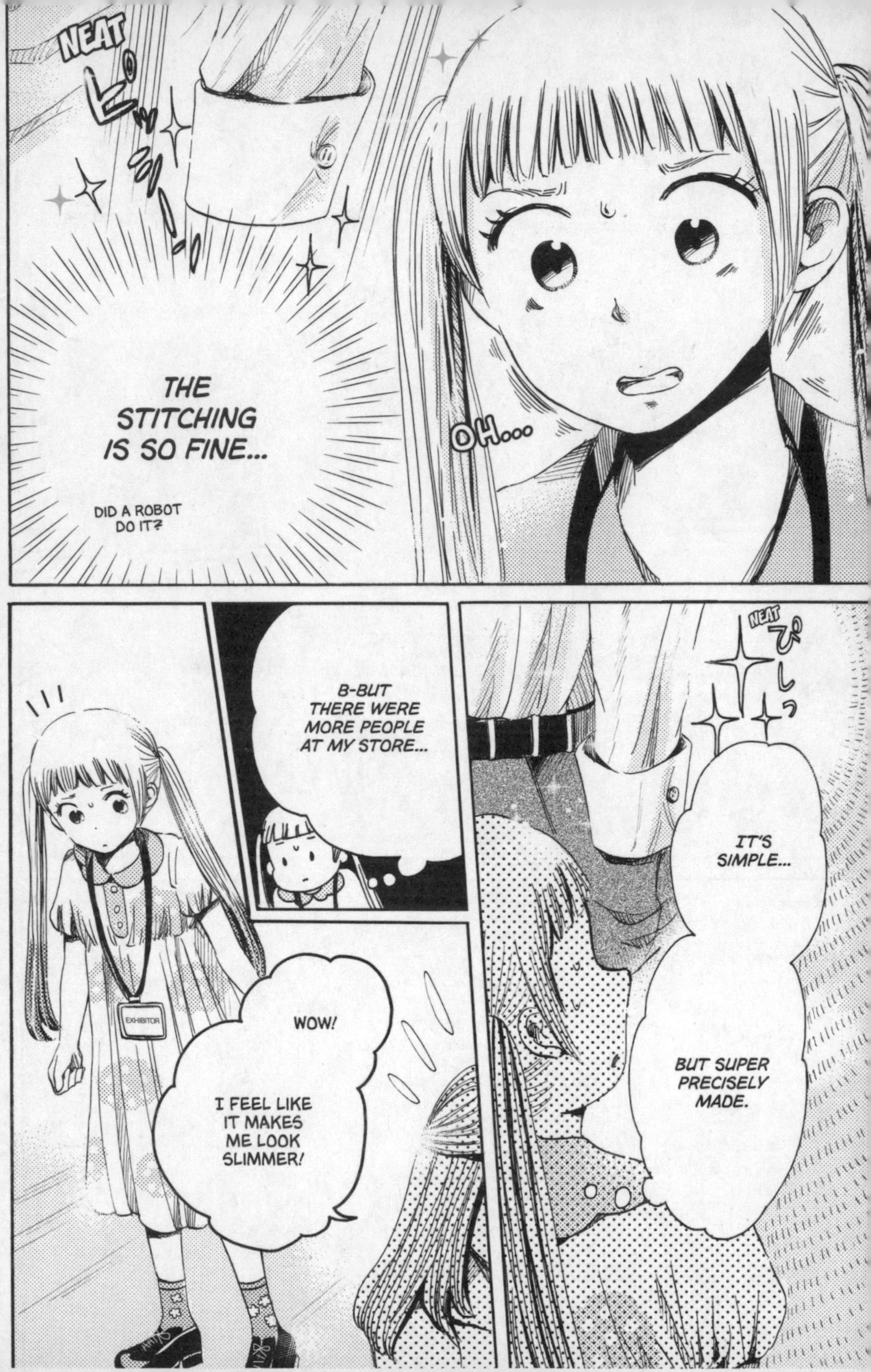
NEAT
THE STITCHING IS SO FINE...
DID A ROBOT DO IT?
OH...
NEAT
ぴしっ
IT'S SIMPLE...
BUT SUPER PRECISELY MADE.
B-BUT THERE WERE MORE PEOPLE AT MY STORE...
WOW!
I FEEL LIKE IT MAKES ME LOOK SLIMMER!
EXHIBITOR

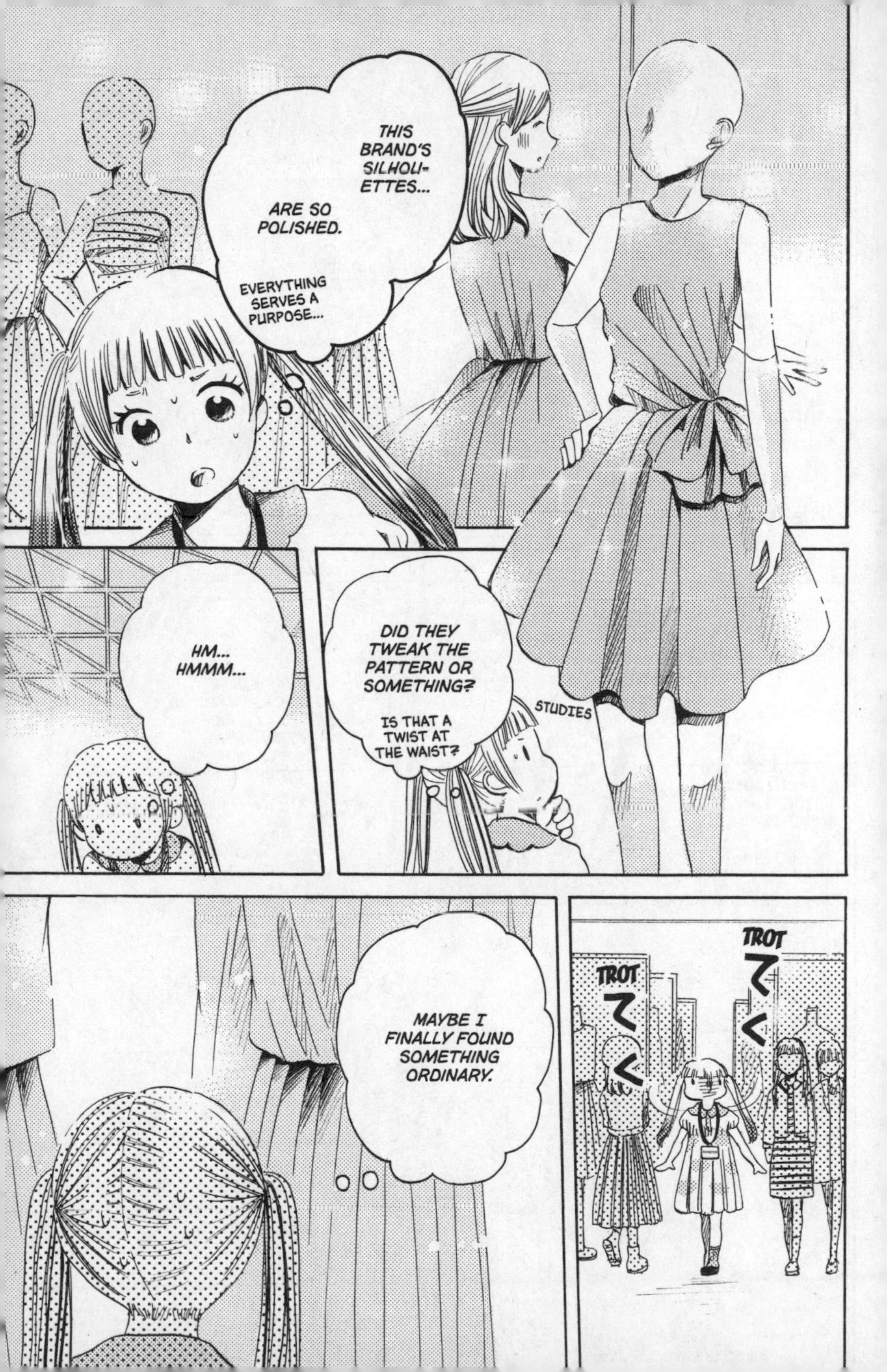
THIS BRAND'S SILHOUETTES...
ARE SO POLISHED.
EVERYTHING SERVES A PURPOSE...
DID THEY TWEAK THE PATTERN OR SOMETHING?
STUDIES
IS THAT A TWIST AT THE WAIST?
HM... HMMM...
TROT
てく
TROT
てく
MAYBE I FINALLY FOUND SOMETHING ORDINARY.

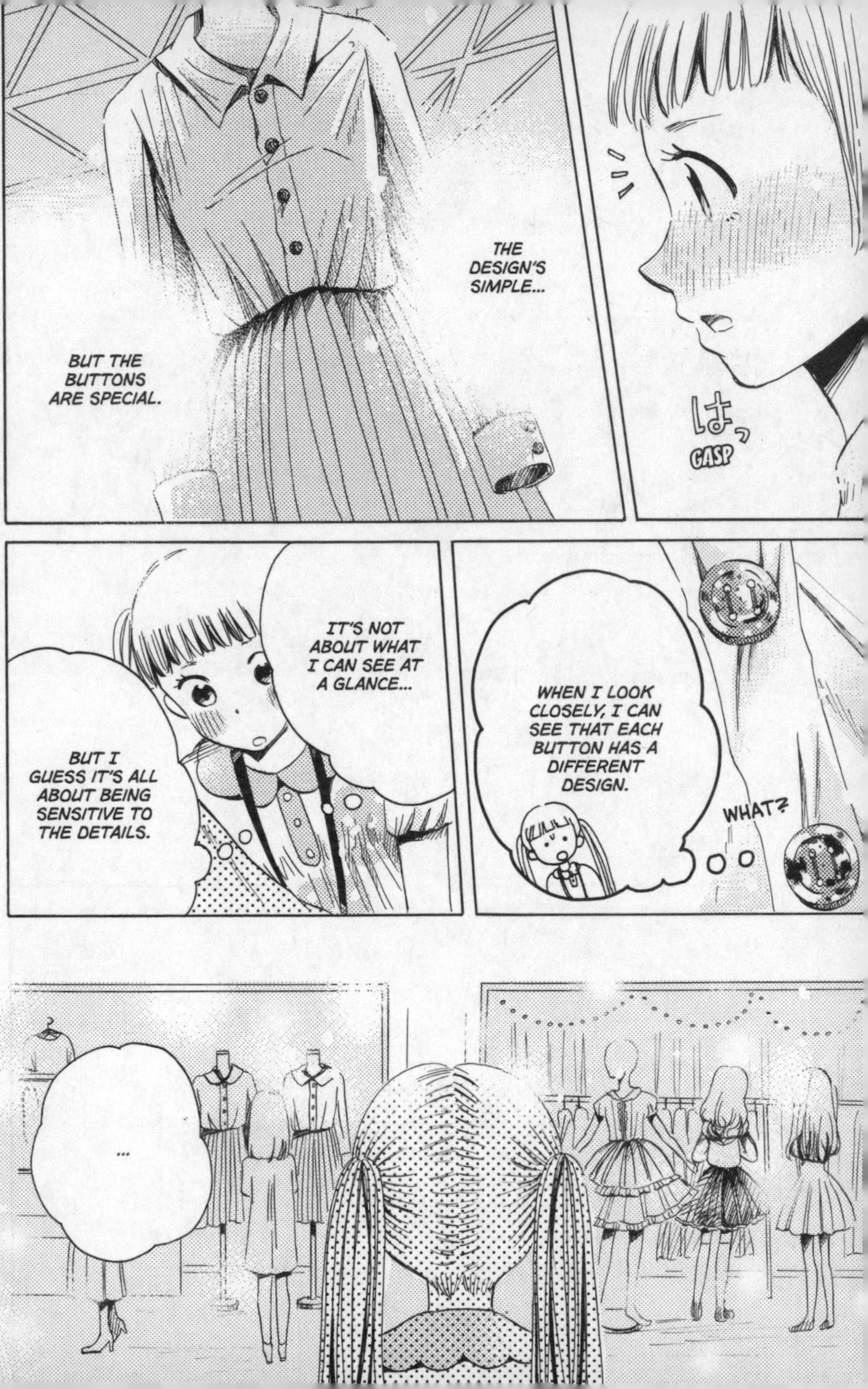

はっ
GASP
THE DESIGN'S SIMPLE...
BUT THE BUTTONS ARE SPECIAL.
WHEN I LOOK CLOSELY, I CAN SEE THAT EACH BUTTON HAS A DIFFERENT DESIGN.
WHAT?
IT'S NOT ABOUT WHAT I CAN SEE AT A GLANCE...
BUT I GUESS IT'S ALL ABOUT BEING SENSITIVE TO THE DETAILS.
...

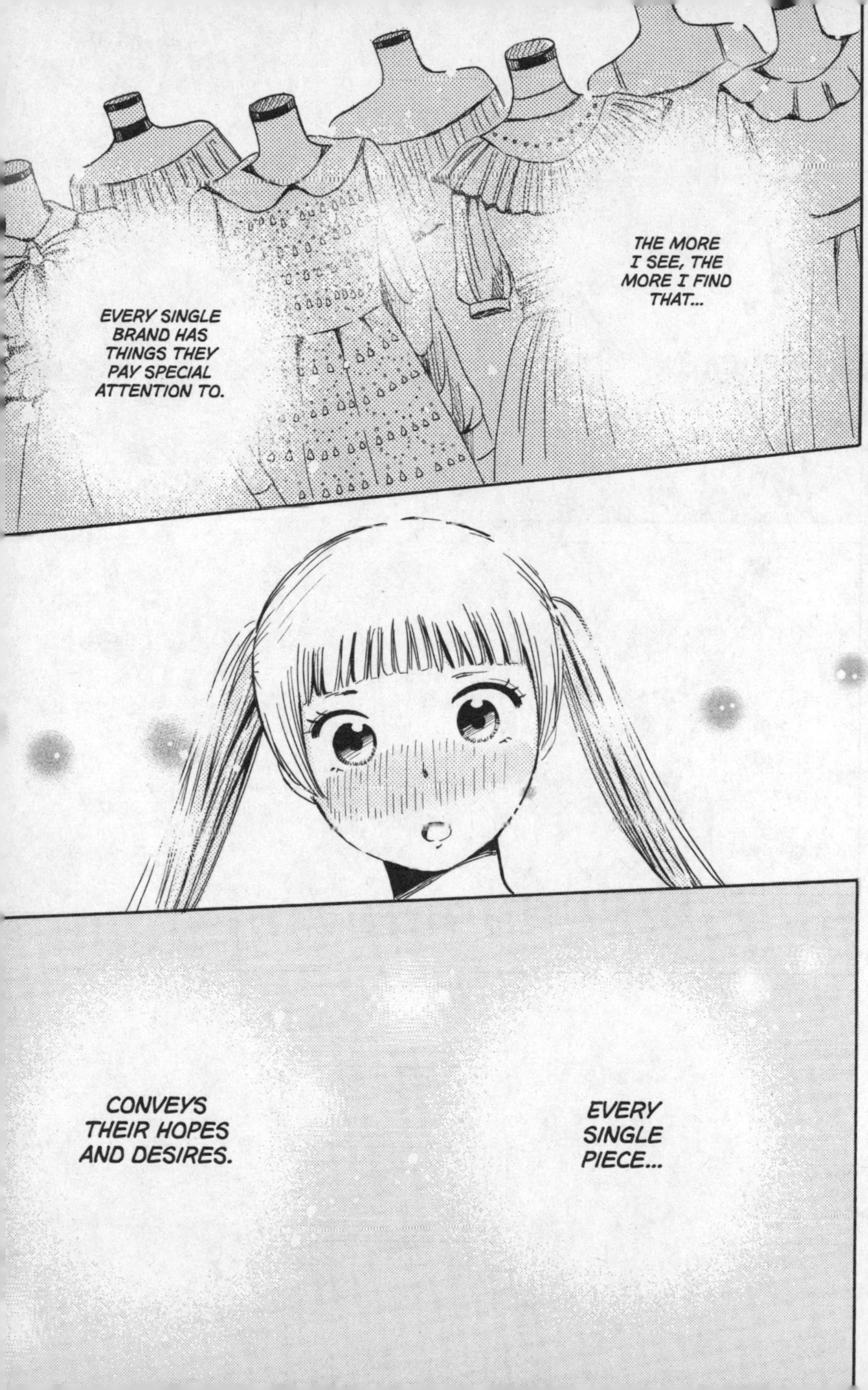
THE MORE I SEE, THE MORE I FIND THAT...
EVERY SINGLE BRAND HAS THINGS THEY PAY SPECIAL ATTENTION TO.
EVERY SINGLE PIECE...
CONVEYS THEIR HOPES AND DESIRES.

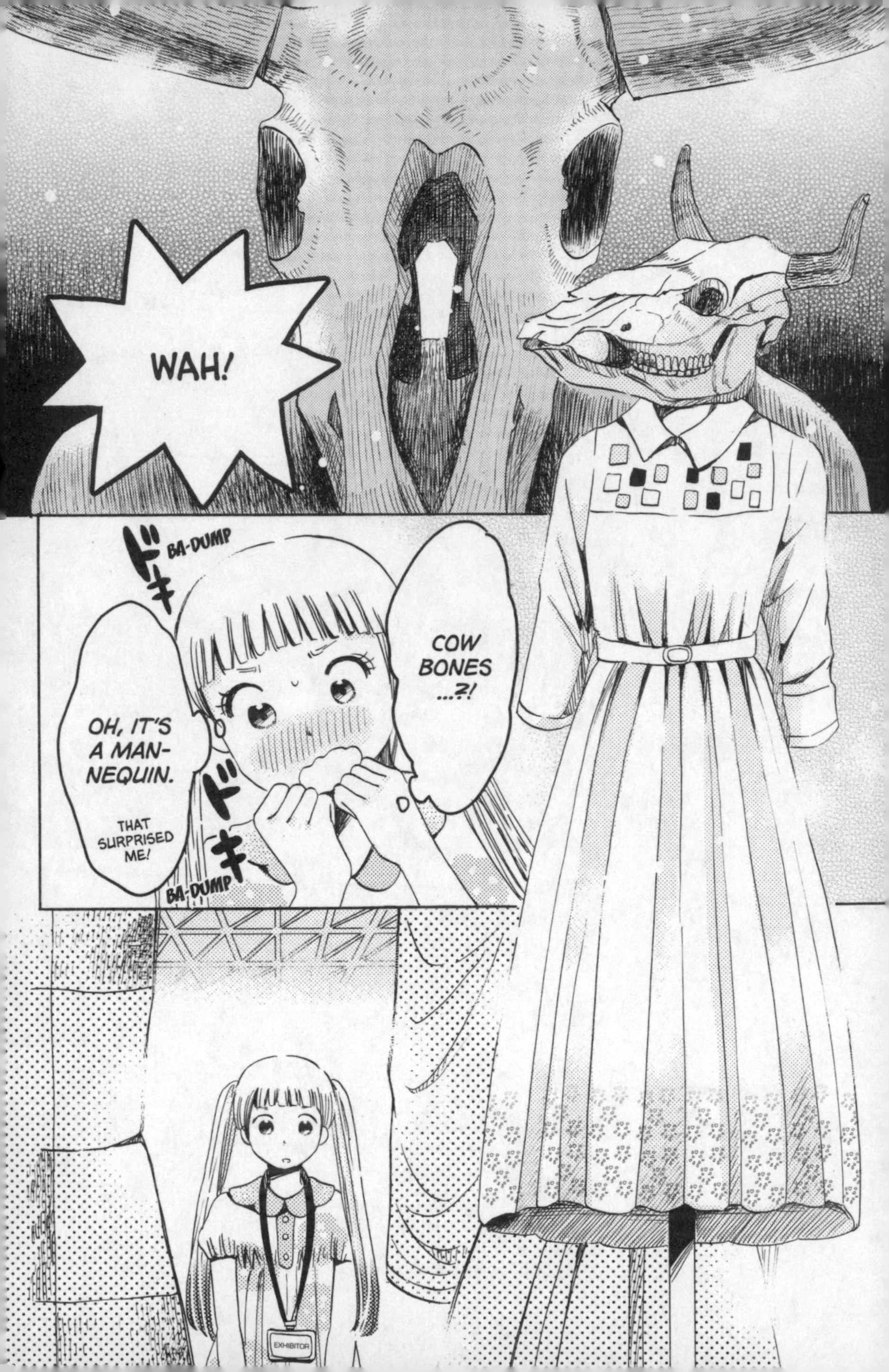
WAH!
COW BONES ...?!
ドキ
BA-DUMP
OH, IT'S A MAN-NEQUIN.
THAT SURPRISED ME!
ドキ
BA-DUMP
EXHIBITOR

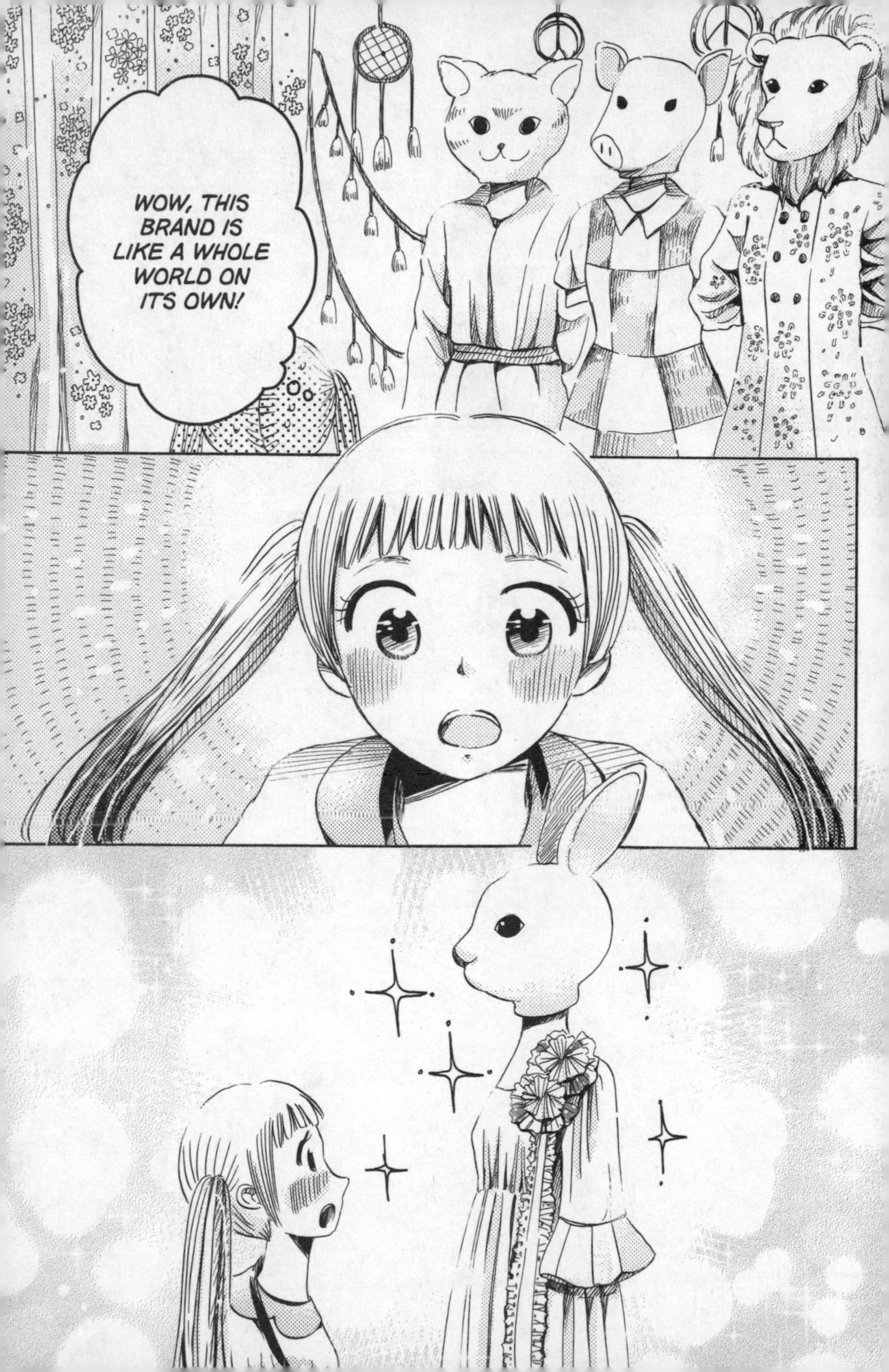
WOW, THIS BRAND IS LIKE A WHOLE WORLD ON ITS OWN!

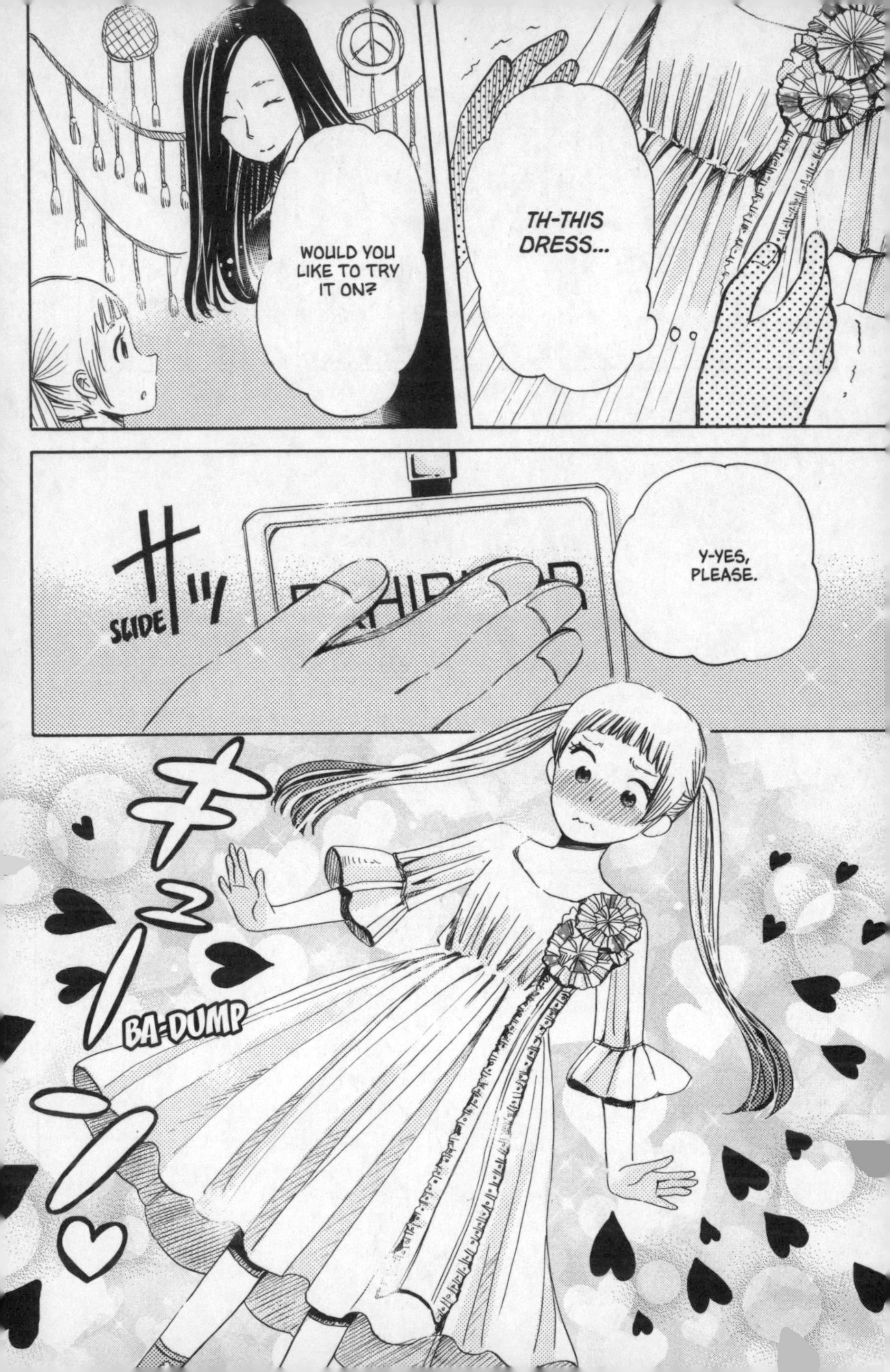
TH-THIS DRESS...
WOULD YOU LIKE TO TRY IT ON?
Y-YES, PLEASE.
SLIDE
BA-DUMP

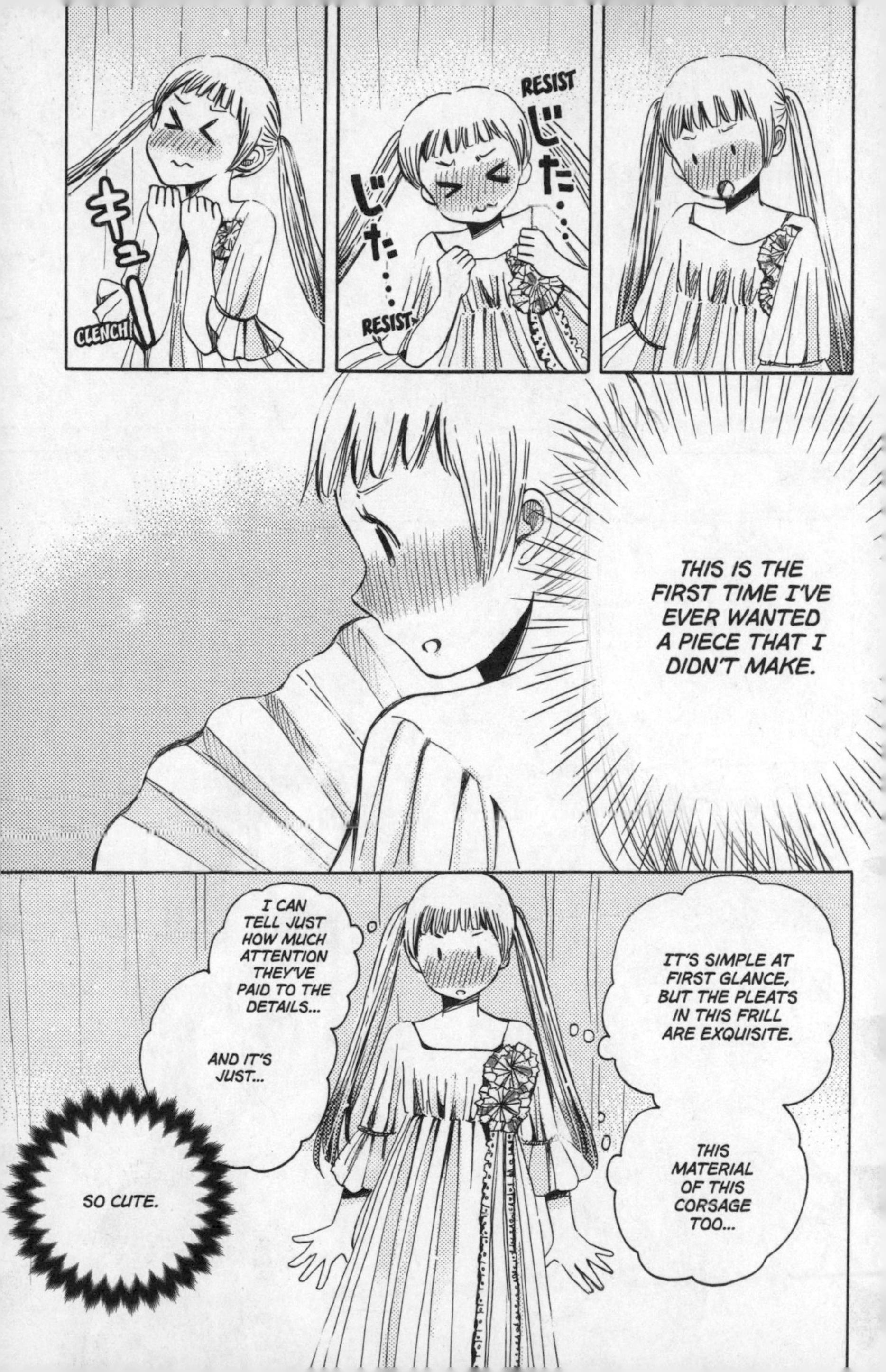
RESIST
じた…
じた…
RESIST
キュ
CLENCH
THIS IS THE FIRST TIME I'VE EVER WANTED A PIECE THAT I DIDN'T MAKE.
IT'S SIMPLE AT FIRST GLANCE, BUT THE PLEATS IN THIS FRILL ARE EXQUISITE.
I CAN TELL JUST HOW MUCH ATTENTION THEY'VE PAID TO THE DETAILS...
THIS MATERIAL OF THIS CORSAGE TOO...
AND IT'S JUST...
SO CUTE.

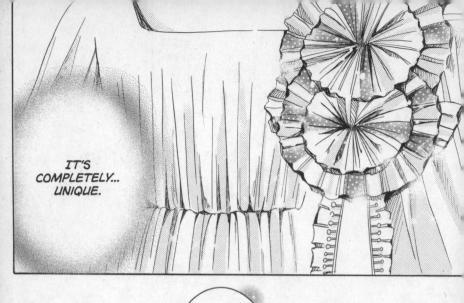

IT'S
COMPLETELY...
UNIQUE.

THANK YOU
SO MUCH.

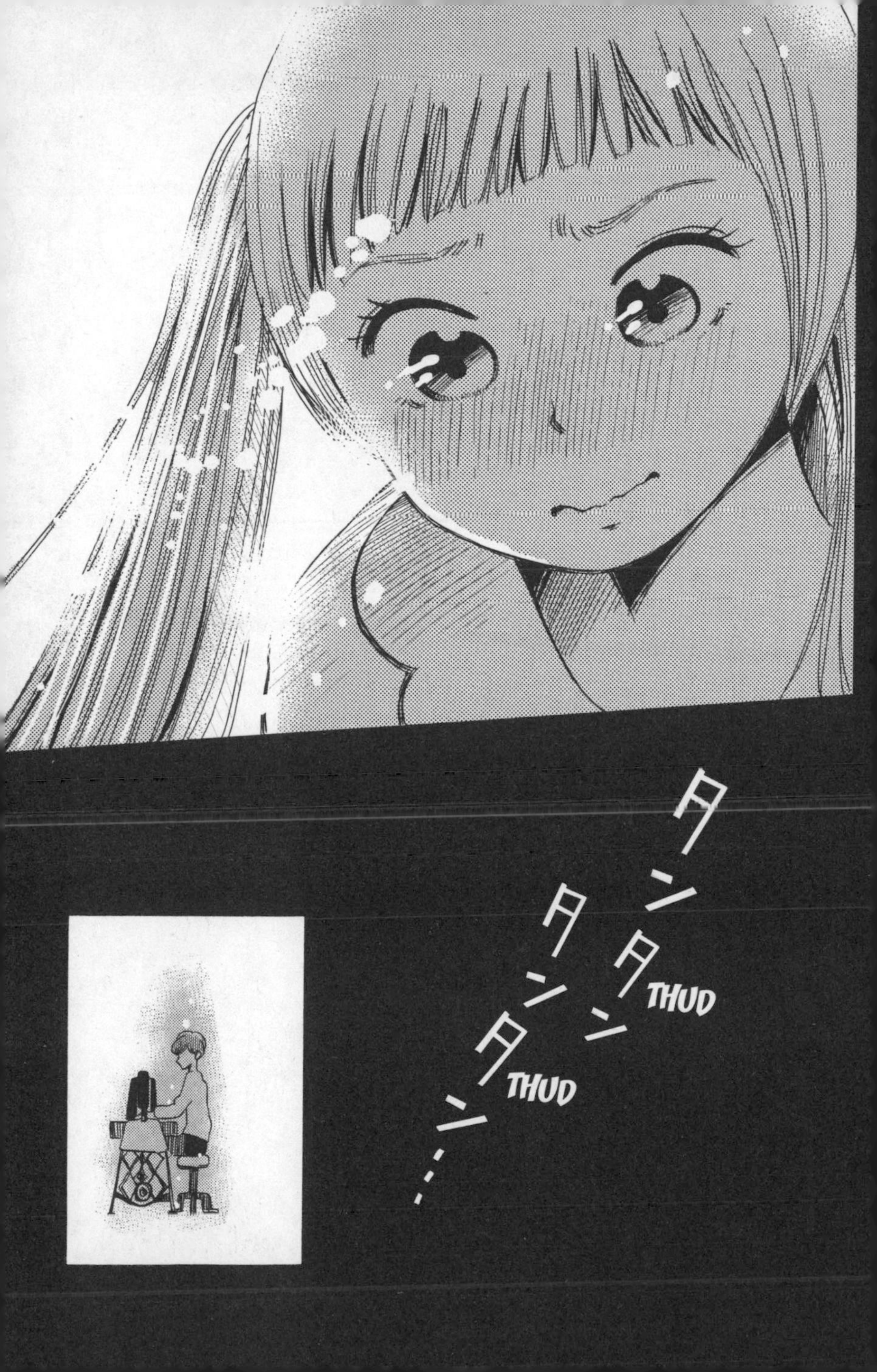
タン
タン
THUD
タンタン…
THUD

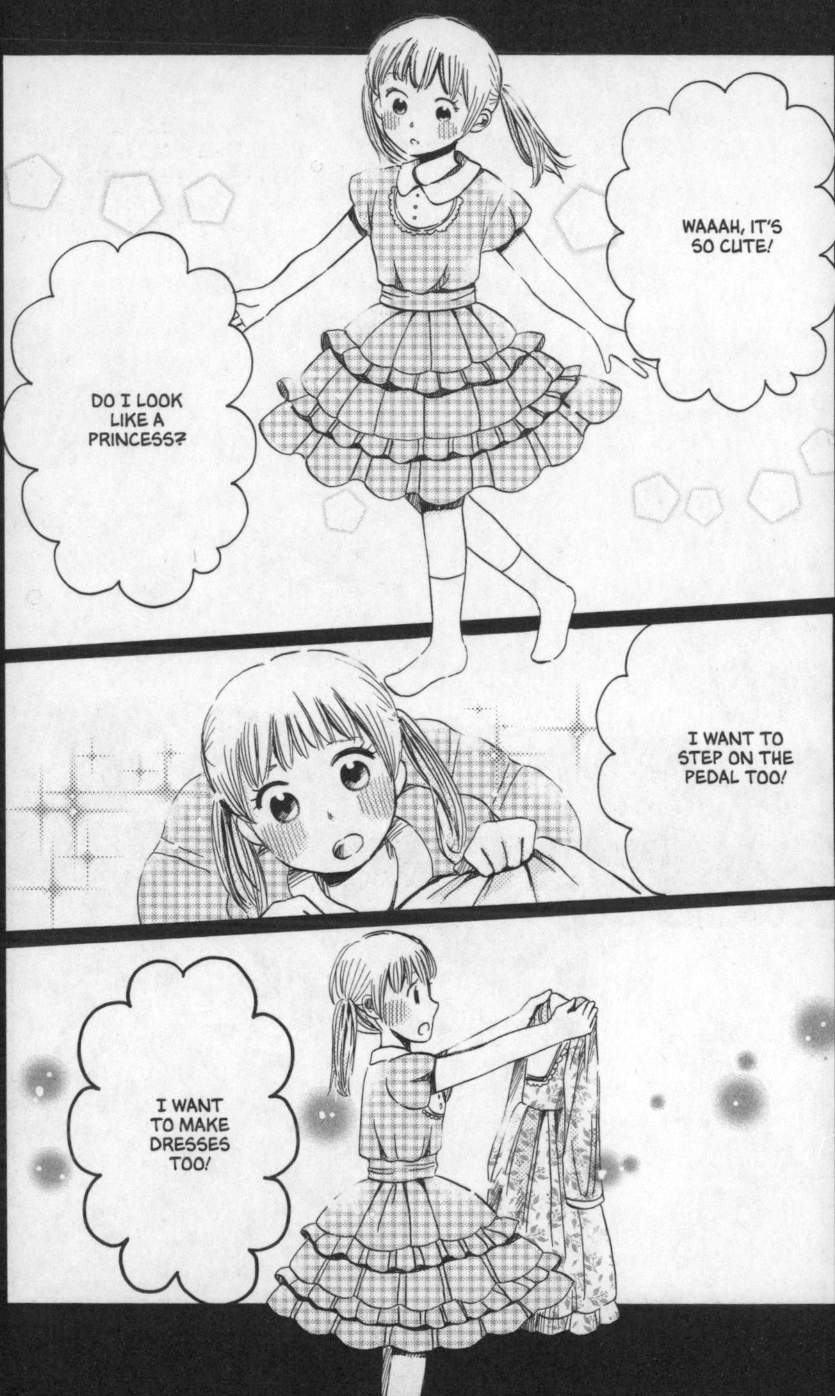
WAAAH, IT'S SO CUTE!
DO I LOOK LIKE A PRINCESS?
I WANT TO STEP ON THE PEDAL TOO!
I WANT TO MAKE DRESSES TOO!

I WANTED TO
BE THE ONE WHO
GAVE OTHERS THE
SAME HEART-RACING
THRILL I FELT...

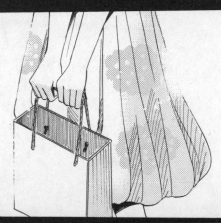

WHEN I
WORE THAT
MAGICAL
DRESS.

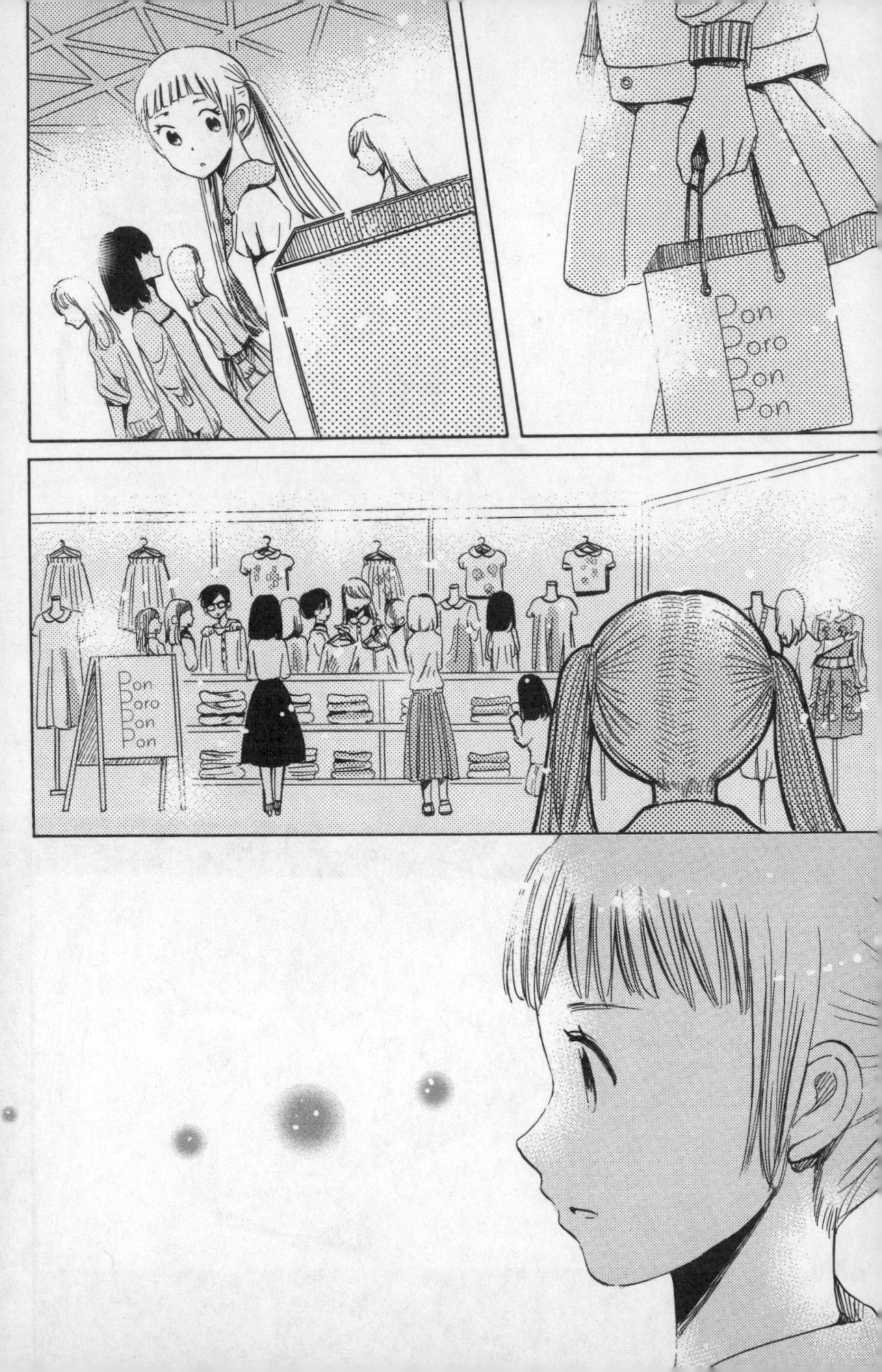
Pon
Poro
Pon
Pon
Pon
Poro
Pon
Pon

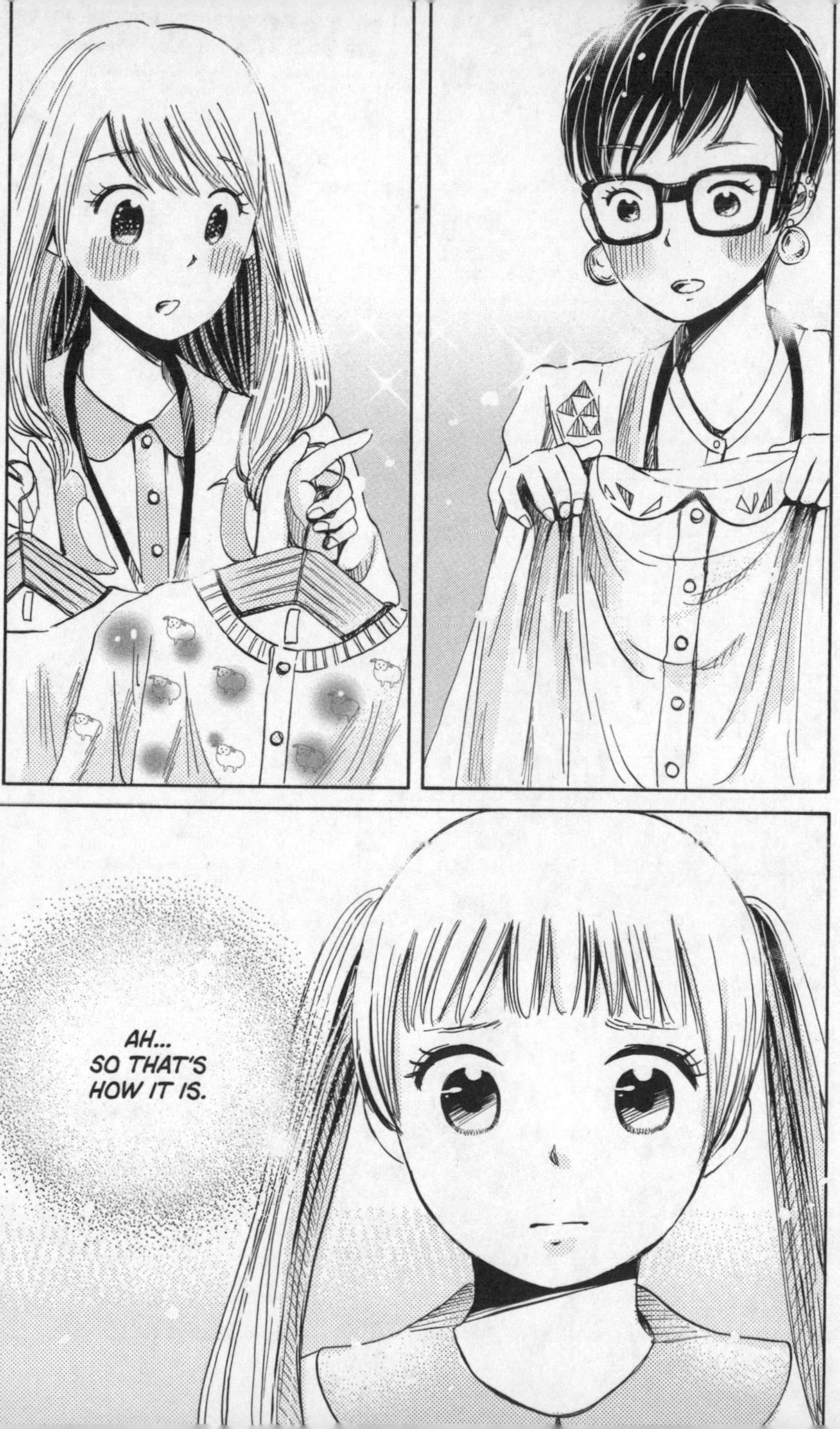
AH... SO THAT'S HOW IT IS.

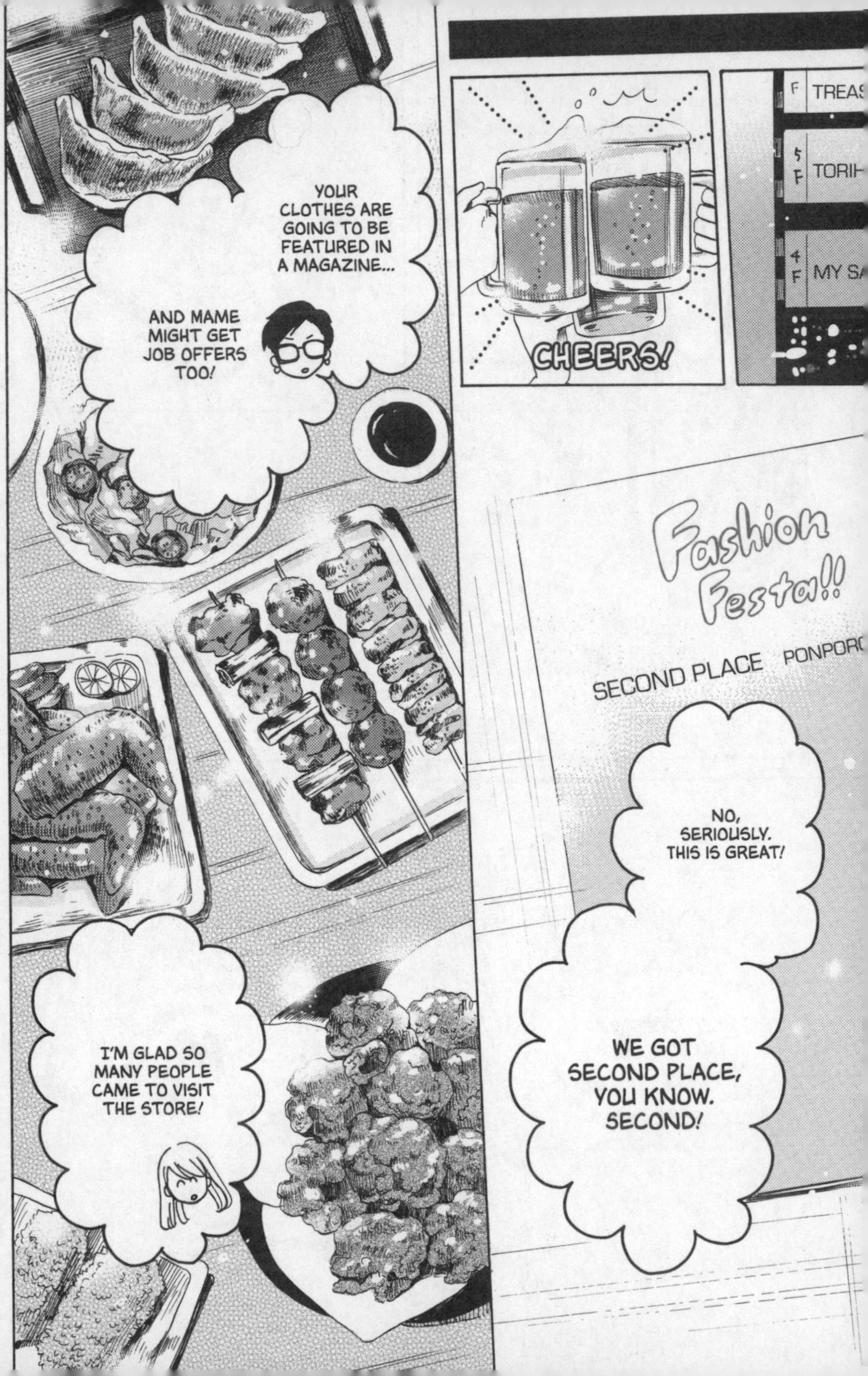
F TREAS
5F TORIH
4F MY SA
CHEERS!
Fashion Festa!!
SECOND PLACE PONPOR
NO, SERIOUSLY. THIS IS GREAT!
WE GOT SECOND PLACE, YOU KNOW. SECOND!
YOUR CLOTHES ARE GOING TO BE FEATURED IN A MAGAZINE...
AND MAME MIGHT GET JOB OFFERS TOO!
I'M GLAD SO MANY PEOPLE CAME TO VISIT THE STORE!

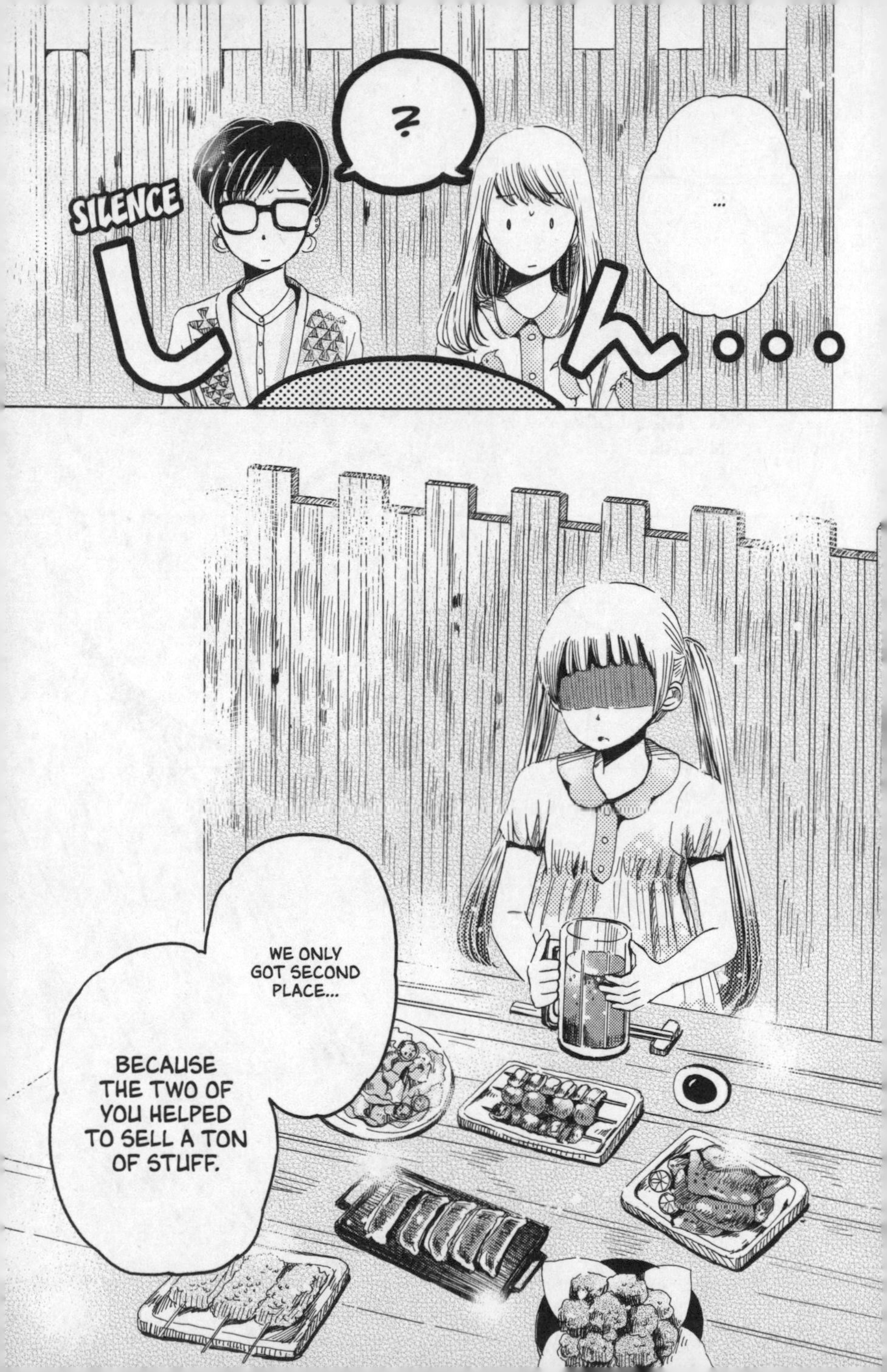

...
しん…
?
SILENCE
WE ONLY GOT SECOND PLACE...
BECAUSE THE TWO OF YOU HELPED TO SELL A TON OF STUFF.

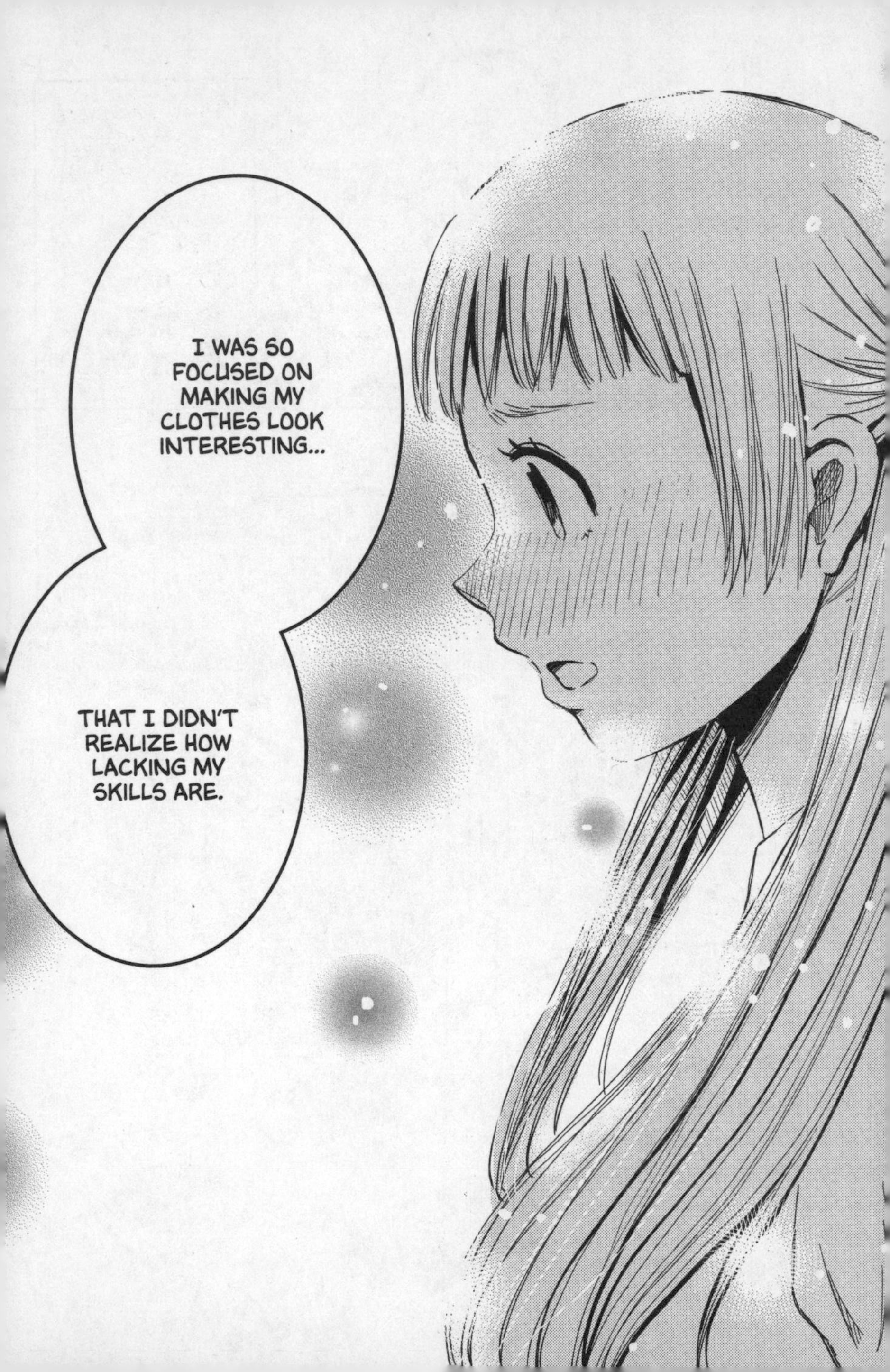
I WAS SO FOCUSED ON MAKING MY CLOTHES LOOK INTERESTING...
THAT I DIDN'T REALIZE HOW LACKING MY SKILLS ARE.

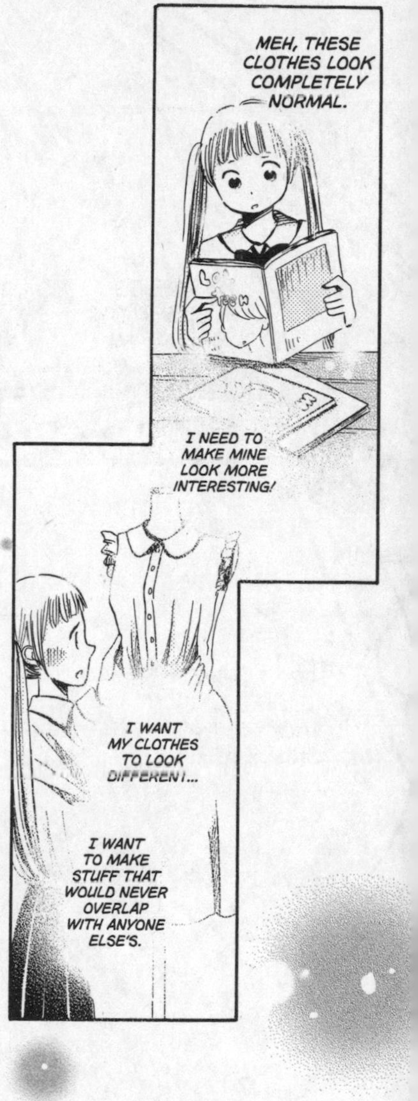
MEH, THESE CLOTHES LOOK COMPLETELY NORMAL.
I NEED TO MAKE MINE LOOK MORE INTERESTING!
I WANT MY CLOTHES TO LOOK DIFFERENT...
I WANT TO MAKE STUFF THAT WOULD NEVER OVERLAP WITH ANYONE ELSE'S.

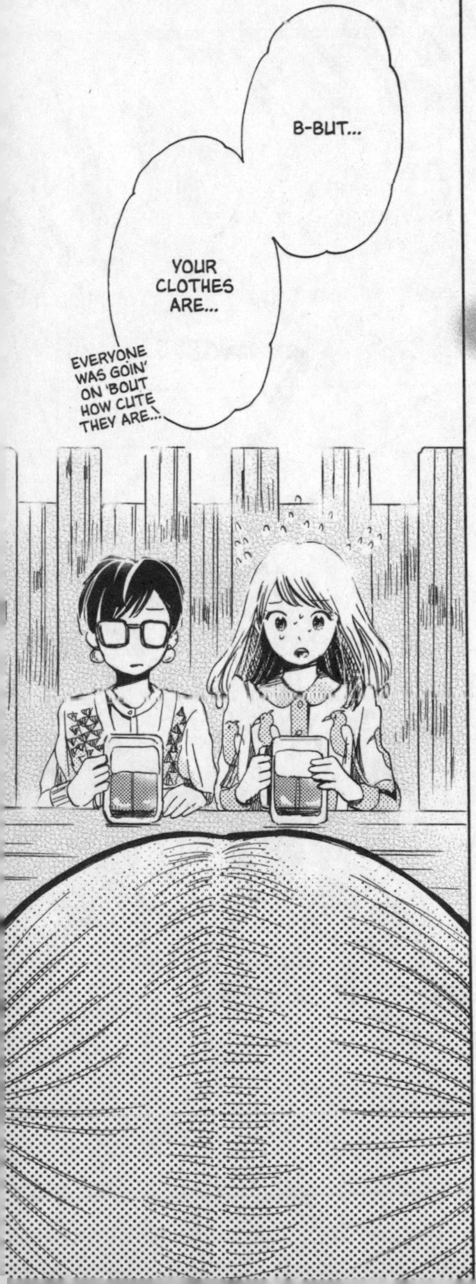
B-BUT...
YOUR CLOTHES ARE...
EVERYONE WAS GOIN' ON 'BOUT HOW CUTE THEY ARE...

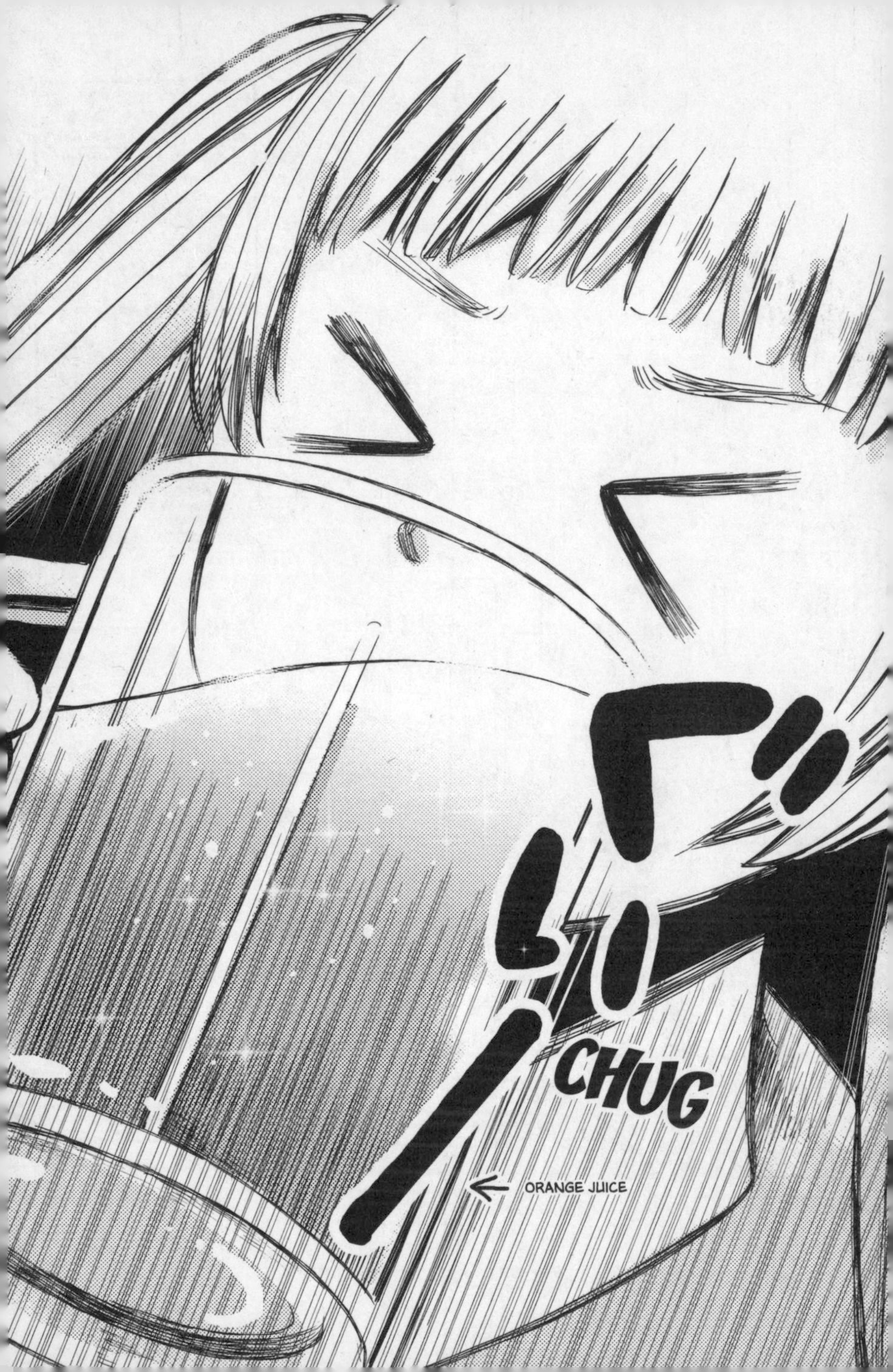
CHUG
ORANGE JUICE

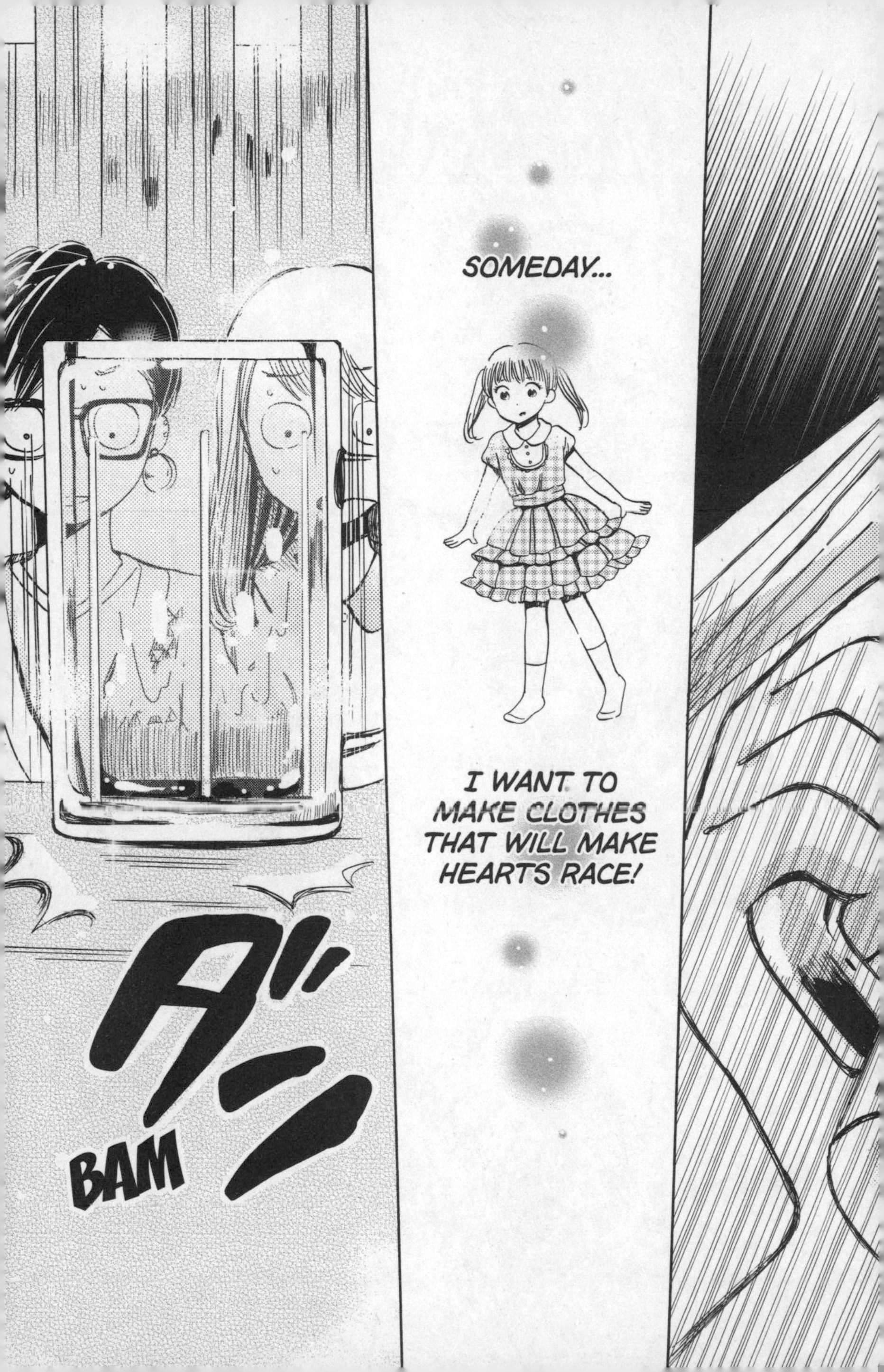
SOMEDAY...
I WANT TO MAKE CLOTHES THAT WILL MAKE HEARTS RACE!
ダン
BAM

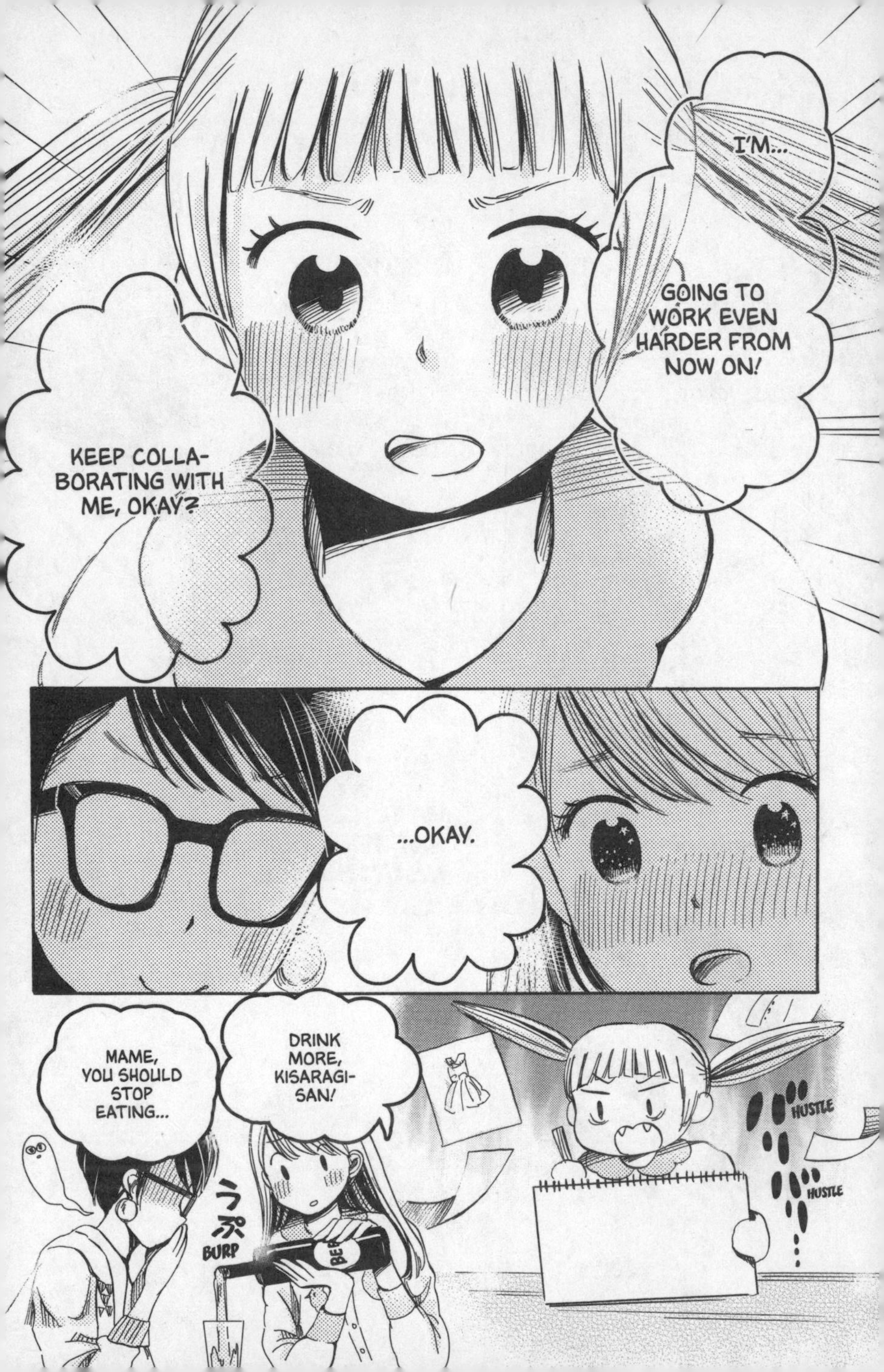
I'M...
GOING TO WORK EVEN HARDER FROM NOW ON!
KEEP COLLA-BORATING WITH ME, OKAY?
...OKAY.
HUSTLE
HUSTLE
DRINK MORE, KISARAGI-SAN!
MAME, YOU SHOULD STOP EATING...
うぷ
BURP

M A M E
coordinate

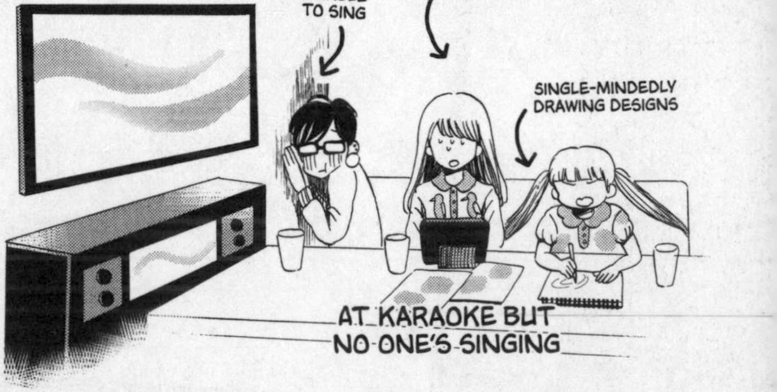
AFTER-PARTY
NOT SURE WHAT TO SING
LIMP AND UNABLE TO SING
SINGLE-MINDEDLY DRAWING DESIGNS
AT KARAOKE BUT NO-ONE'S SINGING

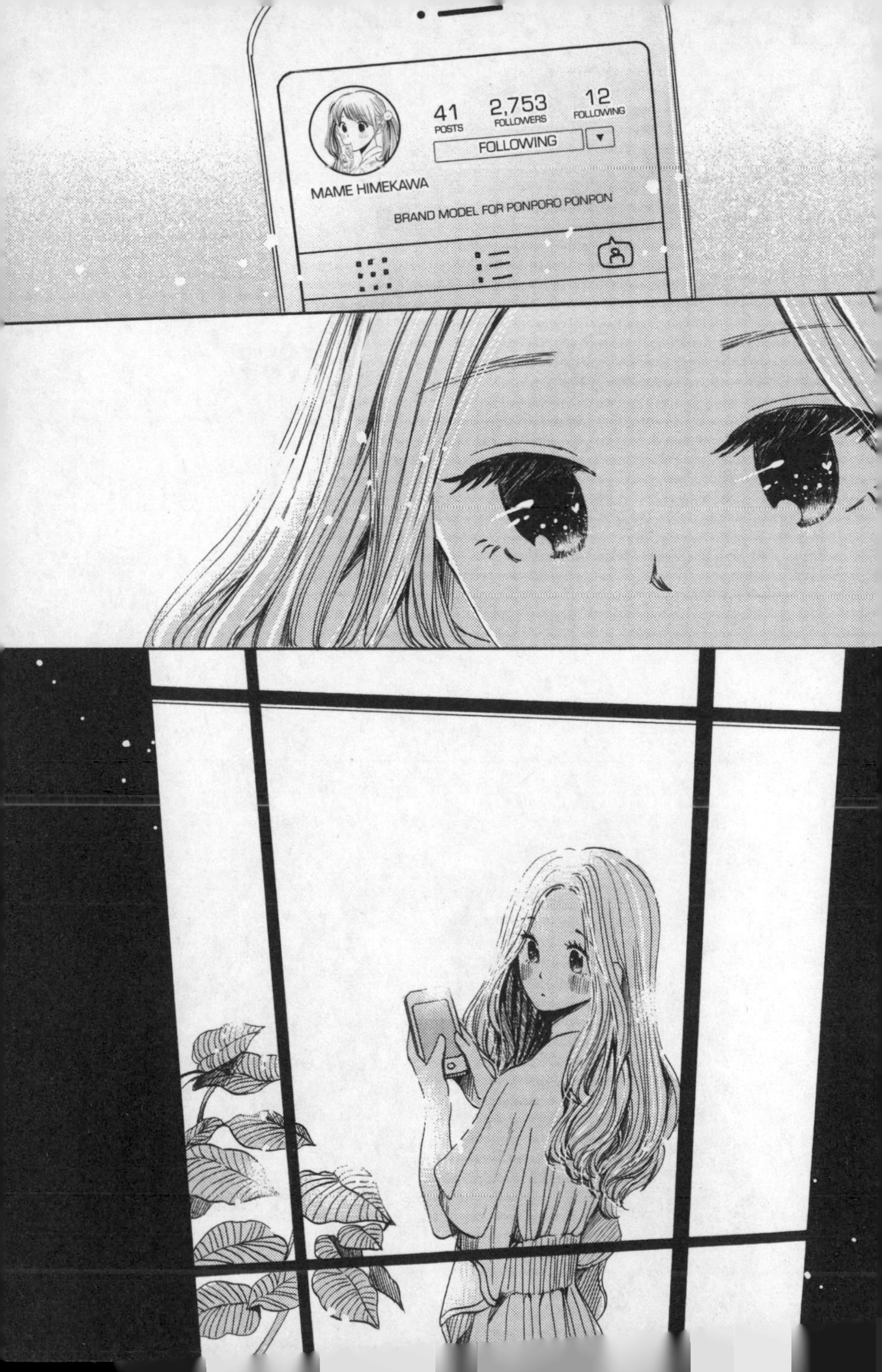
41
POSTS
2,753
FOLLOWERS
12
FOLLOWING
FOLLOWING
MAME HIMEKAWA
BRAND MODEL FOR PONPORO PONPON

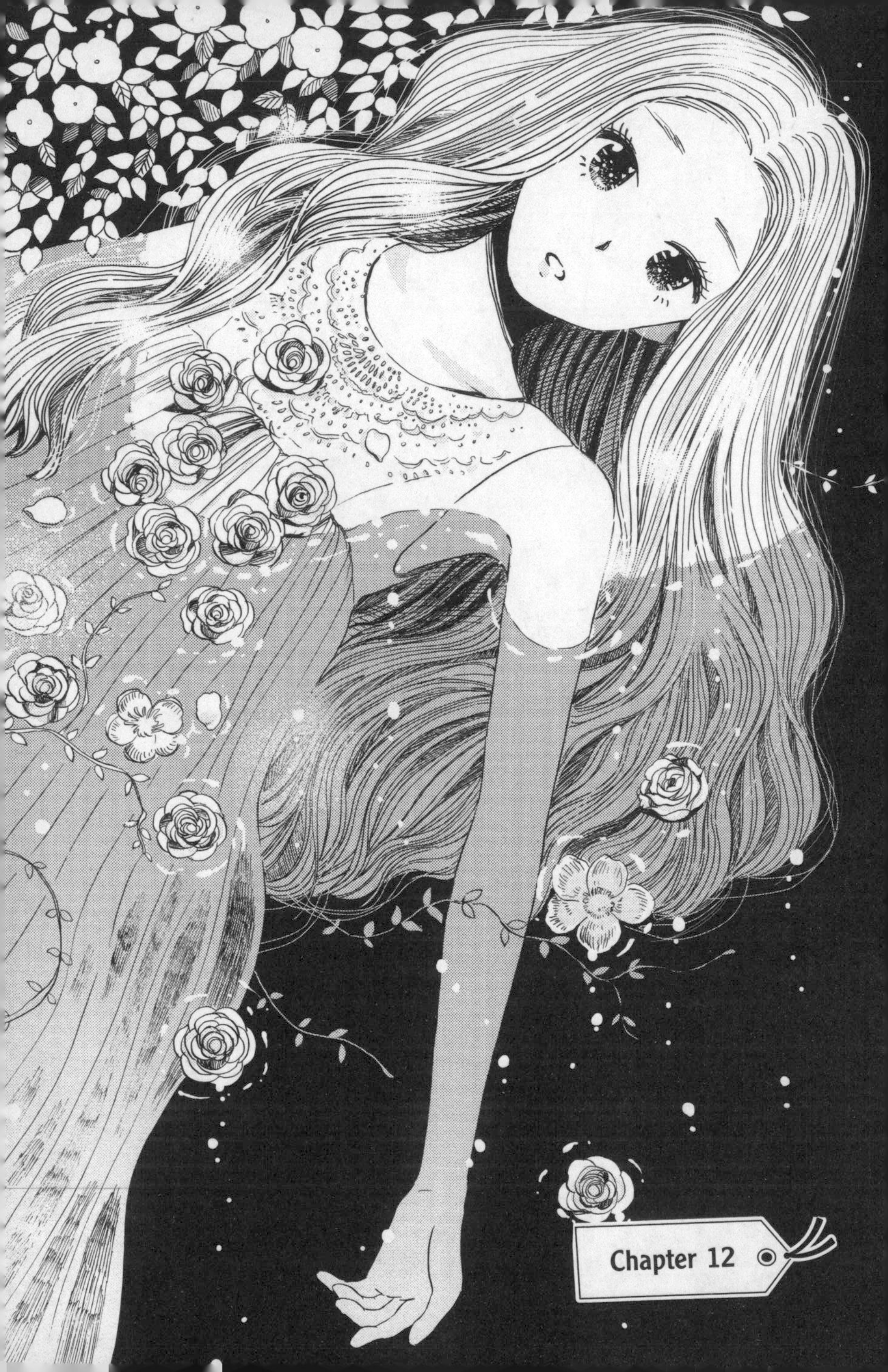
Chapter 12

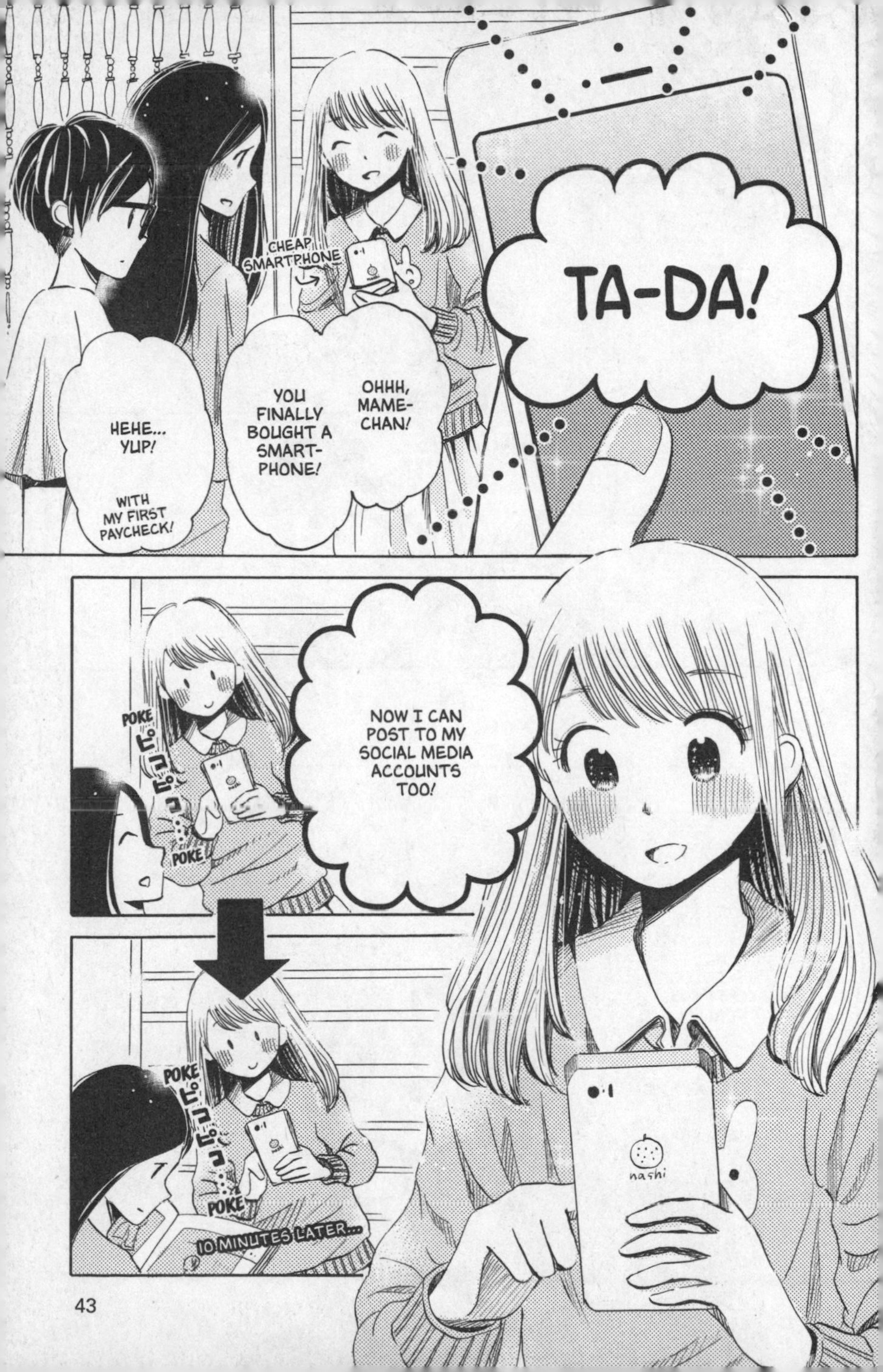
TA-DA!
CHEAP SMARTPHONE
OHHH, MAME-CHAN!
YOU FINALLY BOUGHT A SMARTPHONE!
HEHE... YUP!
WITH MY FIRST PAYCHECK!
NOW I CAN POST TO MY SOCIAL MEDIA ACCOUNTS TOO!
POKE
POKE
POKE
POKE
10 MINUTES LATER...
nashi

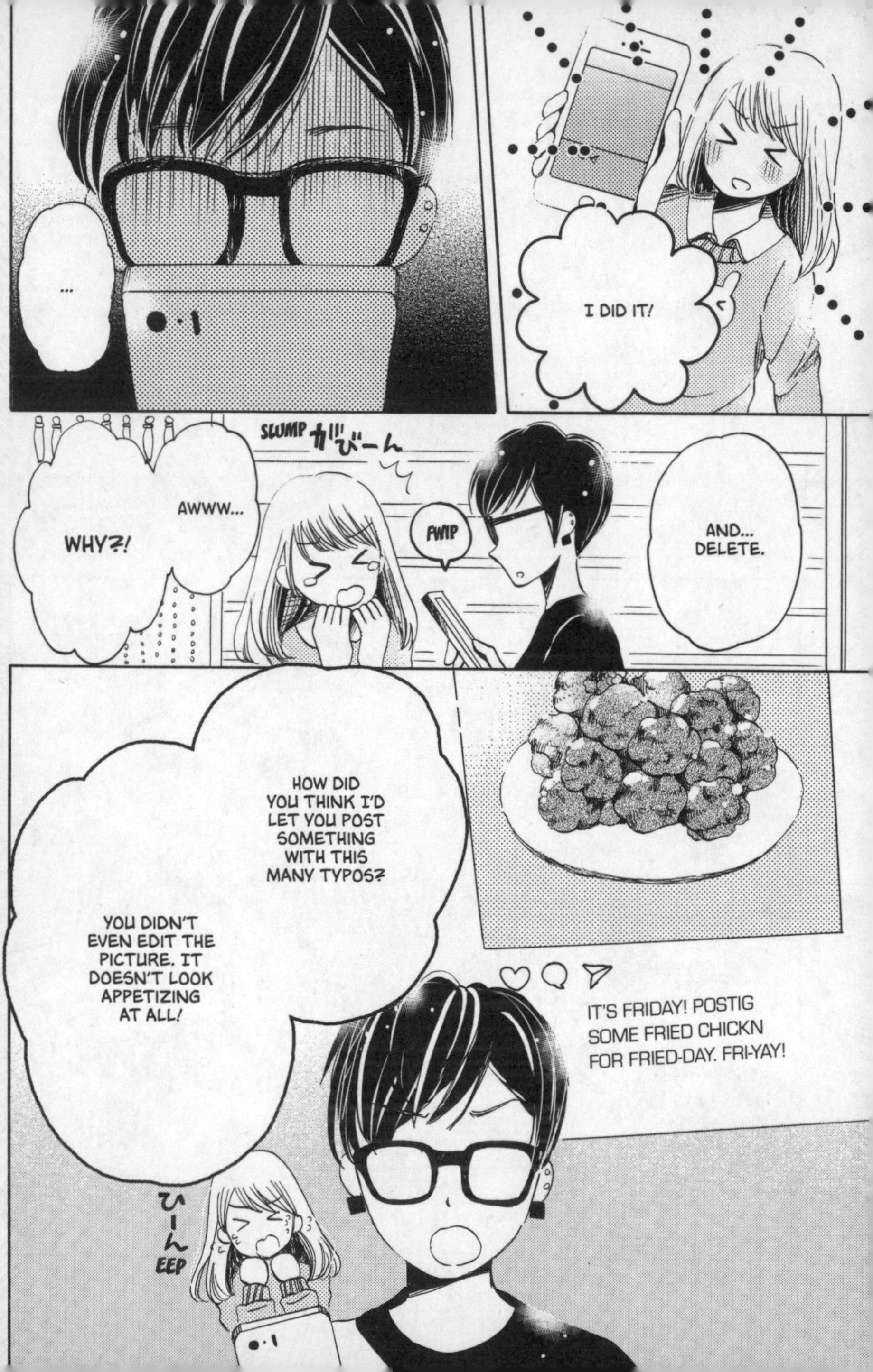
I DID IT!
...
AND... DELETE.
FWIP
SLUMP がびーん
AWWW...
WHY?!
IT'S FRIDAY! POSTIG SOME FRIED CHICKN FOR FRIED-DAY. FRI-YAY!
HOW DID YOU THINK I'D LET YOU POST SOMETHING WITH THIS MANY TYPOS?
YOU DIDN'T EVEN EDIT THE PICTURE. IT DOESN'T LOOK APPETIZING AT ALL!
ひーん EEP

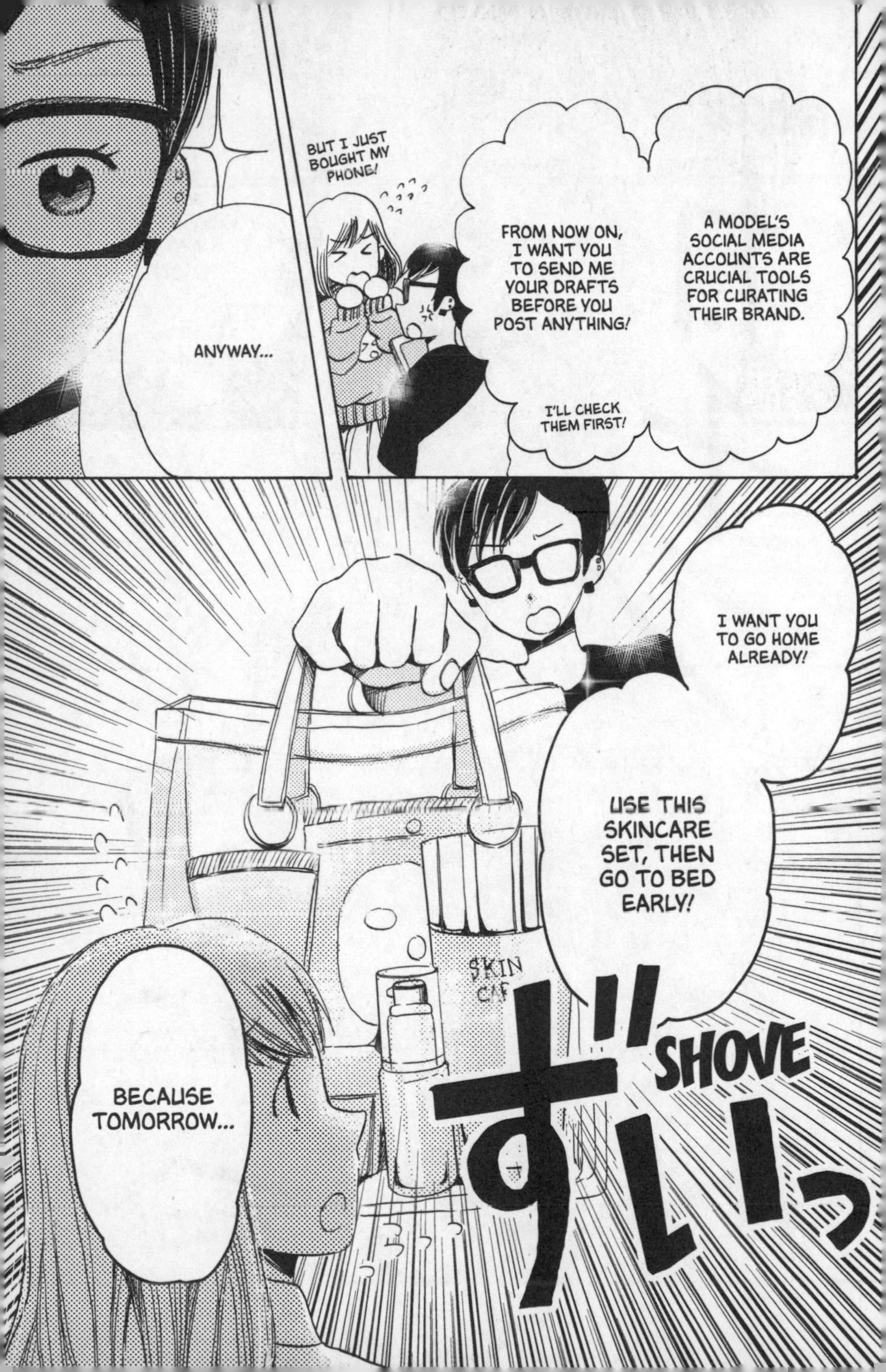
A MODEL'S SOCIAL MEDIA ACCOUNTS ARE CRUCIAL TOOLS FOR CURATING THEIR BRAND.
FROM NOW ON, I WANT YOU TO SEND ME YOUR DRAFTS BEFORE YOU POST ANYTHING!
I'LL CHECK THEM FIRST!
BUT I JUST BOUGHT MY PHONE!
ANYWAY...
I WANT YOU TO GO HOME ALREADY!
USE THIS SKINCARE SET, THEN GO TO BED EARLY!
ずいっ
SHOVE
SKIN CA
BECAUSE TOMORROW...

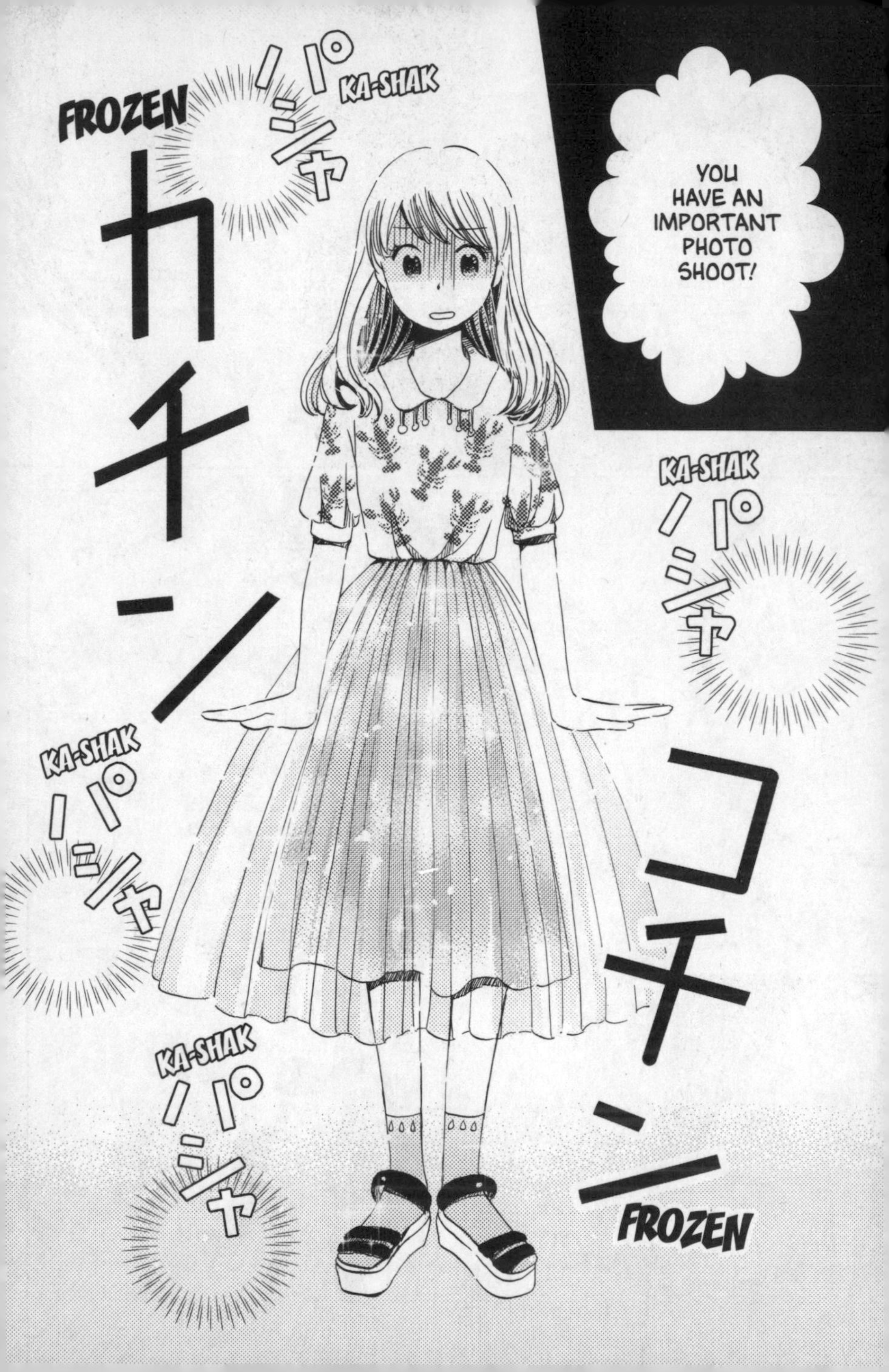
YOU HAVE AN IMPORTANT PHOTO SHOOT!
KA-SHAK
パシャ
FROZEN
カチーン
KA-SHAK
パシャ
KA-SHAK
パシャ
KA-SHAK
パシャ
コチーン
FROZEN

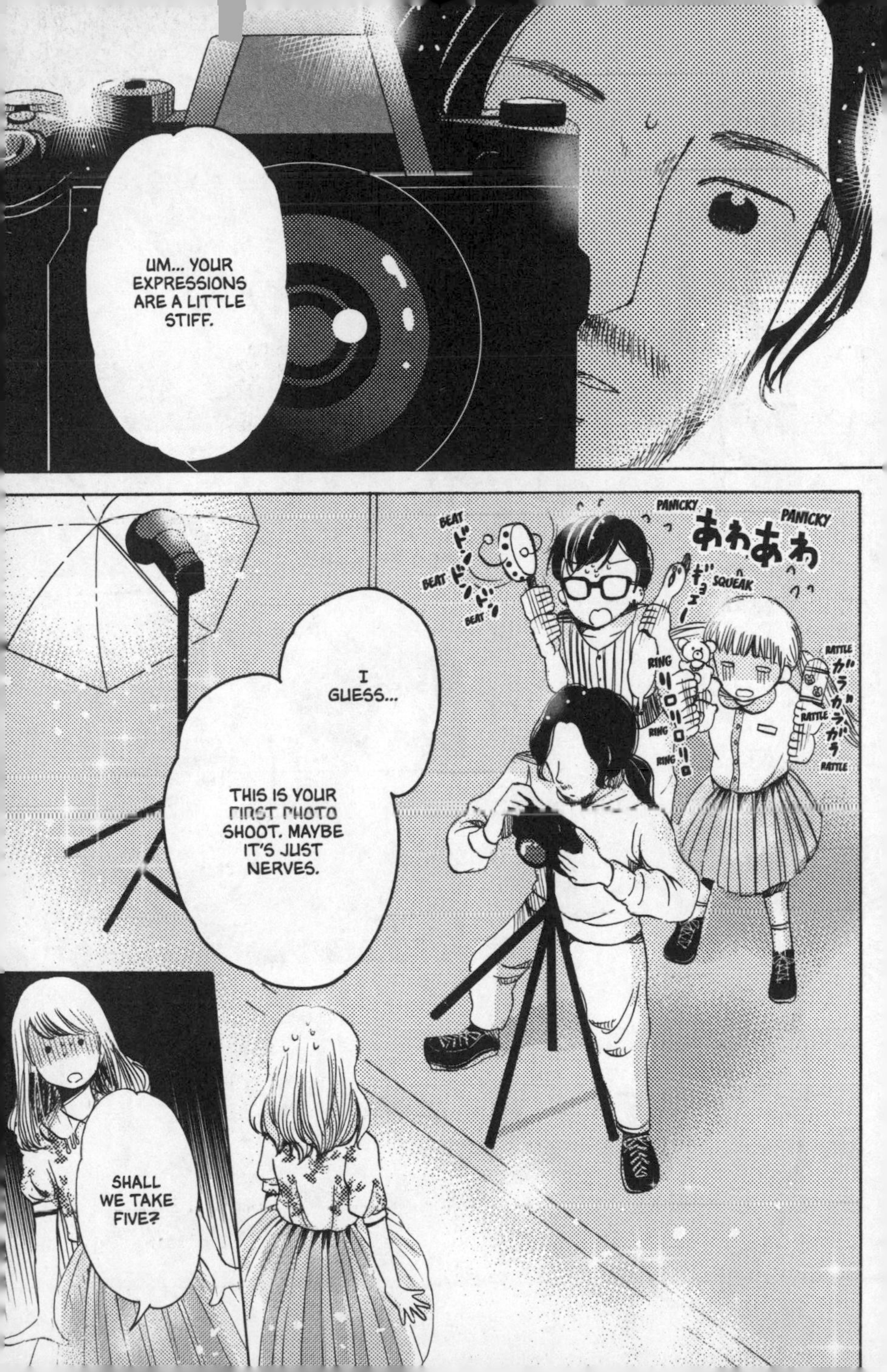
UM... YOUR EXPRESSIONS ARE A LITTLE STIFF.
PANICKY
あわあわ
PANICKY
SQUEAK
BEAT
BEAT
BEAT
RING
RING
RING
RATTLE
RATTLE
RATTLE
I GUESS...
THIS IS YOUR FIRST PHOTO SHOOT. MAYBE IT'S JUST NERVES.
SHALL WE TAKE FIVE?

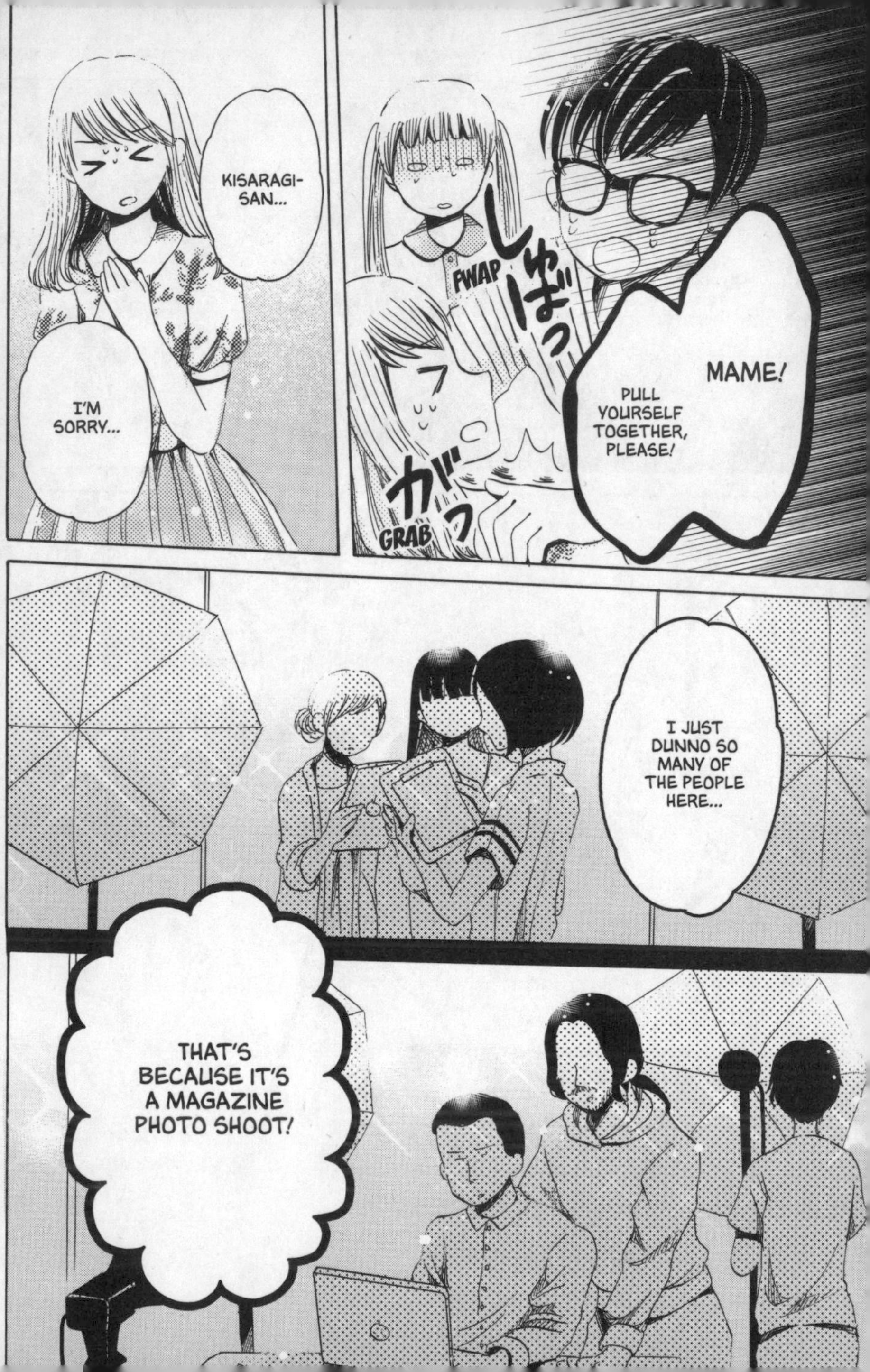
MAME! PULL YOURSELF TOGETHER, PLEASE!
しゅぼっ
FWAP
ガッ
GRAB
KISARAGI-SAN...
I'M SORRY...
I JUST DUNNO SO MANY OF THE PEOPLE HERE...
THAT'S BECAUSE IT'S A MAGAZINE PHOTO SHOOT!

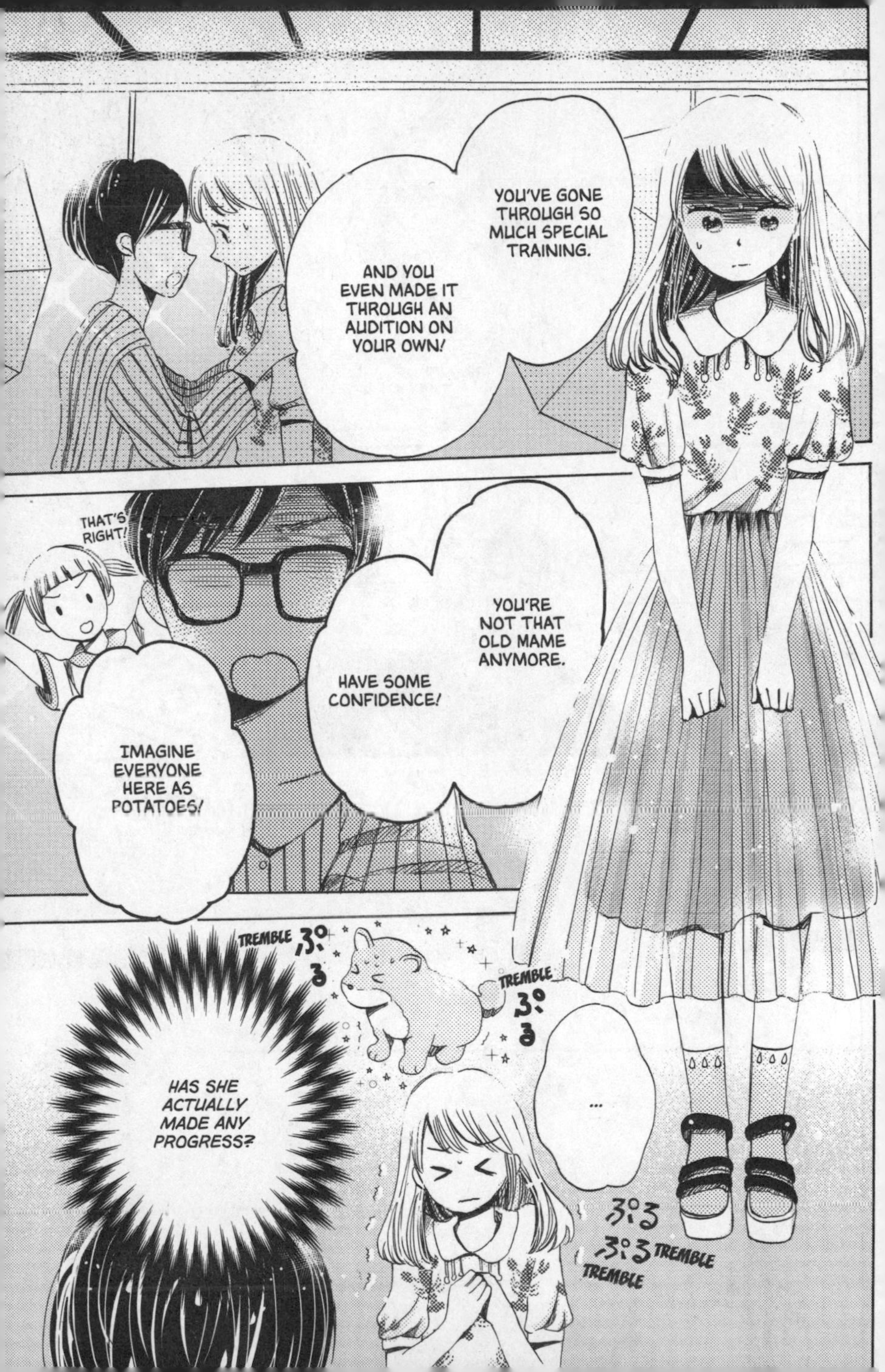
YOU'VE GONE THROUGH SO MUCH SPECIAL TRAINING.
AND YOU EVEN MADE IT THROUGH AN AUDITION ON YOUR OWN!
YOU'RE NOT THAT OLD MAME ANYMORE.
HAVE SOME CONFIDENCE!
THAT'S RIGHT!
IMAGINE EVERYONE HERE AS POTATOES!
...
ぷる ぷる
TREMBLE TREMBLE
ぷる TREMBLE
ぷる TREMBLE
HAS SHE ACTUALLY MADE ANY PROGRESS?

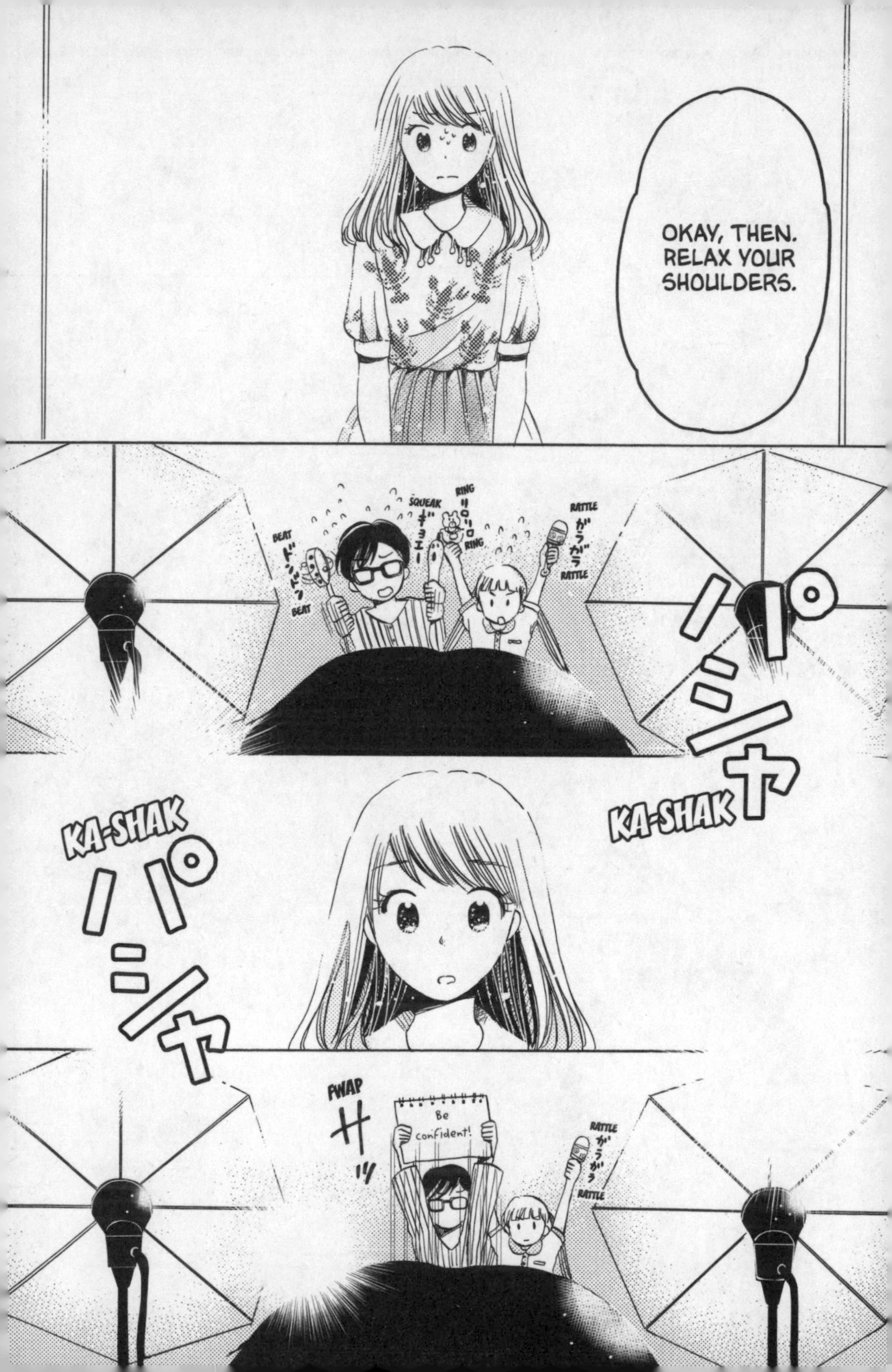
OKAY, THEN. RELAX YOUR SHOULDERS.
RATTLE
RATTLE
RING
RING
SQUEAK
BEAT
BEAT
KA-SHAK
パシャ
KA-SHAK
パシャ
RATTLE
RATTLE
Be confident!
PWAP
サッ

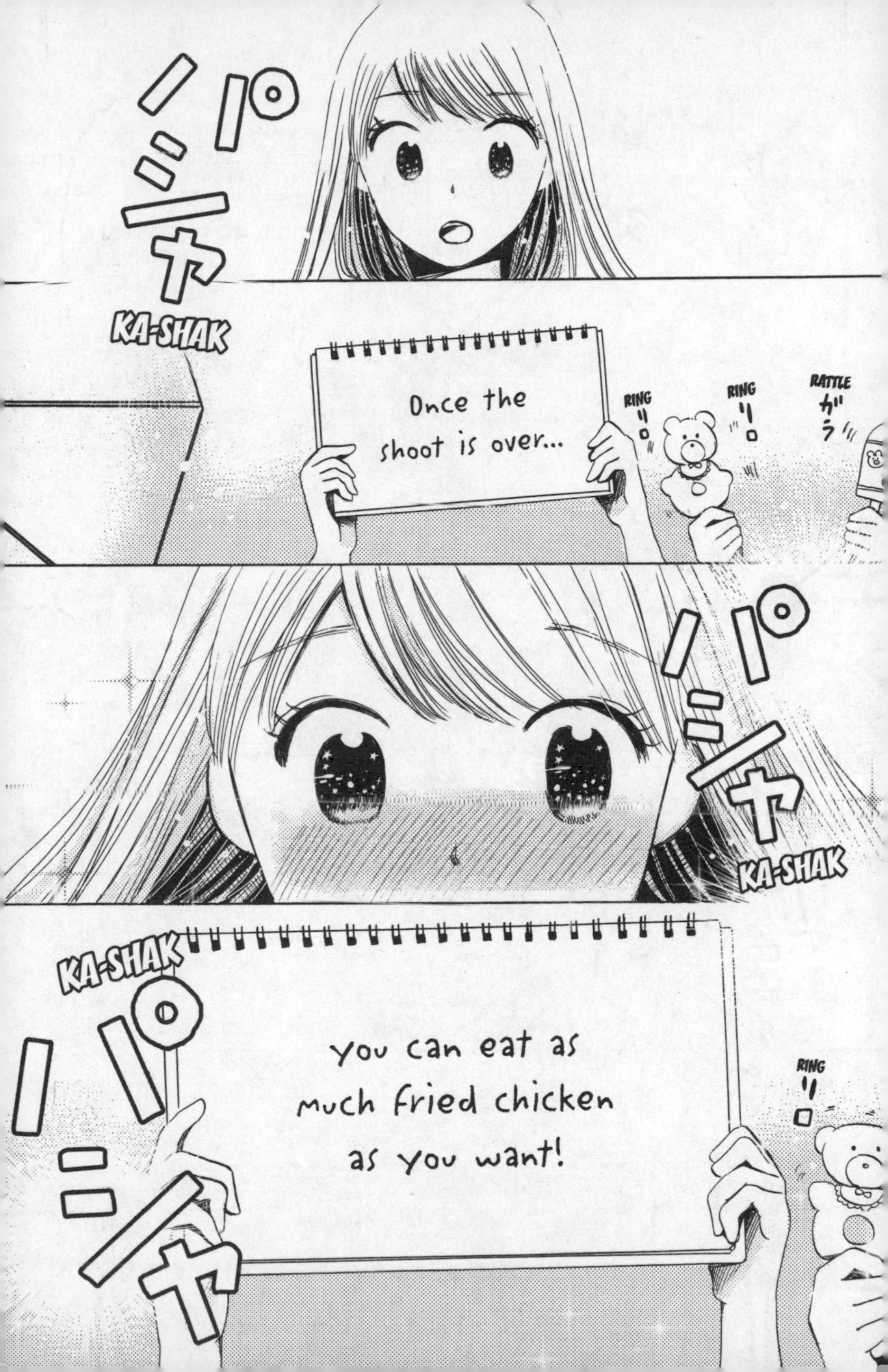
パシャ
KA-SHAK
RATTLE
ガラ
RING
RING
Once the shoot is over...
パシャ
KA-SHAK
RING
you can eat as much fried chicken as you want!
KA-SHAK
パシャ

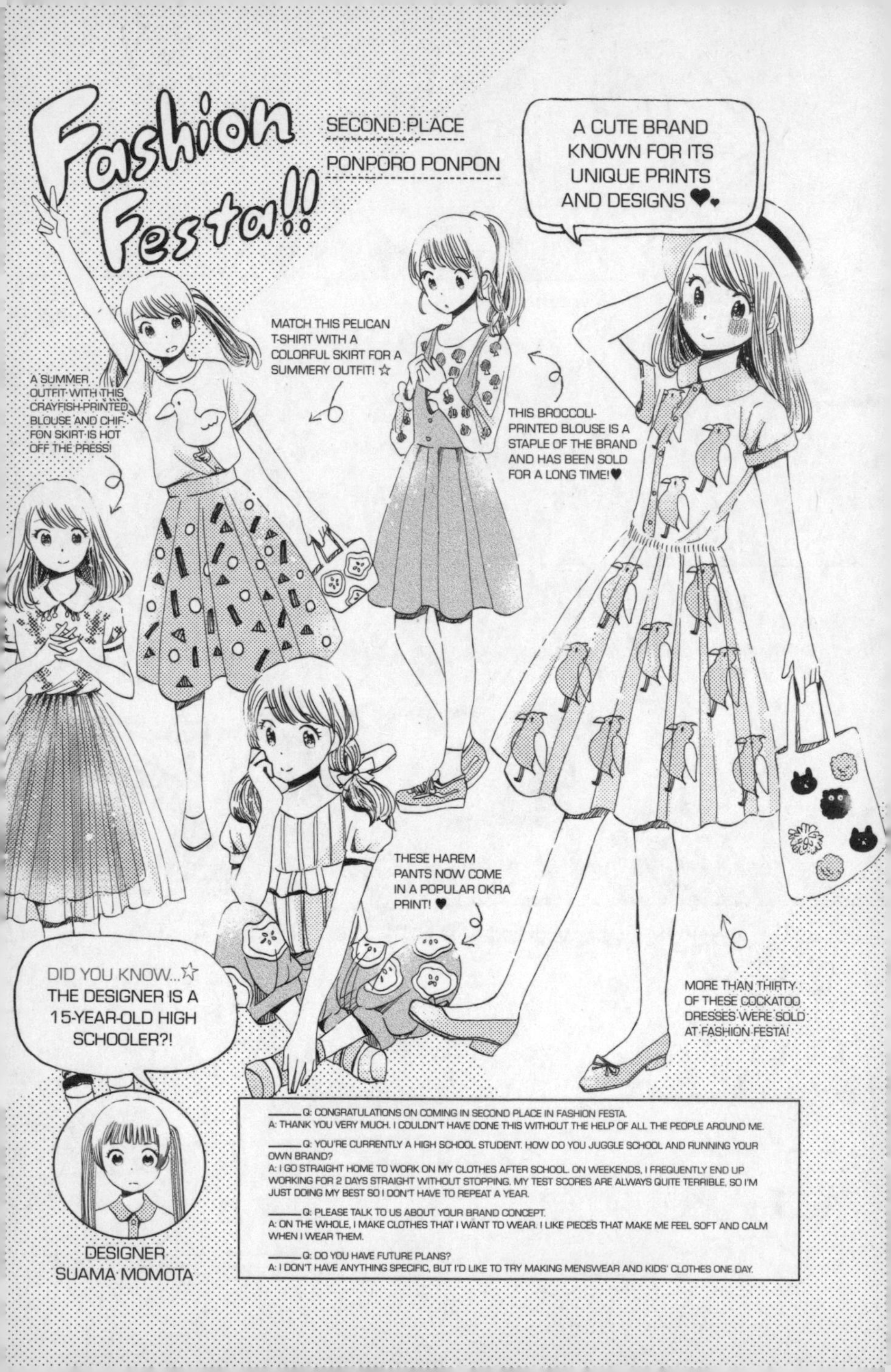
Fashion Festa!!
SECOND PLACE
PONPORO PONPON
A CUTE BRAND KNOWN FOR ITS UNIQUE PRINTS AND DESIGNS ♥
THIS BROCCOLI-PRINTED BLOUSE IS A STAPLE OF THE BRAND AND HAS BEEN SOLD FOR A LONG TIME! ♥
MATCH THIS PELICAN T-SHIRT WITH A COLORFUL SKIRT FOR A SUMMERY OUTFIT! ☆
A SUMMER OUTFIT WITH THIS CRAYFISH-PRINTED BLOUSE AND CHIFFON SKIRT IS HOT OFF THE PRESS!
THESE HAREM PANTS NOW COME IN A POPULAR OKRA PRINT! ♥
MORE THAN THIRTY OF THESE COCKATOO DRESSES WERE SOLD AT FASHION FESTA!
DID YOU KNOW...☆ THE DESIGNER IS A 15-YEAR-OLD HIGH SCHOOLER?!
DESIGNER SUAMA MOMOTA
——Q: CONGRATULATIONS ON COMING IN SECOND PLACE IN FASHION FESTA.
A: THANK YOU VERY MUCH. I COULDN'T HAVE DONE THIS WITHOUT THE HELP OF ALL THE PEOPLE AROUND ME.
——Q: YOU'RE CURRENTLY A HIGH SCHOOL STUDENT. HOW DO YOU JUGGLE SCHOOL AND RUNNING YOUR OWN BRAND?
A: I GO STRAIGHT HOME TO WORK ON MY CLOTHES AFTER SCHOOL. ON WEEKENDS, I FREQUENTLY END UP WORKING FOR 2 DAYS STRAIGHT WITHOUT STOPPING. MY TEST SCORES ARE ALWAYS QUITE TERRIBLE, SO I'M JUST DOING MY BEST SO I DON'T HAVE TO REPEAT A YEAR.
——Q: PLEASE TALK TO US ABOUT YOUR BRAND CONCEPT.
A: ON THE WHOLE, I MAKE CLOTHES THAT I WANT TO WEAR. I LIKE PIECES THAT MAKE ME FEEL SOFT AND CALM WHEN I WEAR THEM.
——Q: DO YOU HAVE FUTURE PLANS?
A: I DON'T HAVE ANYTHING SPECIFIC, BUT I'D LIKE TO TRY MAKING MENSWEAR AND KIDS' CLOTHES ONE DAY.

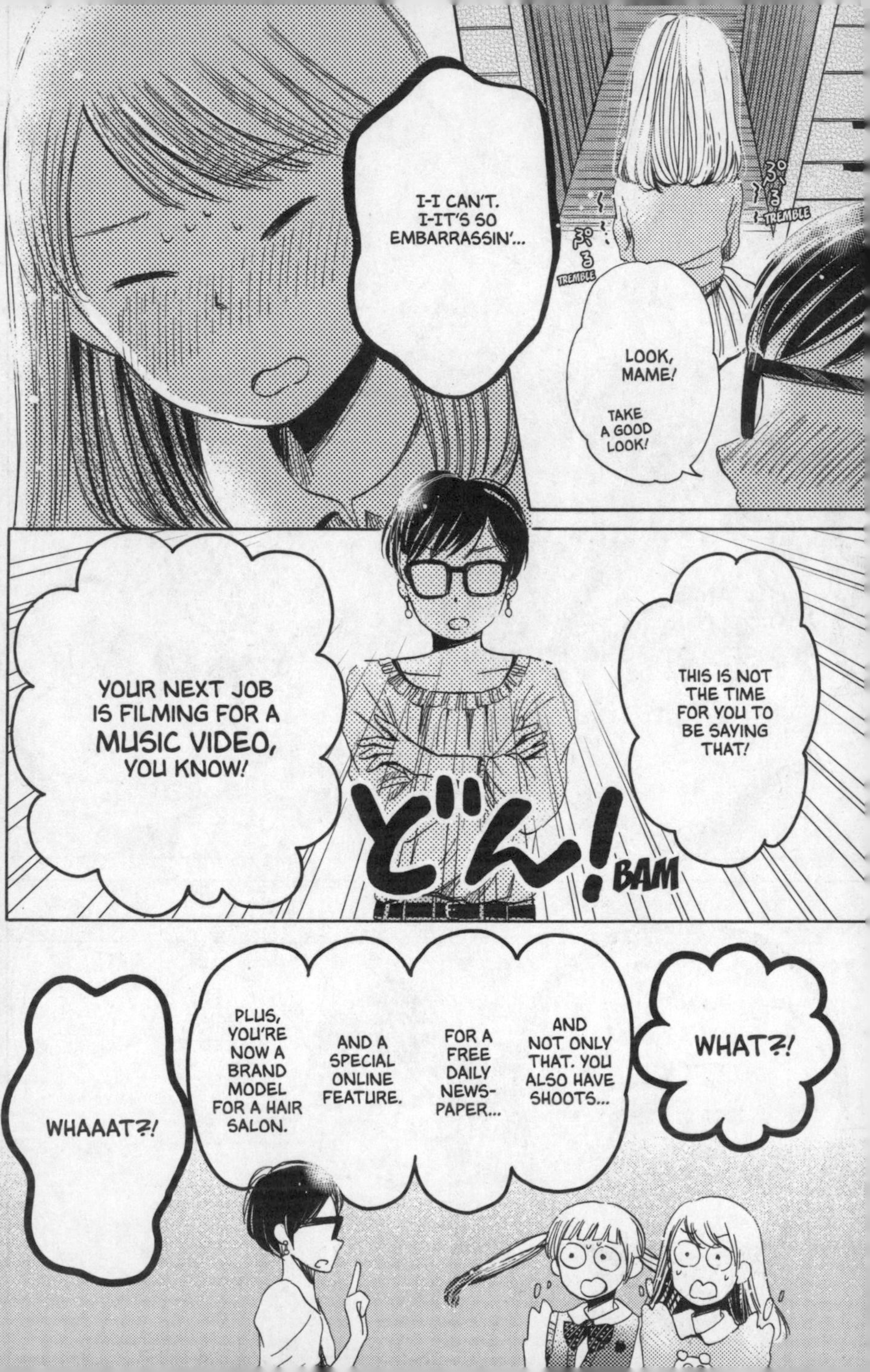
ぷるぷる TREMBLE
ぷる TREMBLE
LOOK, MAME!
TAKE A GOOD LOOK!
I-I CAN'T. I-IT'S SO EMBARRASSIN'...
THIS IS NOT THE TIME FOR YOU TO BE SAYING THAT!
YOUR NEXT JOB IS FILMING FOR A MUSIC VIDEO, YOU KNOW!
どん! BAM
WHAT?!
AND NOT ONLY THAT. YOU ALSO HAVE SHOOTS...
FOR A FREE DAILY NEWS-PAPER...
AND A SPECIAL ONLINE FEATURE.
PLUS, YOU'RE NOW A BRAND MODEL FOR A HAIR SALON.
WHAAAT?!

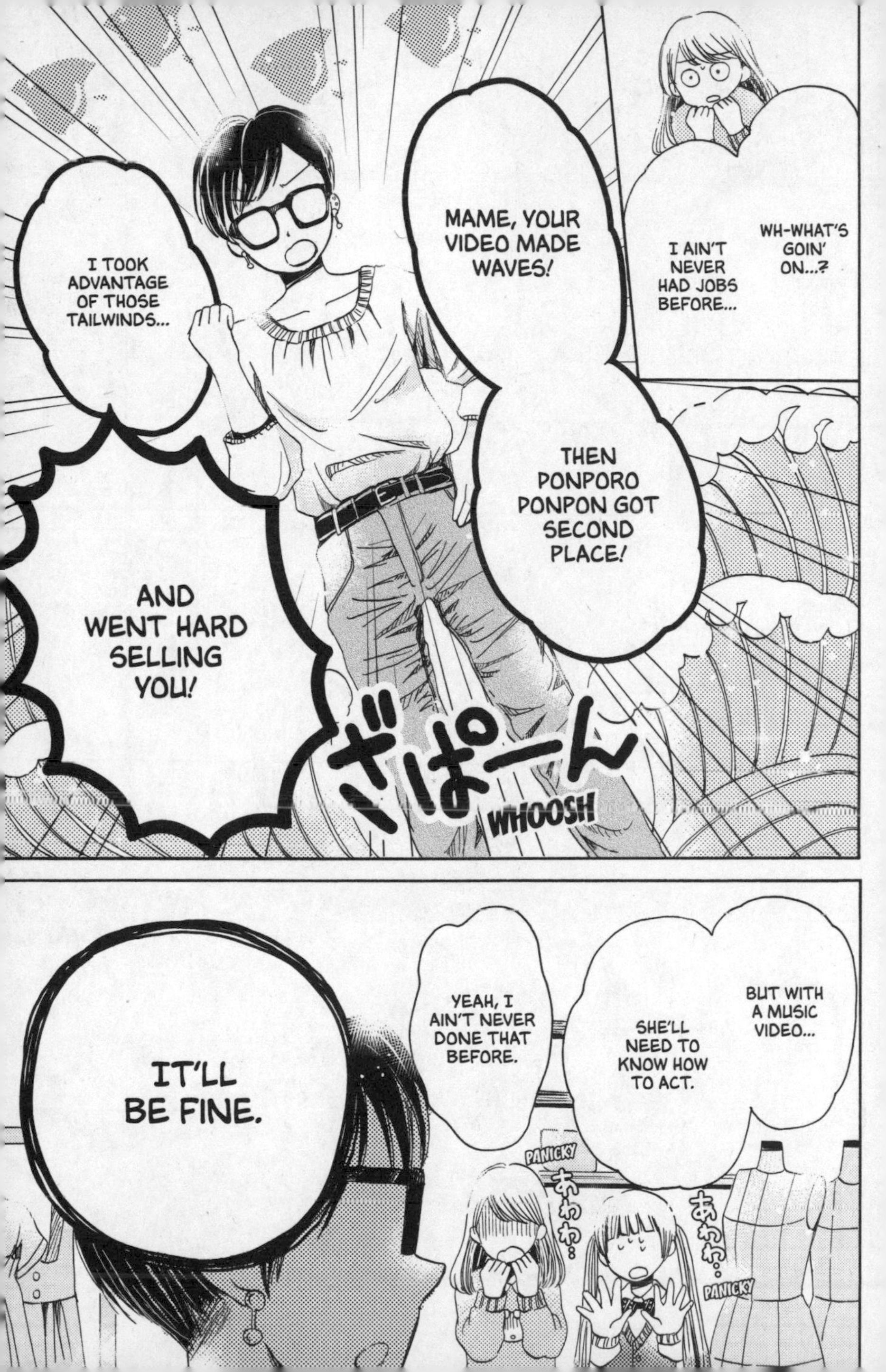
WH-WHAT'S GOIN' ON...?
I AIN'T NEVER HAD JOBS BEFORE...
MAME, YOUR VIDEO MADE WAVES!
THEN PONPORO PONPON GOT SECOND PLACE!
I TOOK ADVANTAGE OF THOSE TAILWINDS...
AND WENT HARD SELLING YOU!
ざぱーん
WHOOSH
BUT WITH A MUSIC VIDEO...
SHE'LL NEED TO KNOW HOW TO ACT.
YEAH, I AIN'T NEVER DONE THAT BEFORE.
あわわ・・
PANICKY
あわわ・・
PANICKY
IT'LL BE FINE.

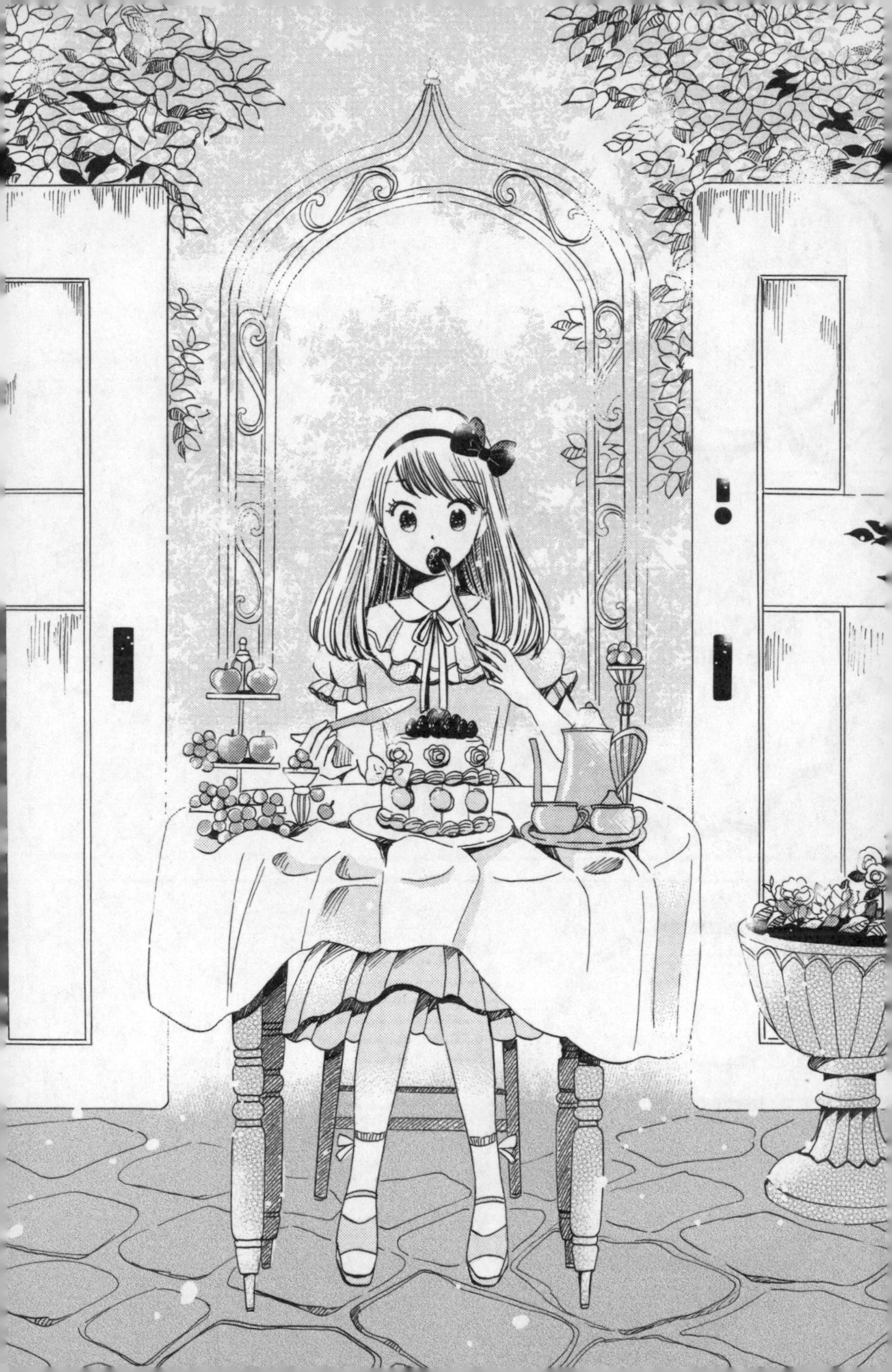

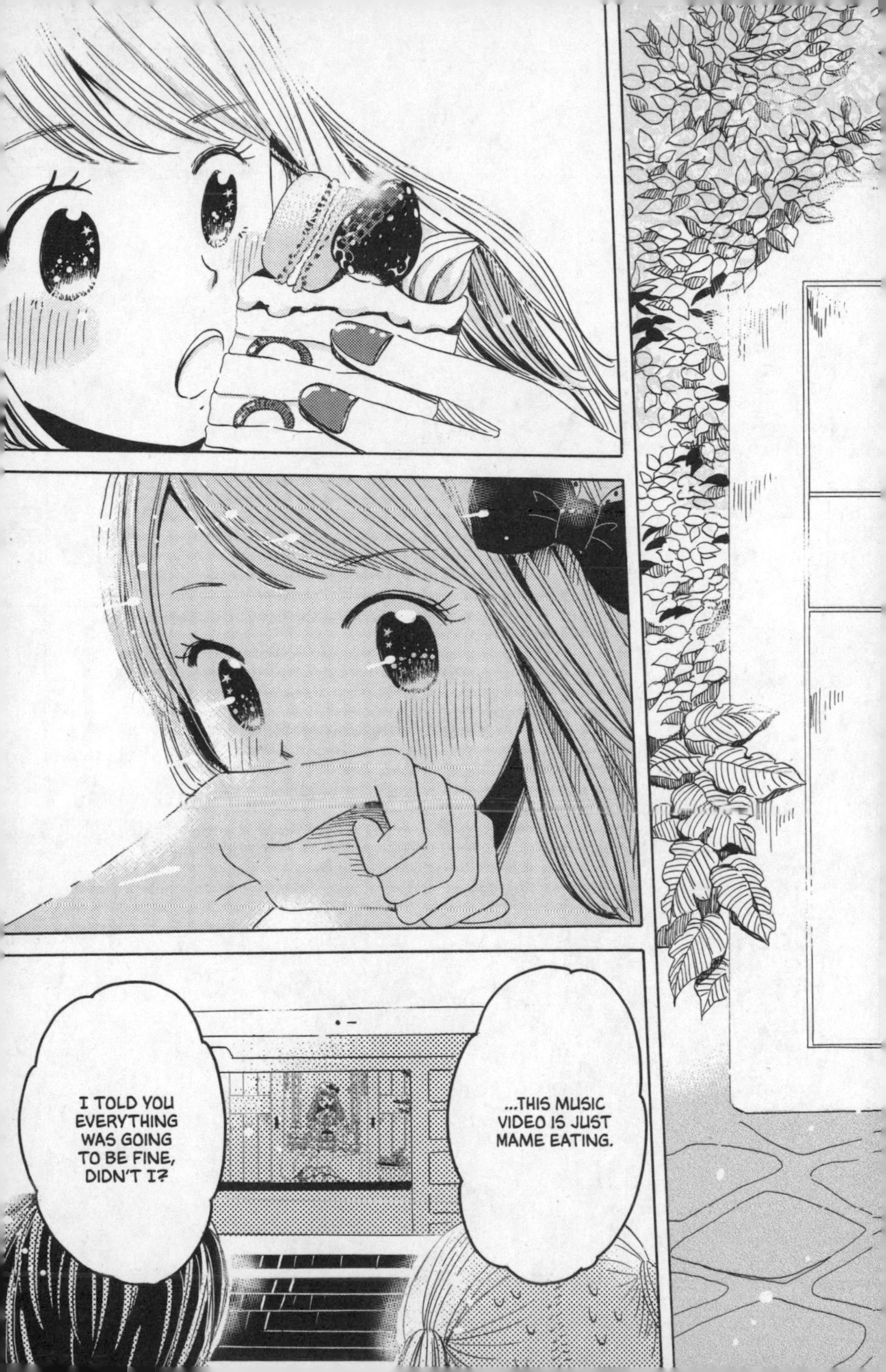
...THIS MUSIC VIDEO IS JUST MAME EATING.
I TOLD YOU EVERYTHING WAS GOING TO BE FINE, DIDN'T I?

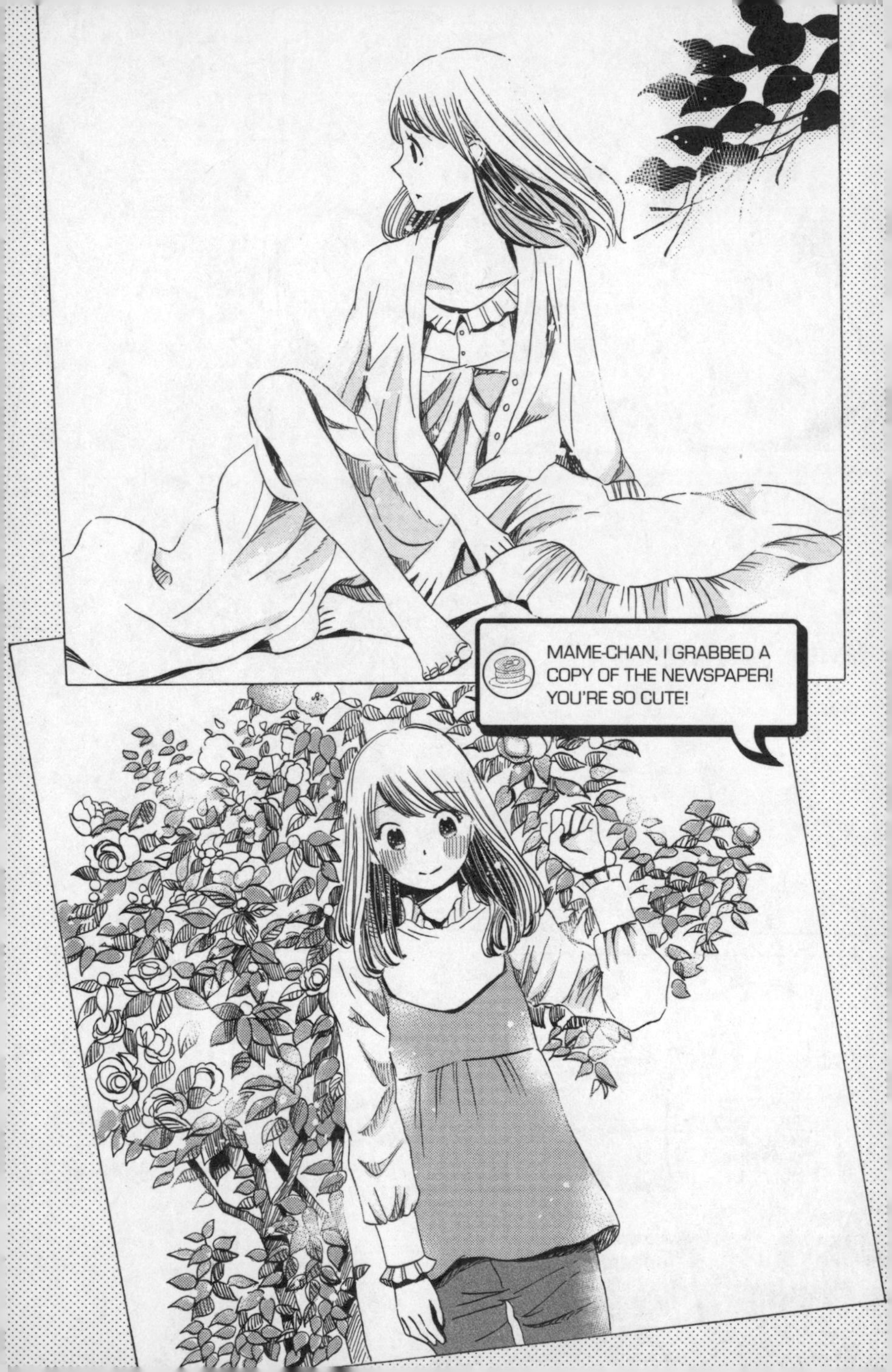
MAME-CHAN, I GRABBED A COPY OF THE NEWSPAPER! YOU'RE SO CUTE!

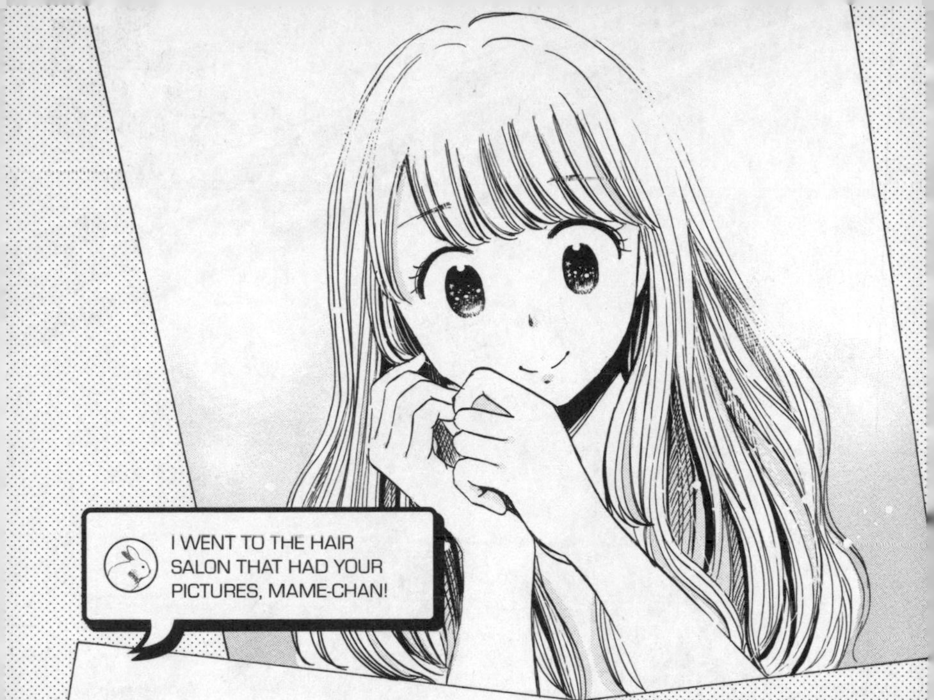
I WENT TO THE HAIR SALON THAT HAD YOUR PICTURES, MAME-CHAN!

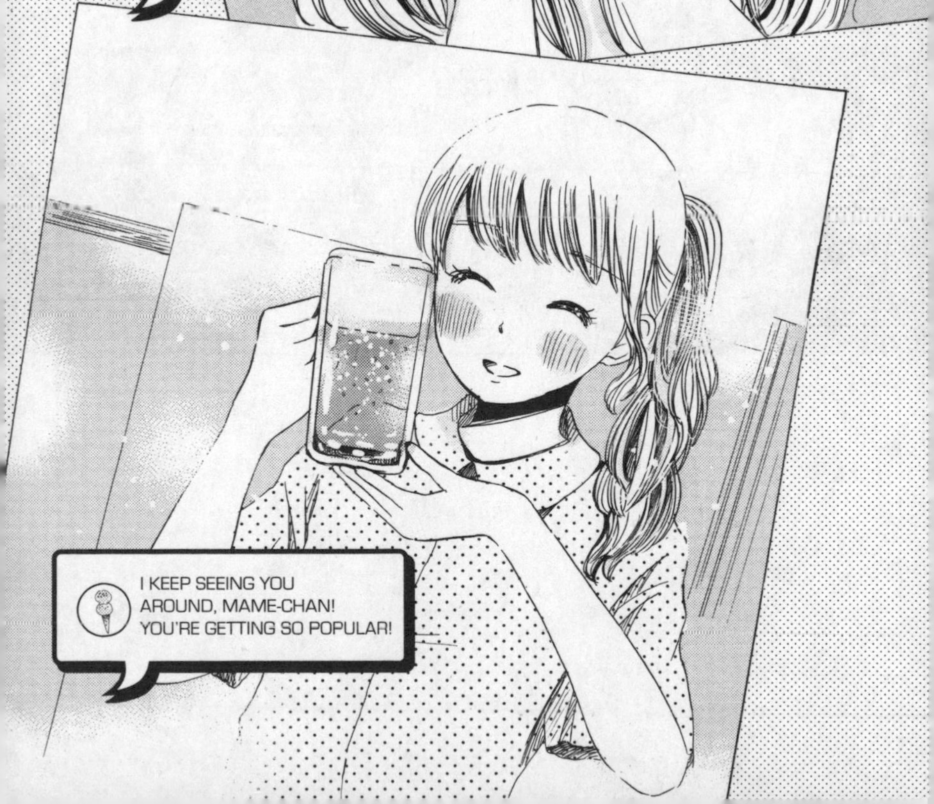
I KEEP SEEING YOU AROUND, MAME-CHAN! YOU'RE GETTING SO POPULAR!

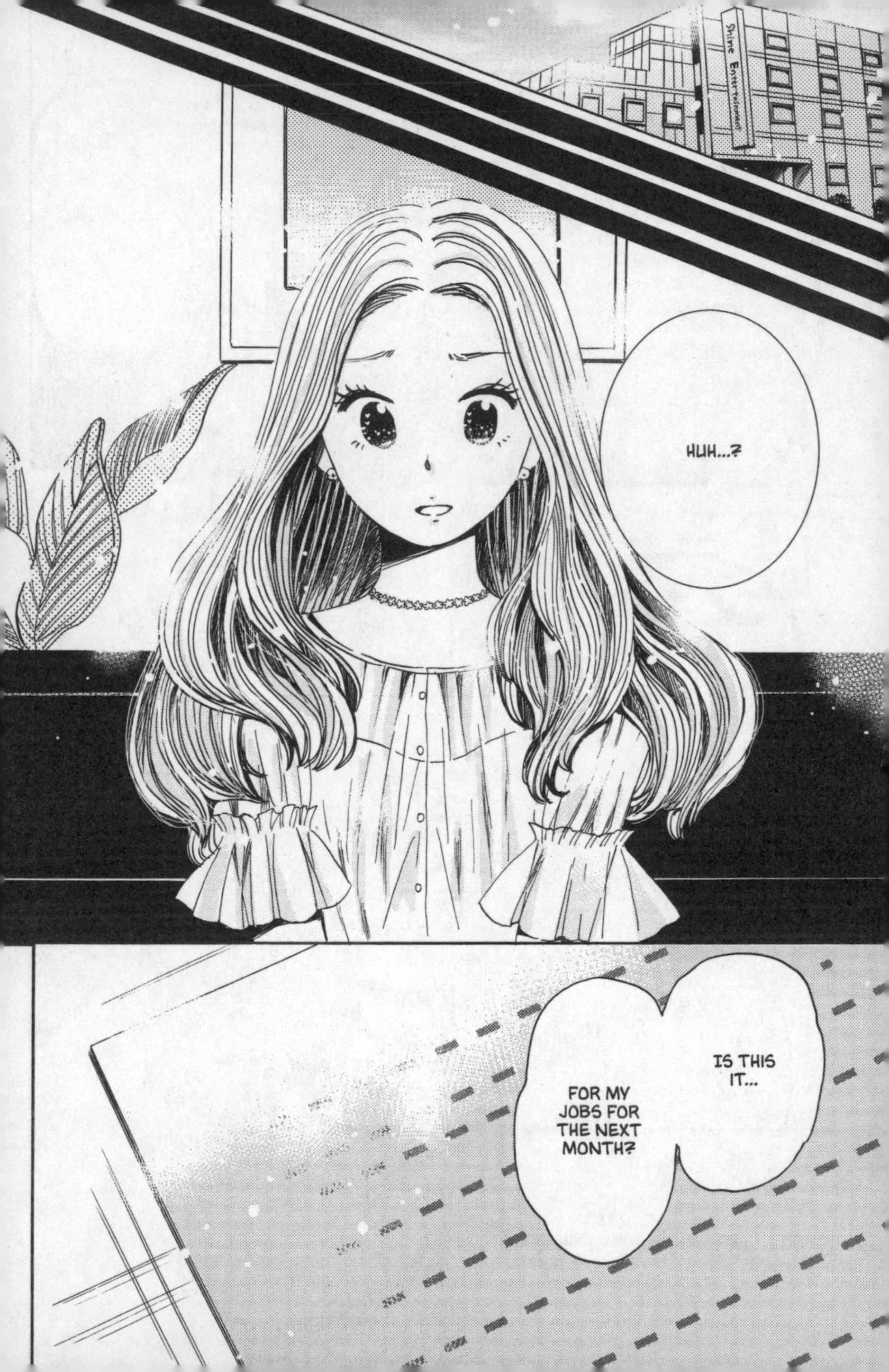
Shine Entertainment
HUH...?
IS THIS IT...
FOR MY JOBS FOR THE NEXT MONTH?

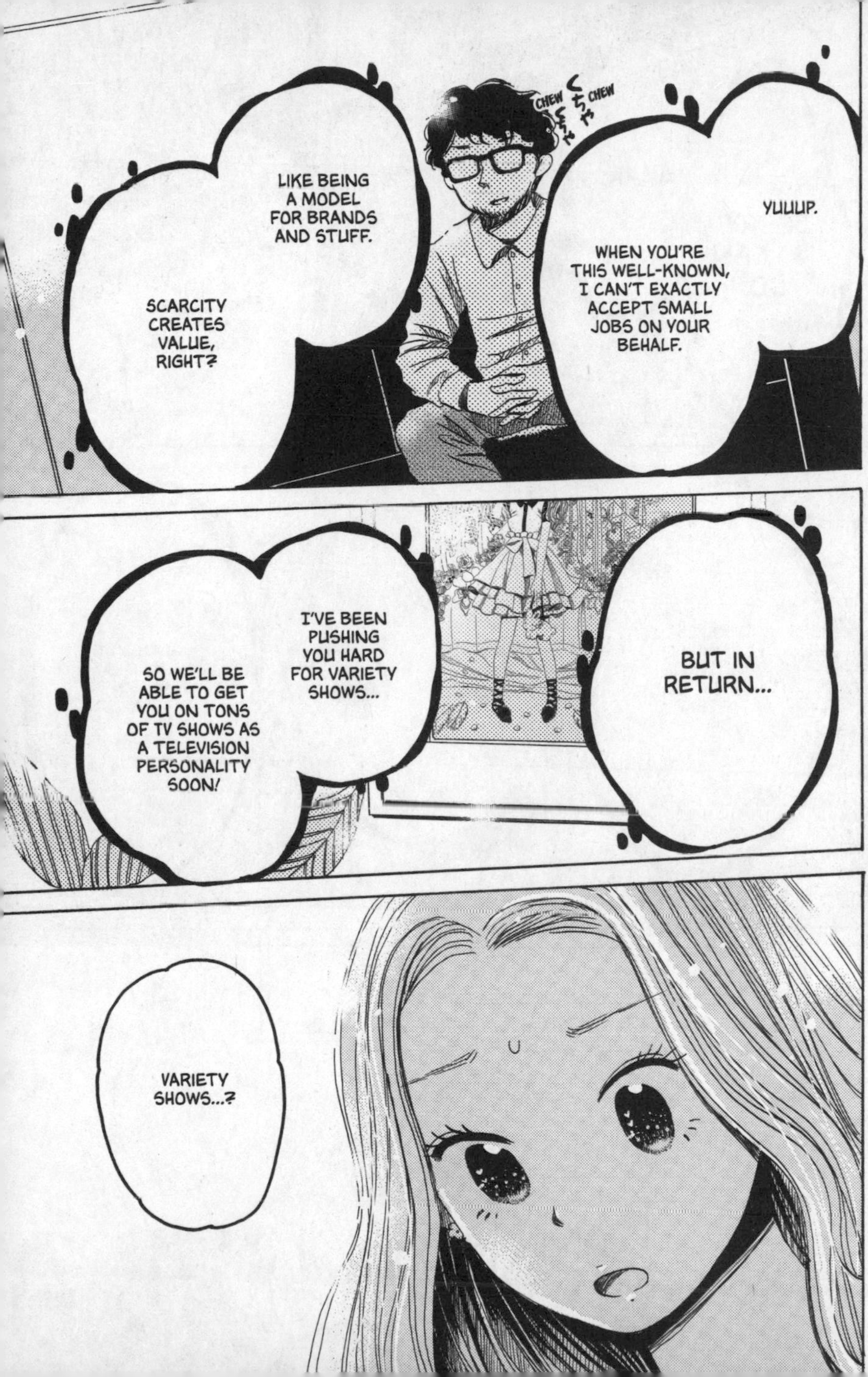
CHEW くちゃ CHEW くちゃ
YUUUP.
WHEN YOU'RE THIS WELL-KNOWN, I CAN'T EXACTLY ACCEPT SMALL JOBS ON YOUR BEHALF.
LIKE BEING A MODEL FOR BRANDS AND STUFF.
SCARCITY CREATES VALUE, RIGHT?
BUT IN RETURN...
I'VE BEEN PUSHING YOU HARD FOR VARIETY SHOWS...
SO WE'LL BE ABLE TO GET YOU ON TONS OF TV SHOWS AS A TELEVISION PERSONALITY SOON!
VARIETY SHOWS...?

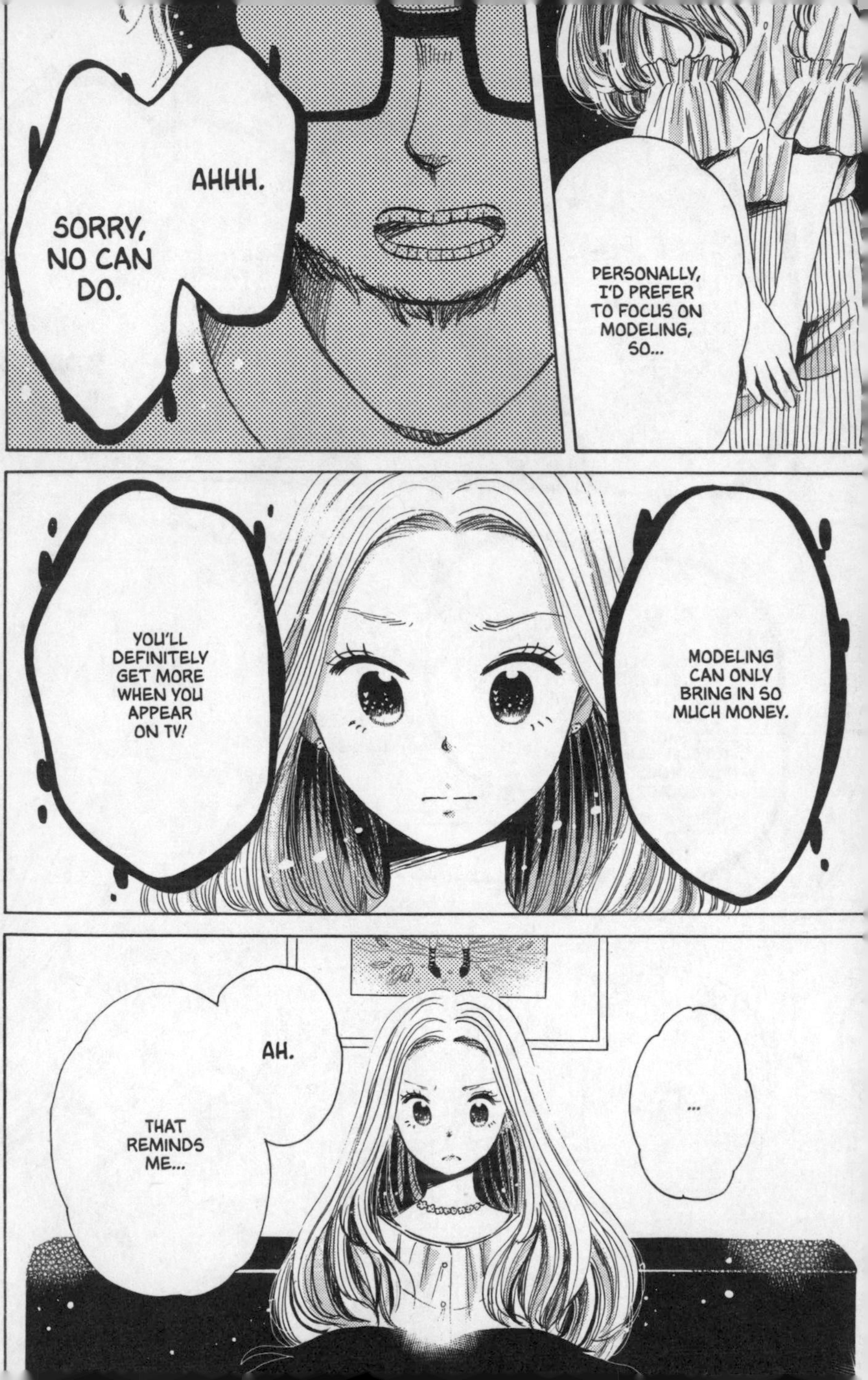
PERSONALLY, I'D PREFER TO FOCUS ON MODELING, SO...
AHHH.
SORRY, NO CAN DO.
MODELING CAN ONLY BRING IN SO MUCH MONEY.
YOU'LL DEFINITELY GET MORE WHEN YOU APPEAR ON TV!
...
AH.
THAT REMINDS ME...

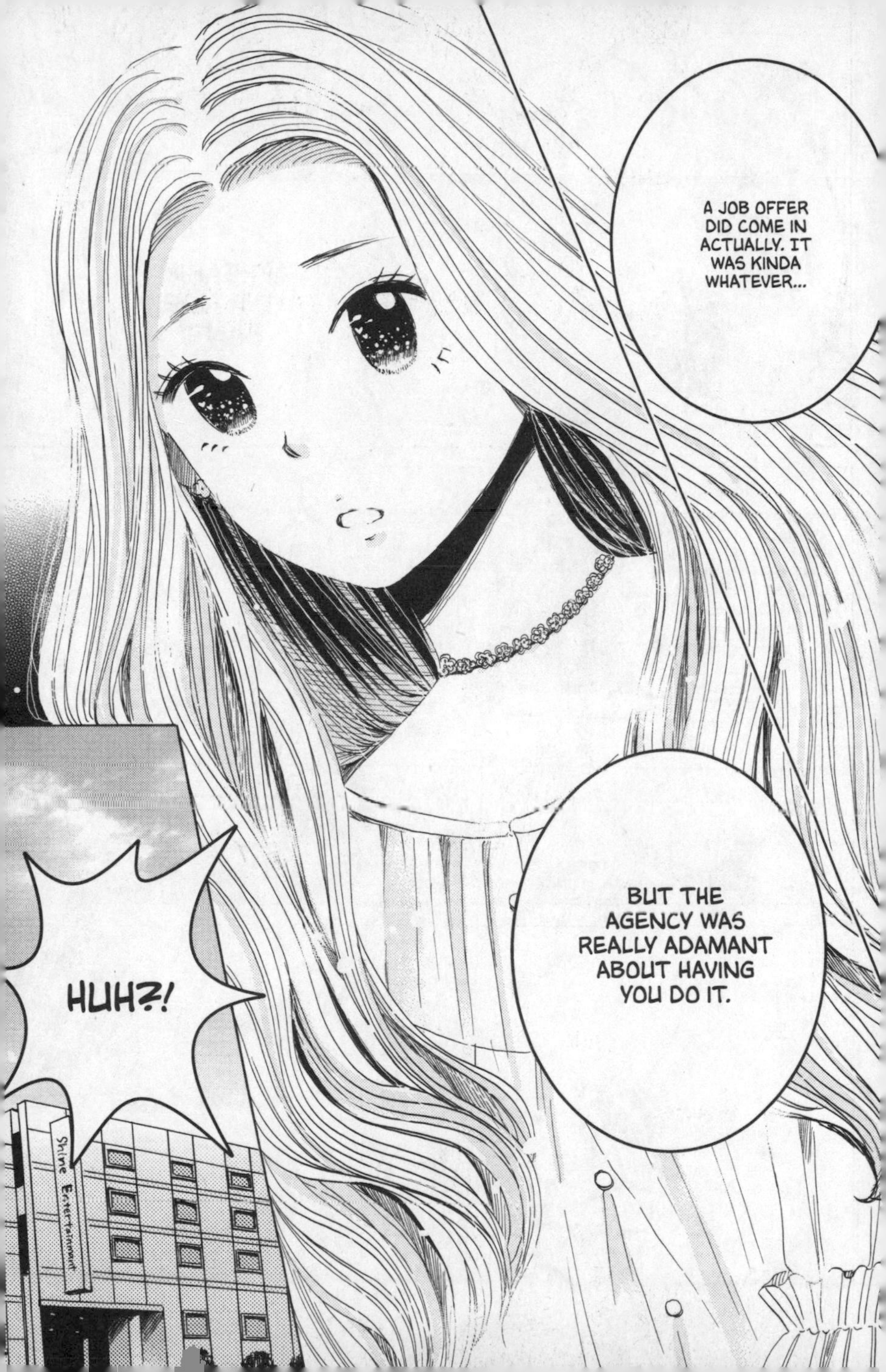
A JOB OFFER DID COME IN ACTUALLY. IT WAS KINDA WHATEVER...
BUT THE AGENCY WAS REALLY ADAMANT ABOUT HAVING YOU DO IT.
HUH?!
Shine Entertainment

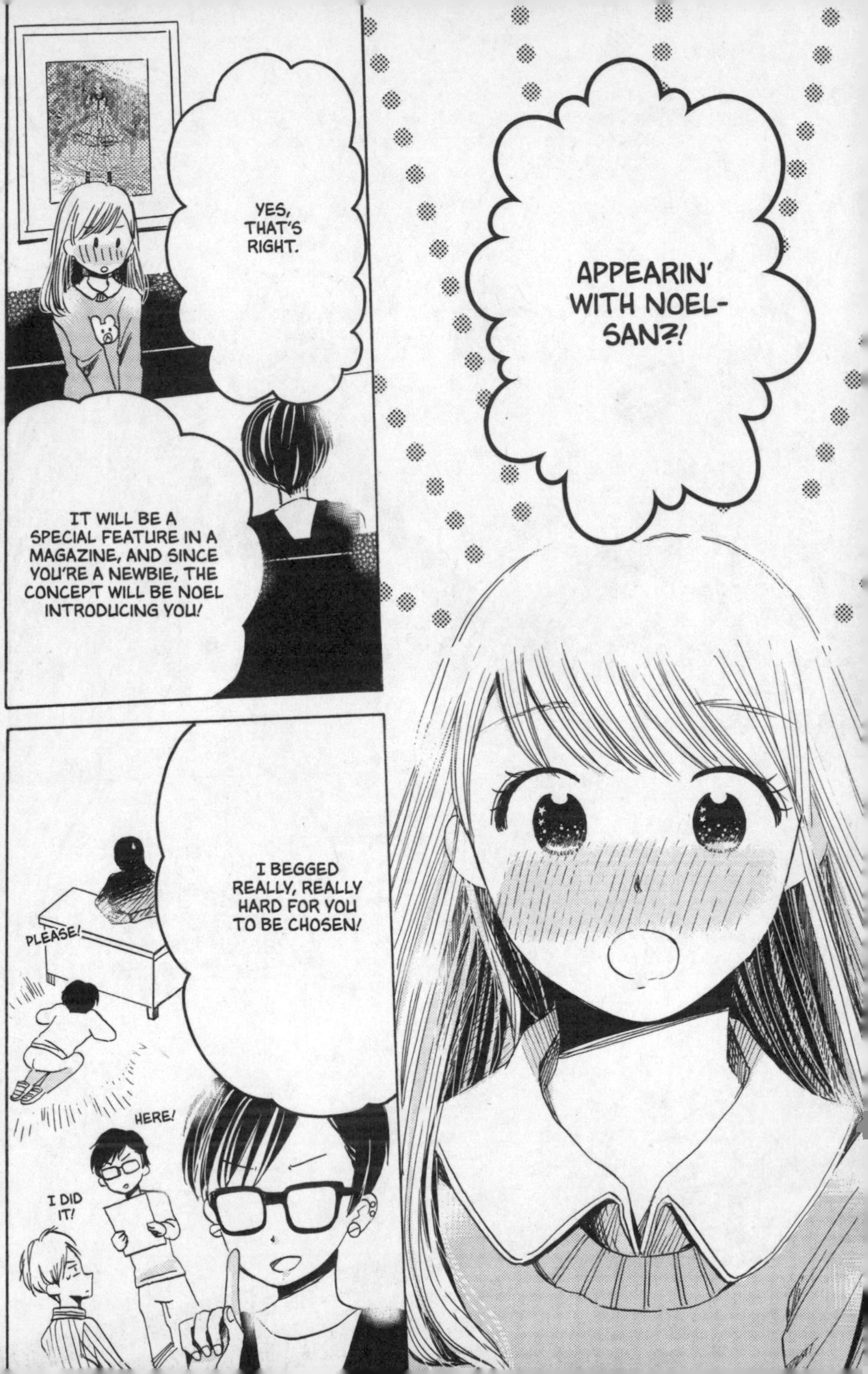
APPEARIN' WITH NOEL-SAN?!
YES, THAT'S RIGHT.
IT WILL BE A SPECIAL FEATURE IN A MAGAZINE, AND SINCE YOU'RE A NEWBIE, THE CONCEPT WILL BE NOEL INTRODUCING YOU!
I BEGGED REALLY, REALLY HARD FOR YOU TO BE CHOSEN!
PLEASE!
HERE!
I DID IT!

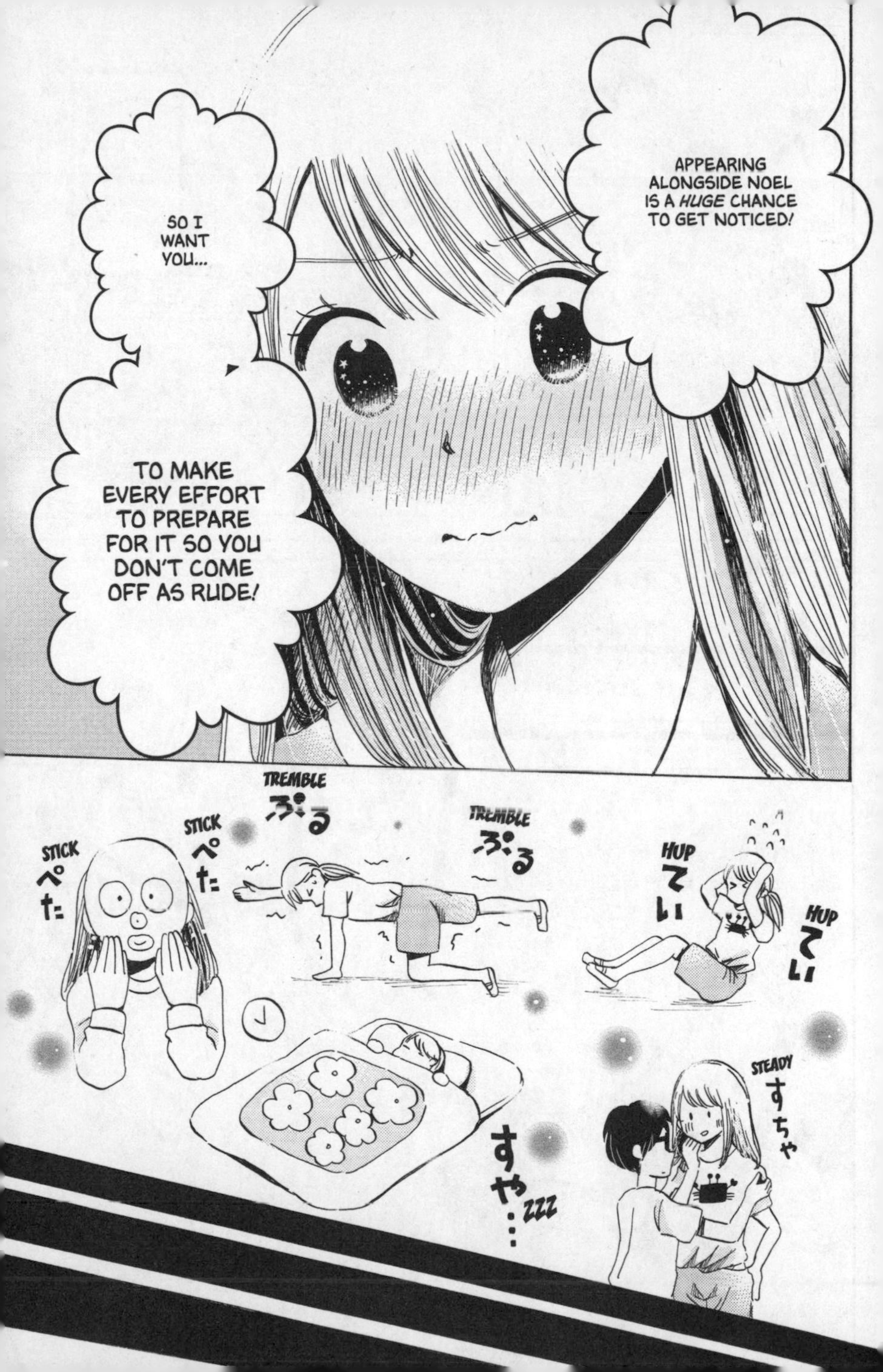
APPEARING ALONGSIDE NOEL IS A *HUGE* CHANCE TO GET NOTICED!
SO I WANT YOU...
TO MAKE EVERY EFFORT TO PREPARE FOR IT SO YOU DON'T COME OFF AS RUDE!
HUP てい
HUP てい
TREMBLE ぷる
TREMBLE ぷる
STICK ぺた
STICK ぺた
STEADY すちゃ
すや... ZZZ

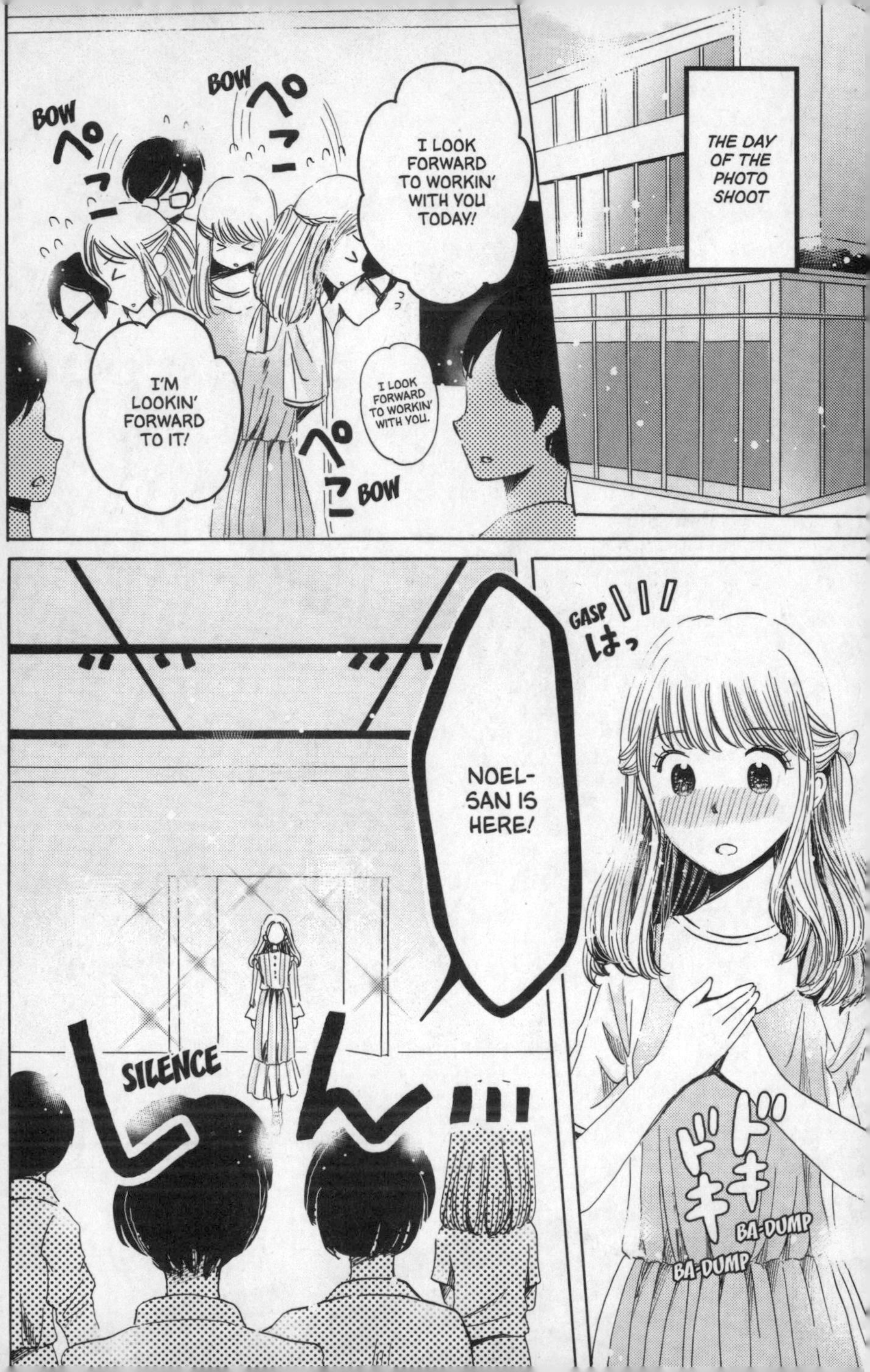
THE DAY OF THE PHOTO SHOOT
I LOOK FORWARD TO WORKIN' WITH YOU TODAY!
BOW ぺこ
BOW ぺこ
I LOOK FORWARD TO WORKIN' WITH YOU.
ぺこ BOW
I'M LOOKIN' FORWARD TO IT!
GASP はっ
NOEL-SAN IS HERE!
ドキドキ
BA-DUMP
BA-DUMP
SILENCE
しん…

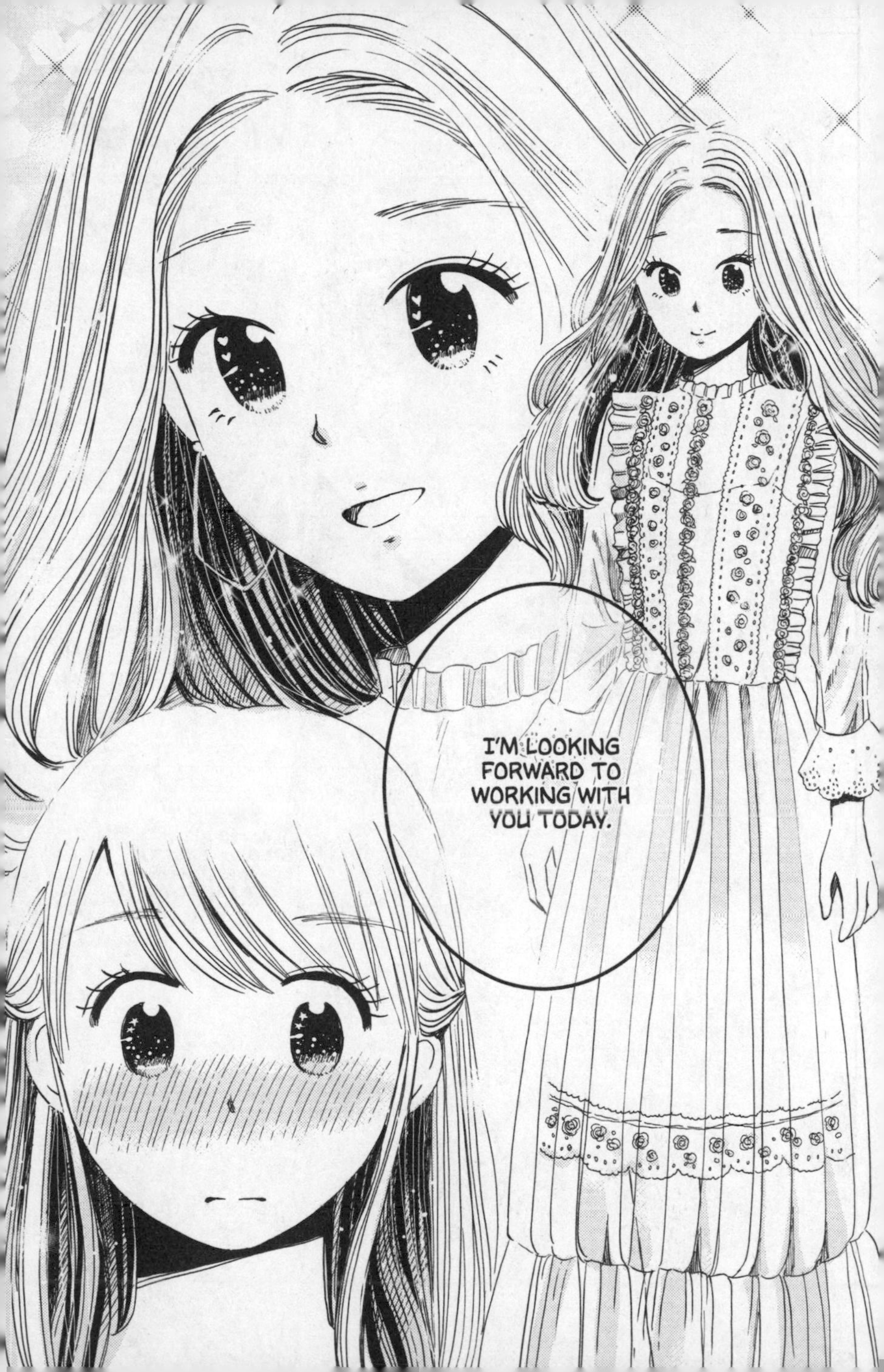
I'M LOOKING FORWARD TO WORKING WITH YOU TODAY.

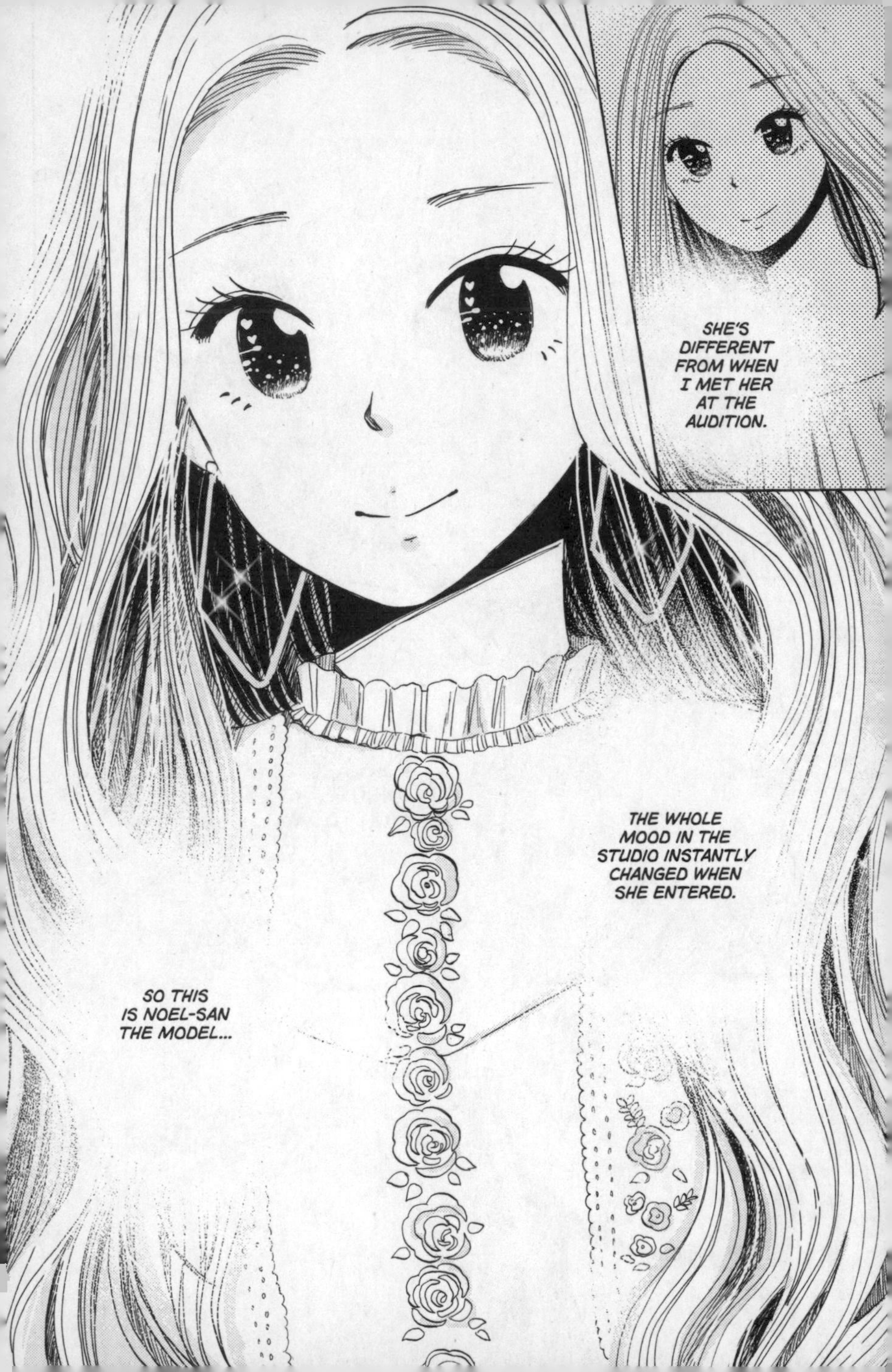
SHE'S DIFFERENT FROM WHEN I MET HER AT THE AUDITION.
THE WHOLE MOOD IN THE STUDIO INSTANTLY CHANGED WHEN SHE ENTERED.
SO THIS IS NOEL-SAN THE MODEL...

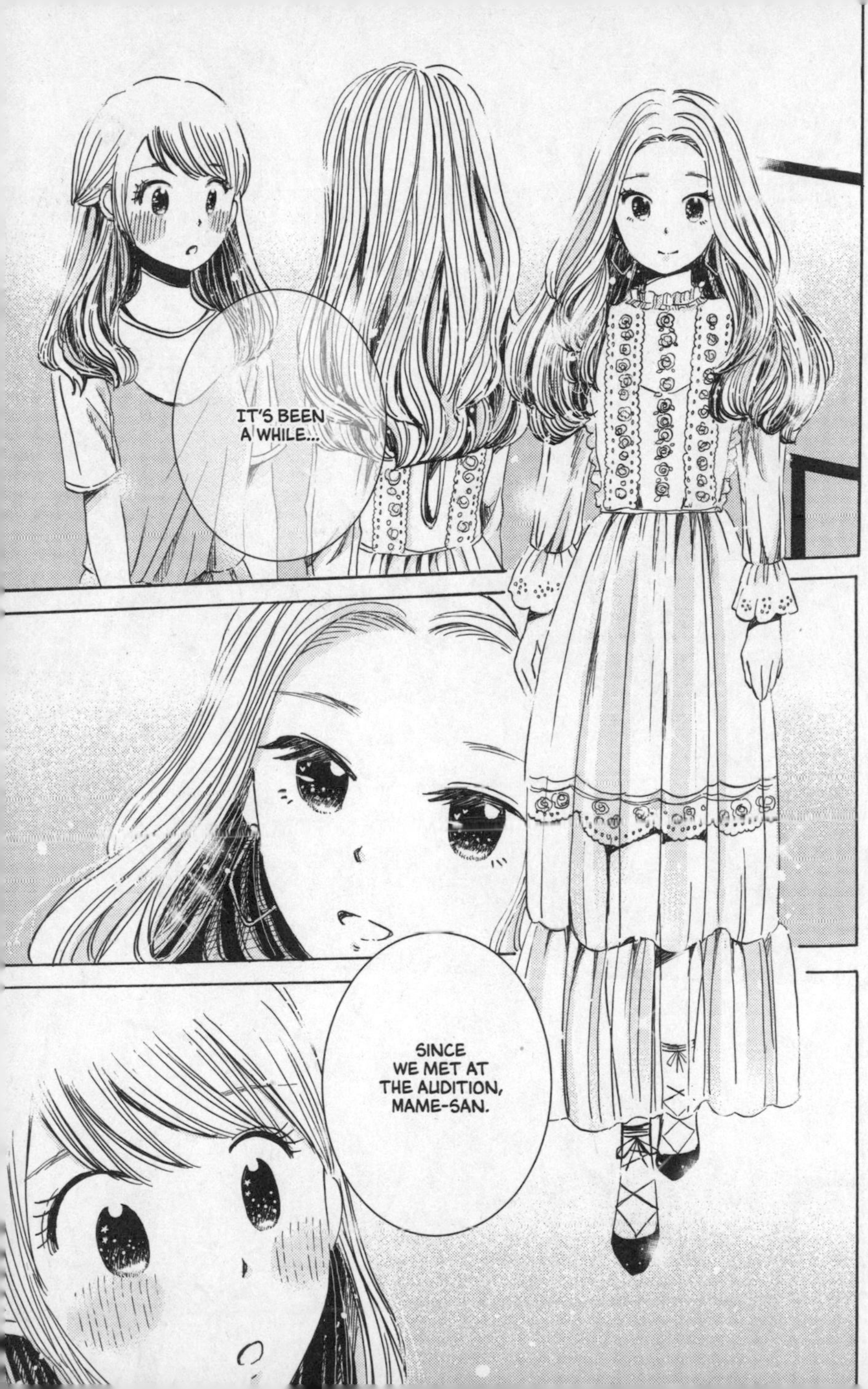
IT'S BEEN A WHILE...
SINCE WE MET AT THE AUDITION, MAME-SAN.

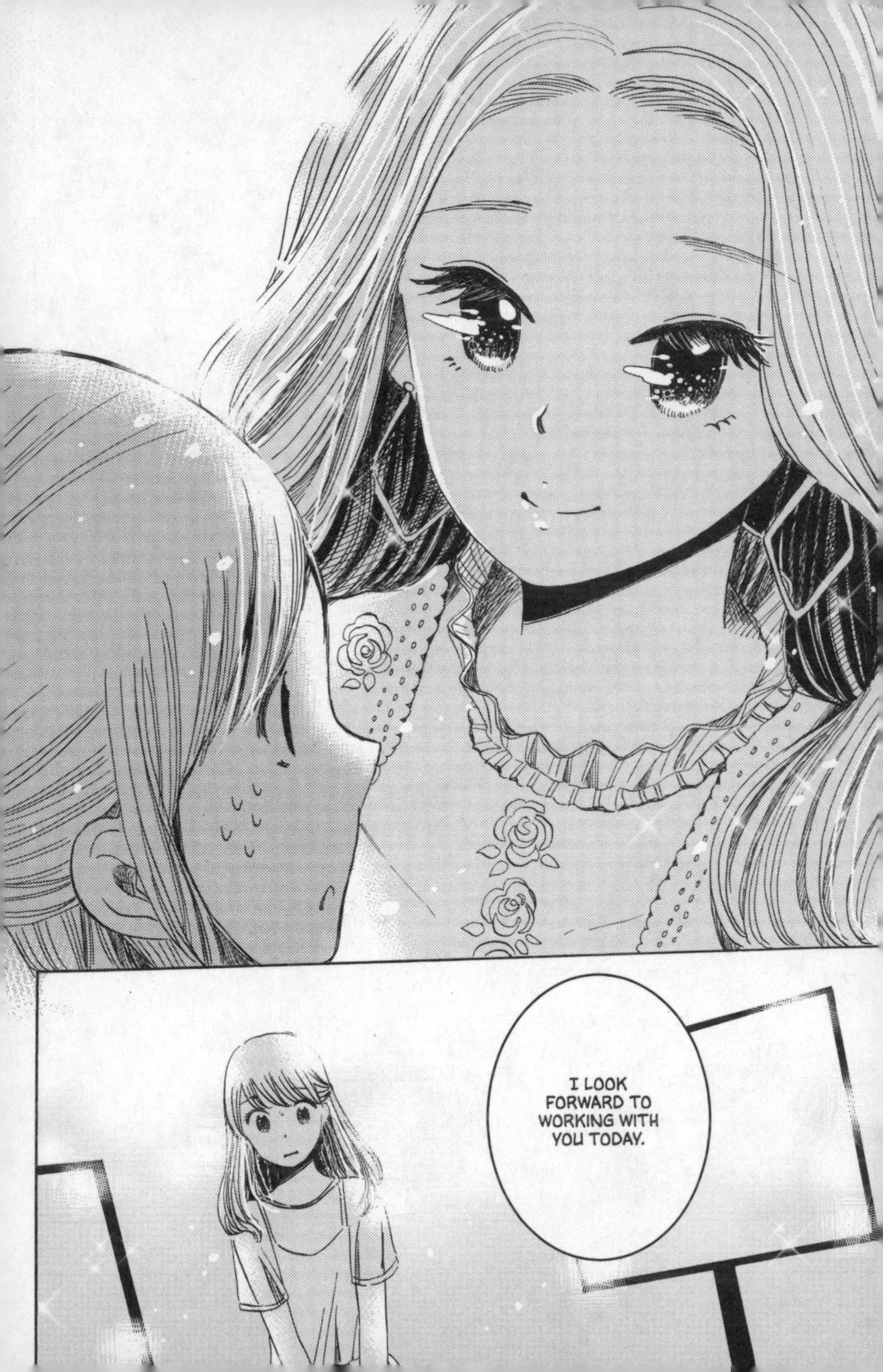
I LOOK FORWARD TO WORKING WITH YOU TODAY.

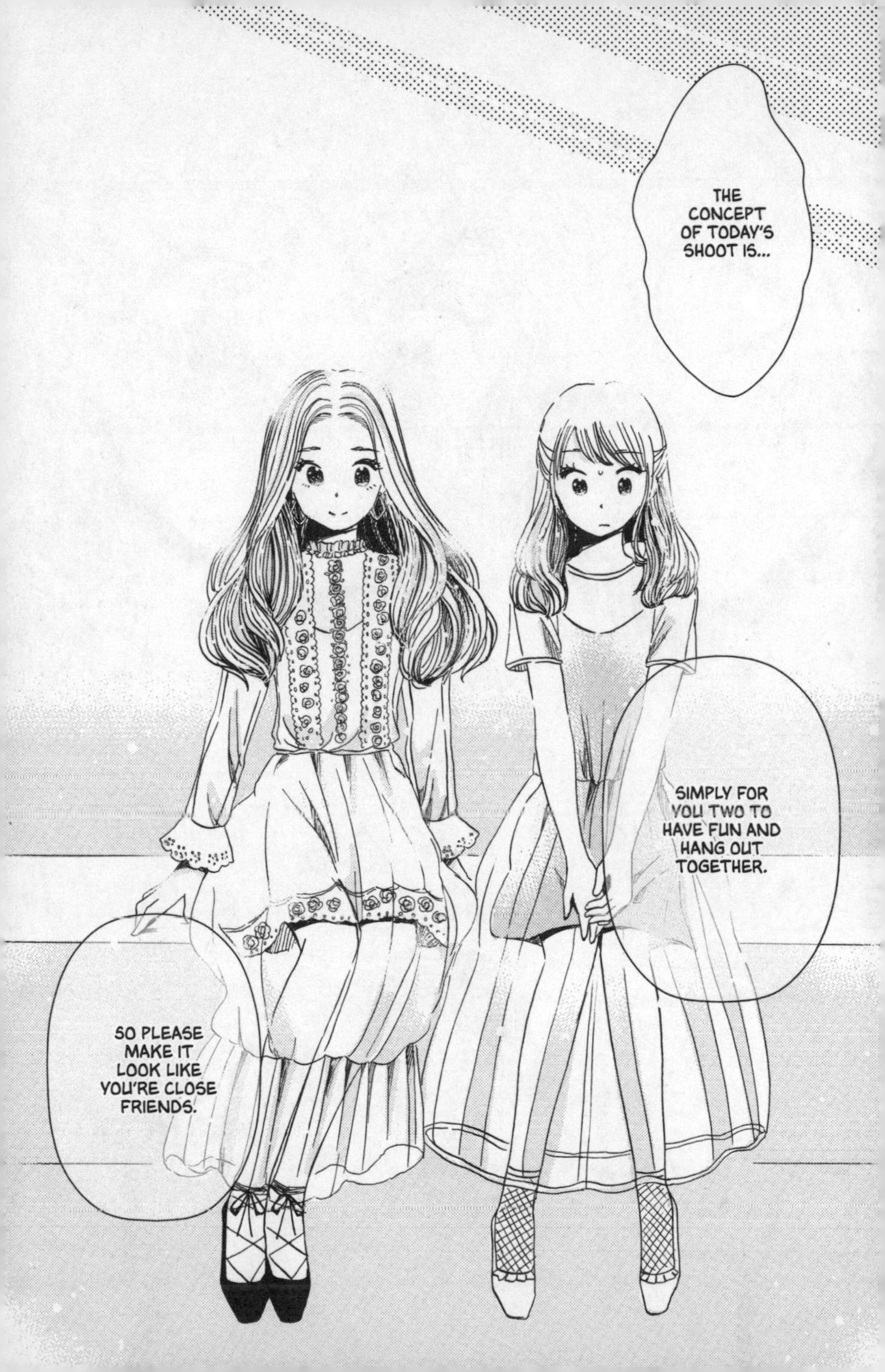
THE CONCEPT OF TODAY'S SHOOT IS...
SIMPLY FOR YOU TWO TO HAVE FUN AND HANG OUT TOGETHER.
SO PLEASE MAKE IT LOOK LIKE YOU'RE CLOSE FRIENDS.

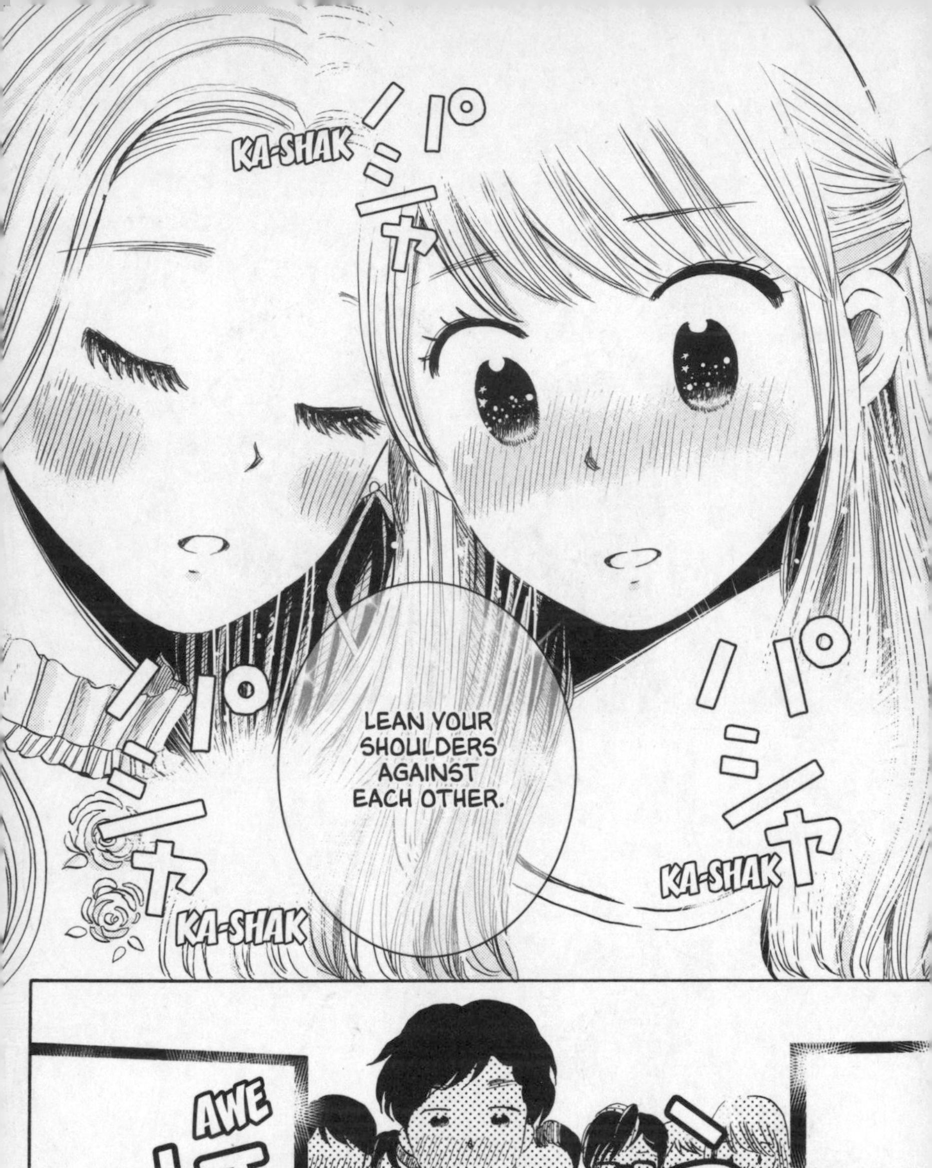
パシャ
KA-SHAK
パシャ
KA-SHAK
LEAN YOUR SHOULDERS AGAINST EACH OTHER.
パシャ
KA-SHAK
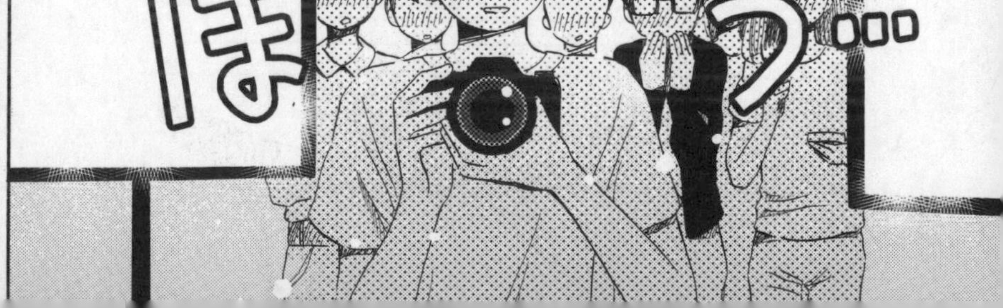
ほう…
AWE

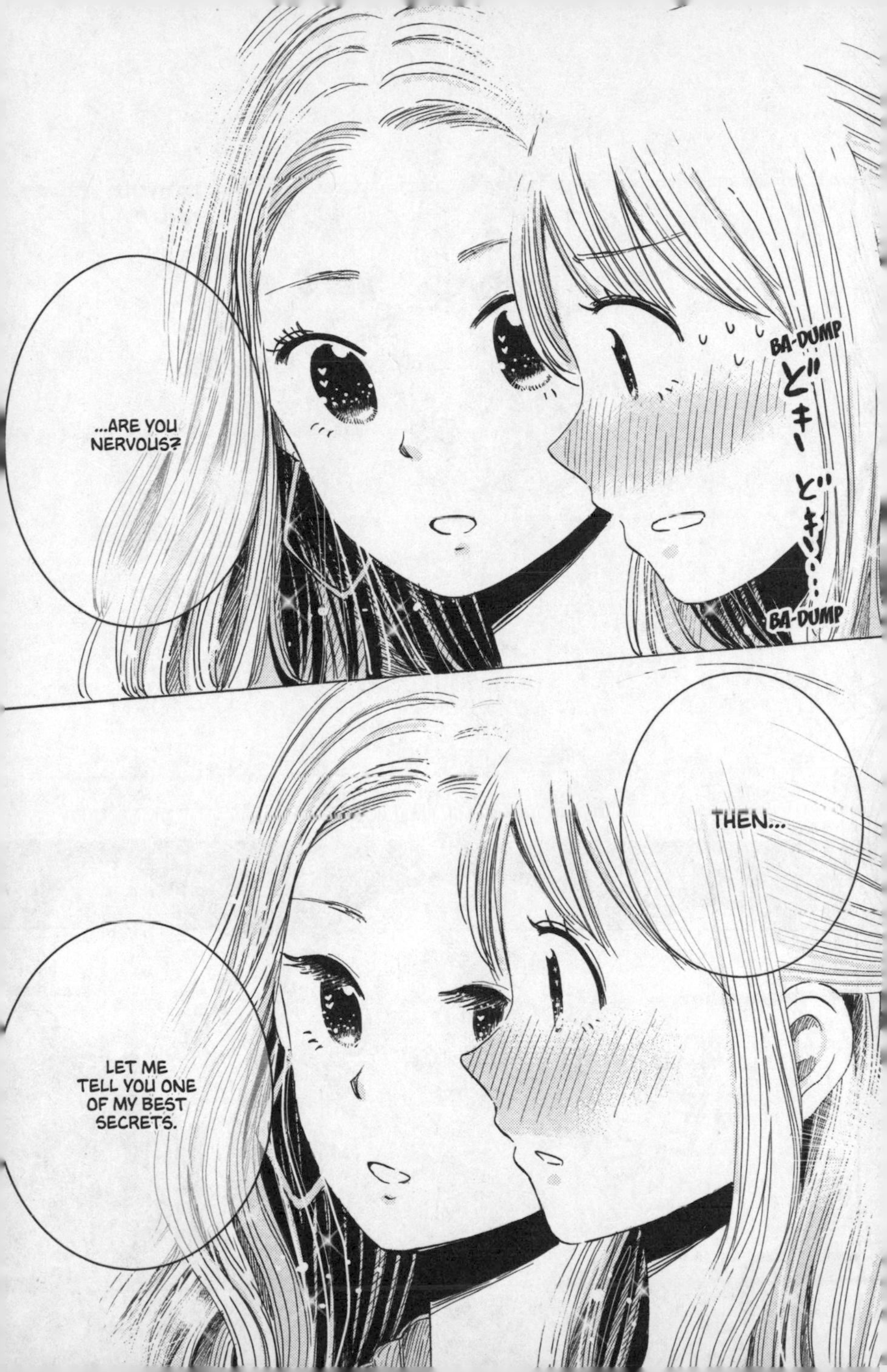
BA-DUMP
どき
どき…
BA-DUMP
...ARE YOU NERVOUS?
THEN...
LET ME TELL YOU ONE OF MY BEST SECRETS.

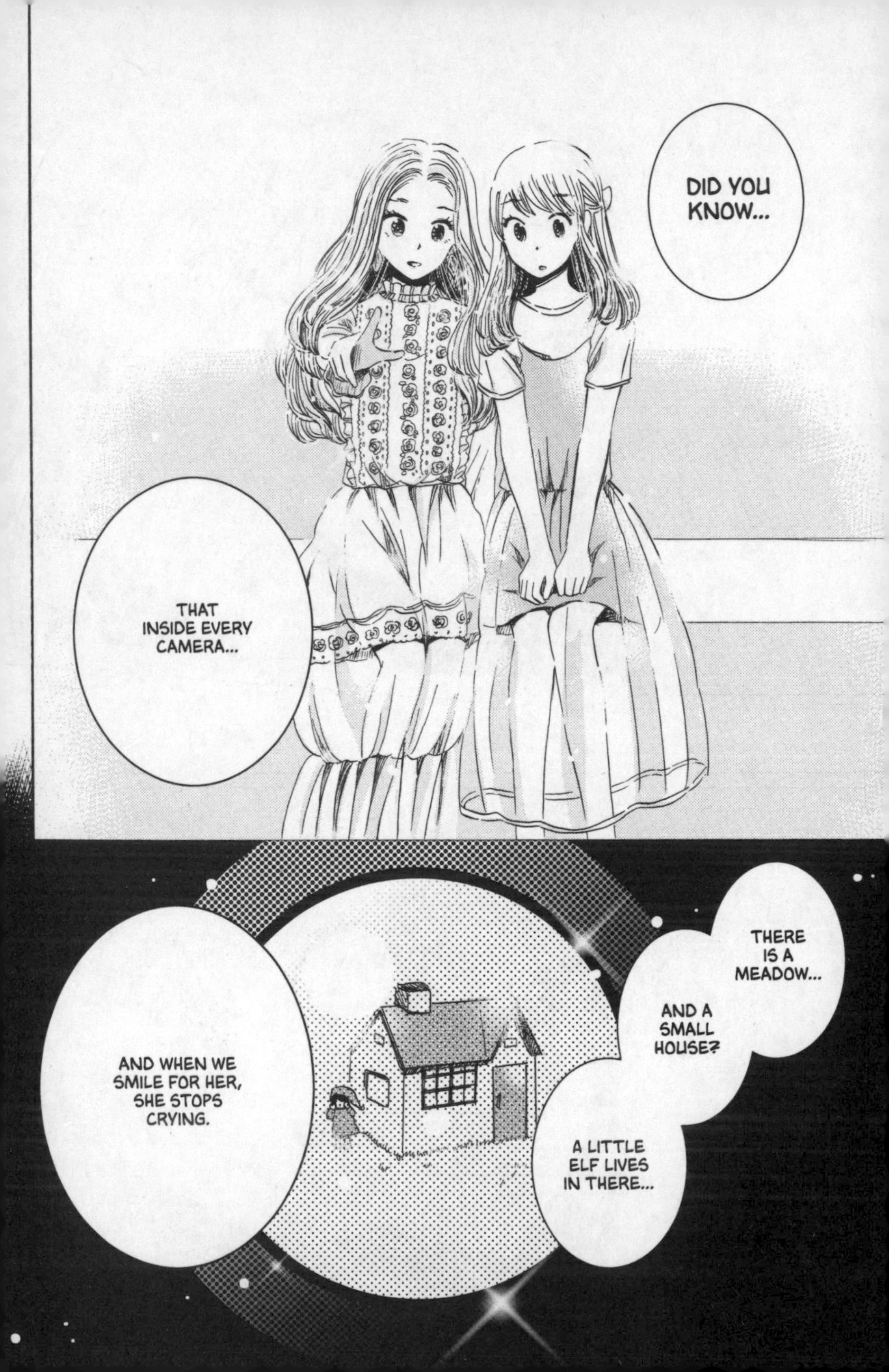
DID YOU KNOW...
THAT INSIDE EVERY CAMERA...
THERE IS A MEADOW...
AND A SMALL HOUSE?
A LITTLE ELF LIVES IN THERE...
AND WHEN WE SMILE FOR HER, SHE STOPS CRYING.

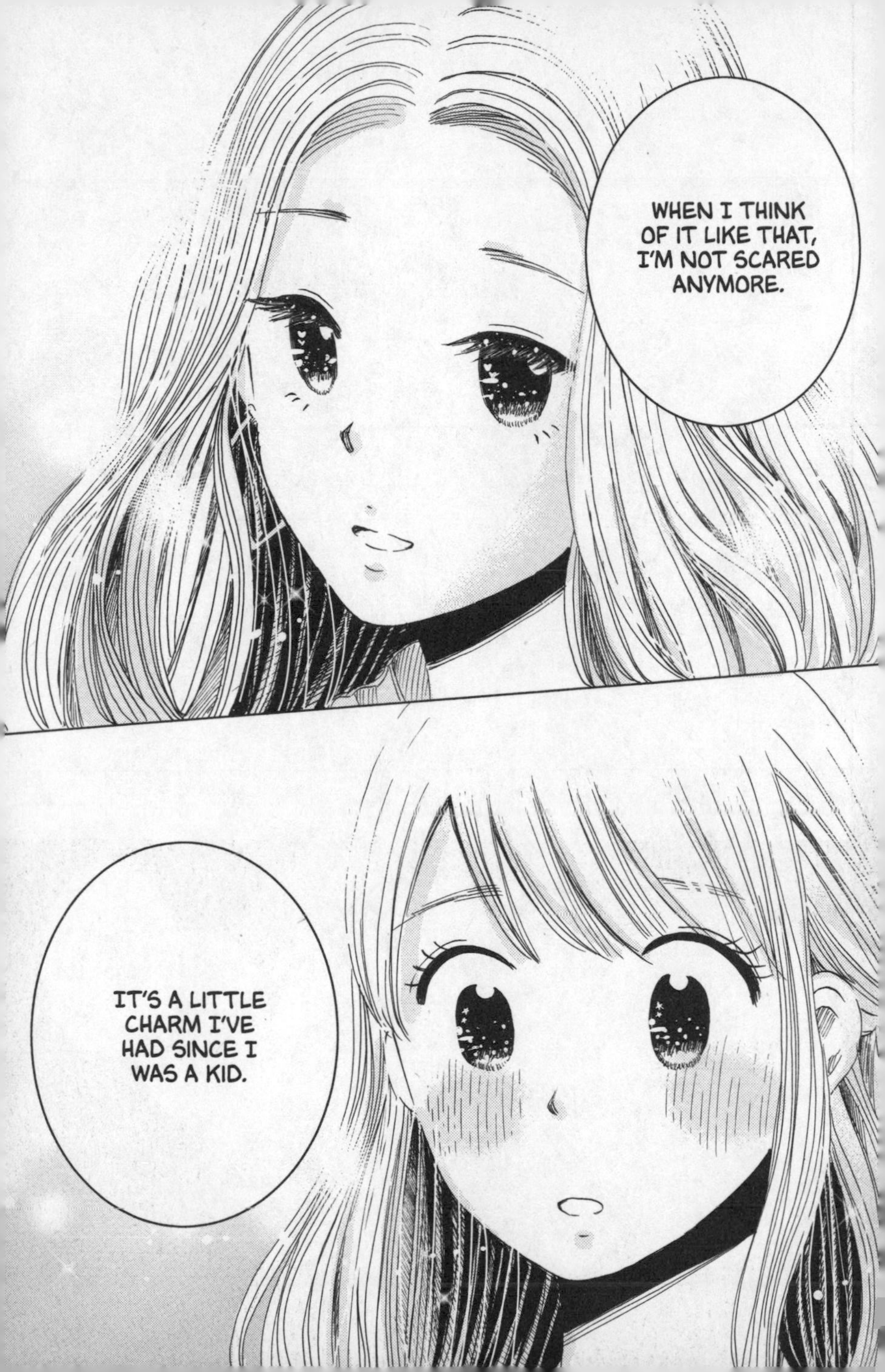
WHEN I THINK OF IT LIKE THAT, I'M NOT SCARED ANYMORE.
IT'S A LITTLE CHARM I'VE HAD SINCE I WAS A KID.

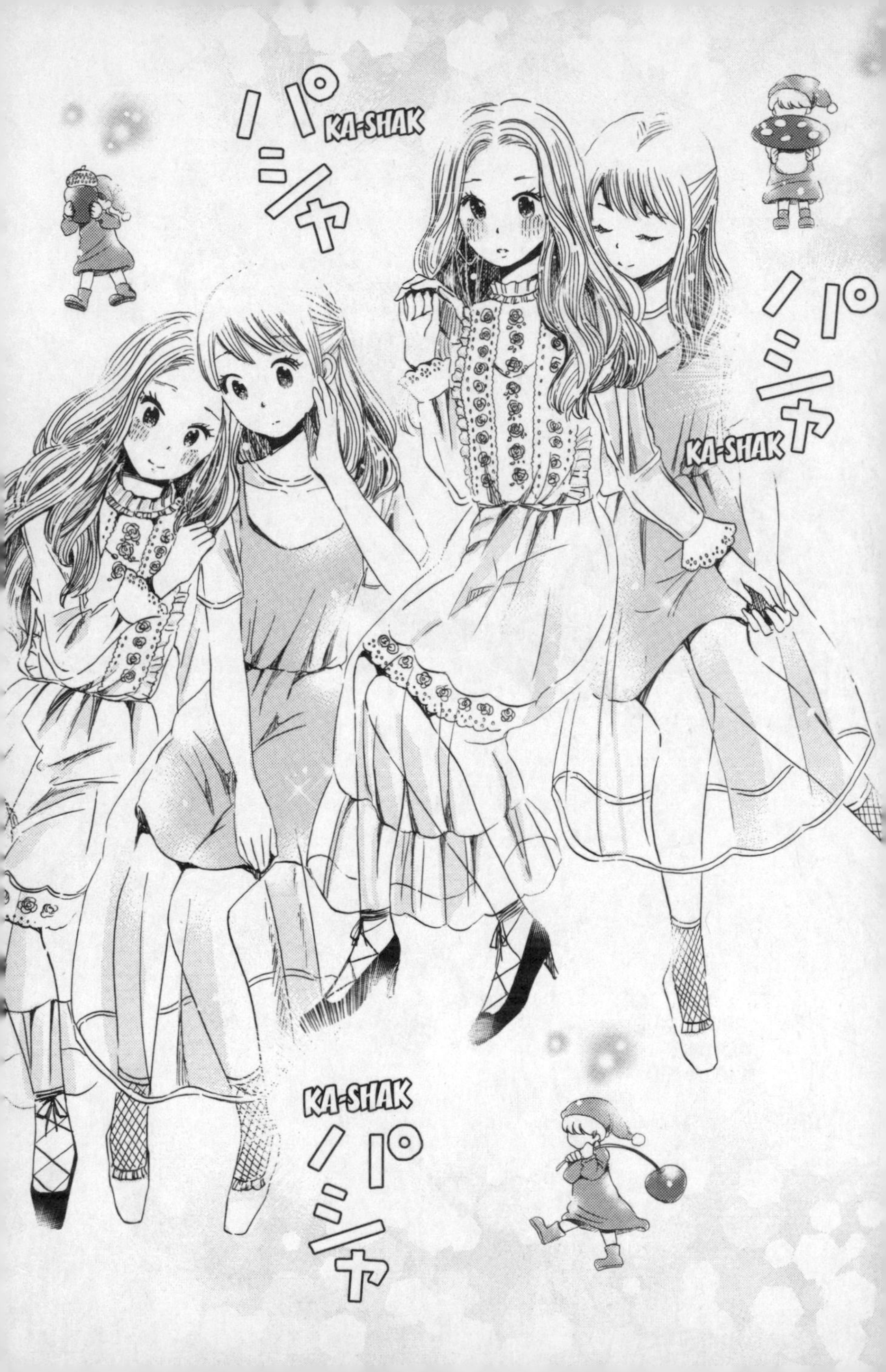
パシャ
KA-SHAK
パシャ
KA-SHAK
KA-SHAK
パシャ

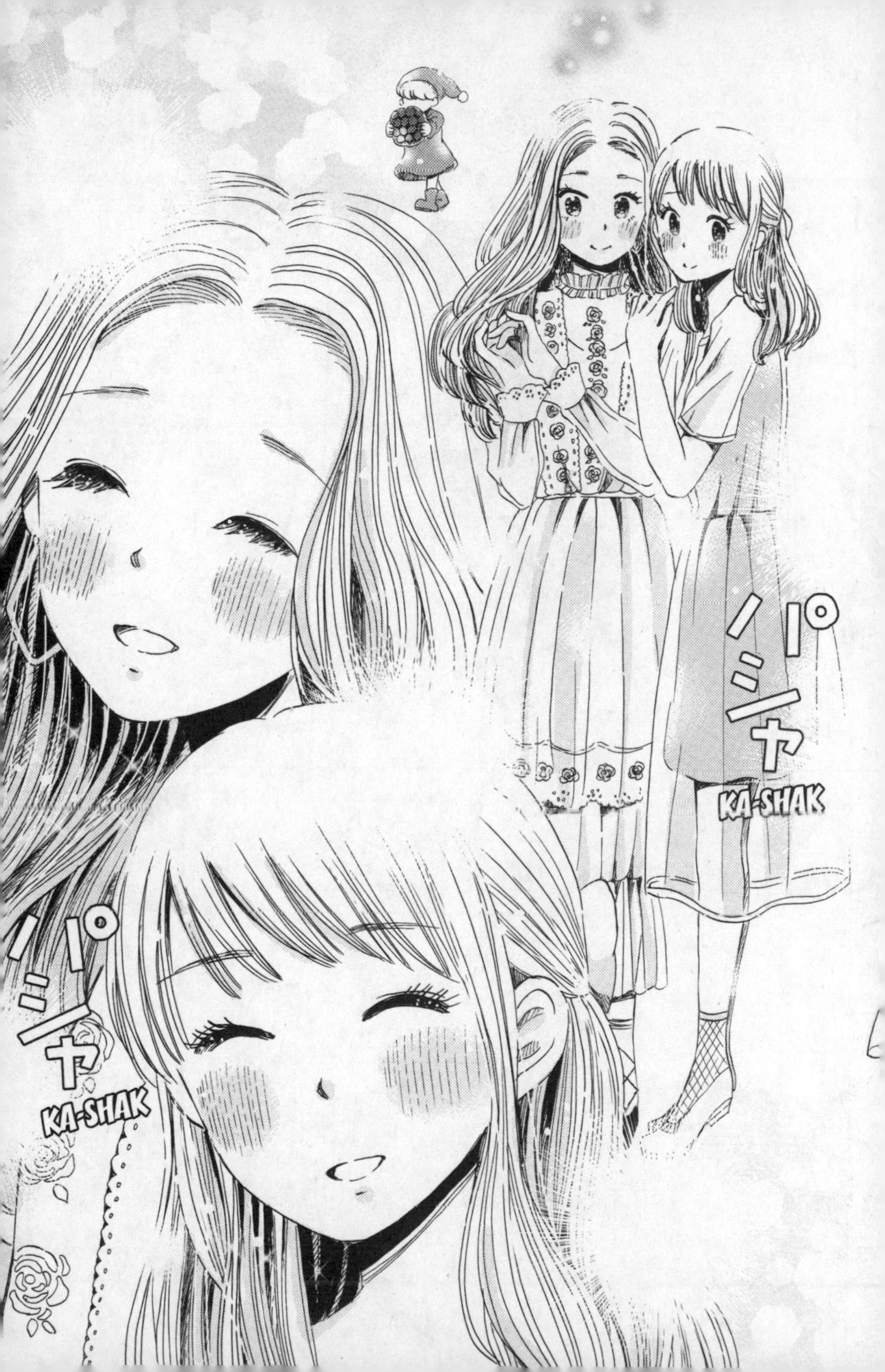
パシャ
KA-SHAK
パシャ
KA-SHAK

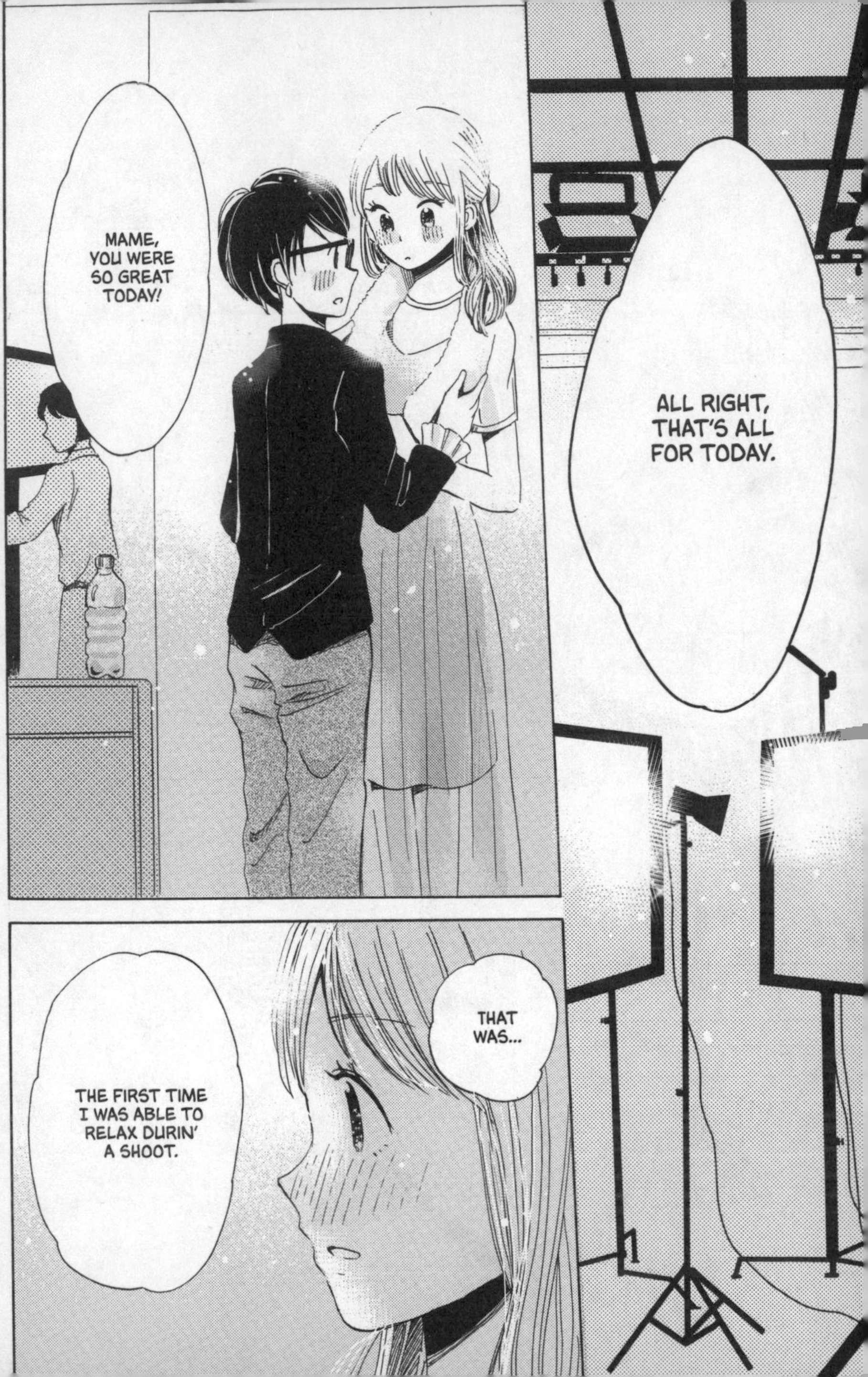
ALL RIGHT, THAT'S ALL FOR TODAY.
MAME, YOU WERE SO GREAT TODAY!
THAT WAS...
THE FIRST TIME I WAS ABLE TO RELAX DURIN' A SHOOT.

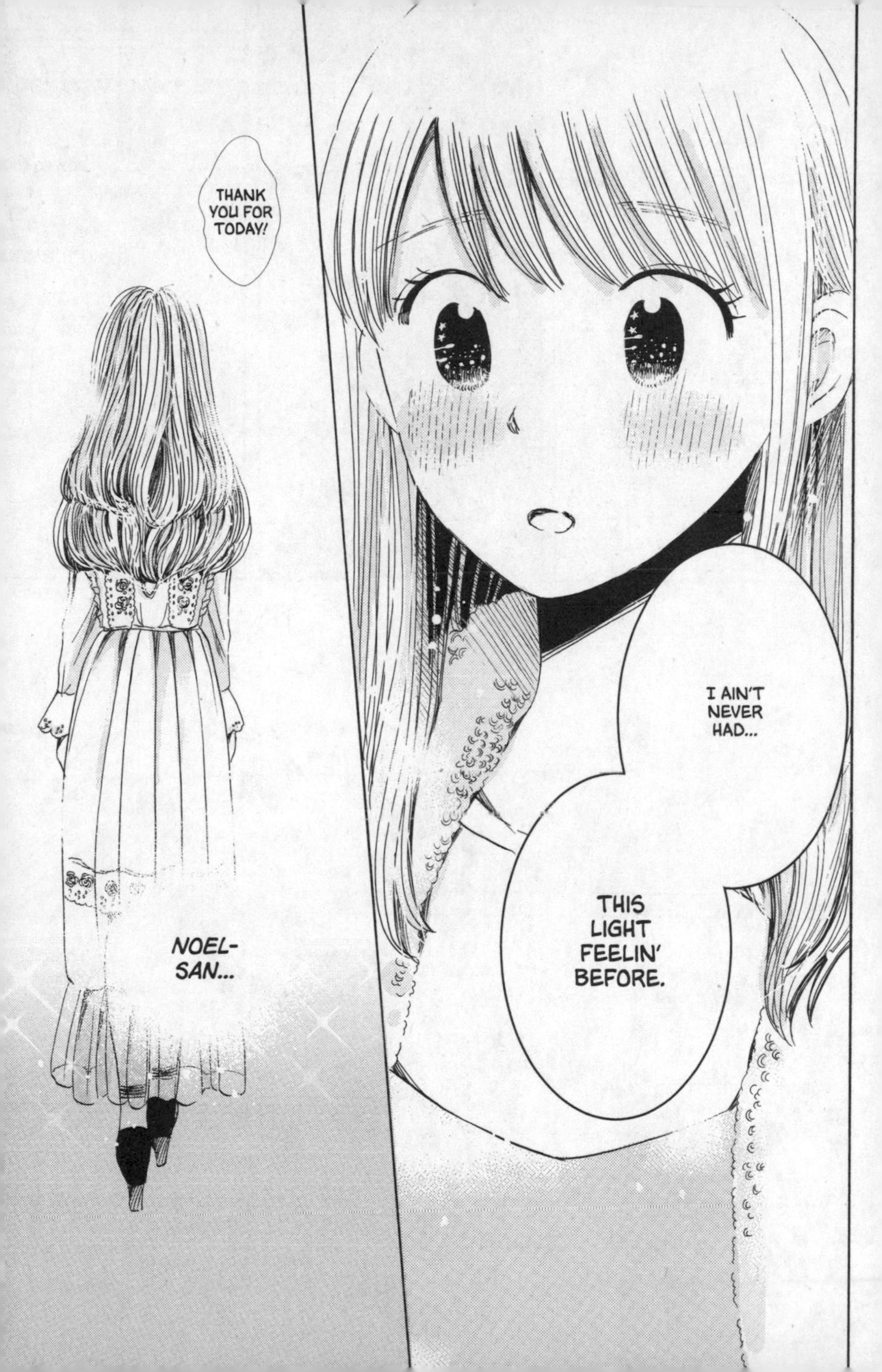
I AIN'T NEVER HAD...
THIS LIGHT FEELIN' BEFORE.
THANK YOU FOR TODAY!
NOEL-SAN...

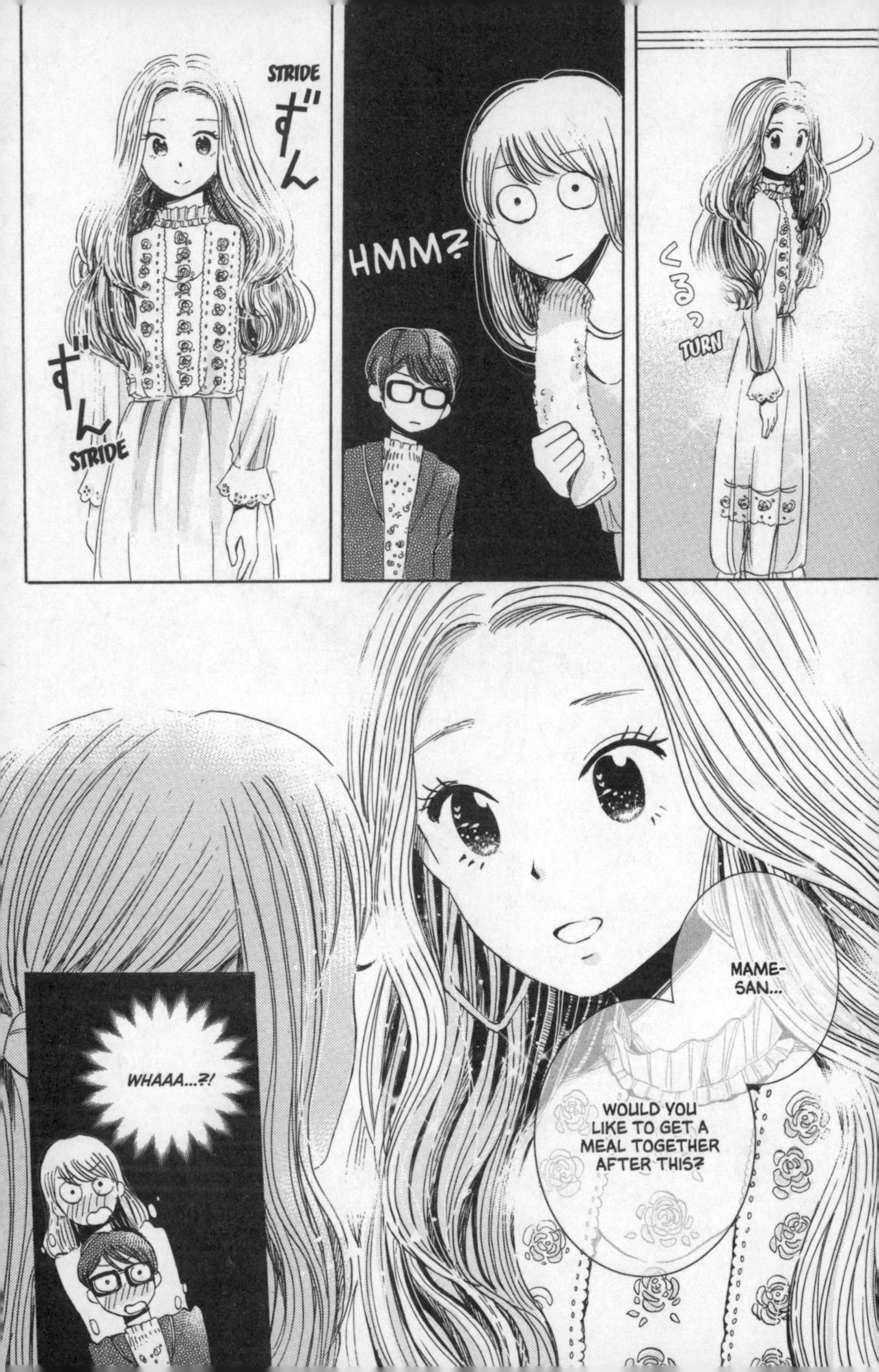
くるっ
TURN
HMM?
STRIDE
ずん
ずん
STRIDE
MAME-SAN...
WOULD YOU LIKE TO GET A MEAL TOGETHER AFTER THIS?
WHAAA...?!

M A M E
coordinate

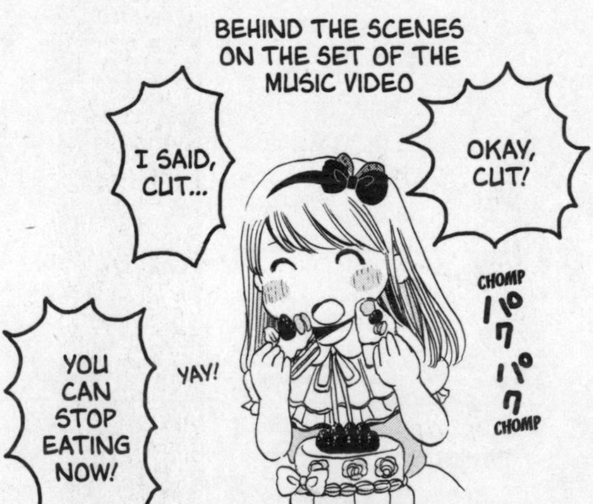
BEHIND THE SCENES ON THE SET OF THE MUSIC VIDEO
OKAY, CUT!
I SAID, CUT...
CHOMP パク パク CHOMP
YAY!
YOU CAN STOP EATING NOW!

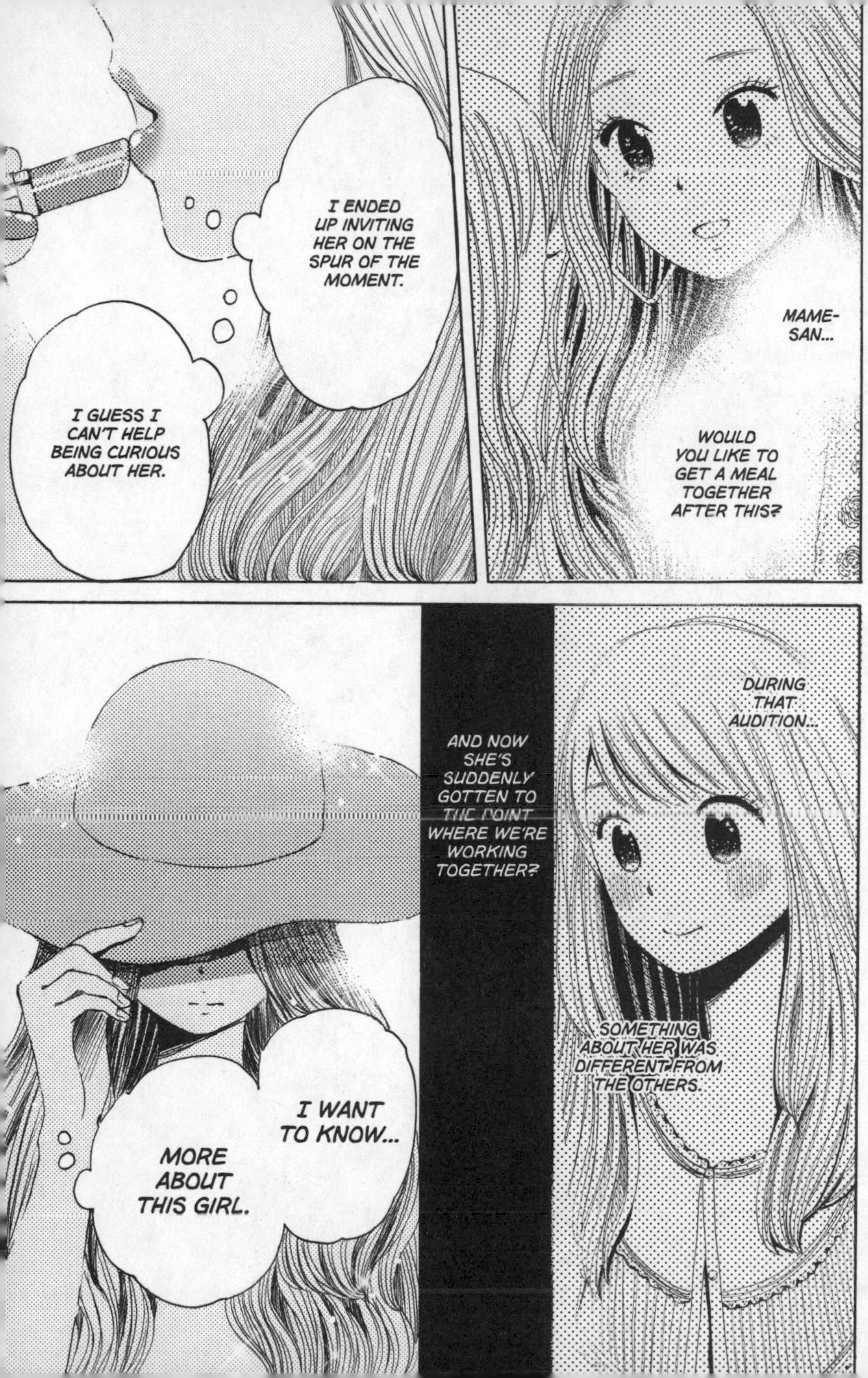
MAME-SAN...
WOULD YOU LIKE TO GET A MEAL TOGETHER AFTER THIS?
I ENDED UP INVITING HER ON THE SPUR OF THE MOMENT.
I GUESS I CAN'T HELP BEING CURIOUS ABOUT HER.
DURING THAT AUDITION...
SOMETHING ABOUT HER WAS DIFFERENT FROM THE OTHERS.
AND NOW SHE'S SUDDENLY GOTTEN TO THE POINT WHERE WE'RE WORKING TOGETHER?
I WANT TO KNOW...
MORE ABOUT THIS GIRL.

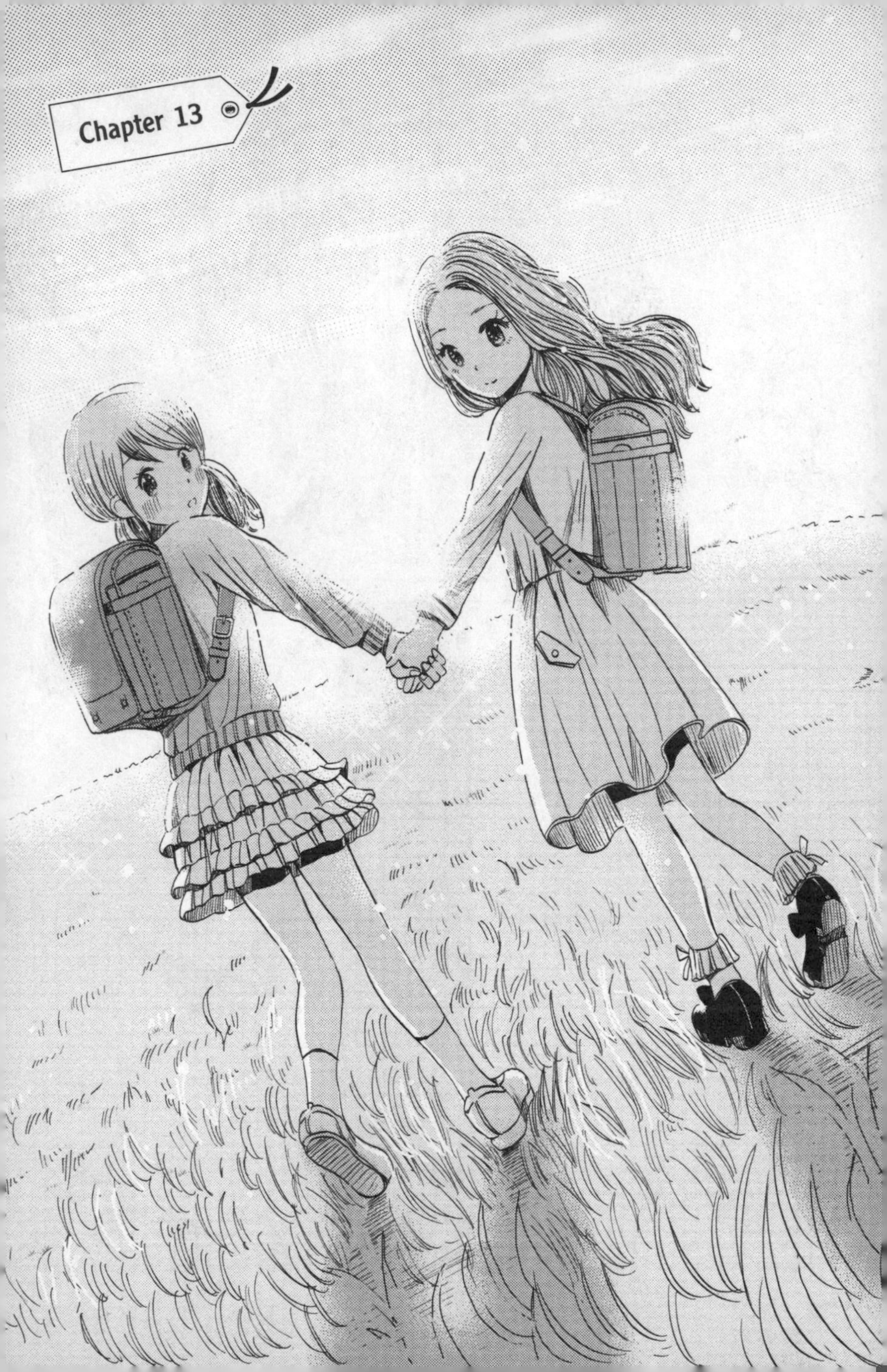
Chapter 13

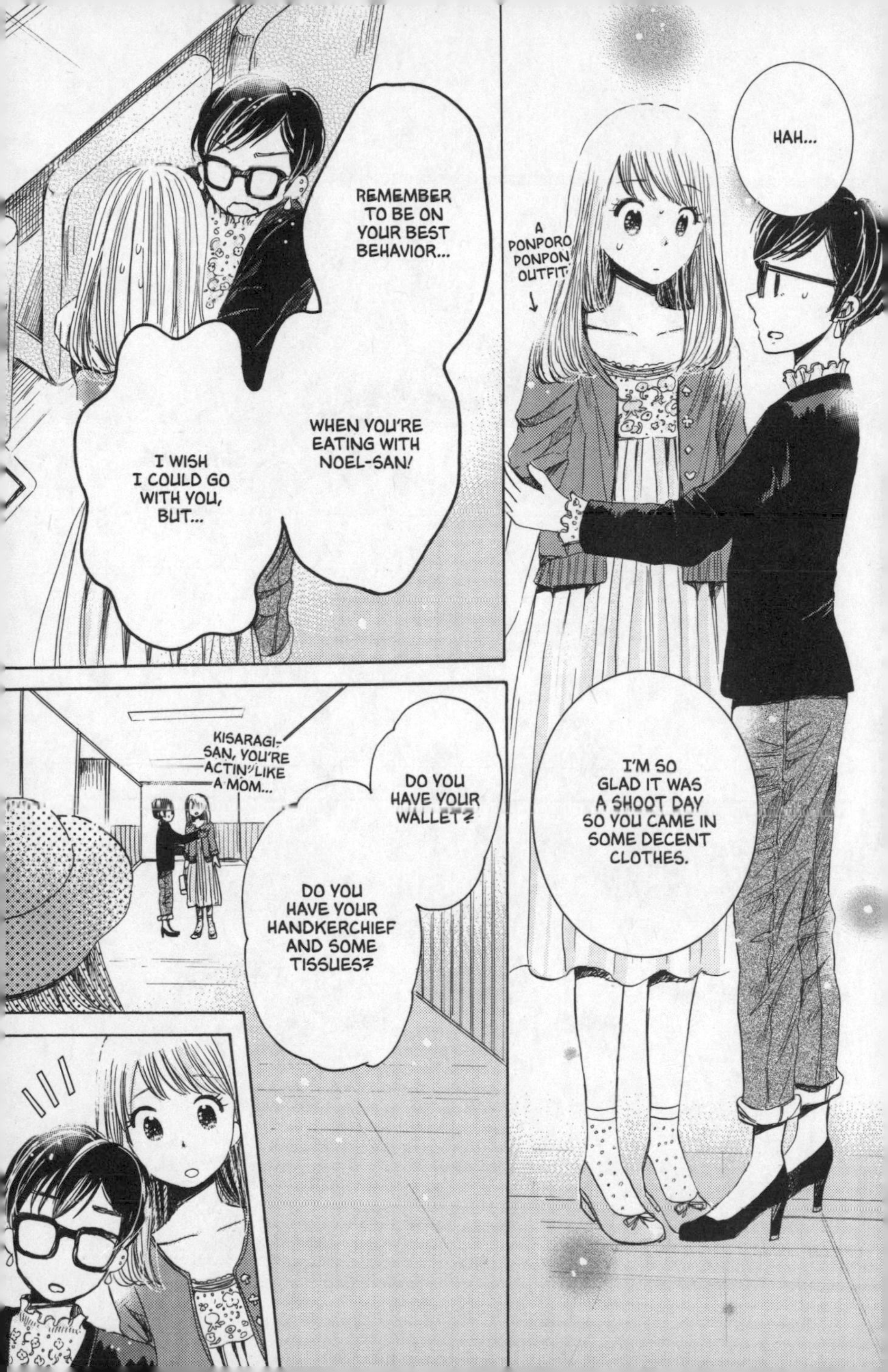
HAH...
A PONPORO PONPON OUTFIT
I'M SO GLAD IT WAS A SHOOT DAY SO YOU CAME IN SOME DECENT CLOTHES.
REMEMBER TO BE ON YOUR BEST BEHAVIOR...
WHEN YOU'RE EATING WITH NOEL-SAN!
I WISH I COULD GO WITH YOU, BUT...
DO YOU HAVE YOUR WALLET?
DO YOU HAVE YOUR HANDKERCHIEF AND SOME TISSUES?
KISARAGI-SAN, YOU'RE ACTIN' LIKE A MOM...

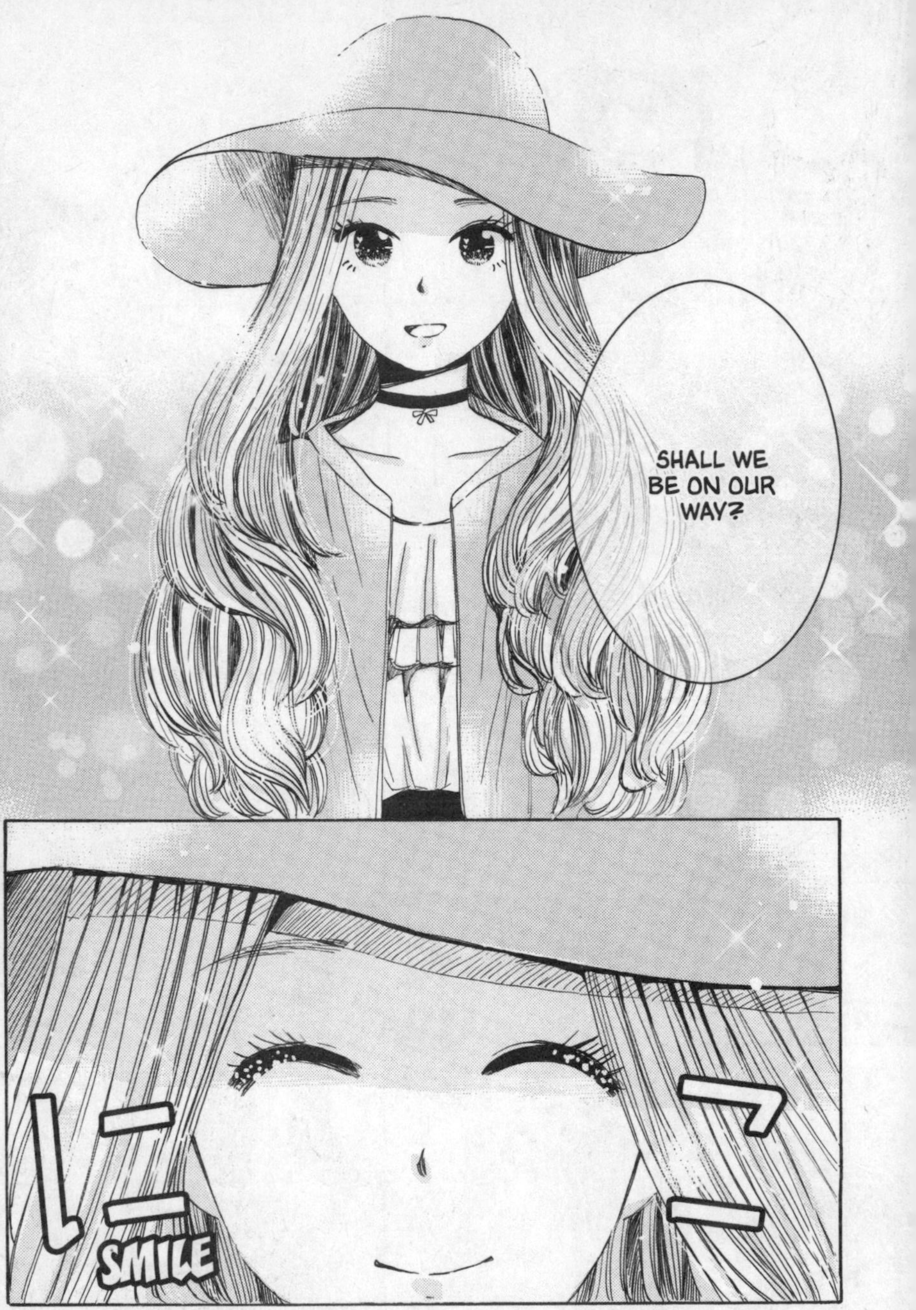
SHALL WE BE ON OUR WAY?
SMILE

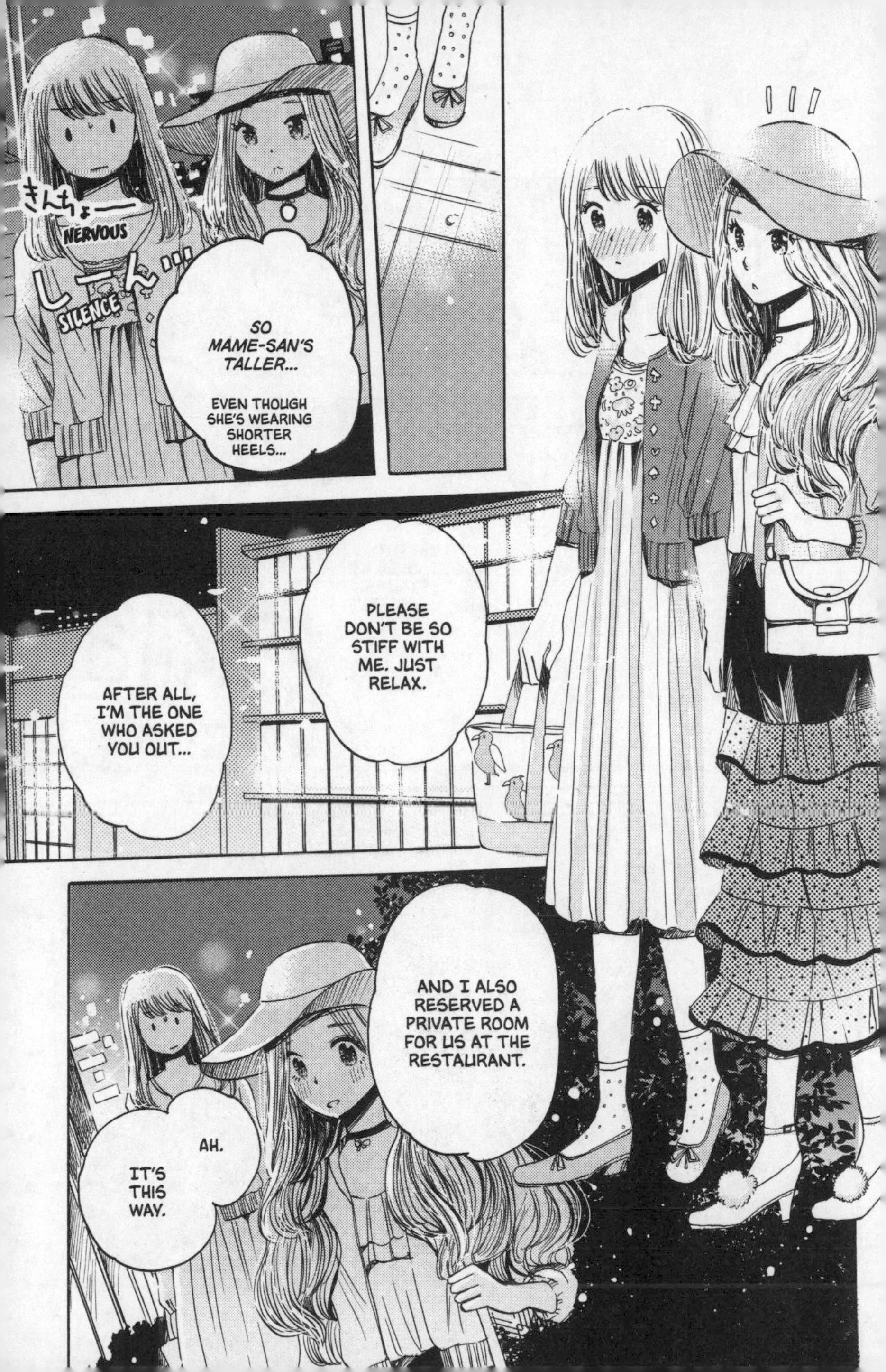
きんちょー
NERVOUS
しーん…
SILENCE
SO MAME-SAN'S TALLER... EVEN THOUGH SHE'S WEARING SHORTER HEELS...
PLEASE DON'T BE SO STIFF WITH ME. JUST RELAX.
AFTER ALL, I'M THE ONE WHO ASKED YOU OUT...
AND I ALSO RESERVED A PRIVATE ROOM FOR US AT THE RESTAURANT.
AH. IT'S THIS WAY.

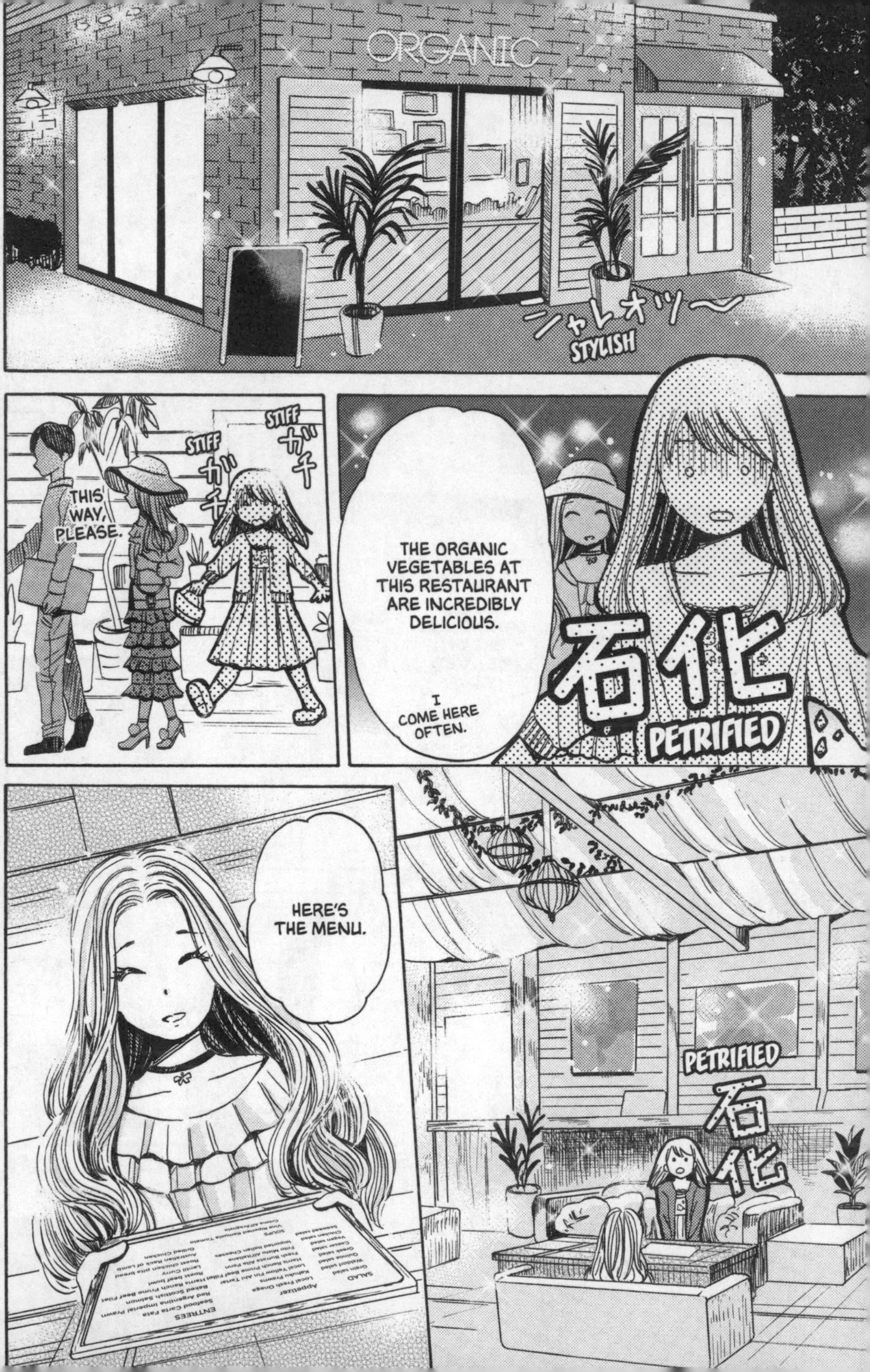
ORGANIC
シャレオツ〜
STYLISH
THE ORGANIC VEGETABLES AT THIS RESTAURANT ARE INCREDIBLY DELICIOUS.
I COME HERE OFTEN.
石化
PETRIFIED
STIFF
ガチ
STIFF
ガチ
THIS WAY, PLEASE.
PETRIFIED
石化
HERE'S THE MENU.

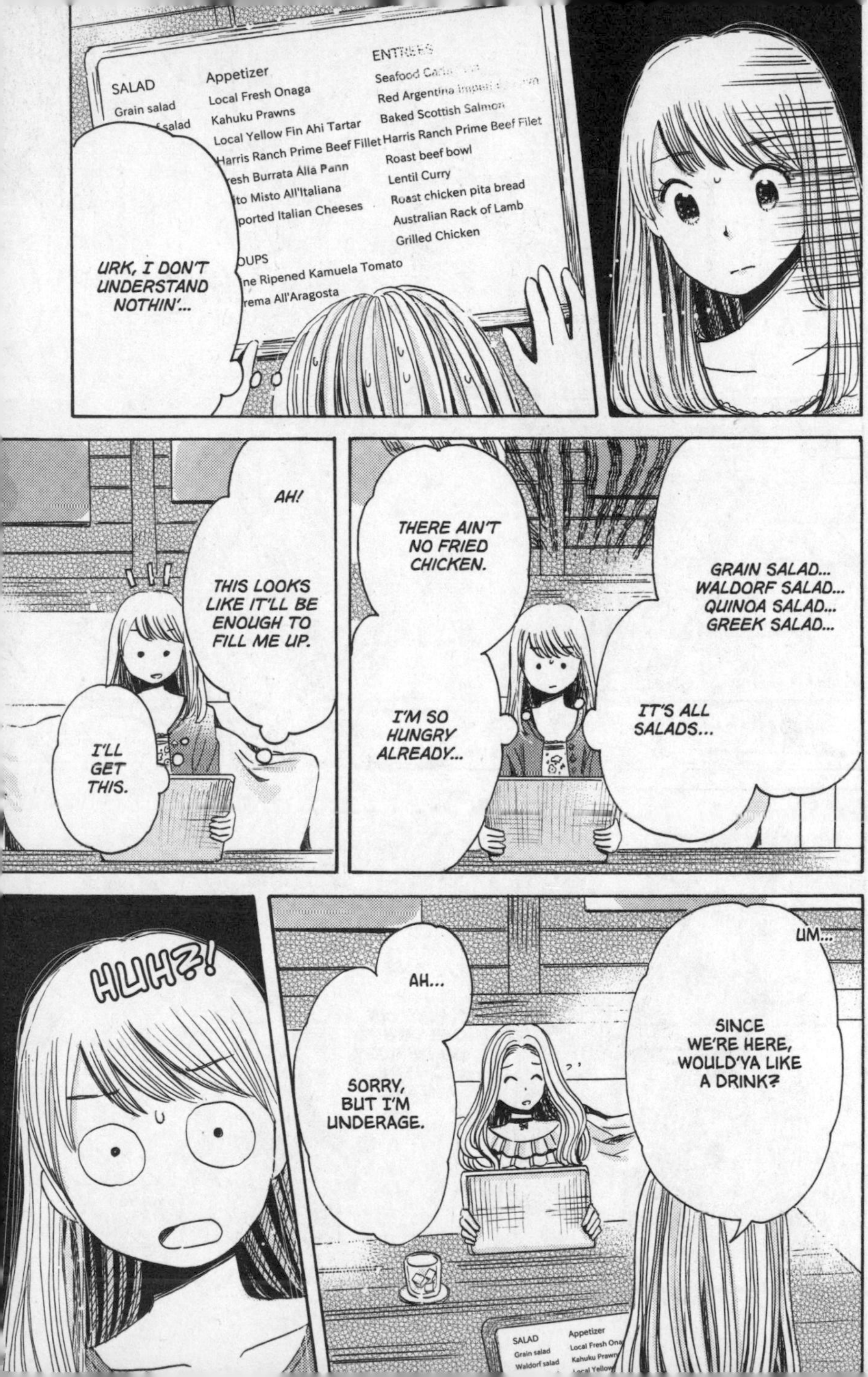
SALAD
Grain salad
Appetizer
Local Fresh Onaga
Kahuku Prawns
Local Yellow Fin Ahi Tartar
Harris Ranch Prime Beef Fillet
ENTREES
Red Argentina
Baked Scottish Salmon
Harris Ranch Prime Beef Filet
Roast beef bowl
Lentil Curry
Roast chicken pita bread
Australian Rack of Lamb
Grilled Chicken
URK, I DON'T UNDERSTAND NOTHIN'...
GRAIN SALAD... WALDORF SALAD... QUINOA SALAD... GREEK SALAD...
IT'S ALL SALADS...
THERE AIN'T NO FRIED CHICKEN.
I'M SO HUNGRY ALREADY...
AH!
THIS LOOKS LIKE IT'LL BE ENOUGH TO FILL ME UP.
I'LL GET THIS.
UM...
SINCE WE'RE HERE, WOULD'YA LIKE A DRINK?
AH...
SORRY, BUT I'M UNDERAGE.
HUH?!

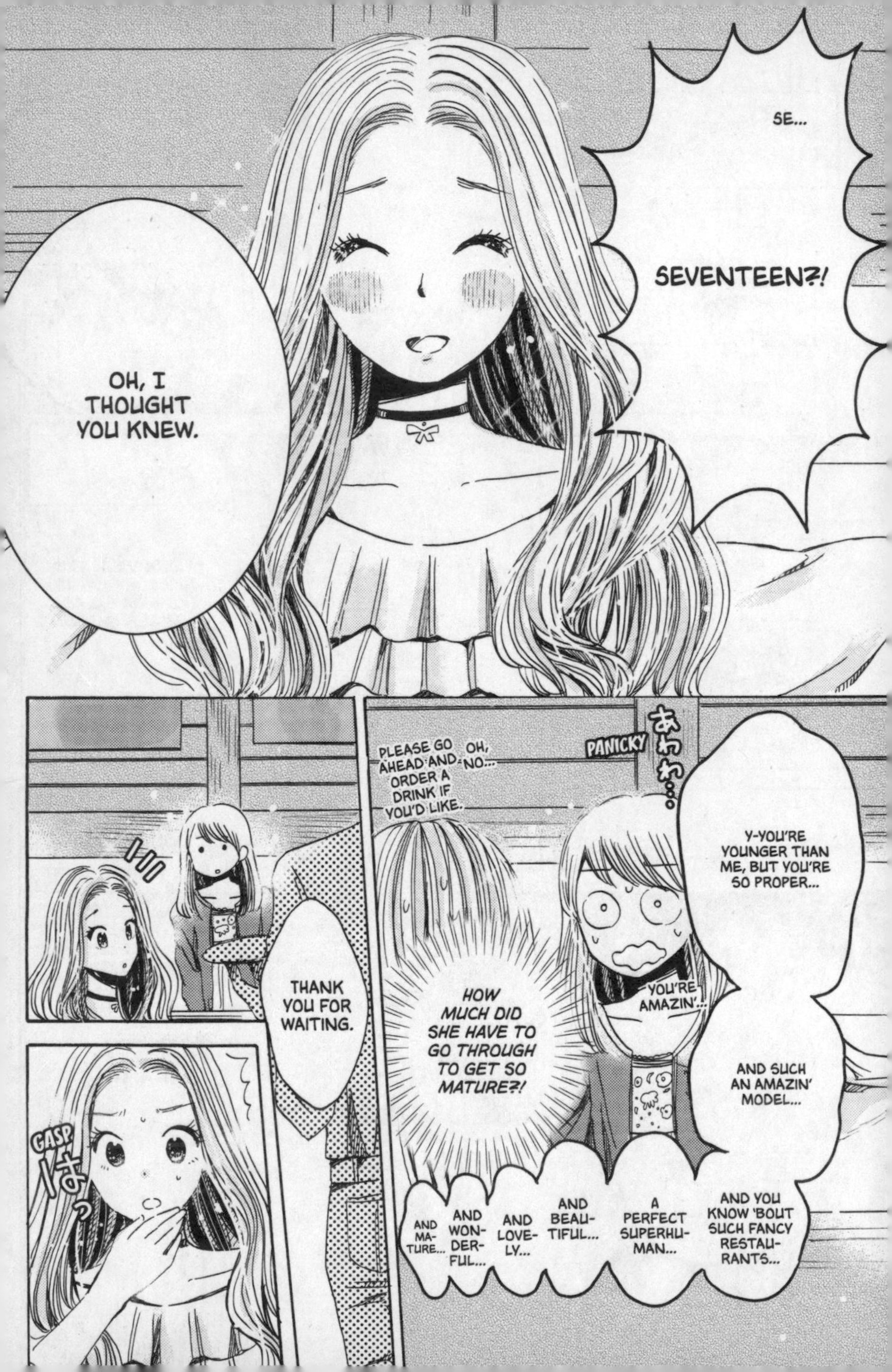
SE...
SEVENTEEN?!
OH, I THOUGHT YOU KNEW.
PANICKY
あわわ…
Y-YOU'RE YOUNGER THAN ME, BUT YOU'RE SO PROPER...
YOU'RE AMAZIN'...
AND SUCH AN AMAZIN' MODEL...
AND YOU KNOW 'BOUT SUCH FANCY RESTAURANTS...
A PERFECT SUPERHUMAN...
AND BEAUTIFUL...
AND LOVELY...
AND WONDERFUL...
AND MATURE...
HOW MUCH DID SHE HAVE TO GO THROUGH TO GET SO MATURE?!
OH, NO...
PLEASE GO AHEAD AND ORDER A DRINK IF YOU'D LIKE.
THANK YOU FOR WAITING.
GASP
はっ

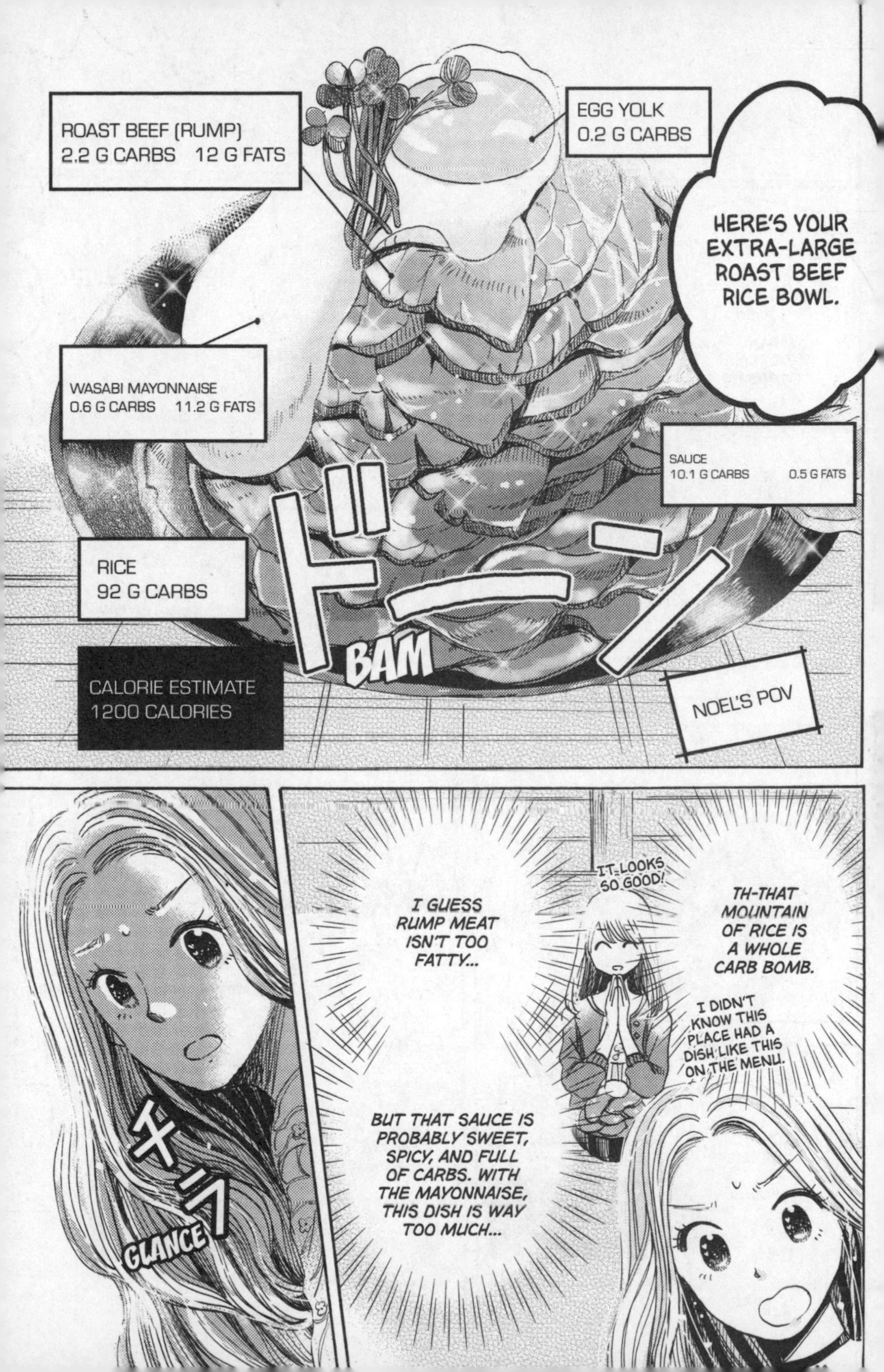
EGG YOLK
0.2 G CARBS
HERE'S YOUR EXTRA-LARGE ROAST BEEF RICE BOWL.
ROAST BEEF (RUMP)
2.2 G CARBS 12 G FATS
SAUCE
10.1 G CARBS 0.5 G FATS
WASABI MAYONNAISE
0.6 G CARBS 11.2 G FATS
RICE
92 G CARBS
BAM
NOEL'S POV
CALORIE ESTIMATE
1200 CALORIES
TH-THAT MOUNTAIN OF RICE IS A WHOLE CARB BOMB.
IT LOOKS SO GOOD!
I GUESS RUMP MEAT ISN'T TOO FATTY...
I DIDN'T KNOW THIS PLACE HAD A DISH LIKE THIS ON THE MENU.
BUT THAT SAUCE IS PROBABLY SWEET, SPICY, AND FULL OF CARBS. WITH THE MAYONNAISE, THIS DISH IS WAY TOO MUCH...
GLANCE

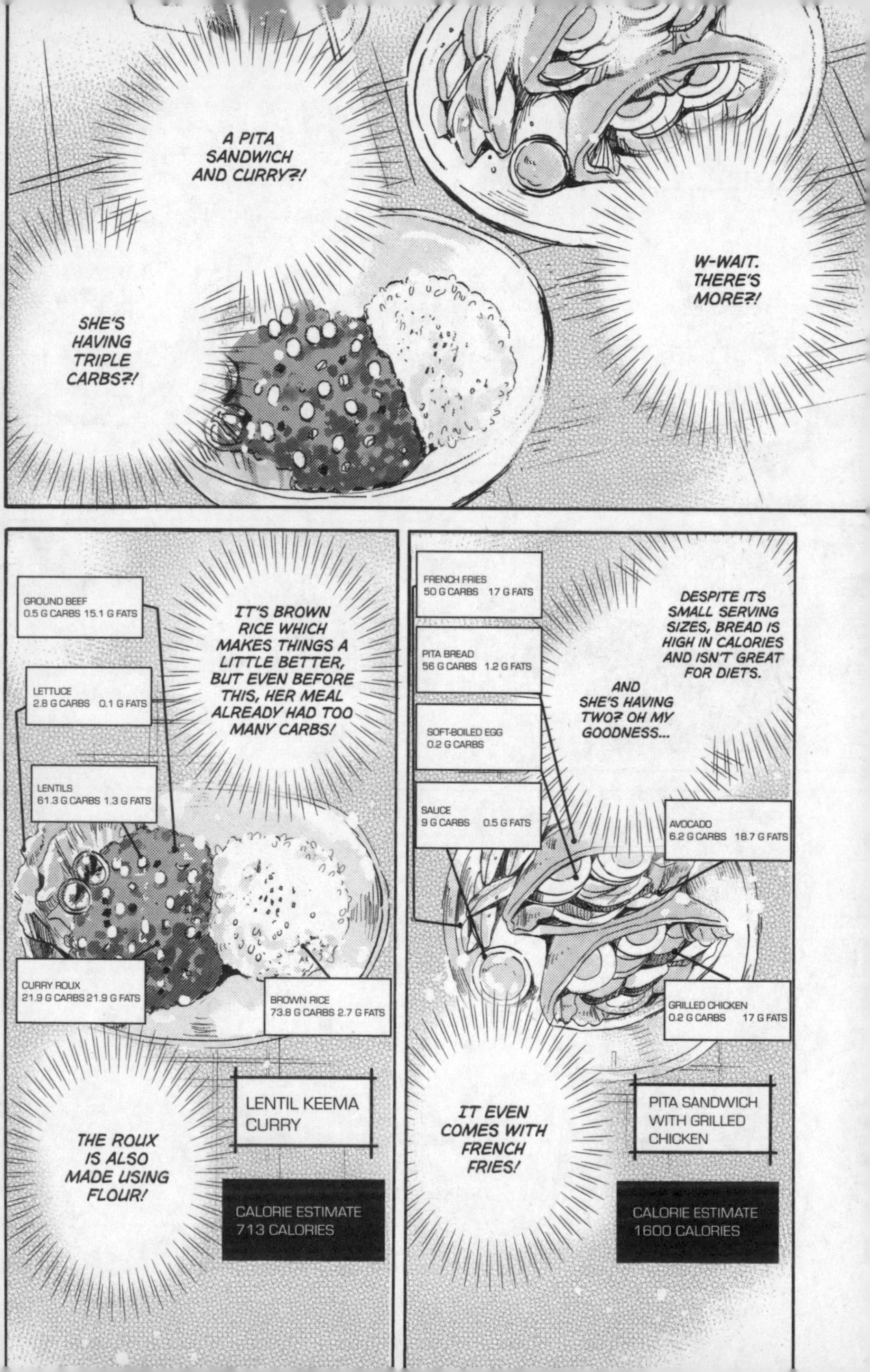
A PITA SANDWICH AND CURRY?!
W-WAIT. THERE'S MORE?!
SHE'S HAVING TRIPLE CARBS?!
FRENCH FRIES 50 G CARBS 17 G FATS
PITA BREAD 56 G CARBS 1.2 G FATS
SOFT-BOILED EGG 0.2 G CARBS
SAUCE 9 G CARBS 0.5 G FATS
DESPITE ITS SMALL SERVING SIZES, BREAD IS HIGH IN CALORIES AND ISN'T GREAT FOR DIETS.
AND SHE'S HAVING TWO? OH MY GOODNESS...
AVOCADO 6.2 G CARBS 18.7 G FATS
GRILLED CHICKEN 0.2 G CARBS 17 G FATS
PITA SANDWICH WITH GRILLED CHICKEN
IT EVEN COMES WITH FRENCH FRIES!
CALORIE ESTIMATE 1600 CALORIES
GROUND BEEF 0.5 G CARBS 15.1 G FATS
IT'S BROWN RICE WHICH MAKES THINGS A LITTLE BETTER, BUT EVEN BEFORE THIS, HER MEAL ALREADY HAD TOO MANY CARBS!
LETTUCE 2.8 G CARBS 0.1 G FATS
LENTILS 61.3 G CARBS 1.3 G FATS
CURRY ROUX 21.9 G CARBS 21.9 G FATS
BROWN RICE 73.8 G CARBS 2.7 G FATS
LENTIL KEEMA CURRY
THE ROUX IS ALSO MADE USING FLOUR!
CALORIE ESTIMATE 713 CALORIES

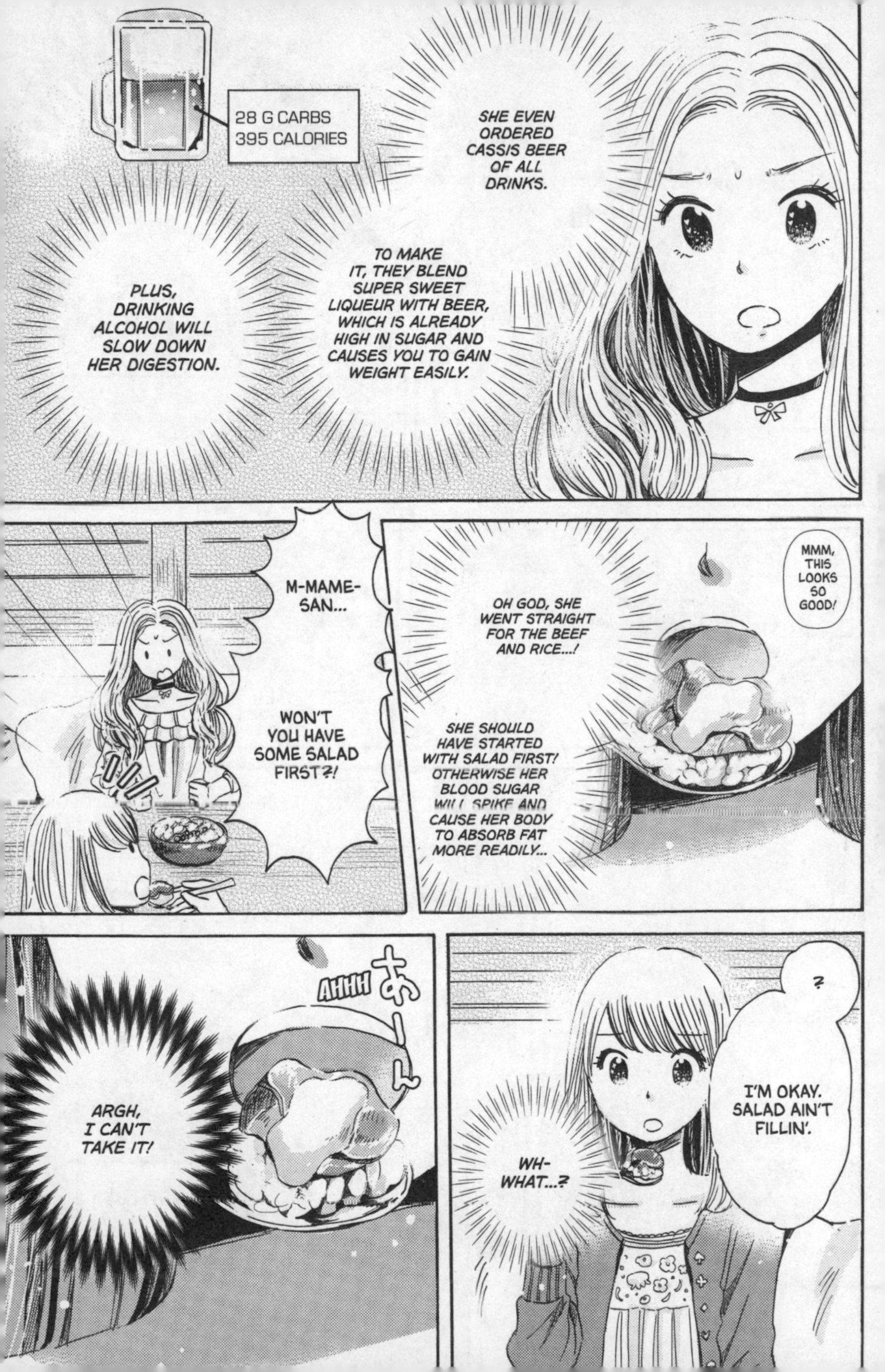
SHE EVEN ORDERED CASSIS BEER OF ALL DRINKS.
28 G CARBS
395 CALORIES
TO MAKE IT, THEY BLEND SUPER SWEET LIQUEUR WITH BEER, WHICH IS ALREADY HIGH IN SUGAR AND CAUSES YOU TO GAIN WEIGHT EASILY.
PLUS, DRINKING ALCOHOL WILL SLOW DOWN HER DIGESTION.
MMM, THIS LOOKS SO GOOD!
OH GOD, SHE WENT STRAIGHT FOR THE BEEF AND RICE...!
SHE SHOULD HAVE STARTED WITH SALAD FIRST! OTHERWISE HER BLOOD SUGAR WILL SPIKE AND CAUSE HER BODY TO ABSORB FAT MORE READILY...
M-MAME-SAN...
WON'T YOU HAVE SOME SALAD FIRST?!
?
I'M OKAY. SALAD AIN'T FILLIN'.
WH-WHAT...?
AHHH
あーん
ARGH, I CAN'T TAKE IT!

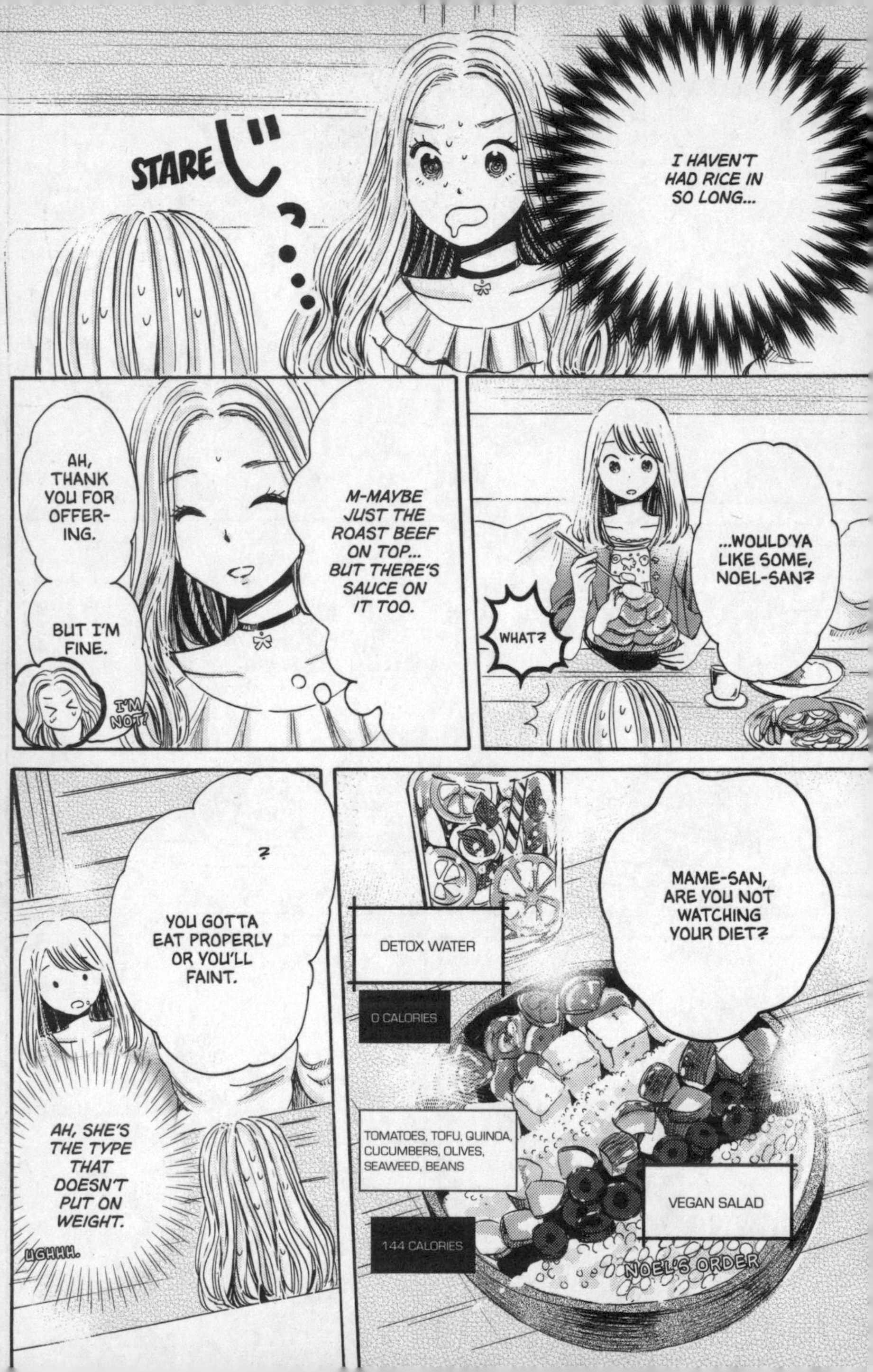
I HAVEN'T HAD RICE IN SO LONG...
STARE じっ...
...WOULD'YA LIKE SOME, NOEL-SAN?
WHAT?
M-MAYBE JUST THE ROAST BEEF ON TOP... BUT THERE'S SAUCE ON IT TOO.
AH, THANK YOU FOR OFFERING.
BUT I'M FINE.
I'M NOT!
MAME-SAN, ARE YOU NOT WATCHING YOUR DIET?
DETOX WATER
0 CALORIES
VEGAN SALAD
TOMATOES, TOFU, QUINOA, CUCUMBERS, OLIVES, SEAWEED, BEANS
144 CALORIES
NOEL'S ORDER
?
YOU GOTTA EAT PROPERLY OR YOU'LL FAINT.
AH, SHE'S THE TYPE THAT DOESN'T PUT ON WEIGHT.
UGHHH.

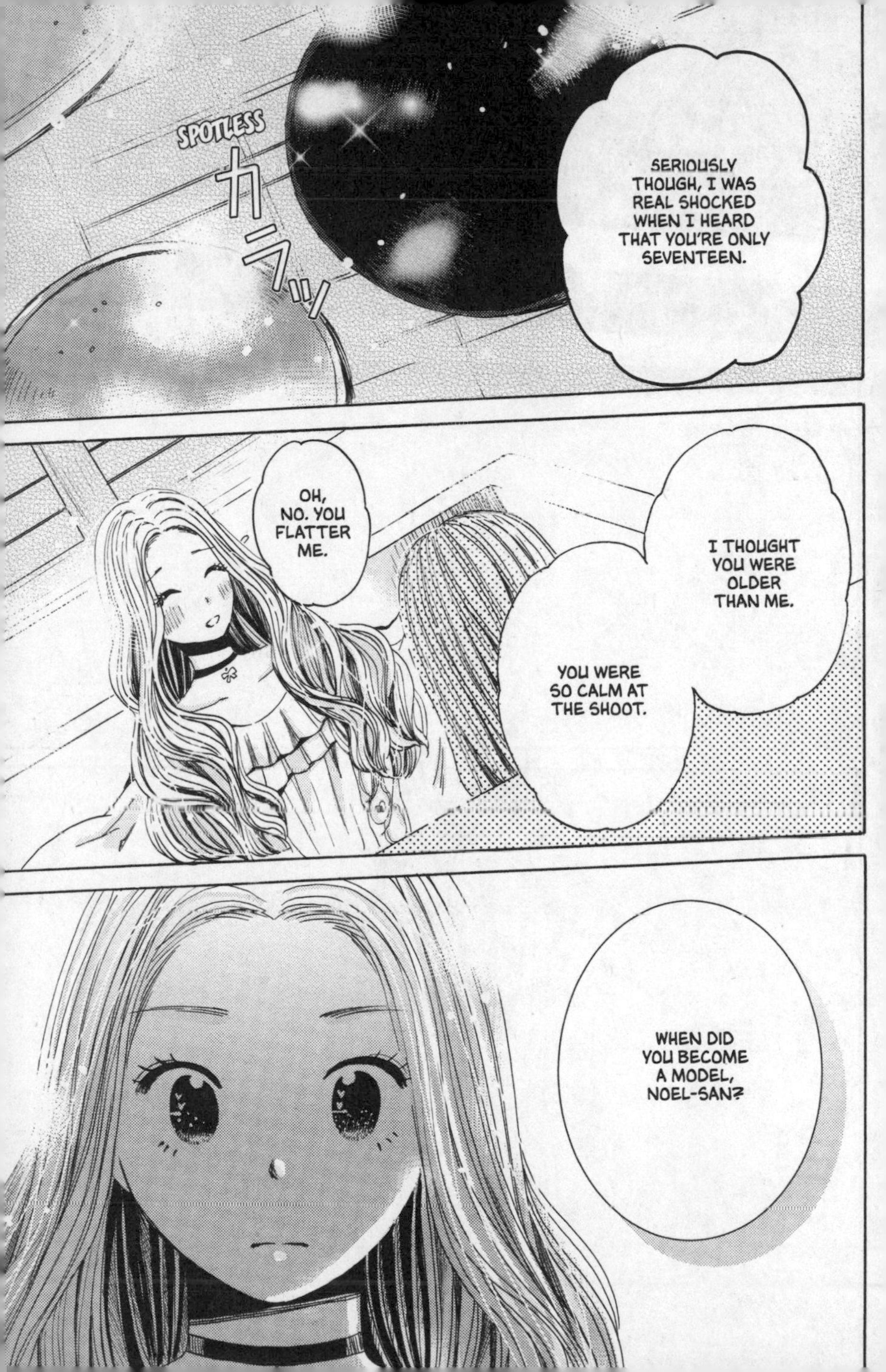
SERIOUSLY THOUGH, I WAS REAL SHOCKED WHEN I HEARD THAT YOU'RE ONLY SEVENTEEN.
SPOTLESS
カラッ
I THOUGHT YOU WERE OLDER THAN ME.
YOU WERE SO CALM AT THE SHOOT.
OH, NO. YOU FLATTER ME.
WHEN DID YOU BECOME A MODEL, NOEL-SAN?

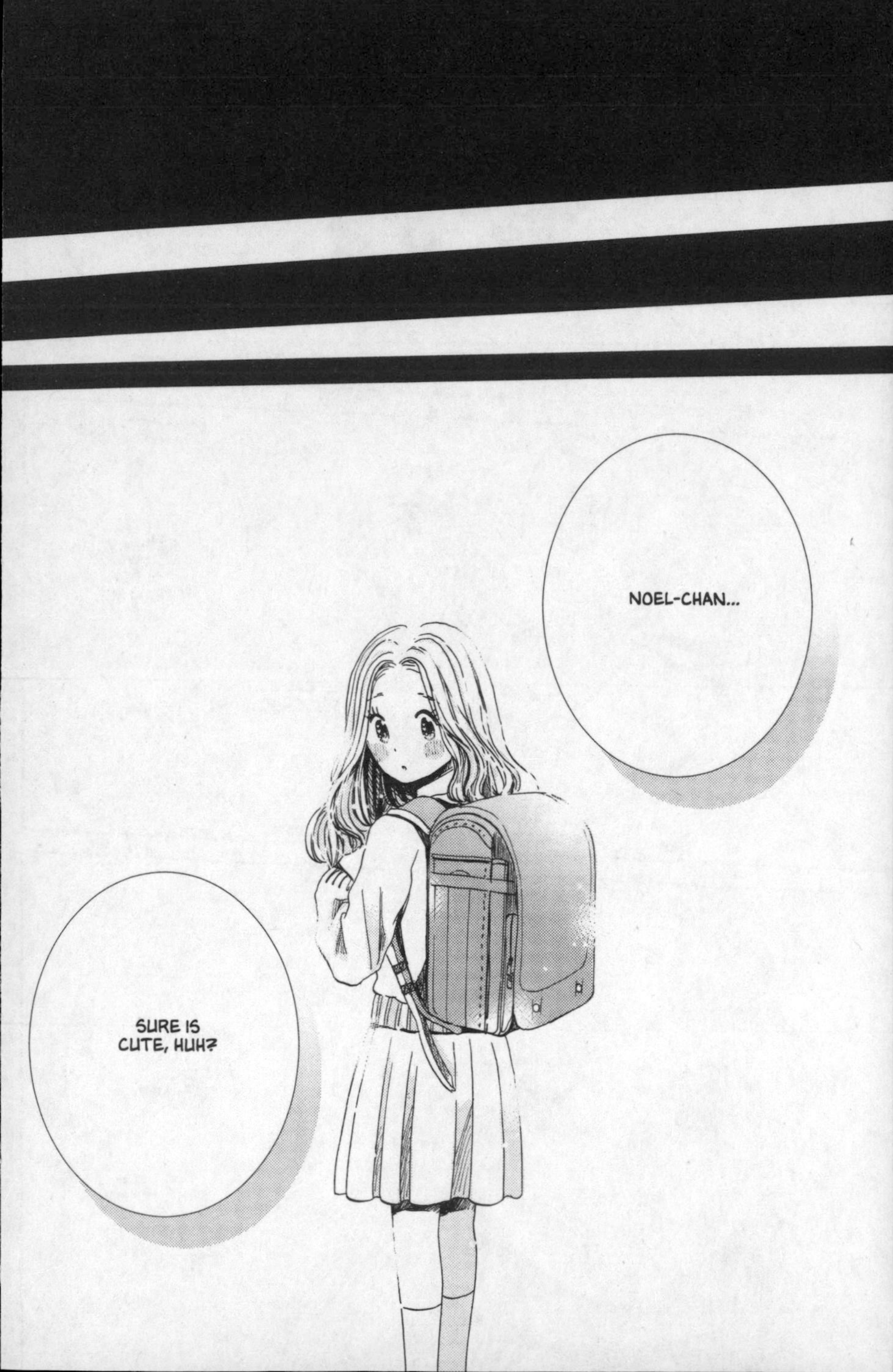
NOEL-CHAN...
SURE IS CUTE, HUH?

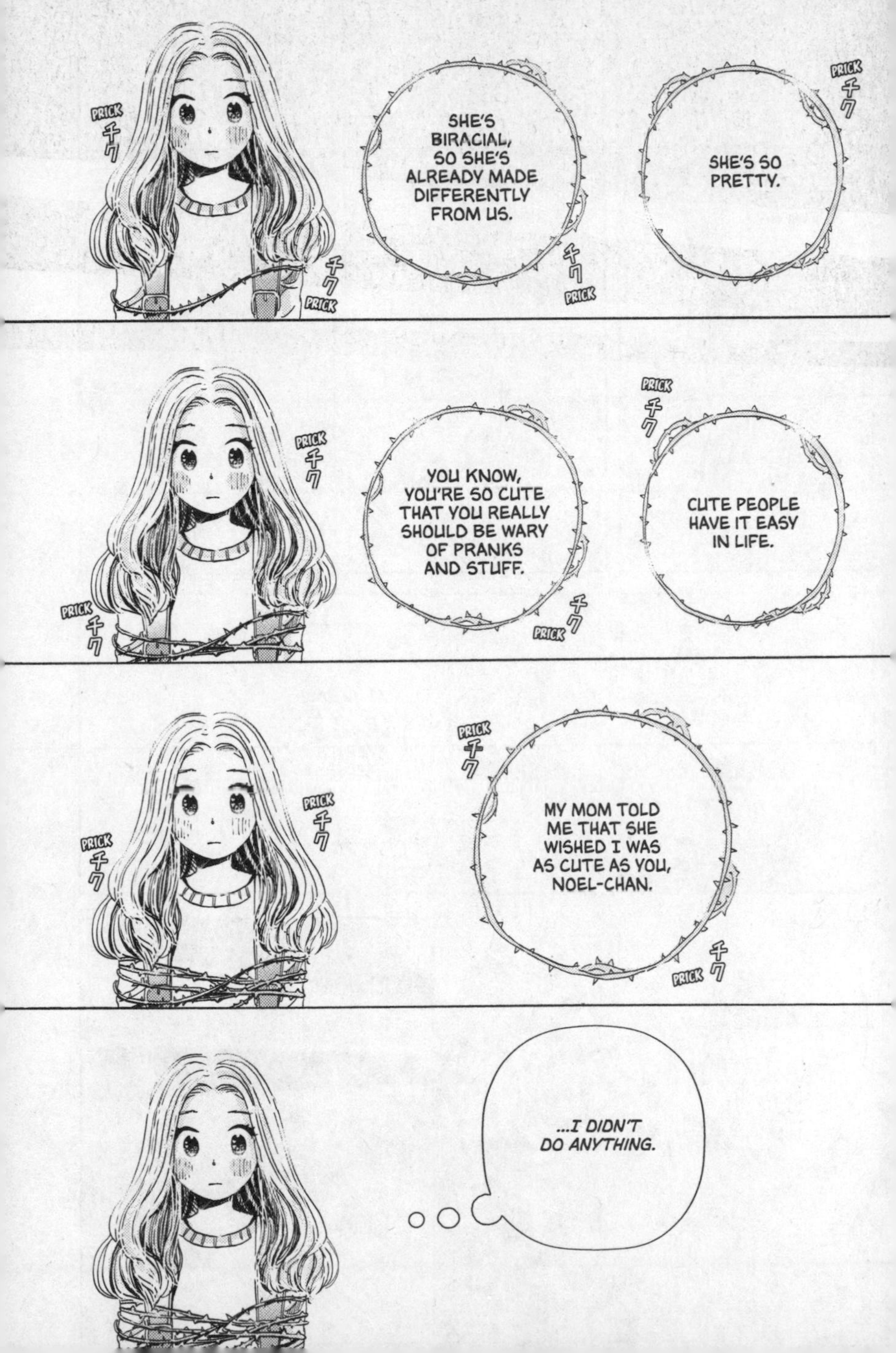
PRICK チク
SHE'S SO PRETTY.
SHE'S BIRACIAL, SO SHE'S ALREADY MADE DIFFERENTLY FROM US.
PRICK チク
PRICK チク
PRICK チク
PRICK チク
CUTE PEOPLE HAVE IT EASY IN LIFE.
YOU KNOW, YOU'RE SO CUTE THAT YOU REALLY SHOULD BE WARY OF PRANKS AND STUFF.
PRICK チク
PRICK チク
PRICK チク
PRICK チク
MY MOM TOLD ME THAT SHE WISHED I WAS AS CUTE AS YOU, NOEL-CHAN.
PRICK チク
PRICK チク
PRICK チク
...I DIDN'T DO ANYTHING.

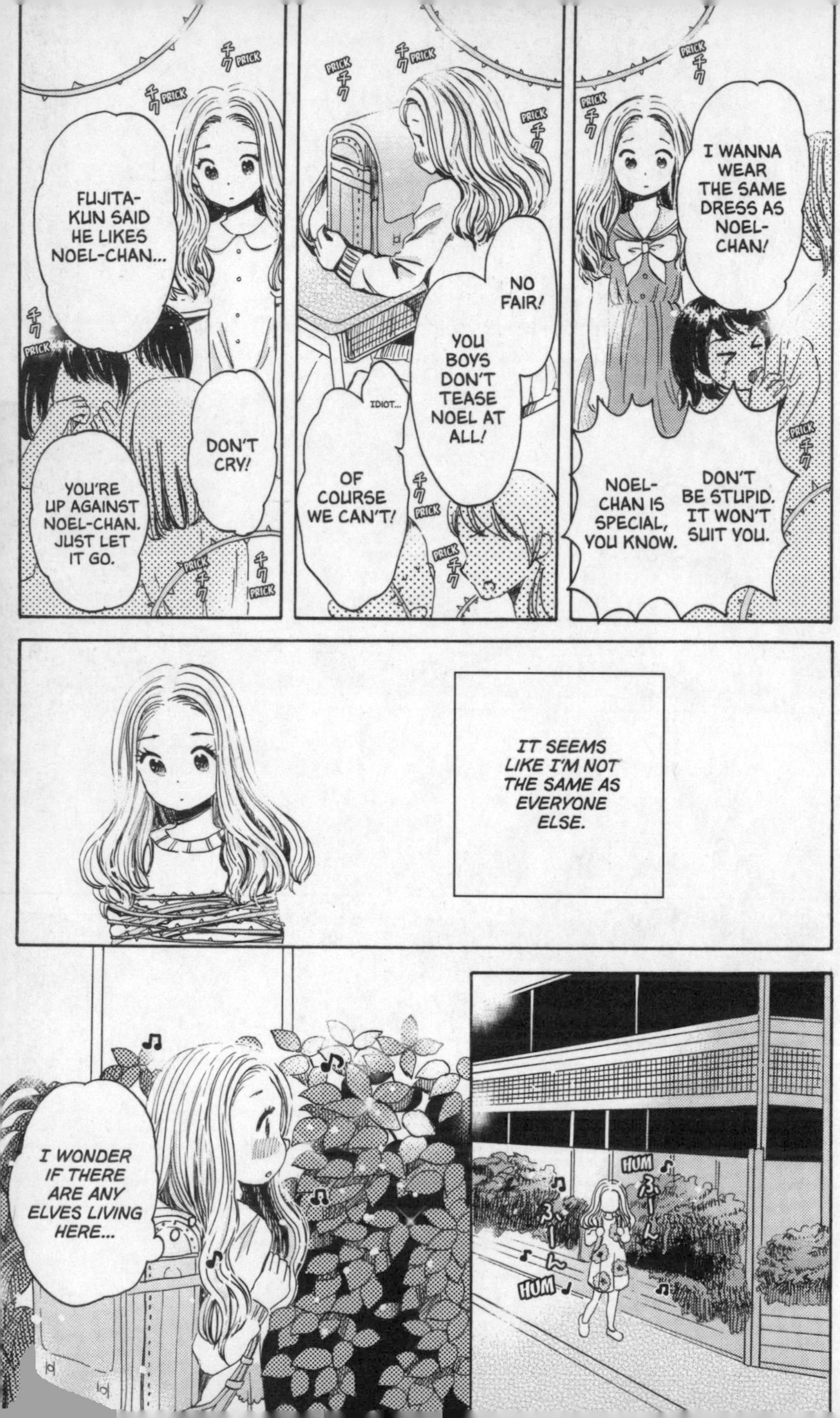
PRICK
チク
I WANNA WEAR THE SAME DRESS AS NOEL-CHAN!
DON'T BE STUPID. IT WON'T SUIT YOU.
NOEL-CHAN IS SPECIAL, YOU KNOW.
PRICK
チク
NO FAIR!
YOU BOYS DON'T TEASE NOEL AT ALL!
IDIOT...
OF COURSE WE CAN'T!
PRICK
チク
FUJITA-KUN SAID HE LIKES NOEL-CHAN...
DON'T CRY!
YOU'RE UP AGAINST NOEL-CHAN. JUST LET IT GO.
IT SEEMS LIKE I'M NOT THE SAME AS EVERYONE ELSE.
HUM
ふ～ん
HUM
I WONDER IF THERE ARE ANY ELVES LIVING HERE...

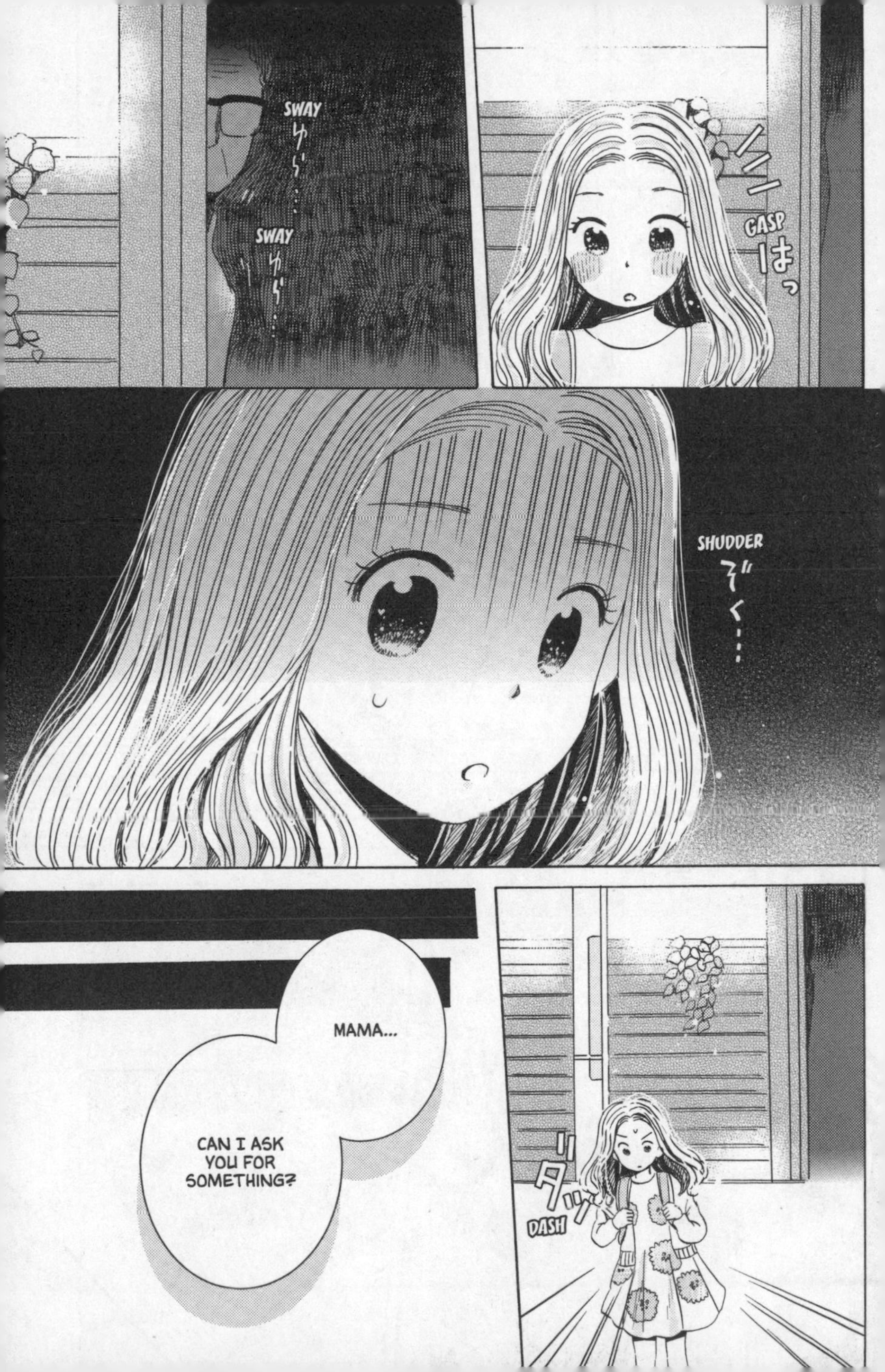
GASP
はっ
SWAY
SWAY
SHUDDER
ぞく…
DASH
ダッ
MAMA...
CAN I ASK YOU FOR SOMETHING?

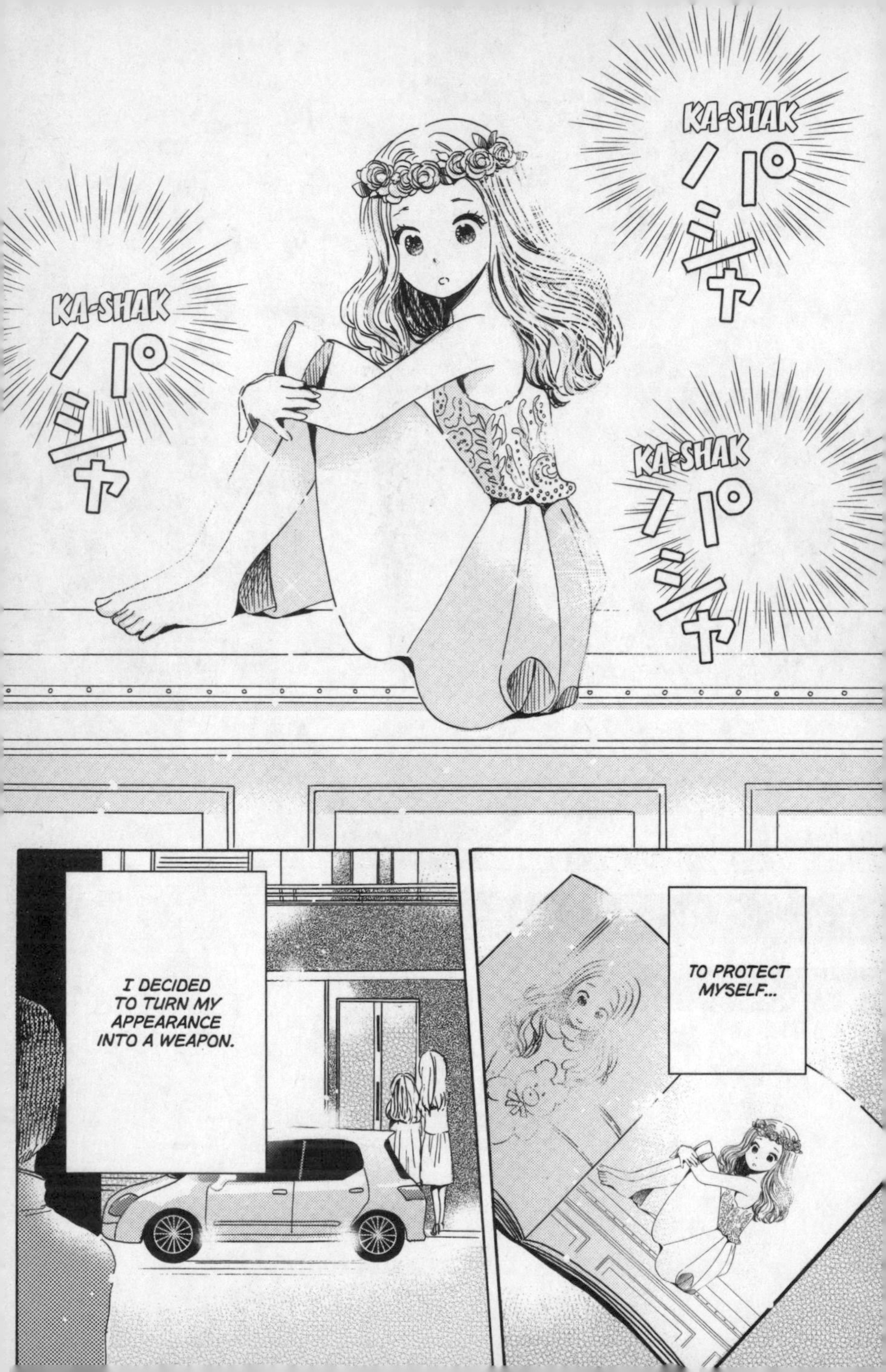
KA-SHAK
パシャ
KA-SHAK
パシャ
KA-SHAK
パシャ
TO PROTECT MYSELF...
I DECIDED TO TURN MY APPEARANCE INTO A WEAPON.

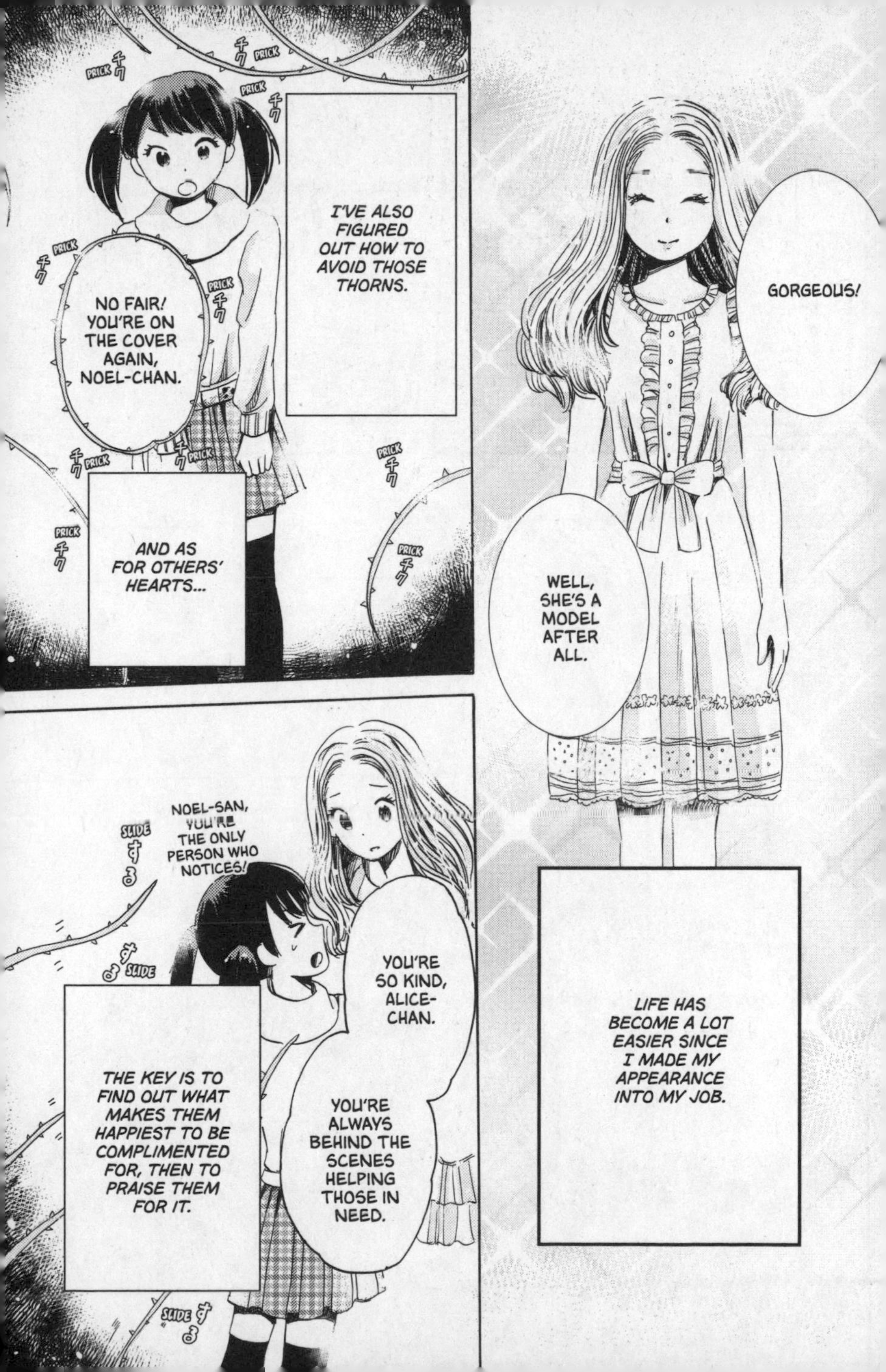
GORGEOUS!
WELL, SHE'S A MODEL AFTER ALL.
LIFE HAS BECOME A LOT EASIER SINCE I MADE MY APPEARANCE INTO MY JOB.
PRICK チク
PRICK チク
PRICK チク
I'VE ALSO FIGURED OUT HOW TO AVOID THOSE THORNS.
NO FAIR! YOU'RE ON THE COVER AGAIN, NOEL-CHAN.
PRICK チク
PRICK チク
PRICK チク
PRICK チク
PRICK チク
PRICK チク
AND AS FOR OTHERS' HEARTS...
YOU'RE SO KIND, ALICE-CHAN.
NOEL-SAN, YOU'RE THE ONLY PERSON WHO NOTICES!
SLIDE する
SLIDE する
YOU'RE ALWAYS BEHIND THE SCENES HELPING THOSE IN NEED.
THE KEY IS TO FIND OUT WHAT MAKES THEM HAPPIEST TO BE COMPLIMENTED FOR, THEN TO PRAISE THEM FOR IT.
SLIDE する

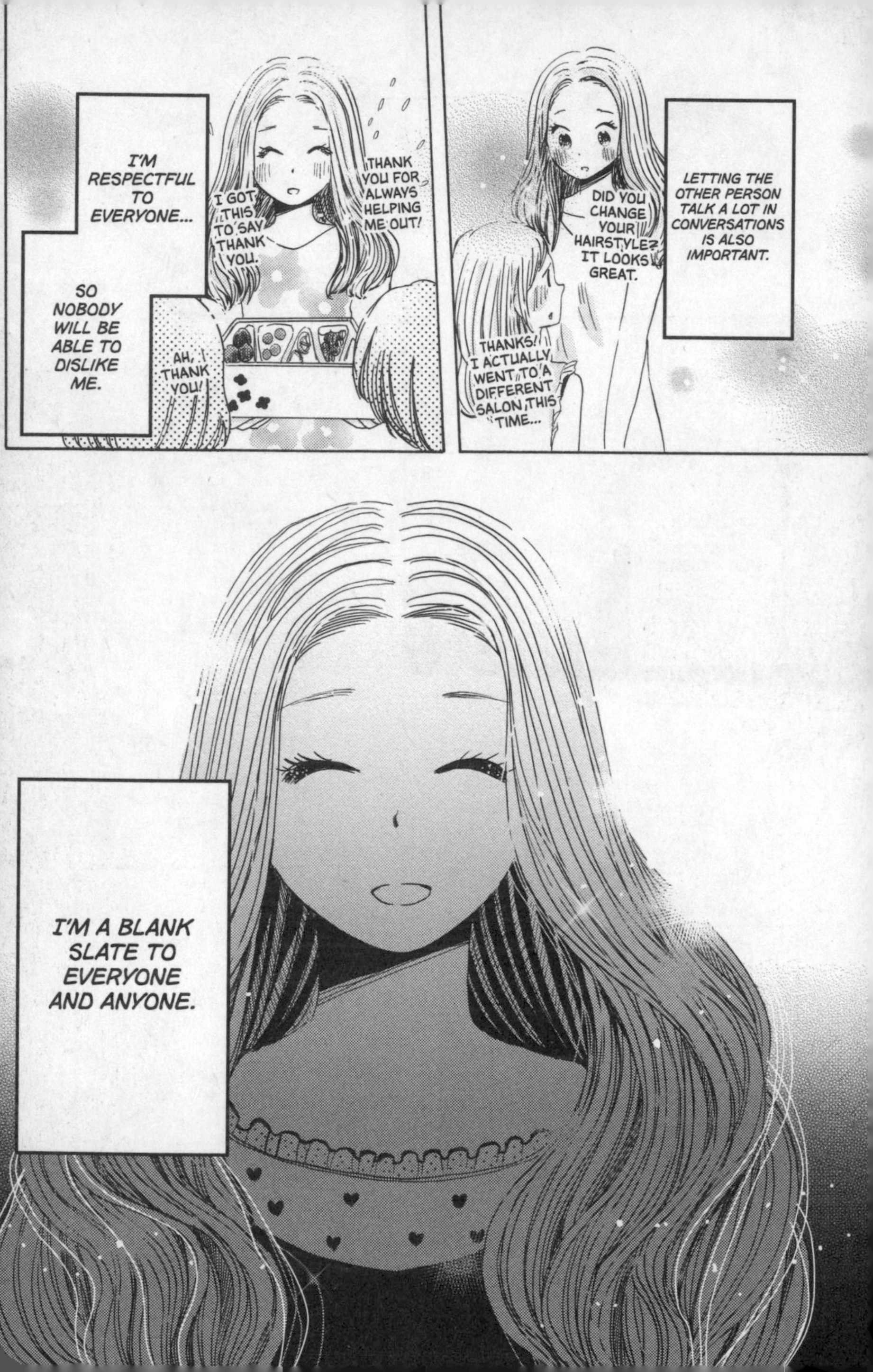
LETTING THE OTHER PERSON TALK A LOT IN CONVERSATIONS IS ALSO IMPORTANT.
DID YOU CHANGE YOUR HAIRSTYLE? IT LOOKS GREAT.
THANKS! I ACTUALLY WENT TO A DIFFERENT SALON THIS TIME...
THANK YOU FOR ALWAYS HELPING ME OUT!
I GOT THIS TO SAY THANK YOU.
I'M RESPECTFUL TO EVERYONE...
SO NOBODY WILL BE ABLE TO DISLIKE ME.
AH, THANK YOU!
I'M A BLANK SLATE TO EVERYONE AND ANYONE.

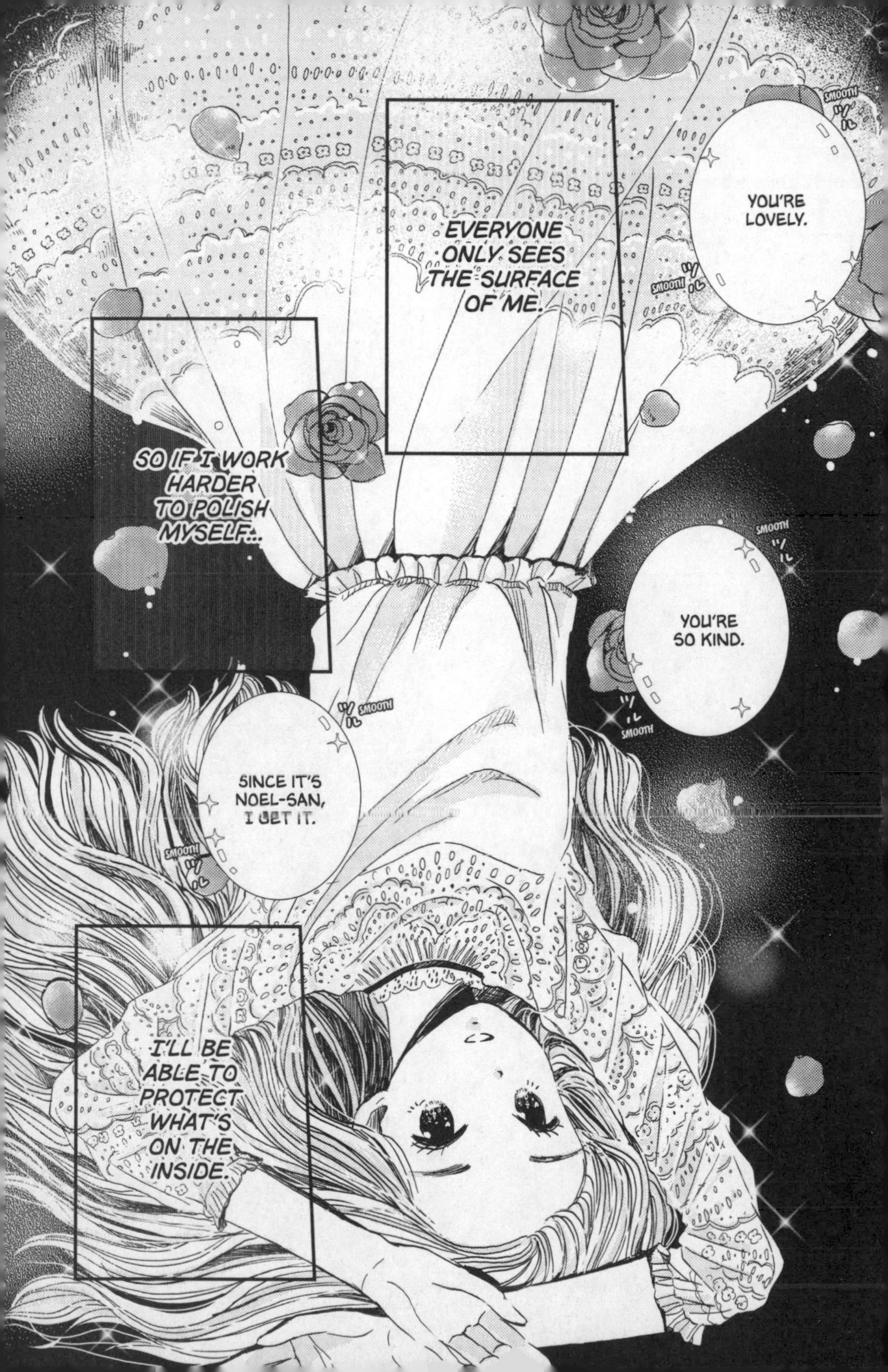

SMOOTH
YOU'RE LOVELY.
SMOOTH
EVERYONE ONLY SEES THE SURFACE OF ME.
SMOOTH
YOU'RE SO KIND.
SMOOTH
SO IF I WORK HARDER TO POLISH MYSELF...
SMOOTH
SINCE IT'S NOEL-SAN, I GET IT.
SMOOTH
I'LL BE ABLE TO PROTECT WHAT'S ON THE INSIDE.

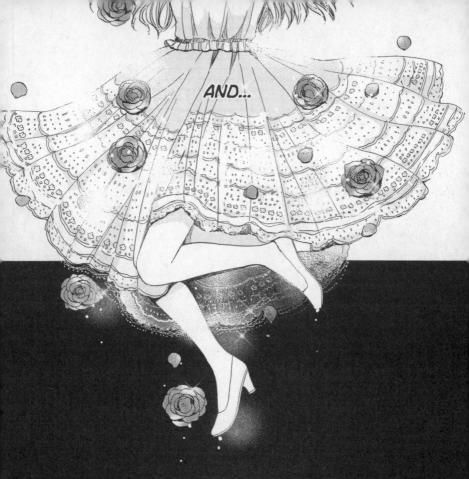

AND...

NO ONE
KNOWS THE
REAL ME.

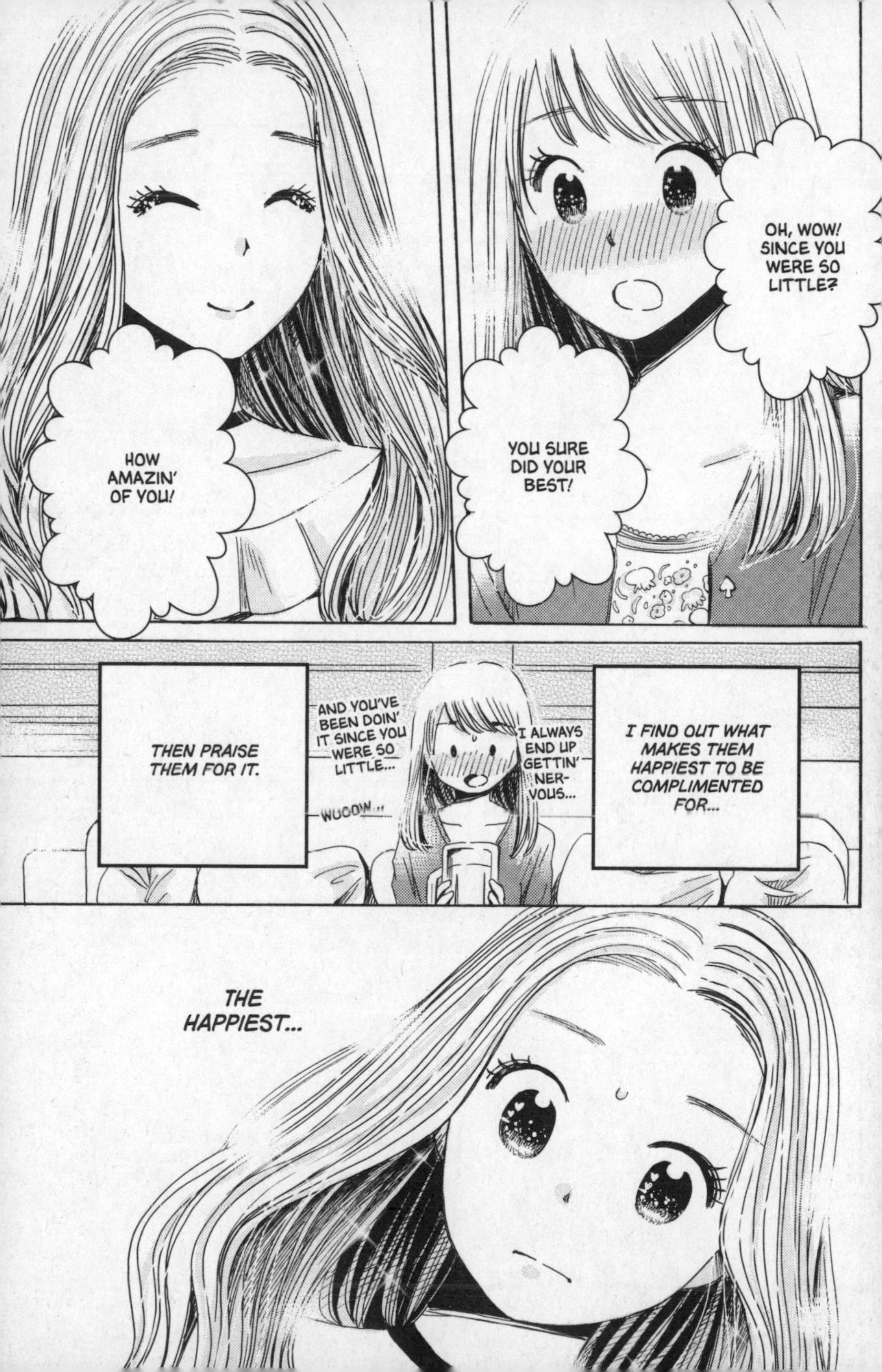
OH, WOW! SINCE YOU WERE SO LITTLE?
YOU SURE DID YOUR BEST!
HOW AMAZIN' OF YOU!
I FIND OUT WHAT MAKES THEM HAPPIEST TO BE COMPLIMENTED FOR...
I ALWAYS END UP GETTIN' NER-VOUS...
AND YOU'VE BEEN DOIN' IT SINCE YOU WERE SO LITTLE...
WUOOW...
THEN PRAISE THEM FOR IT.
THE HAPPIEST...

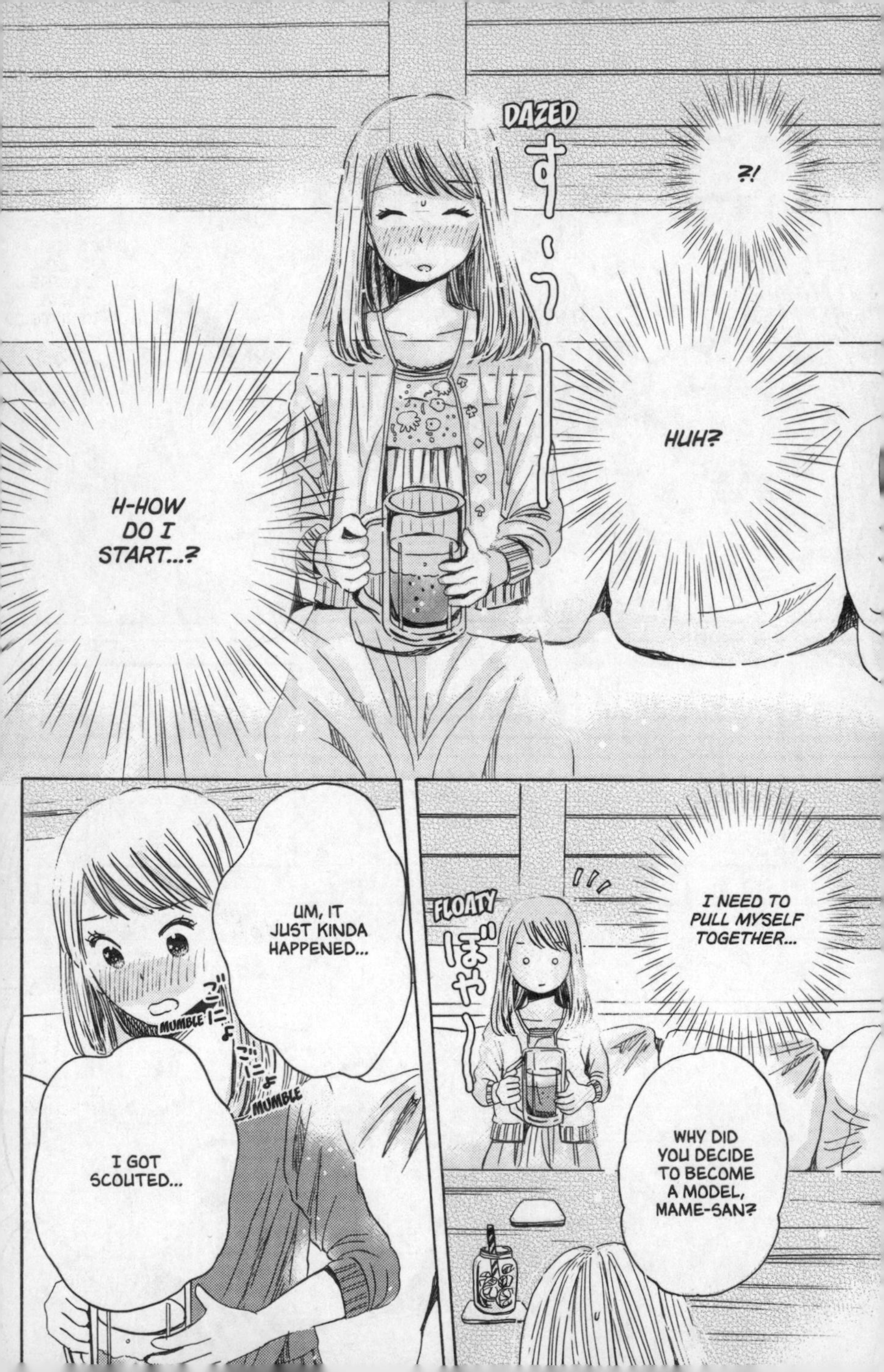
?!
DAZED
すーっ
HUH?
H-HOW DO I START...?
I NEED TO PULL MYSELF TOGETHER...
FLOATY
ぼやー
WHY DID YOU DECIDE TO BECOME A MODEL, MAME-SAN?
UM, IT JUST KINDA HAPPENED...
MUMBLE
ごにょ
ごにょ
MUMBLE
I GOT SCOUTED...

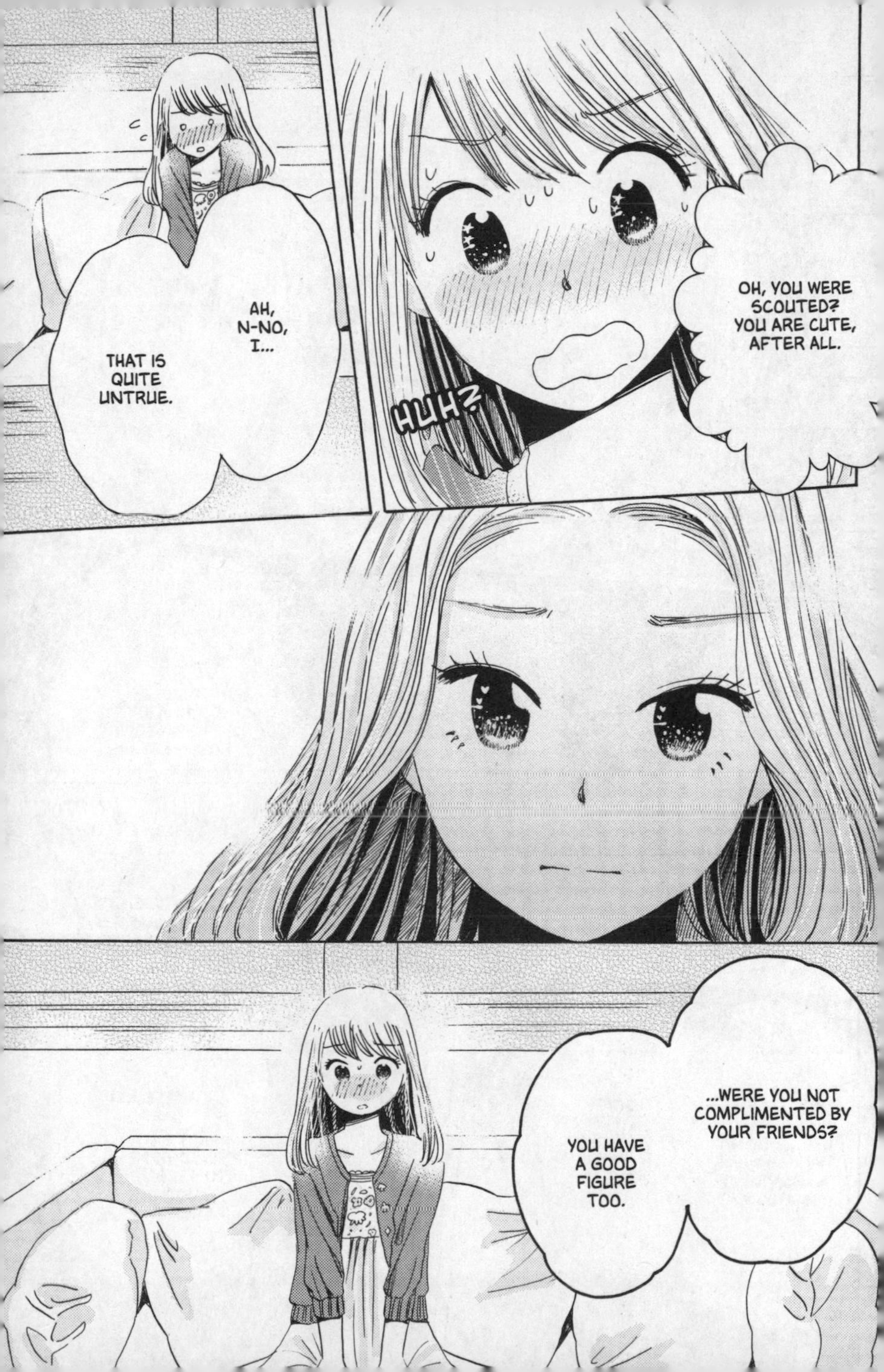
OH, YOU WERE SCOUTED? YOU ARE CUTE, AFTER ALL.
HUH?
AH, N-NO, I...
THAT IS QUITE UNTRUE.
...WERE YOU NOT COMPLIMENTED BY YOUR FRIENDS?
YOU HAVE A GOOD FIGURE TOO.

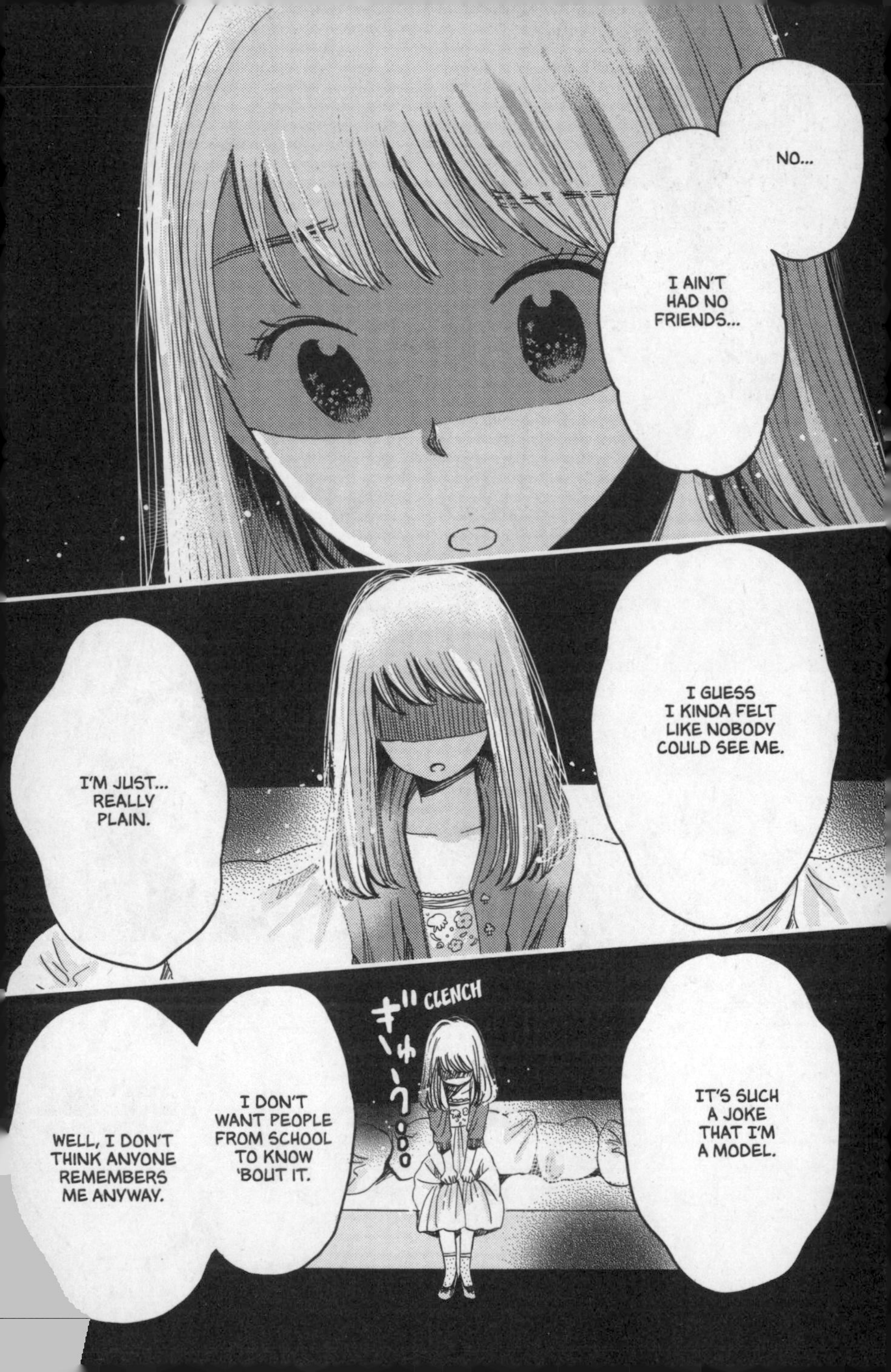
NO...
I AIN'T HAD NO FRIENDS...
I GUESS I KINDA FELT LIKE NOBODY COULD SEE ME.
I'M JUST... REALLY PLAIN.
IT'S SUCH A JOKE THAT I'M A MODEL.
CLENCH
I DON'T WANT PEOPLE FROM SCHOOL TO KNOW 'BOUT IT.
WELL, I DON'T THINK ANYONE REMEMBERS ME ANYWAY.

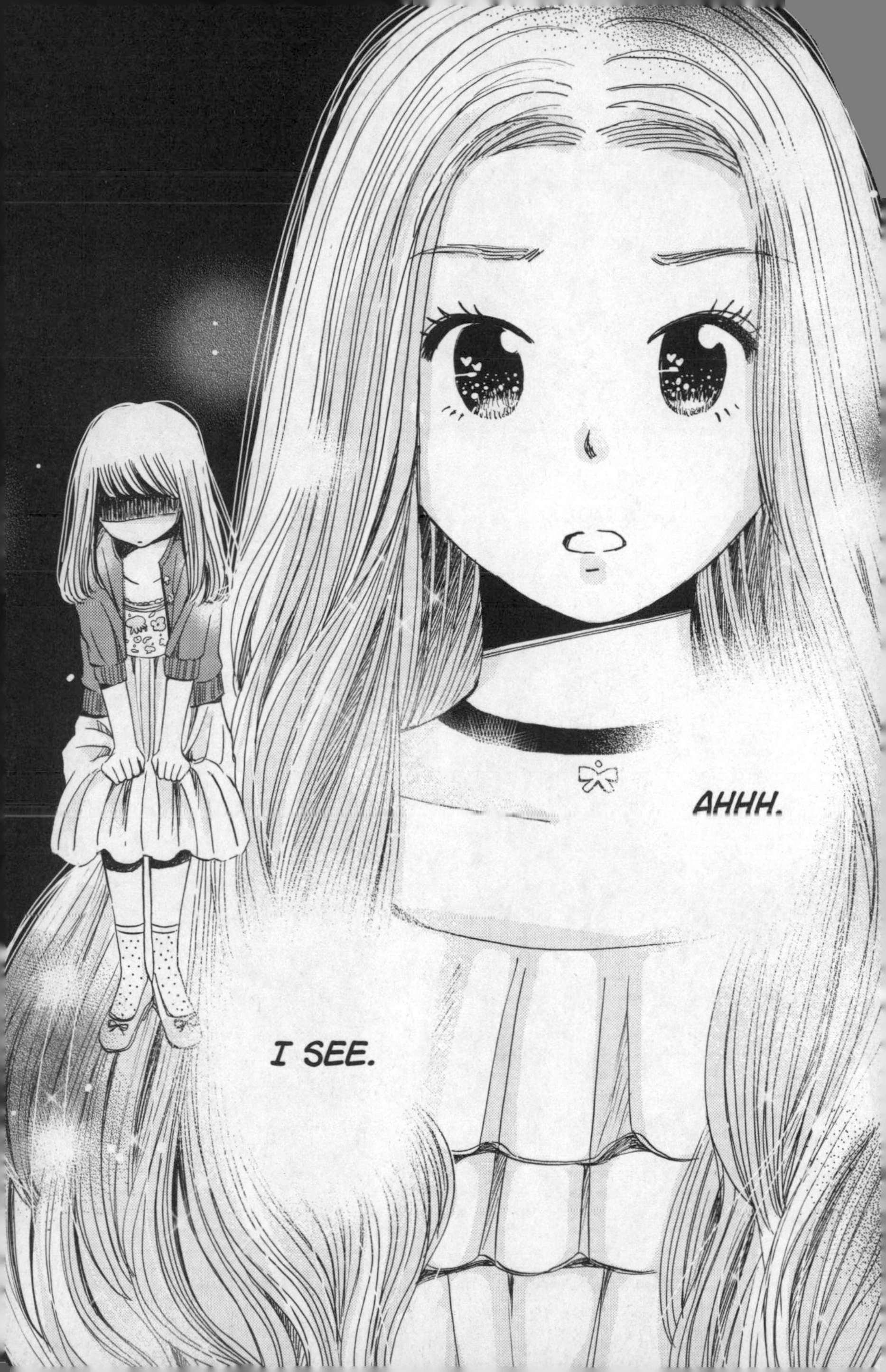
AHHH.
I SEE.

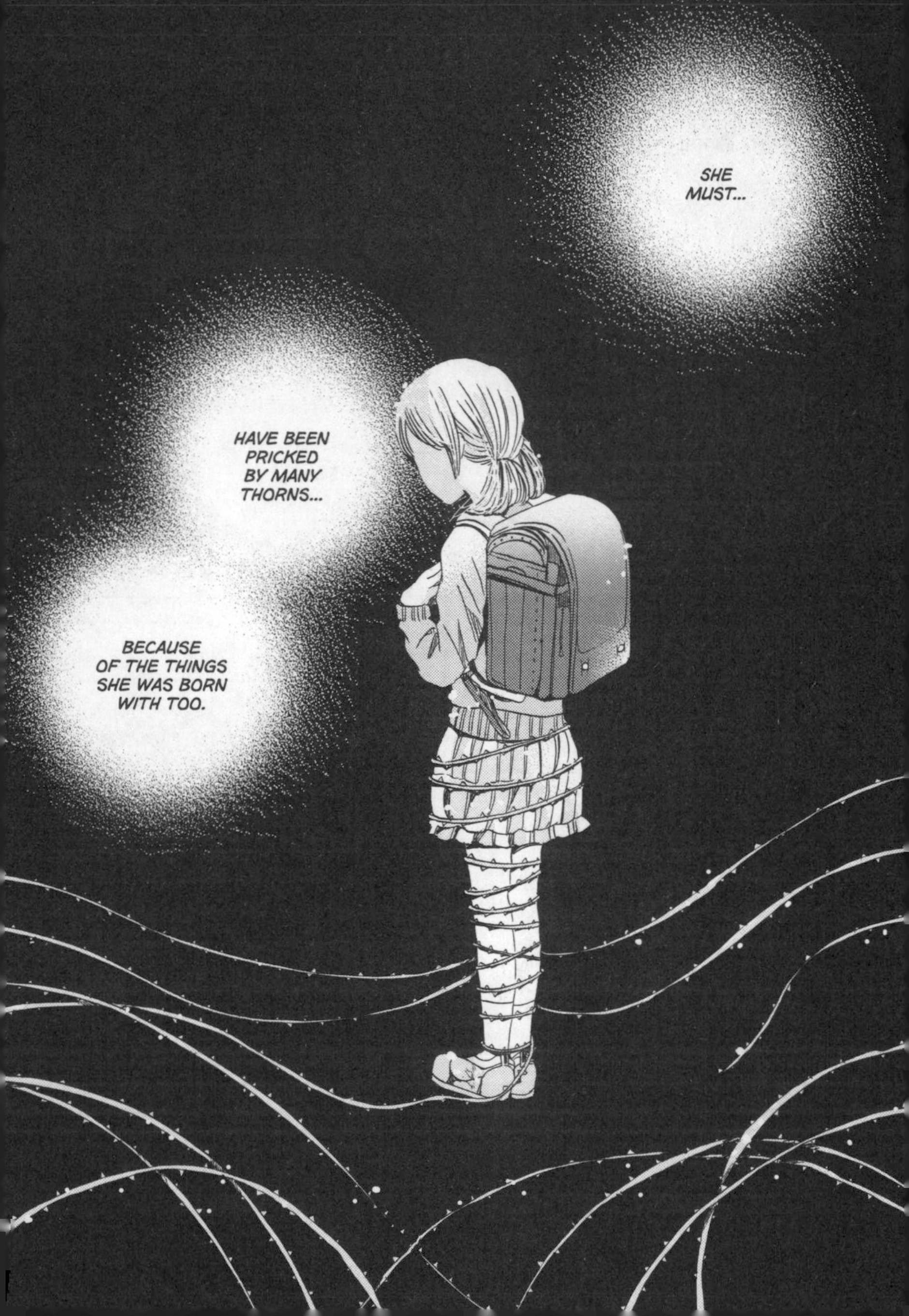
SHE MUST...
HAVE BEEN PRICKED BY MANY THORNS...
BECAUSE OF THE THINGS SHE WAS BORN WITH TOO.

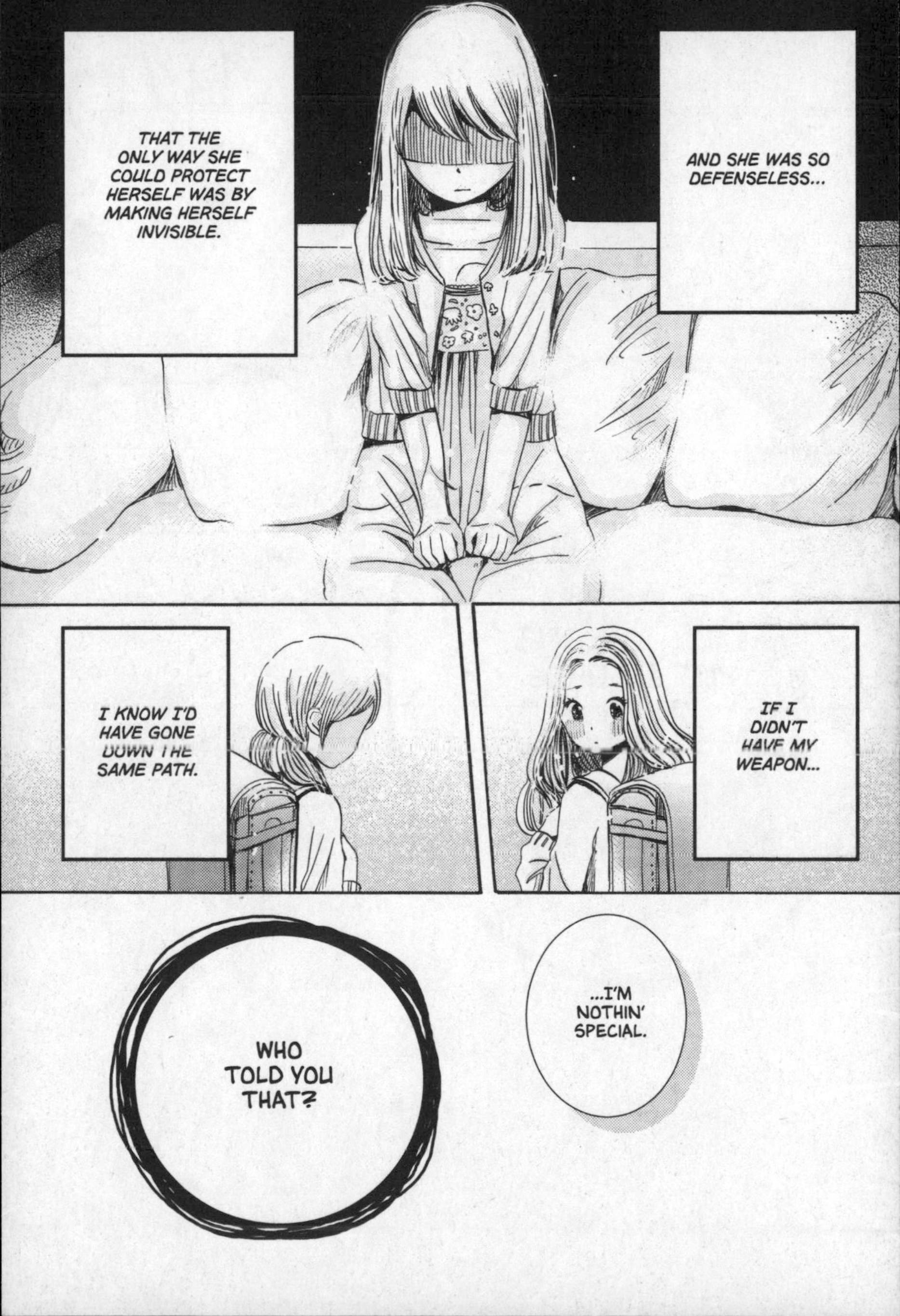
AND SHE WAS SO DEFENSELESS...
THAT THE ONLY WAY SHE COULD PROTECT HERSELF WAS BY MAKING HERSELF INVISIBLE.
IF I DIDN'T HAVE MY WEAPON...
I KNOW I'D HAVE GONE DOWN THE SAME PATH.
...I'M NOTHIN' SPECIAL.
WHO TOLD YOU THAT?

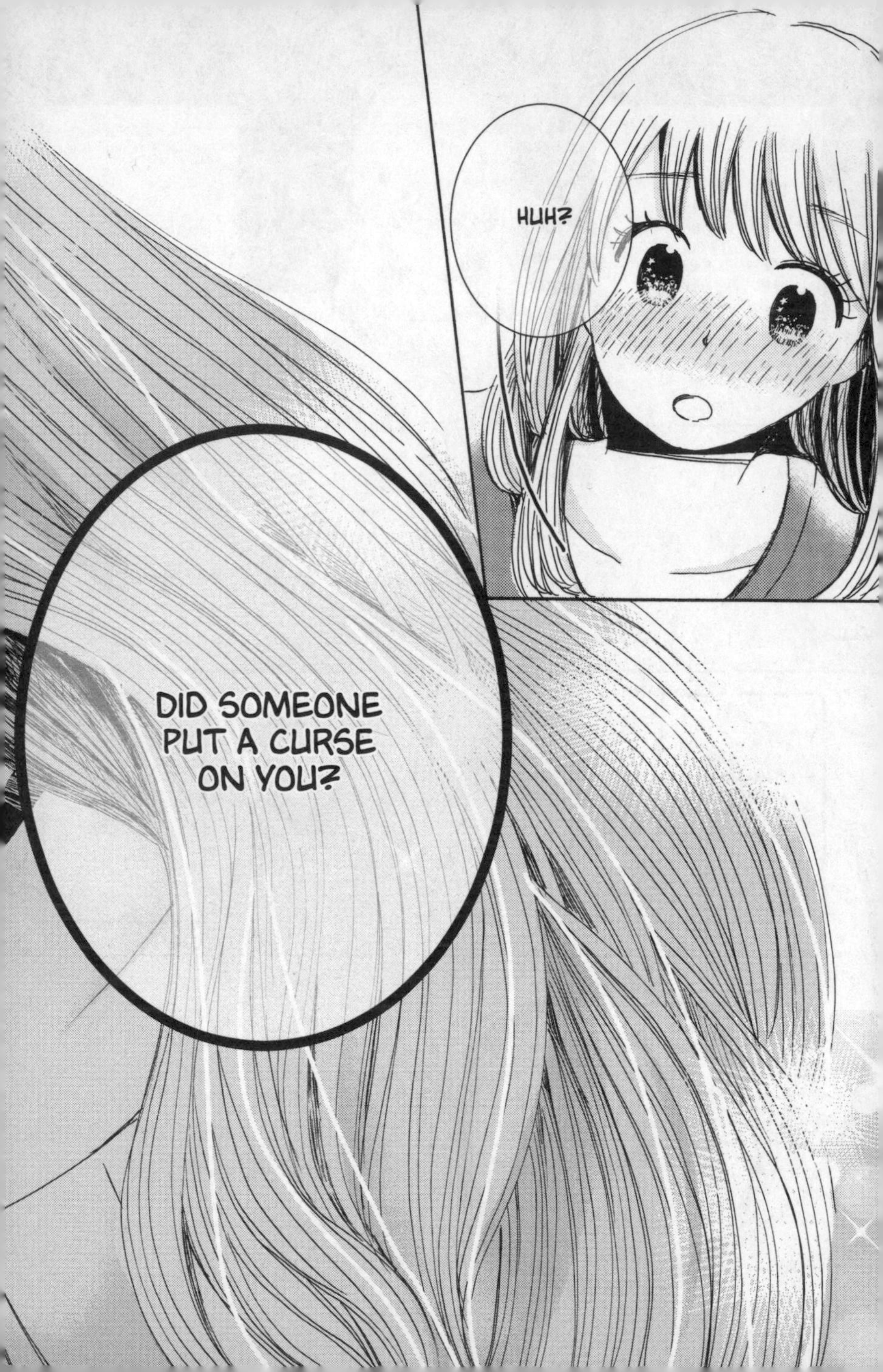
HUH?
DID SOMEONE PUT A CURSE ON YOU?

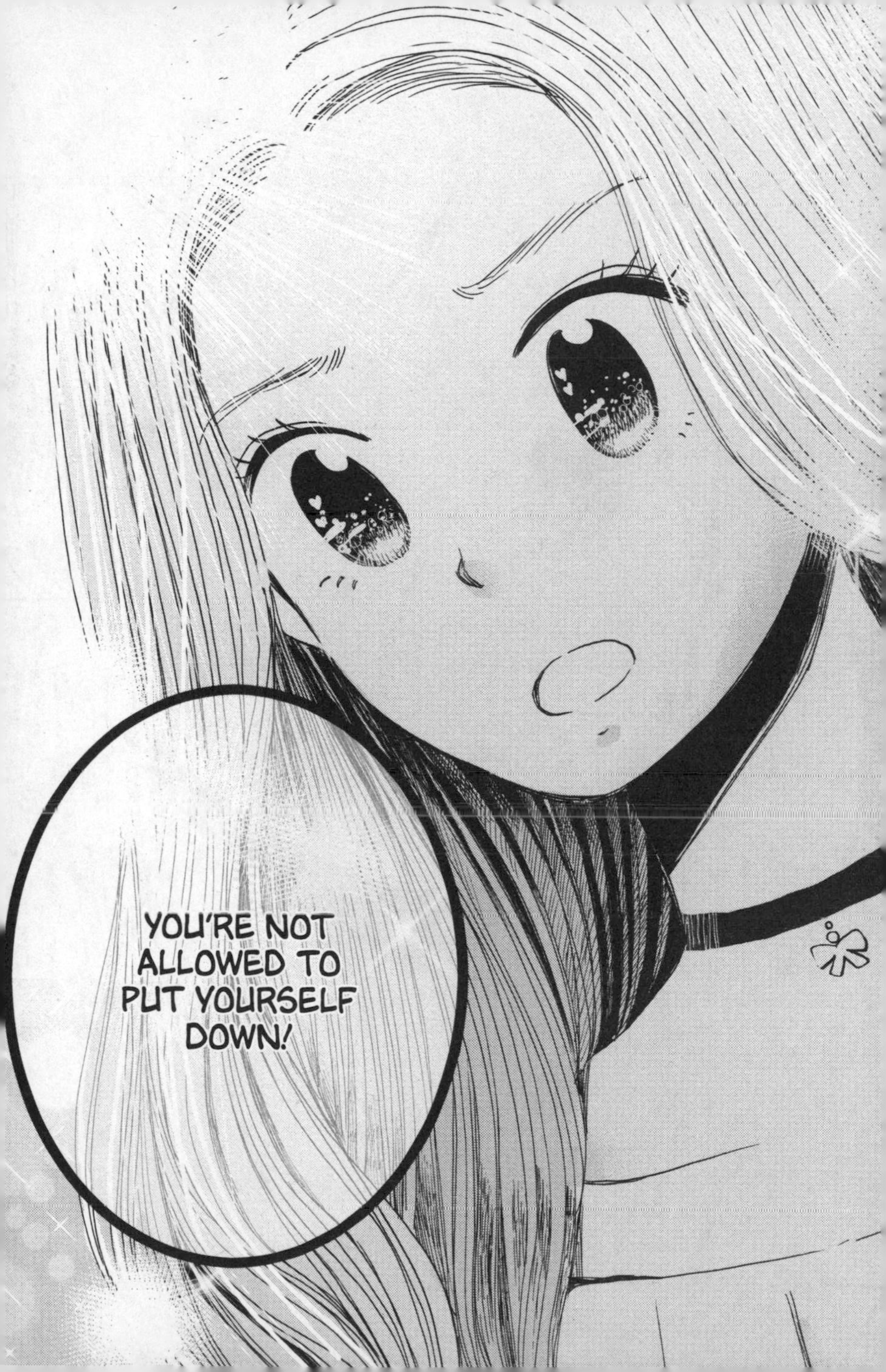
YOU'RE NOT ALLOWED TO PUT YOURSELF DOWN!

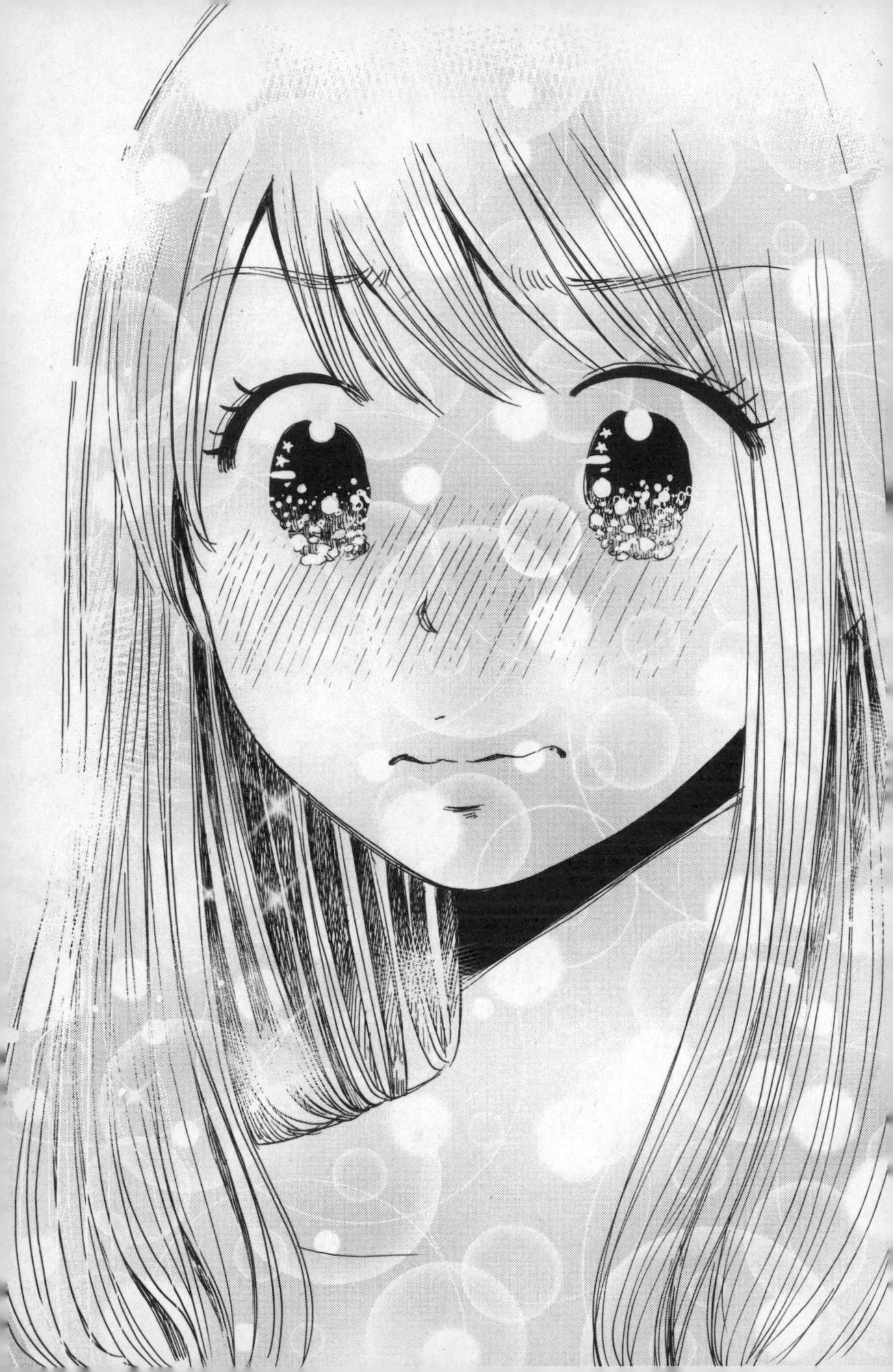

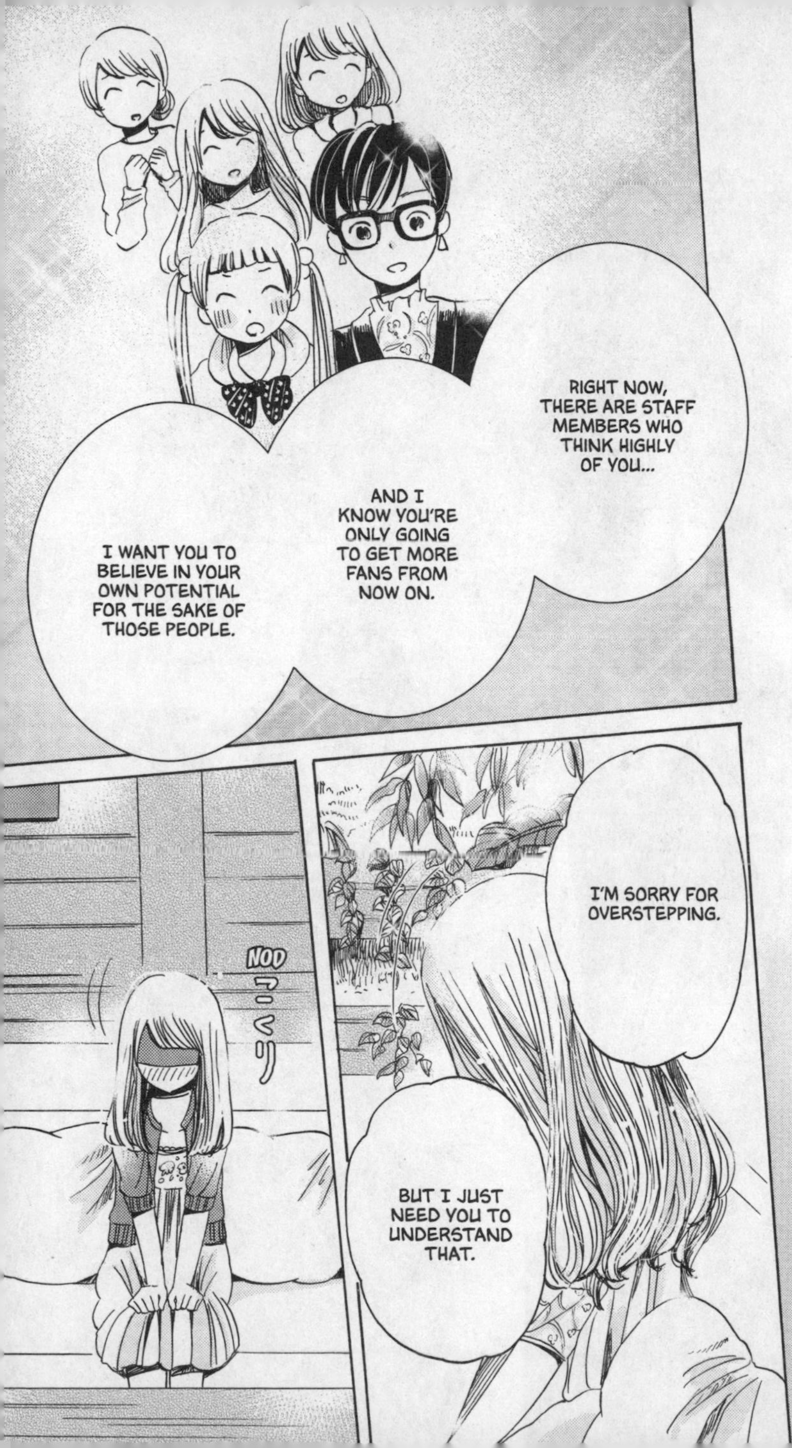
RIGHT NOW, THERE ARE STAFF MEMBERS WHO THINK HIGHLY OF YOU...
AND I KNOW YOU'RE ONLY GOING TO GET MORE FANS FROM NOW ON.
I WANT YOU TO BELIEVE IN YOUR OWN POTENTIAL FOR THE SAKE OF THOSE PEOPLE.
I'M SORRY FOR OVERSTEPPING.
BUT I JUST NEED YOU TO UNDERSTAND THAT.
NOD
こくり

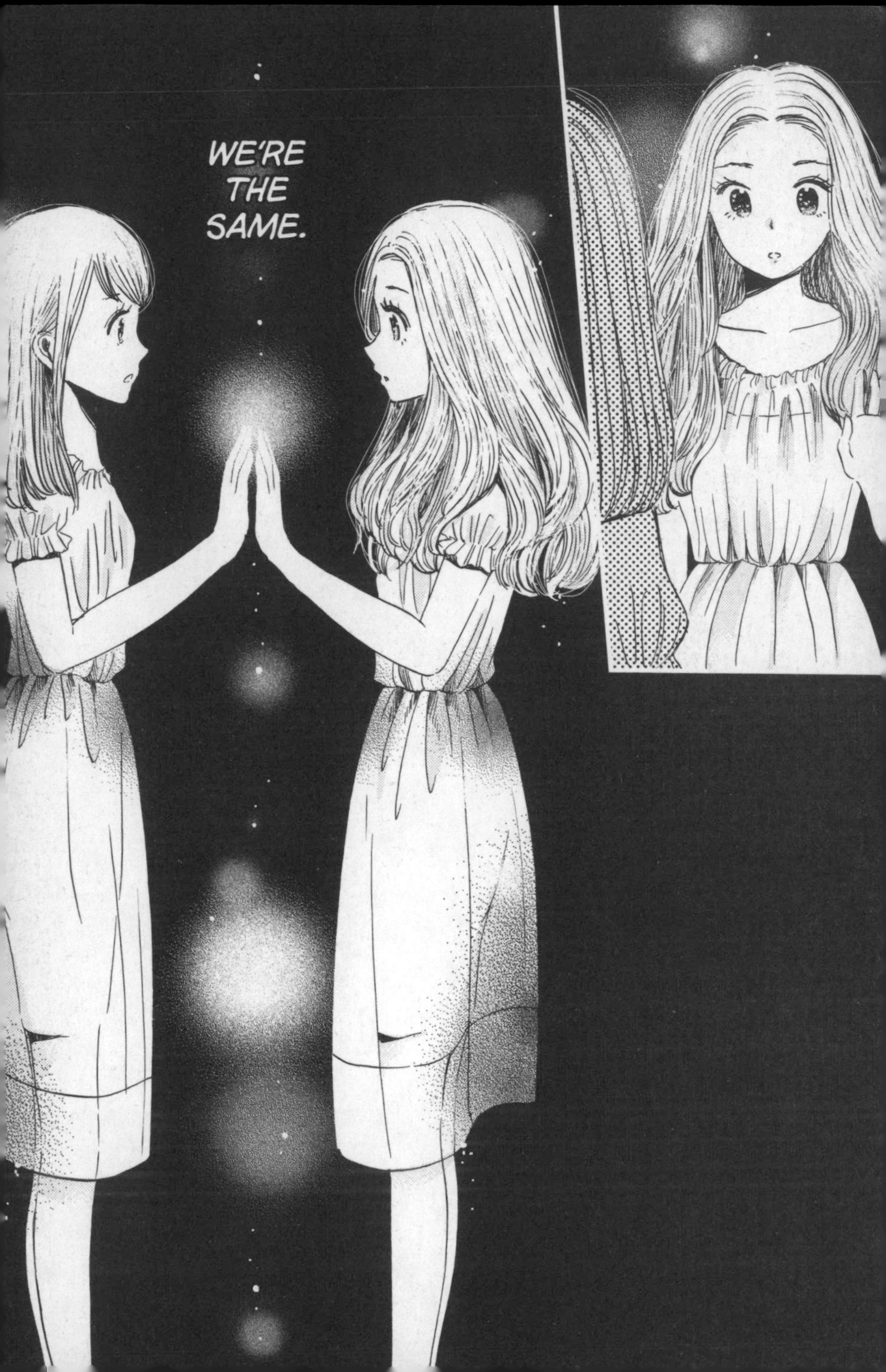
WE'RE THE SAME.

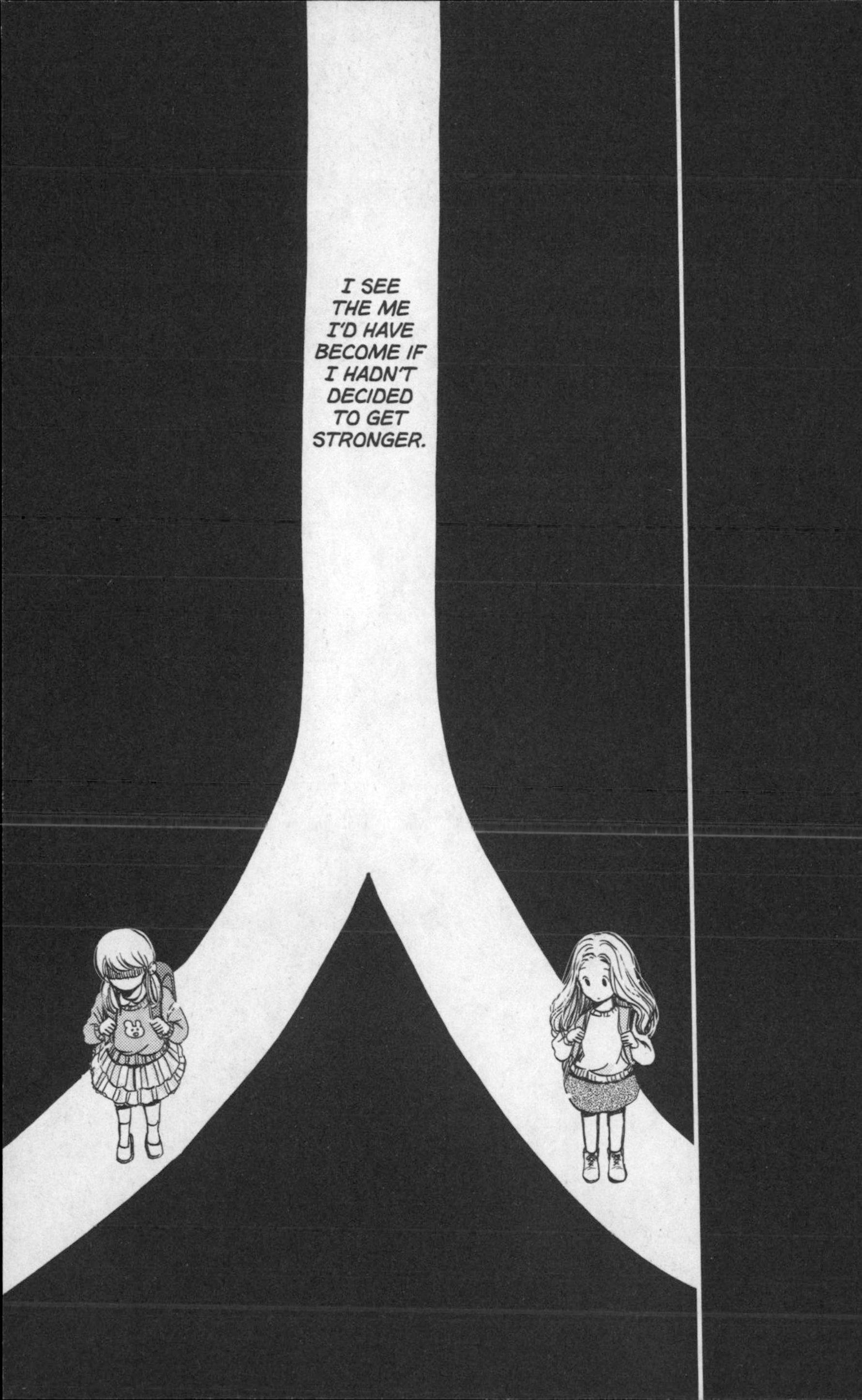
I SEE THE ME I'D HAVE BECOME IF I HADN'T DECIDED TO GET STRONGER.

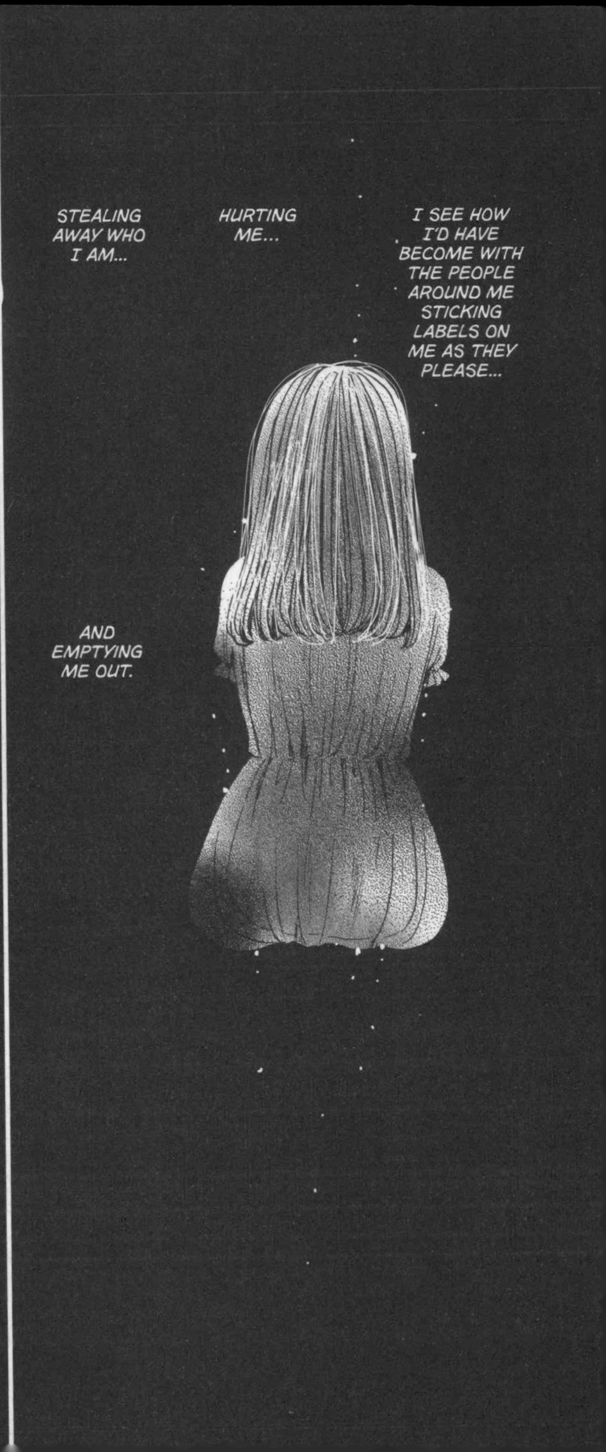
I SEE HOW I'D HAVE BECOME WITH THE PEOPLE AROUND ME STICKING LABELS ON ME AS THEY PLEASE...
HURTING ME...
STEALING AWAY WHO I AM...
AND EMPTYING ME OUT.

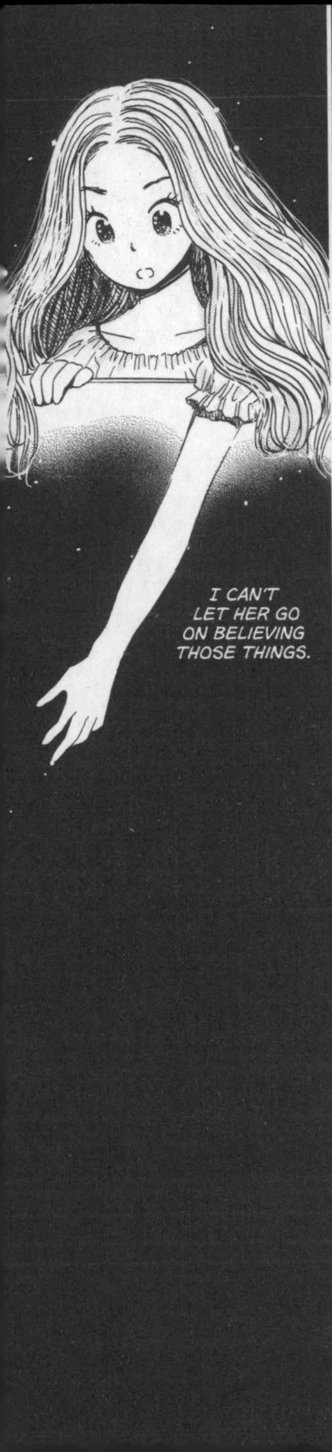
I CAN'T LET HER GO ON BELIEVING THOSE THINGS.

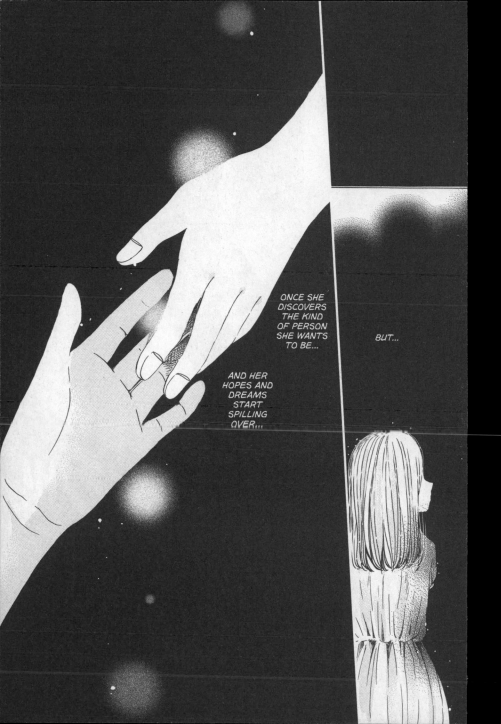

ONCE SHE DISCOVERS THE KIND OF PERSON SHE WANTS TO BE...

BUT...

AND HER HOPES AND DREAMS START SPILLING OVER...

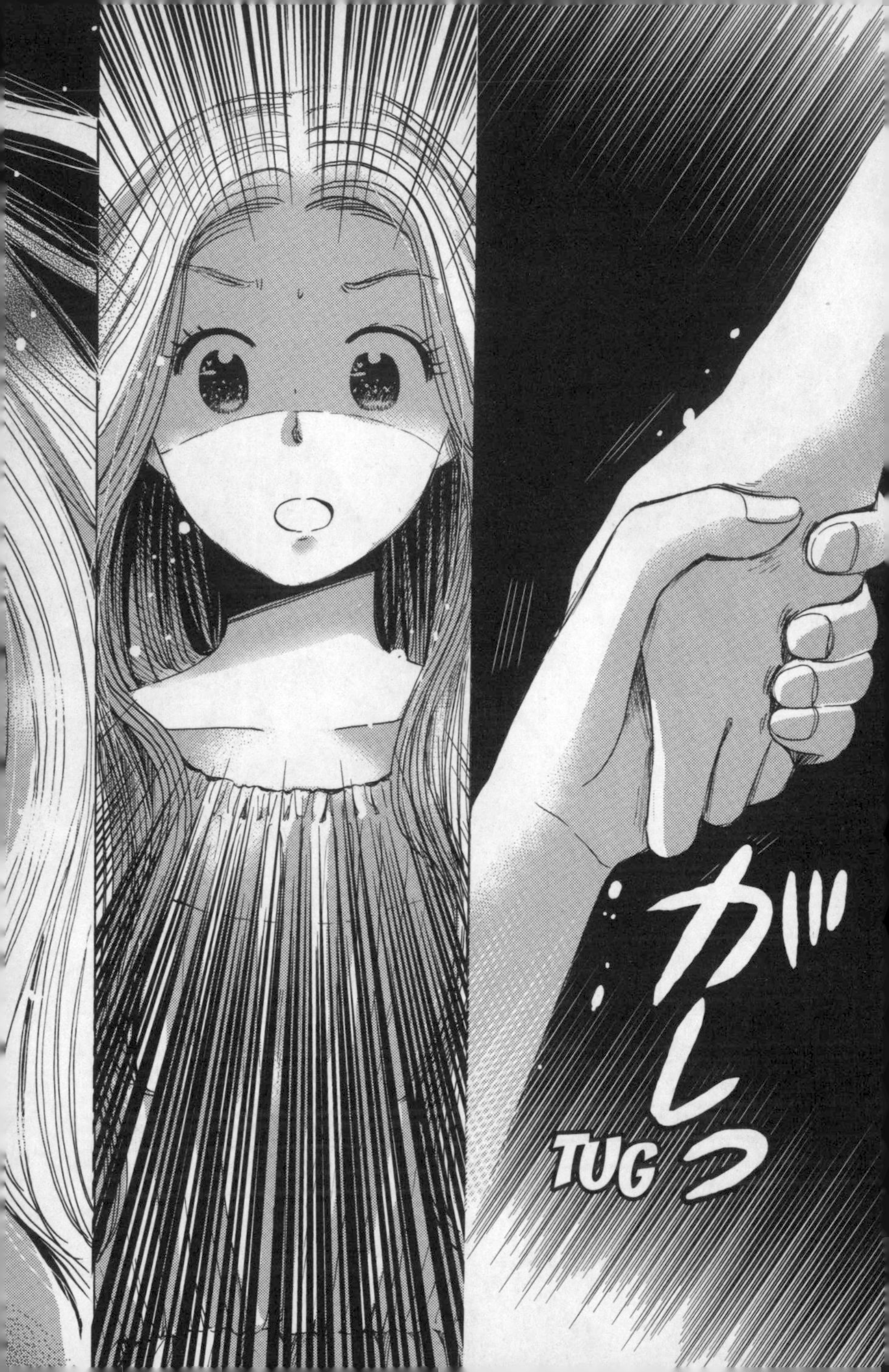
がしっ
TUG

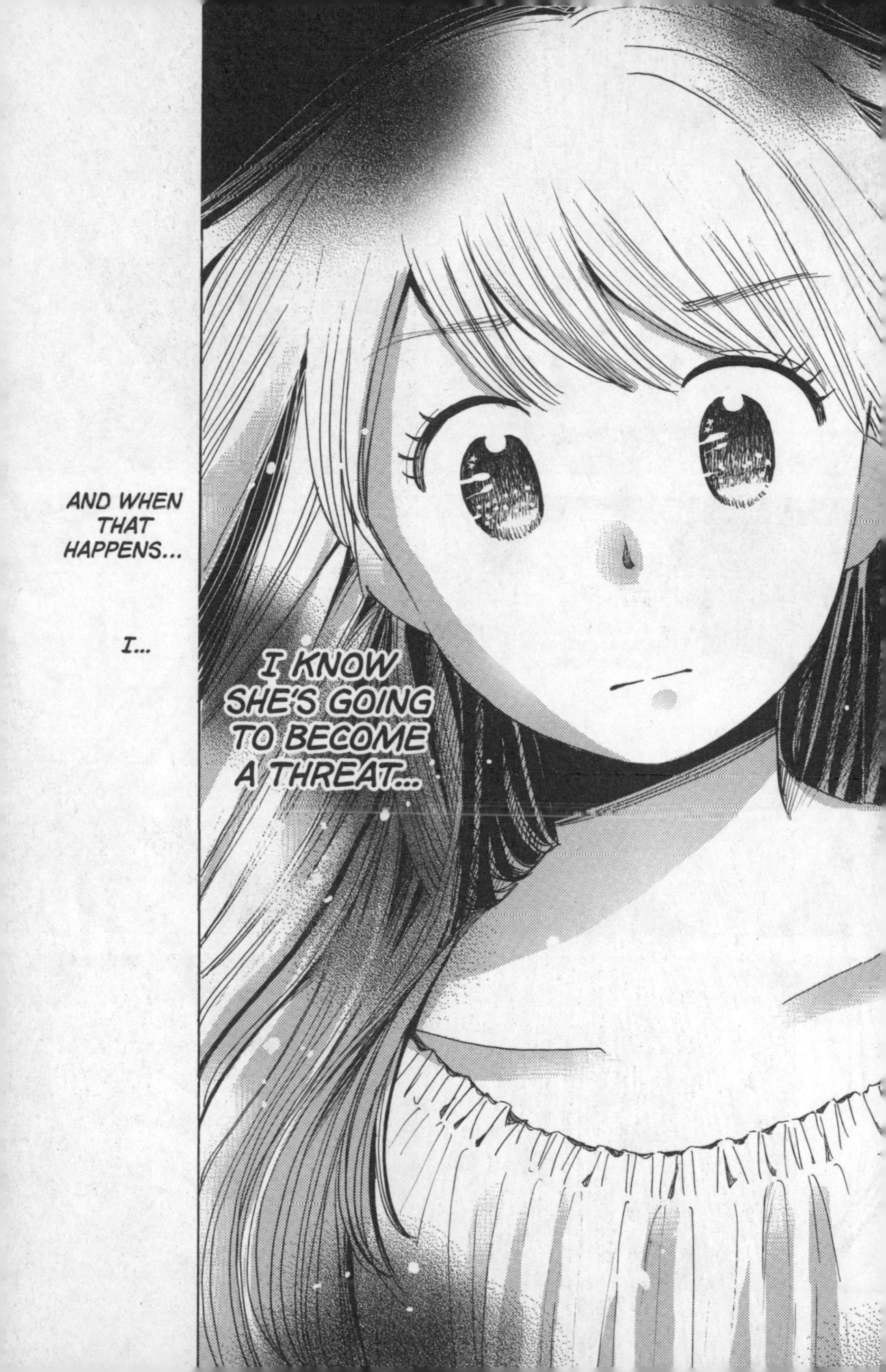
AND WHEN THAT HAPPENS...
I...
I KNOW SHE'S GOING TO BECOME A THREAT...

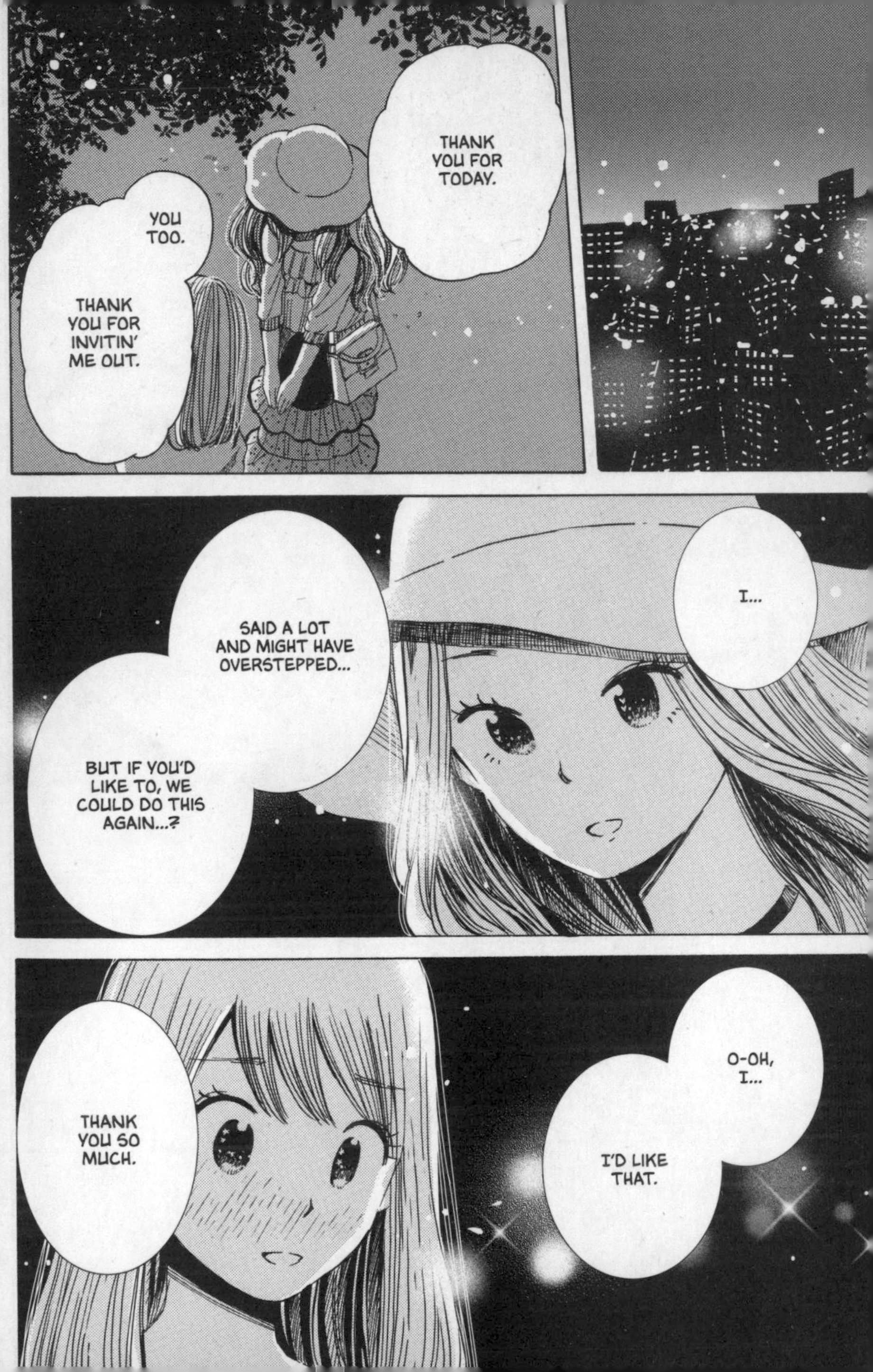
THANK YOU FOR TODAY.
YOU TOO.
THANK YOU FOR INVITIN' ME OUT.
I...
SAID A LOT AND MIGHT HAVE OVERSTEPPED...
BUT IF YOU'D LIKE TO, WE COULD DO THIS AGAIN...?
O-OH, I...
I'D LIKE THAT.
THANK YOU SO MUCH.

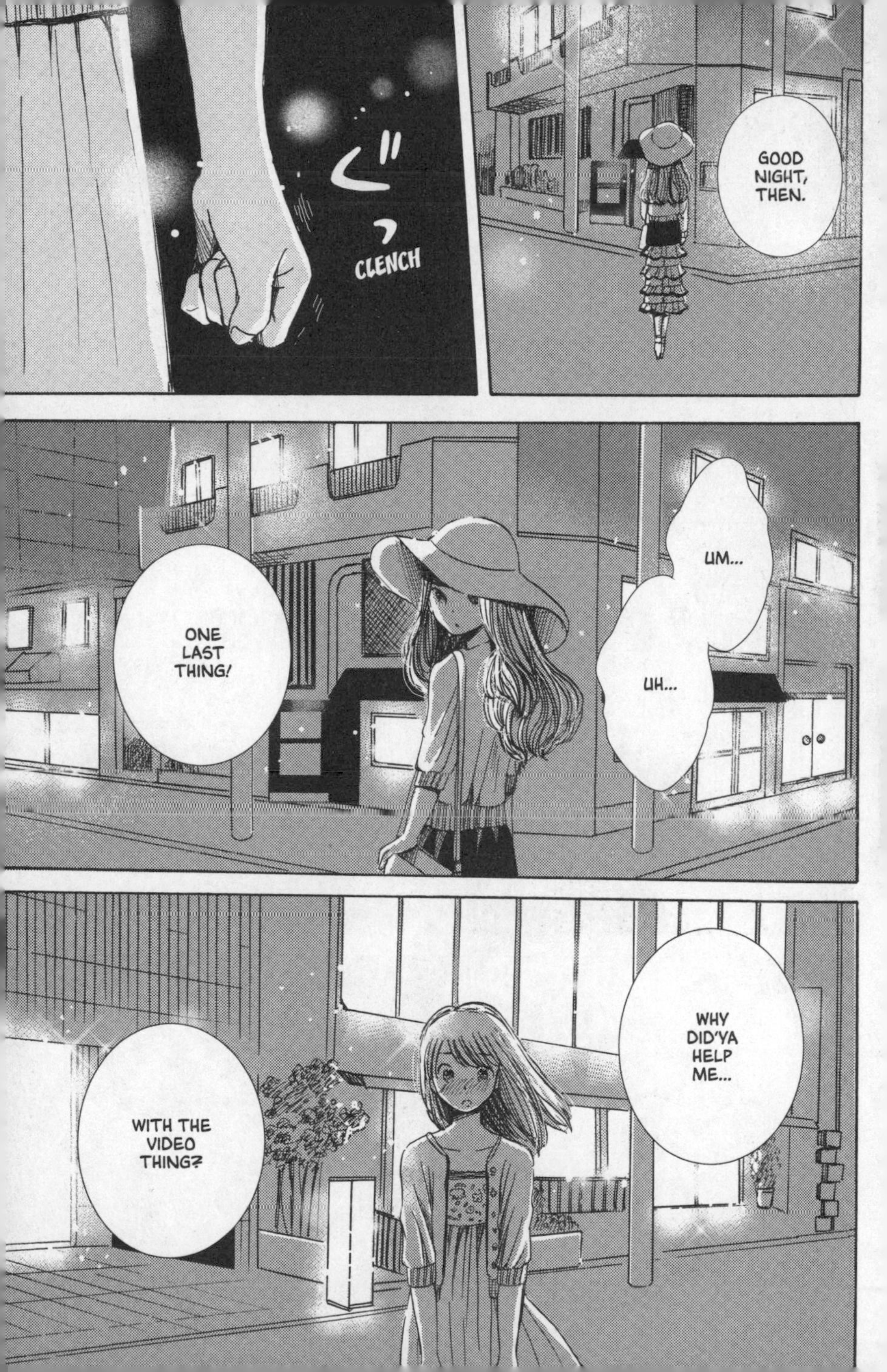
GOOD NIGHT, THEN.
ぐっ
CLENCH
UM...
UH...
ONE LAST THING!
WHY DID'YA HELP ME...
WITH THE VIDEO THING?

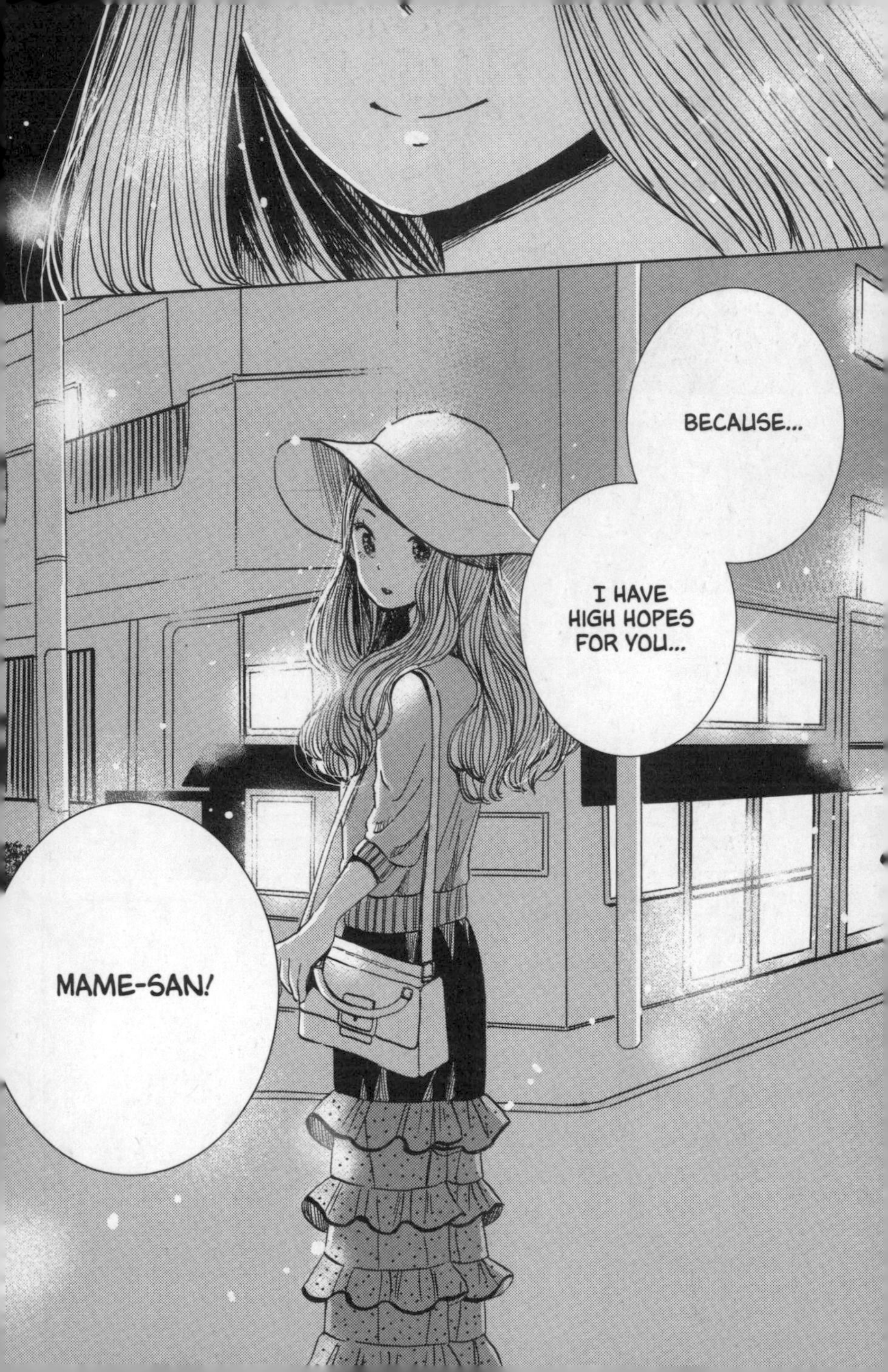
BECAUSE...
I HAVE HIGH HOPES FOR YOU...
MAME-SAN!

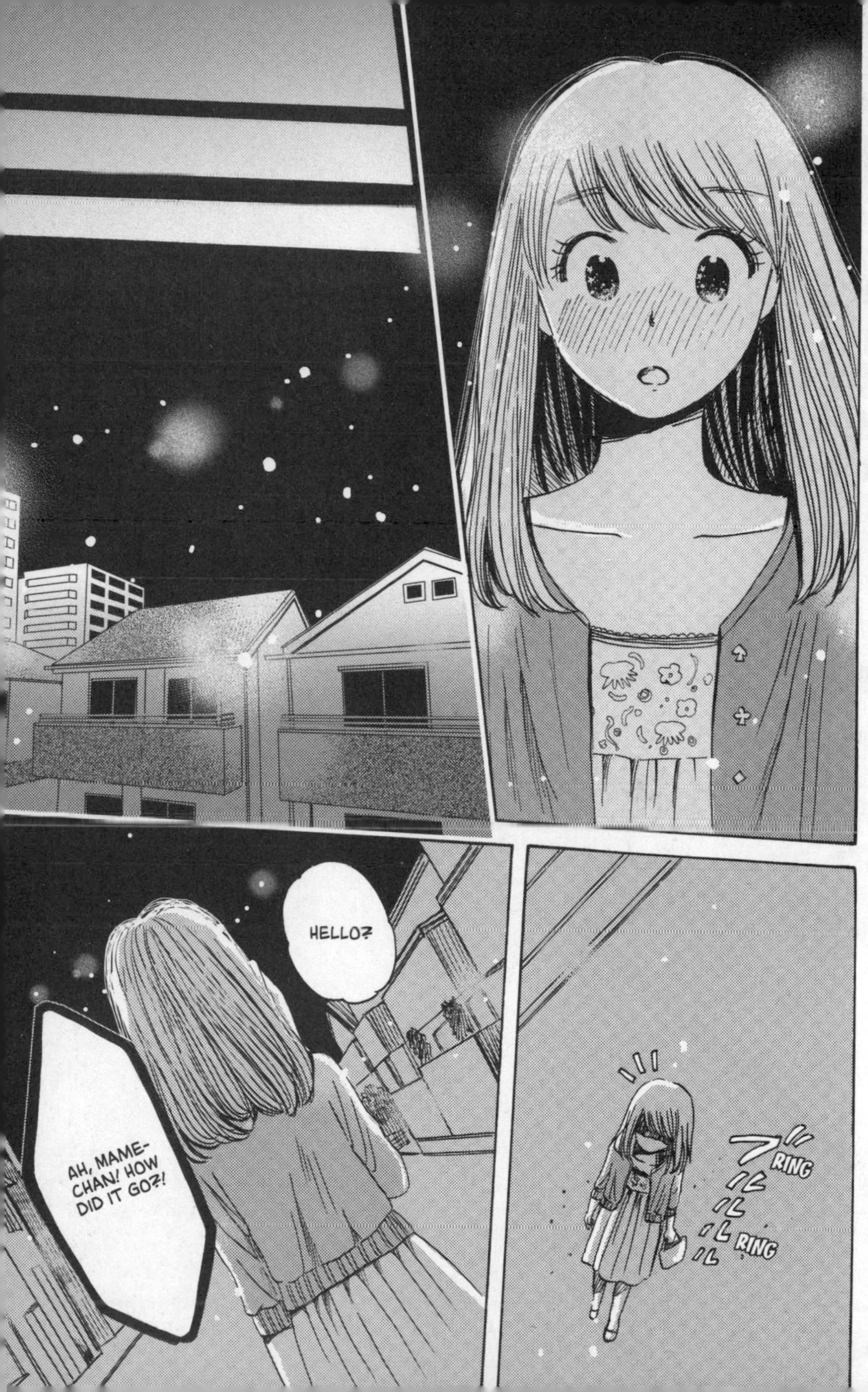
RING
RING
HELLO?
AH, MAME-CHAN! HOW DID IT GO?!

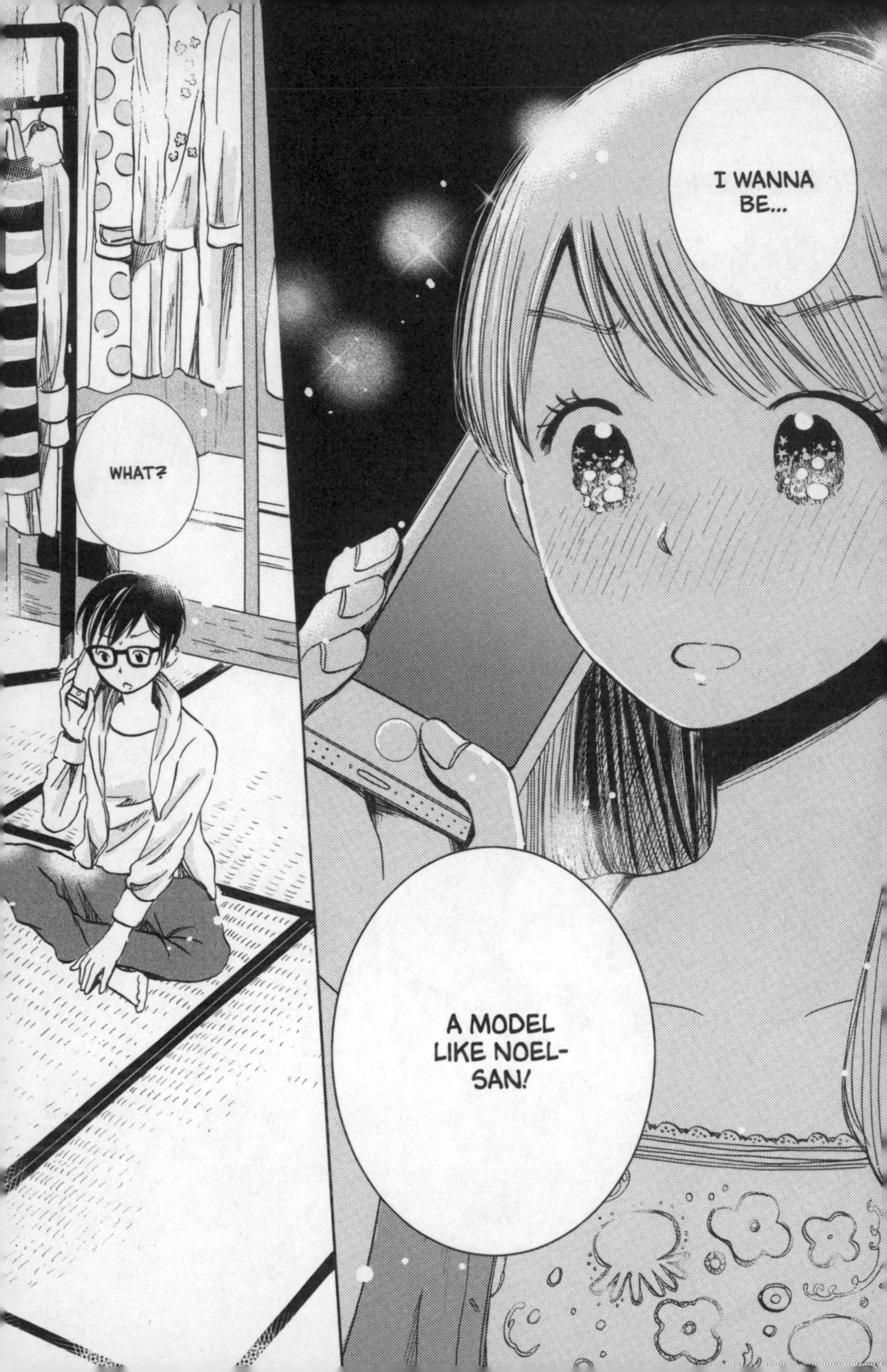
I WANNA BE...
A MODEL LIKE NOEL-SAN!
WHAT?

MAME
coordinate

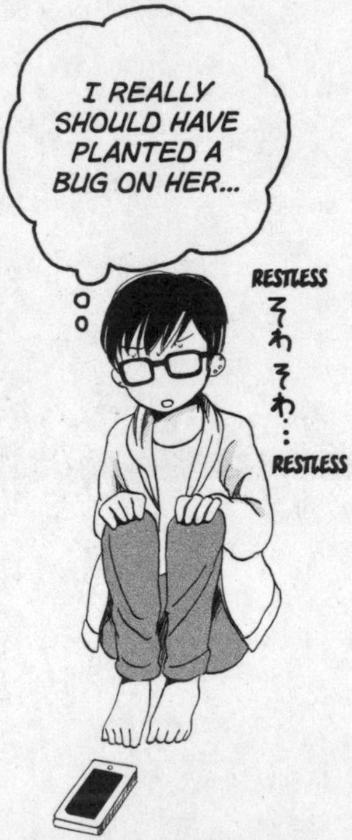
I REALLY SHOULD HAVE PLANTED A BUG ON HER...
RESTLESS
そわ そわ…
RESTLESS

KISARAGI-SAN SPENT THE WHOLE EVENING TRYING TO FIGURE OUT WHEN MAME WAS GOING TO BE DONE WITH DINNER SO THAT SHE COULD CALL.

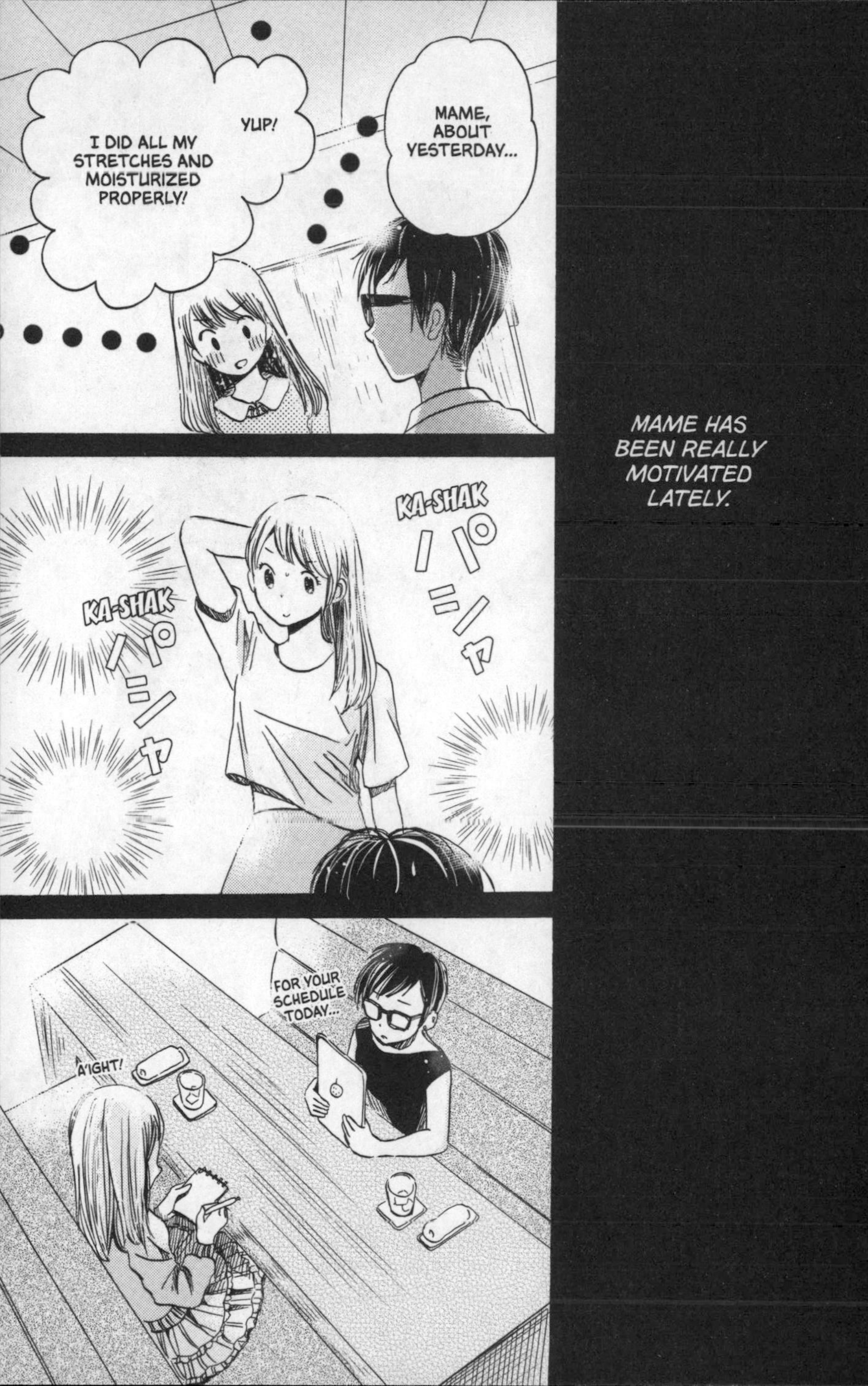
MAME HAS BEEN REALLY MOTIVATED LATELY.
MAME, ABOUT YESTERDAY...
YUP!
I DID ALL MY STRETCHES AND MOISTURIZED PROPERLY!
KA-SHAK
パシャ
KA-SHAK
パシャ
FOR YOUR SCHEDULE TODAY...
A'IGHT!

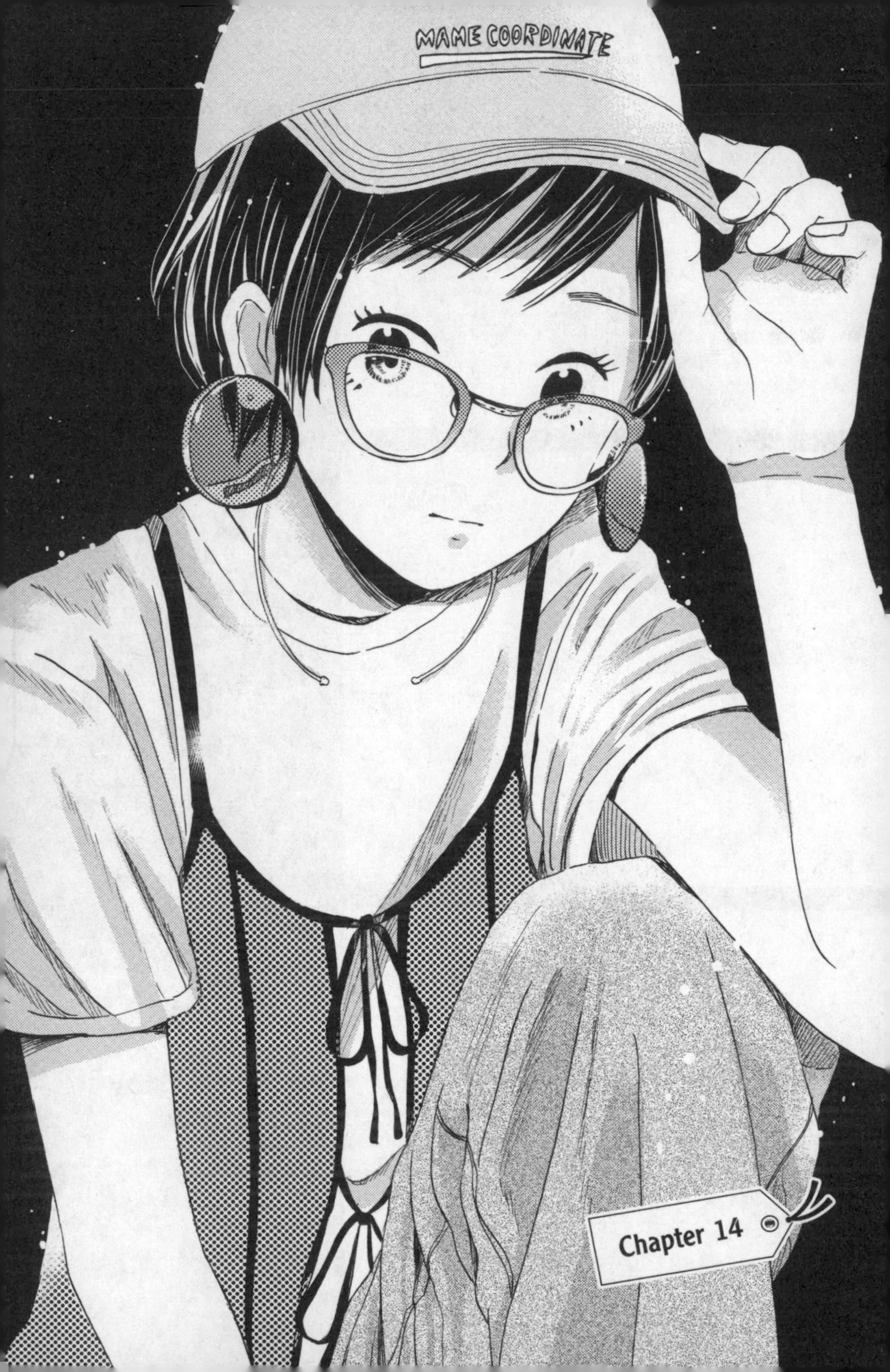
MAME COORDINATE
Chapter 14

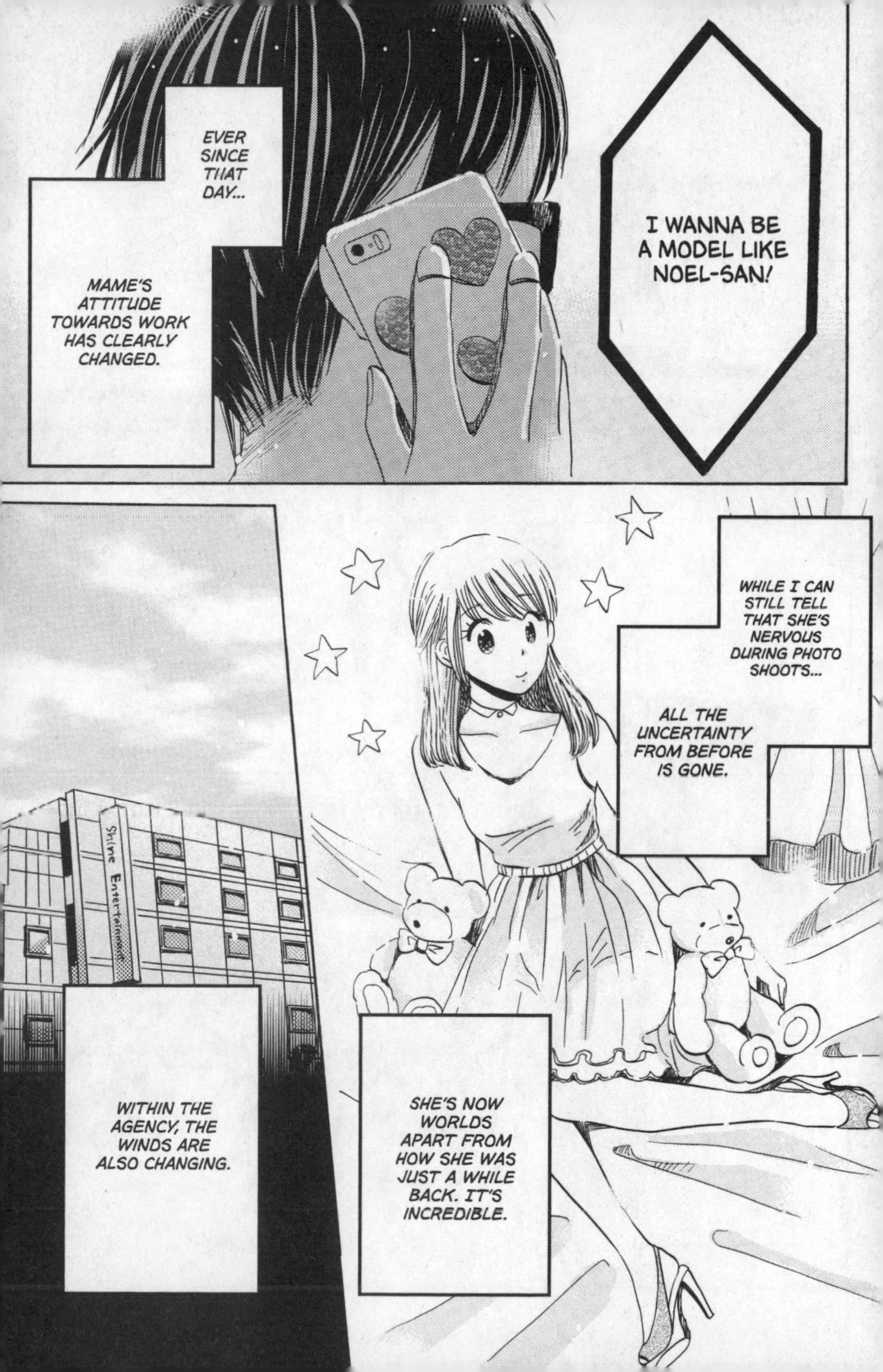
I WANNA BE A MODEL LIKE NOEL-SAN!
EVER SINCE THAT DAY...
MAME'S ATTITUDE TOWARDS WORK HAS CLEARLY CHANGED.
WHILE I CAN STILL TELL THAT SHE'S NERVOUS DURING PHOTO SHOOTS...
ALL THE UNCERTAINTY FROM BEFORE IS GONE.
SHE'S NOW WORLDS APART FROM HOW SHE WAS JUST A WHILE BACK. IT'S INCREDIBLE.
Shine Entertainment
WITHIN THE AGENCY, THE WINDS ARE ALSO CHANGING.

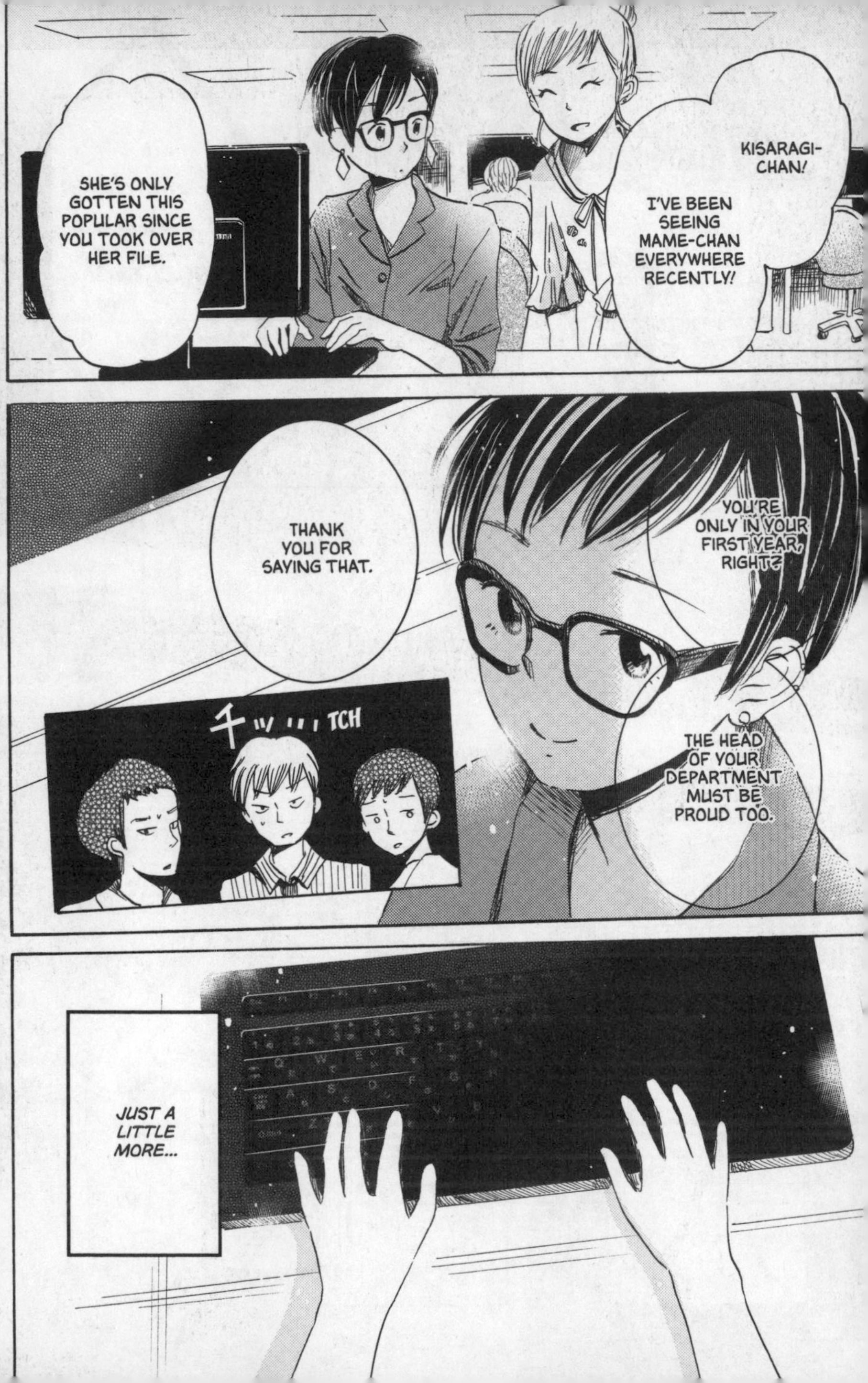
KISARAGI-CHAN!
I'VE BEEN SEEING MAME-CHAN EVERYWHERE RECENTLY!
SHE'S ONLY GOTTEN THIS POPULAR SINCE YOU TOOK OVER HER FILE.
YOU'RE ONLY IN YOUR FIRST YEAR, RIGHT?
THE HEAD OF YOUR DEPARTMENT MUST BE PROUD TOO.
THANK YOU FOR SAYING THAT.
チッ TCH
JUST A LITTLE MORE...

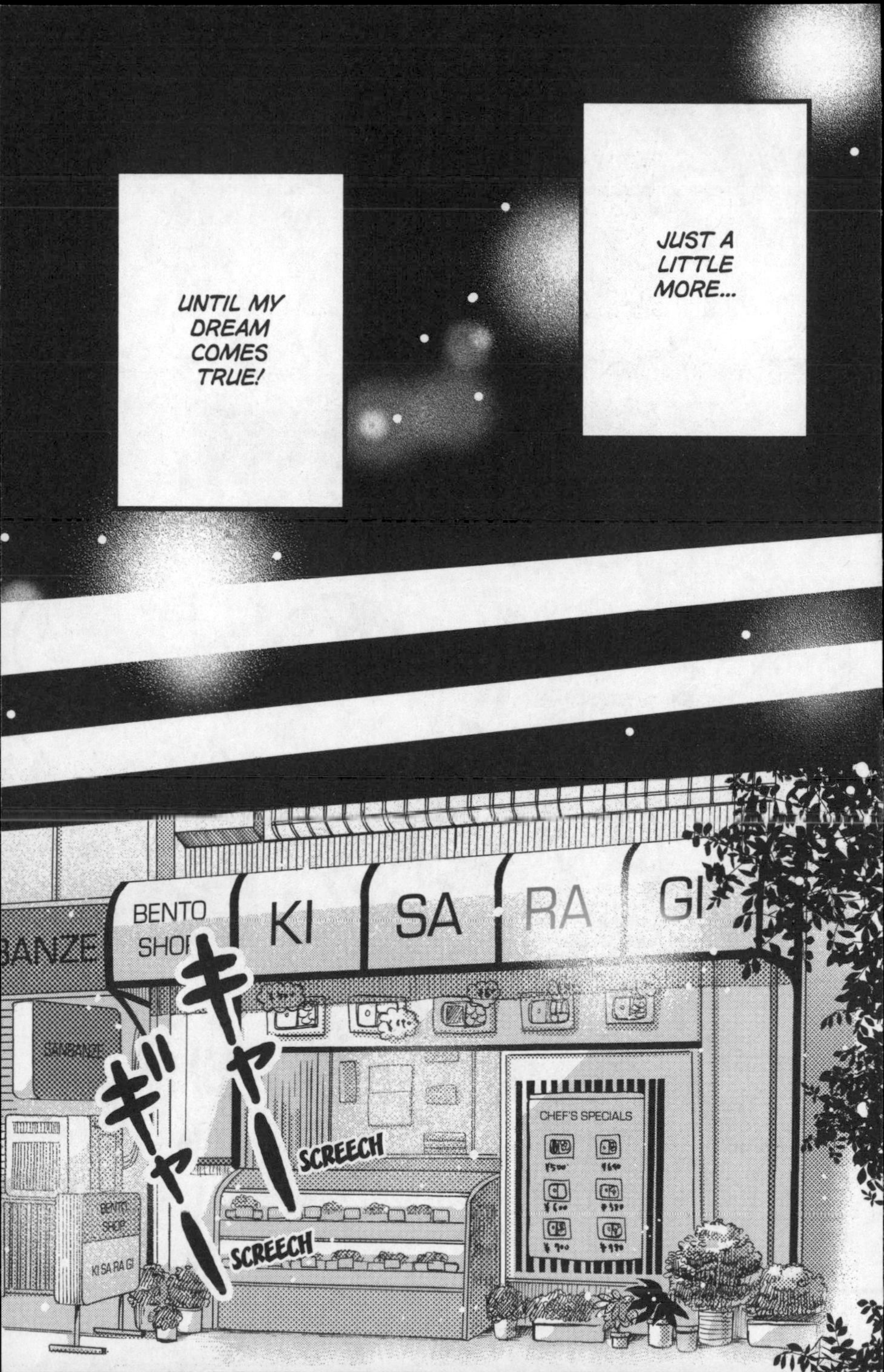
JUST A LITTLE MORE...
UNTIL MY DREAM COMES TRUE!
BENTO SHOP
KI SA RA GI
キャー
SCREECH
ギャー
SCREECH
CHEF'S SPECIALS
BENTO SHOP
KI SA RA GI

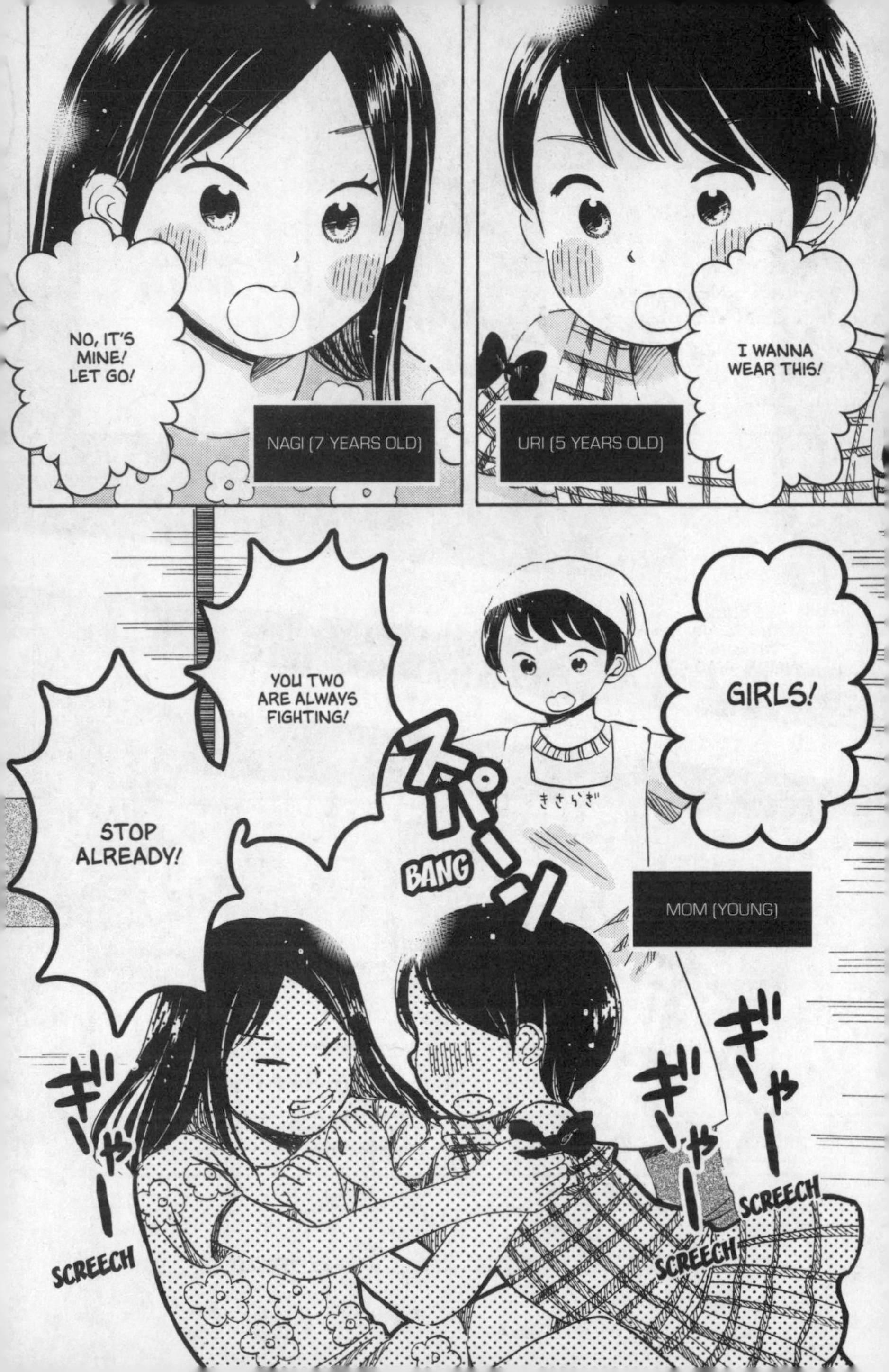
I WANNA WEAR THIS!
URI (5 YEARS OLD)
NO, IT'S MINE! LET GO!
NAGI (7 YEARS OLD)
GIRLS!
MOM (YOUNG)
きさらぎ
YOU TWO ARE ALWAYS FIGHTING!
STOP ALREADY!
スパーン
BANG
ぎゃーぎゃー
SCREECH
SCREECH
ぎゃー
SCREECH

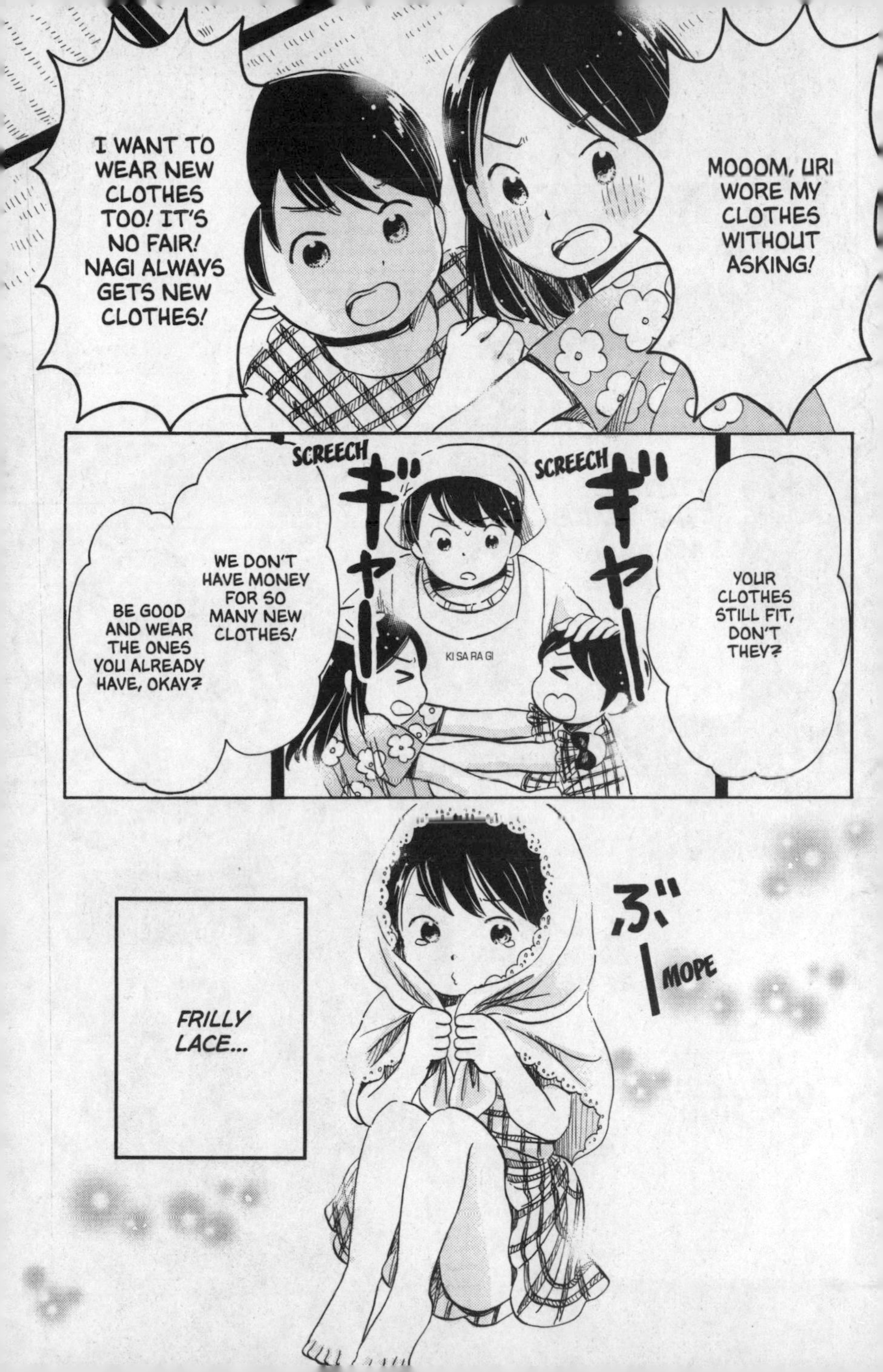
MOOOM, URI WORE MY CLOTHES WITHOUT ASKING!
I WANT TO WEAR NEW CLOTHES TOO! IT'S NO FAIR! NAGI ALWAYS GETS NEW CLOTHES!
YOUR CLOTHES STILL FIT, DON'T THEY?
SCREECH
ギャー
SCREECH
ギャー
KI SA RA GI
WE DON'T HAVE MONEY FOR SO MANY NEW CLOTHES!
BE GOOD AND WEAR THE ONES YOU ALREADY HAVE, OKAY?
ぶー
MOPE
FRILLY LACE...

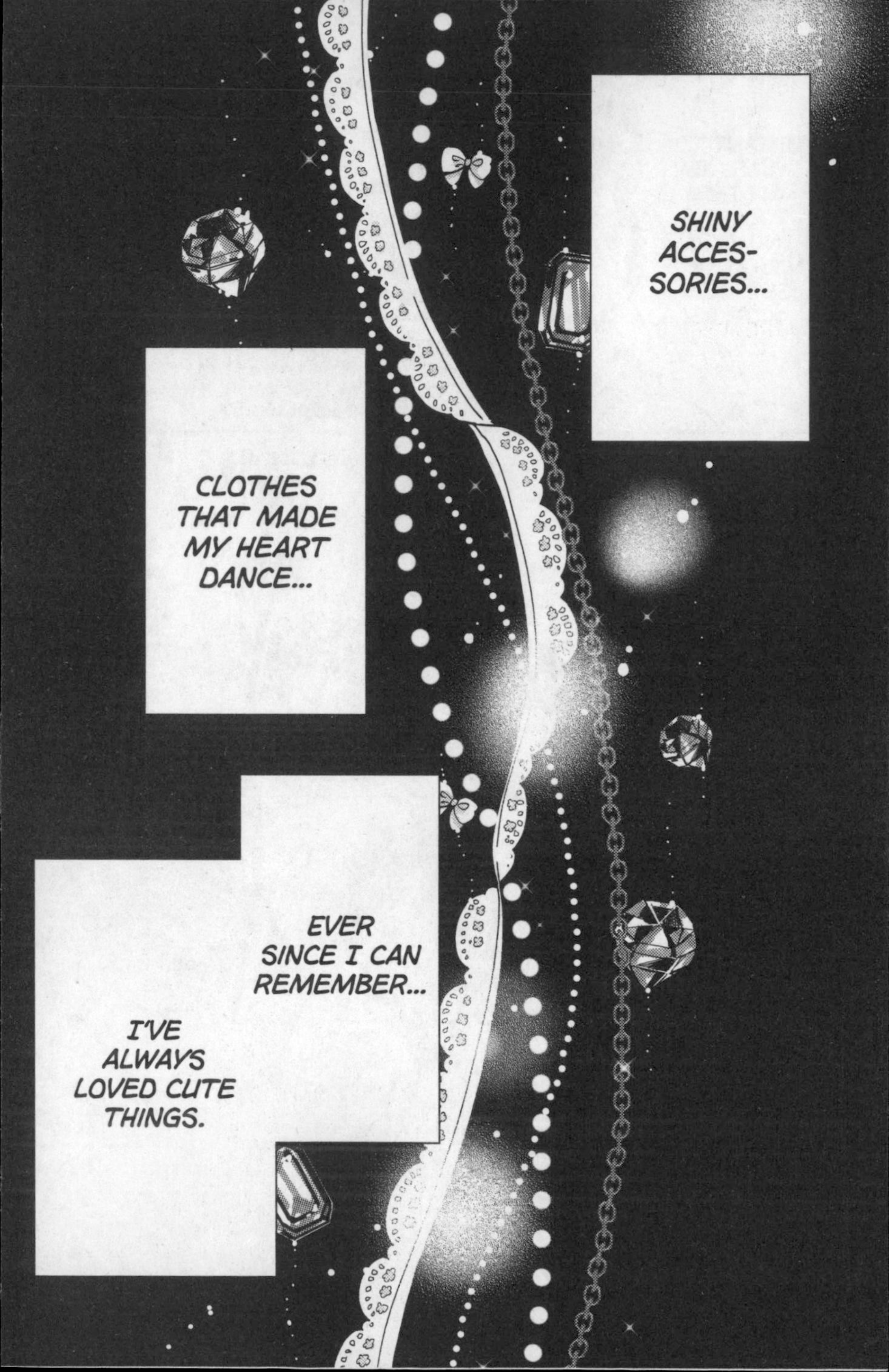
SHINY ACCES-SORIES...
CLOTHES THAT MADE MY HEART DANCE...
EVER SINCE I CAN REMEMBER...
I'VE ALWAYS LOVED CUTE THINGS.

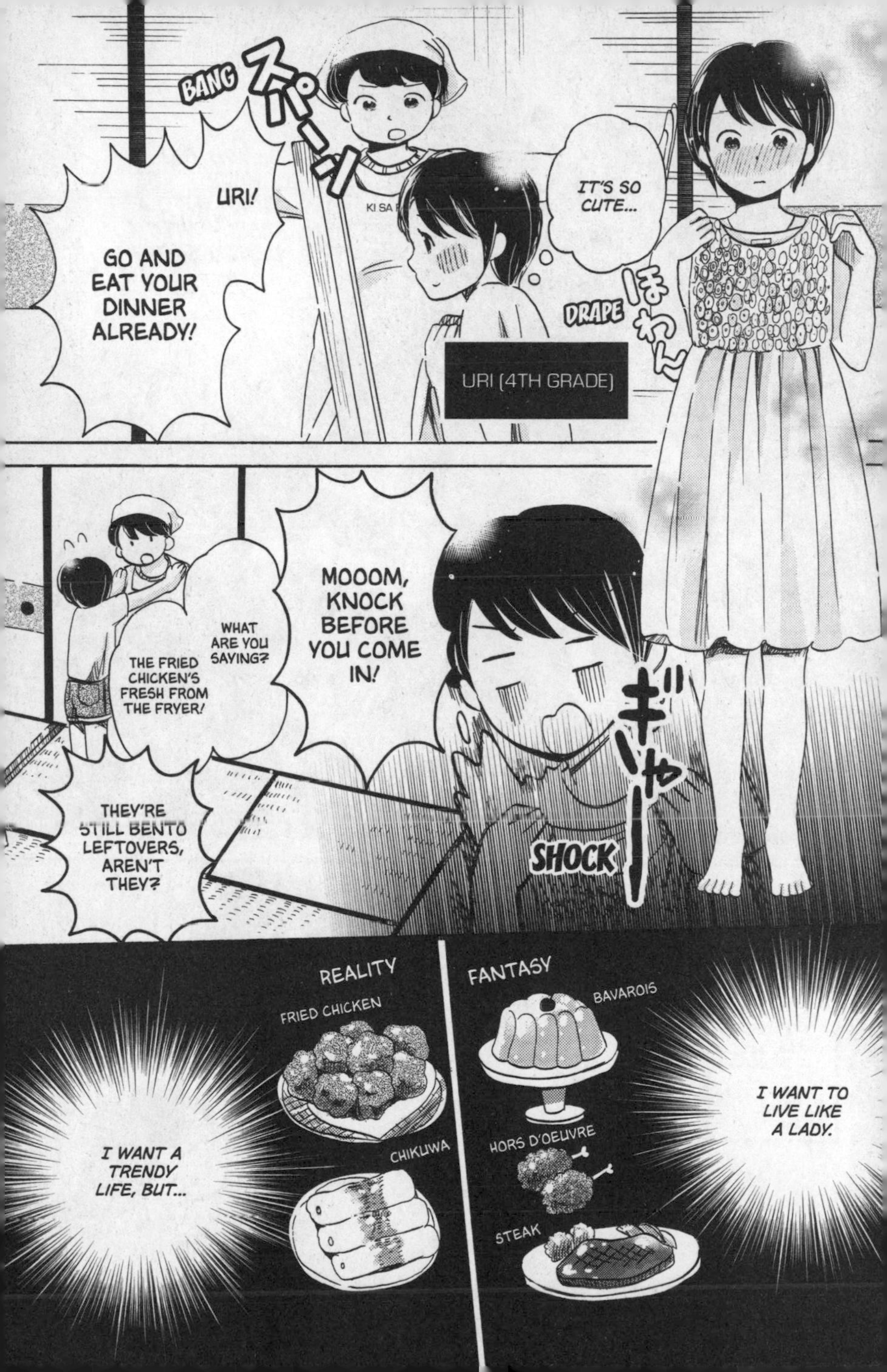
IT'S SO CUTE...
DRAPE
ほわん
URI (4TH GRADE)
BANG
スパーン
URI!
GO AND EAT YOUR DINNER ALREADY!
MOOOM, KNOCK BEFORE YOU COME IN!
SHOCK
ぎゃー
WHAT ARE YOU SAYING?
THE FRIED CHICKEN'S FRESH FROM THE FRYER!
THEY'RE STILL BENTO LEFTOVERS, AREN'T THEY?
I WANT TO LIVE LIKE A LADY.
FANTASY
BAVAROIS
HORS D'OEUVRE
STEAK
REALITY
FRIED CHICKEN
CHIKUWA
I WANT A TRENDY LIFE, BUT...

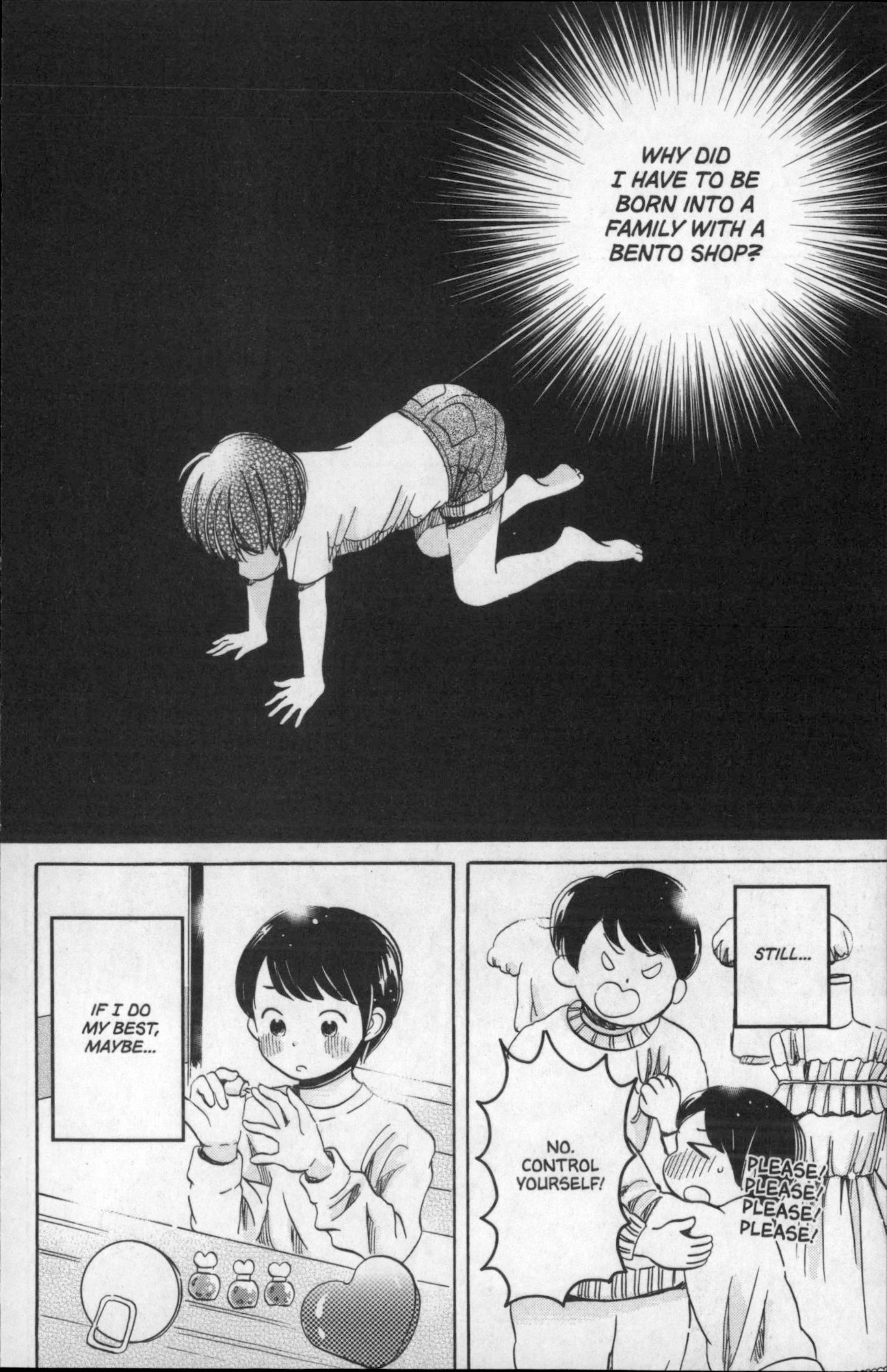
WHY DID I HAVE TO BE BORN INTO A FAMILY WITH A BENTO SHOP?
STILL...
PLEASE! PLEASE! PLEASE! PLEASE!
NO. CONTROL YOURSELF!
IF I DO MY BEST, MAYBE...

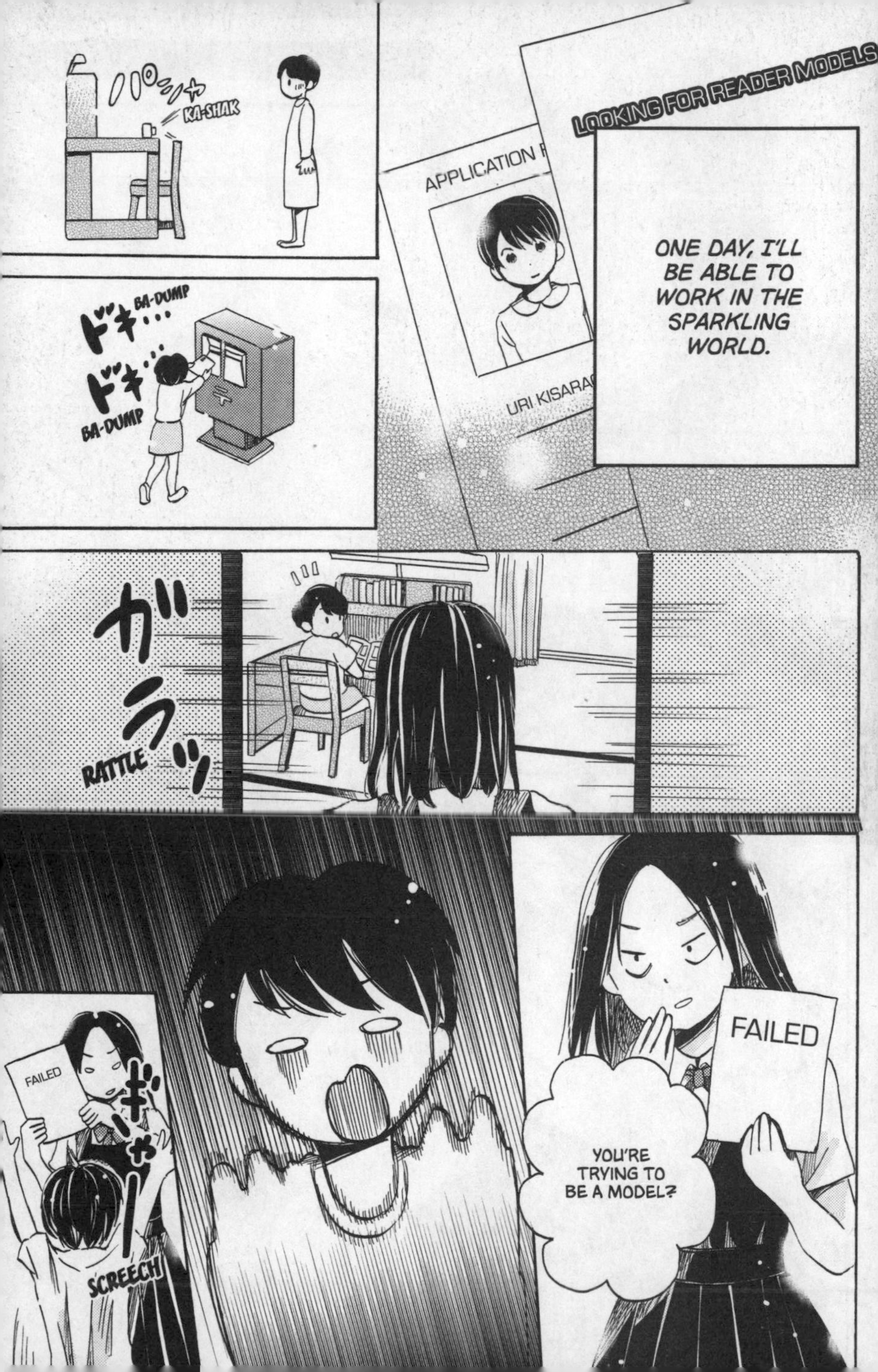
LOOKING FOR READER MODELS
APPLICATION F
URI KISARAG
ONE DAY, I'LL BE ABLE TO WORK IN THE SPARKLING WORLD.
KA-SHAK
BA-DUMP
BA-DUMP
RATTLE
FAILED
YOU'RE TRYING TO BE A MODEL?
FAILED
SCREECH

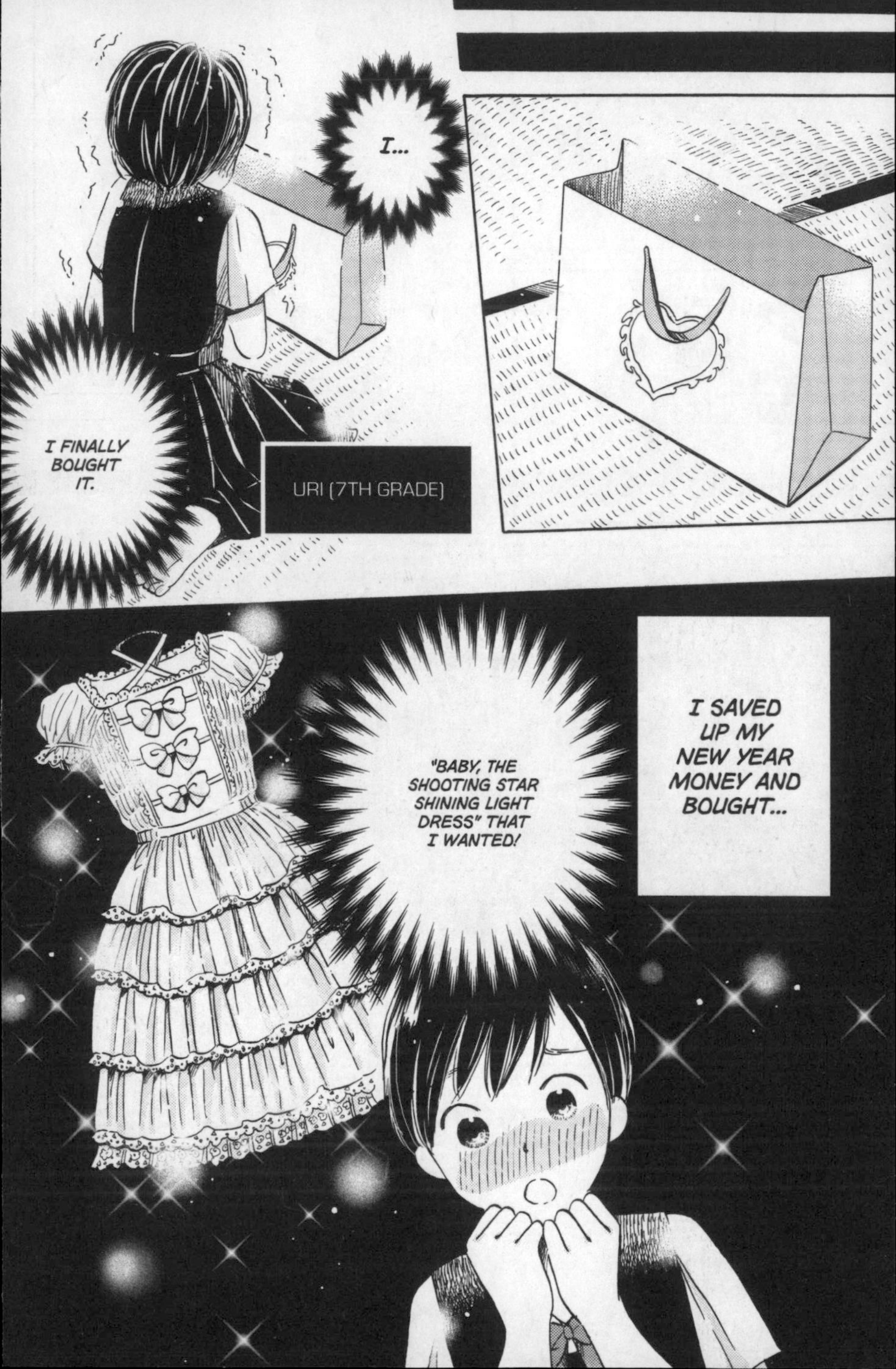
I...
URI (7TH GRADE)
I FINALLY BOUGHT IT.
I SAVED UP MY NEW YEAR MONEY AND BOUGHT...
"BABY, THE SHOOTING STAR SHINING LIGHT DRESS" THAT I WANTED!

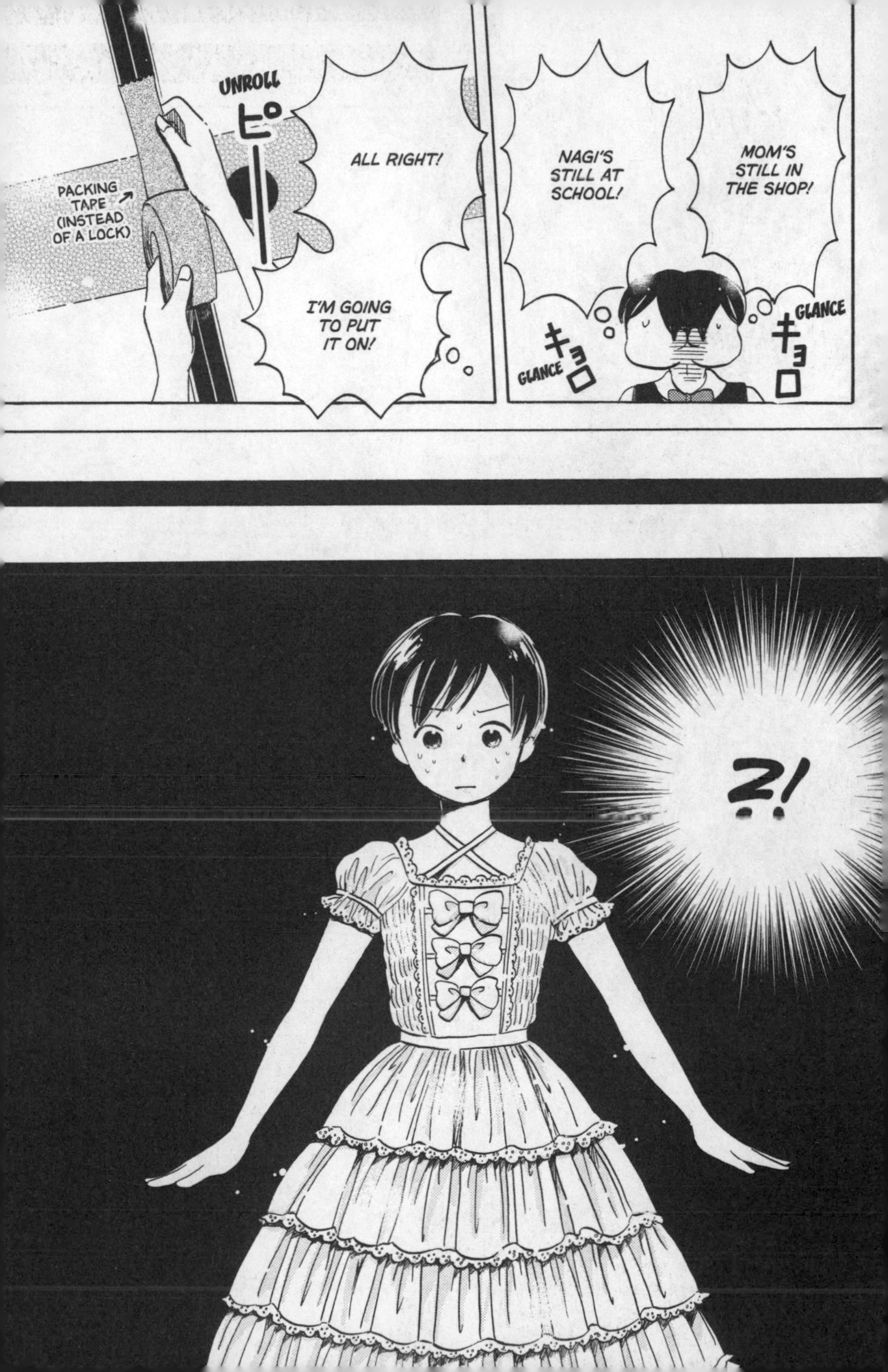
MOM'S STILL IN THE SHOP!
キョロ GLANCE
NAGI'S STILL AT SCHOOL!
キョロ GLANCE
ALL RIGHT!
I'M GOING TO PUT IT ON!
ピー UNROLL
PACKING TAPE (INSTEAD OF A LOCK)
?!

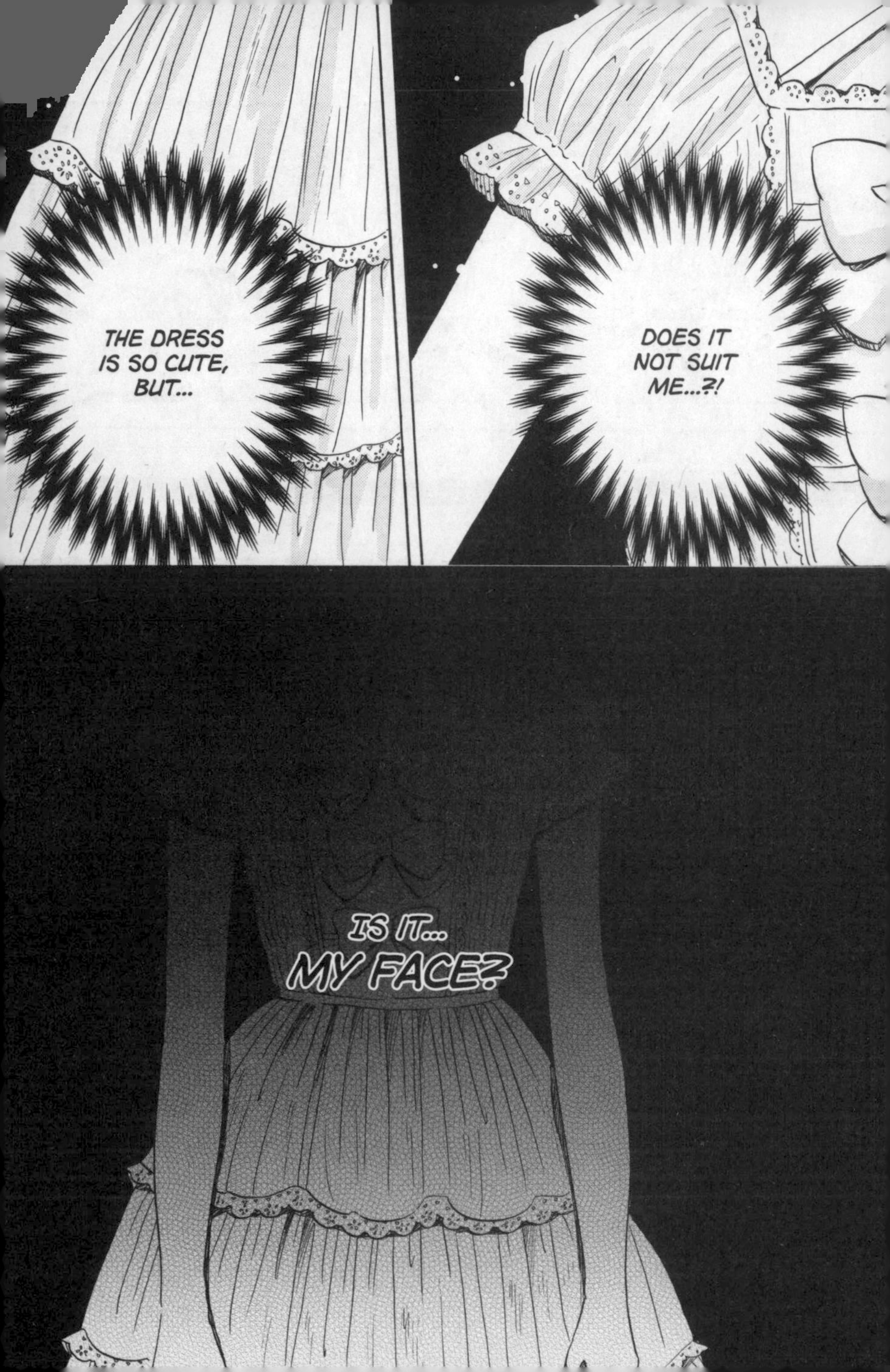
DOES IT NOT SUIT ME...?!
THE DRESS IS SO CUTE, BUT...
IS IT... MY FACE?

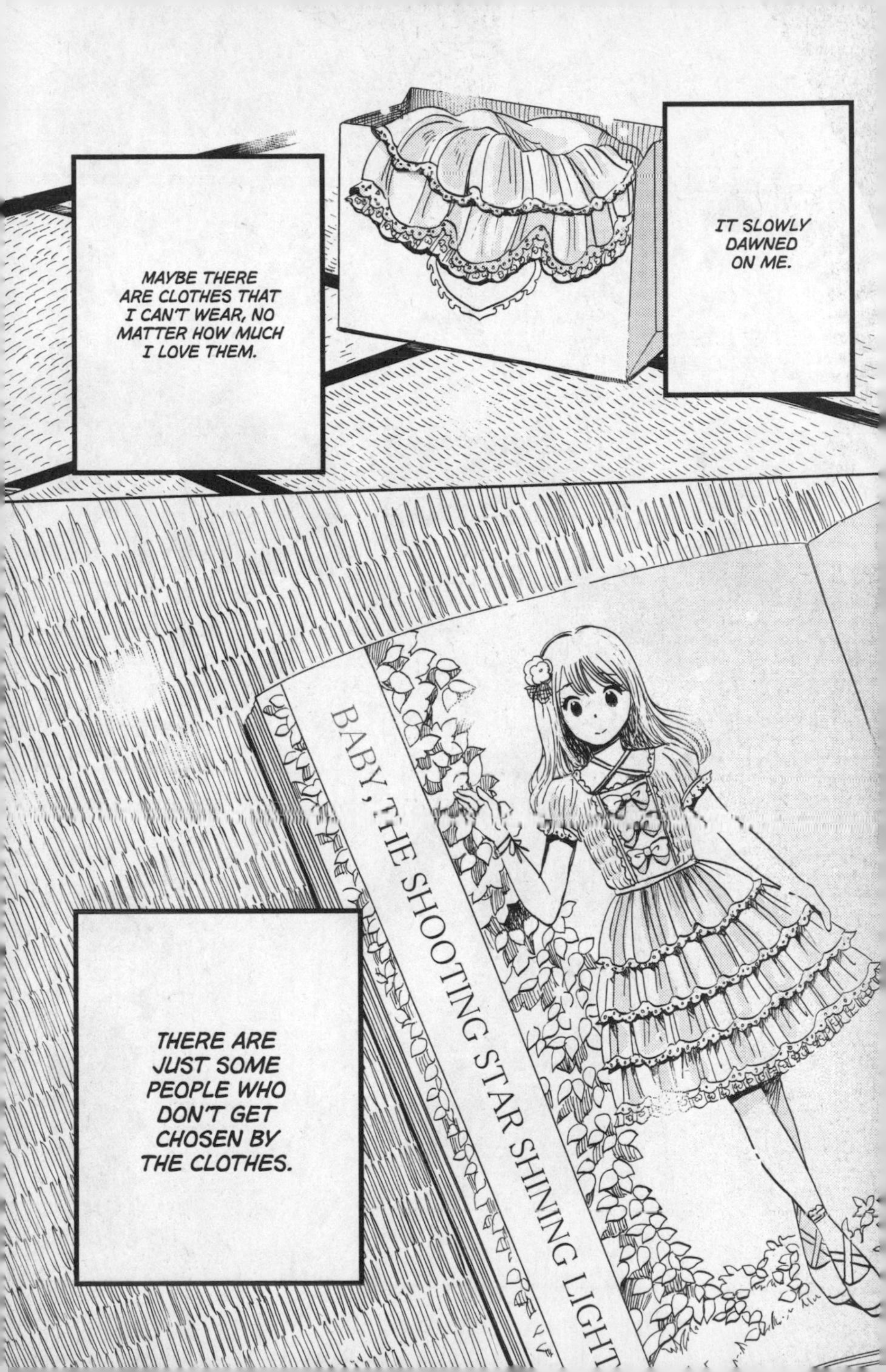
IT SLOWLY DAWNED ON ME.
MAYBE THERE ARE CLOTHES THAT I CAN'T WEAR, NO MATTER HOW MUCH I LOVE THEM.
BABY, THE SHOOTING STAR SHINING LIGHT
THERE ARE JUST SOME PEOPLE WHO DON'T GET CHOSEN BY THE CLOTHES.

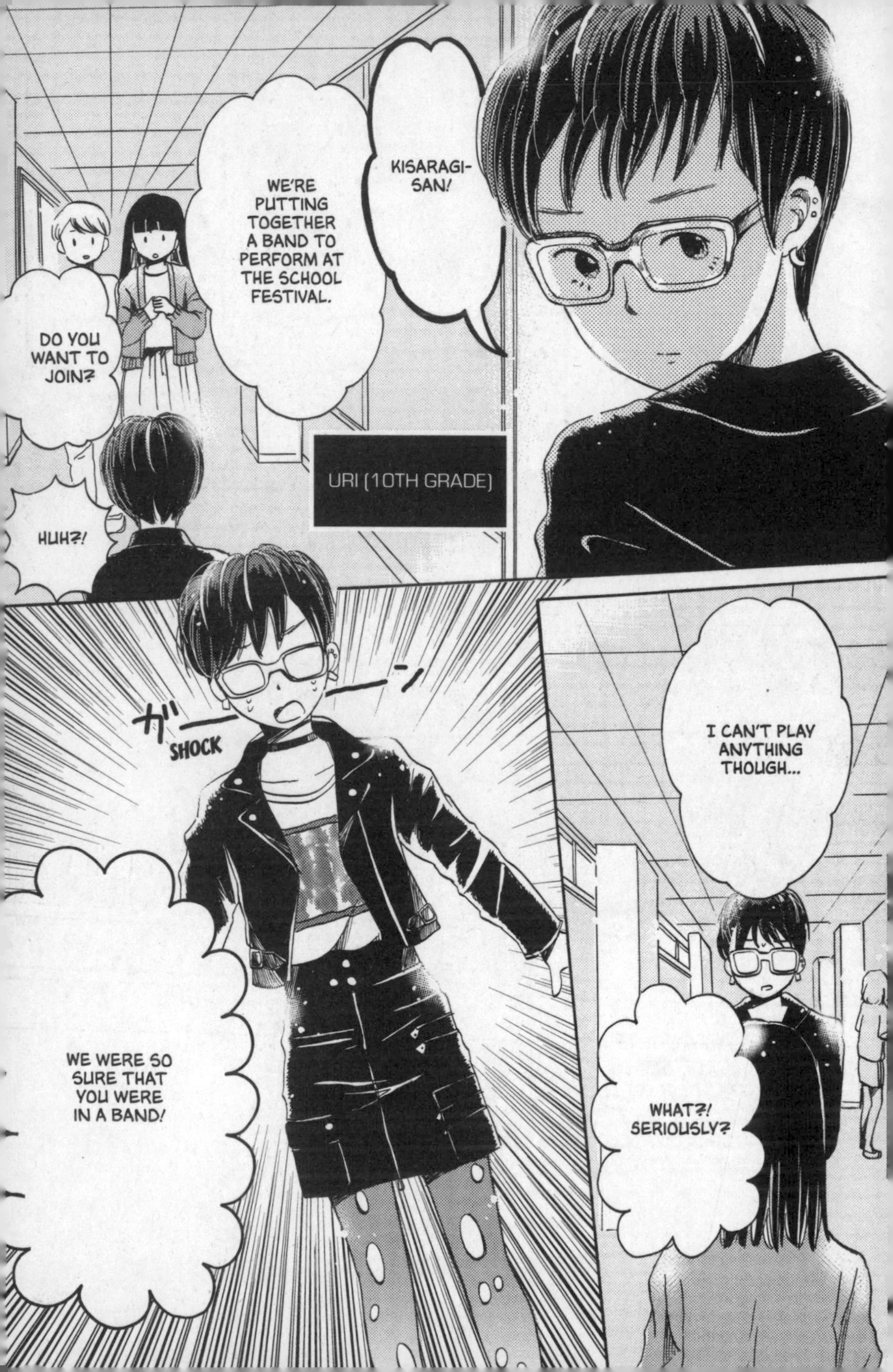
KISARAGI-SAN!
URI (10TH GRADE)
WE'RE PUTTING TOGETHER A BAND TO PERFORM AT THE SCHOOL FESTIVAL.
DO YOU WANT TO JOIN?
HUH?!
I CAN'T PLAY ANYTHING THOUGH...
WHAT?! SERIOUSLY?
ガー
SHOCK
WE WERE SO SURE THAT YOU WERE IN A BAND!

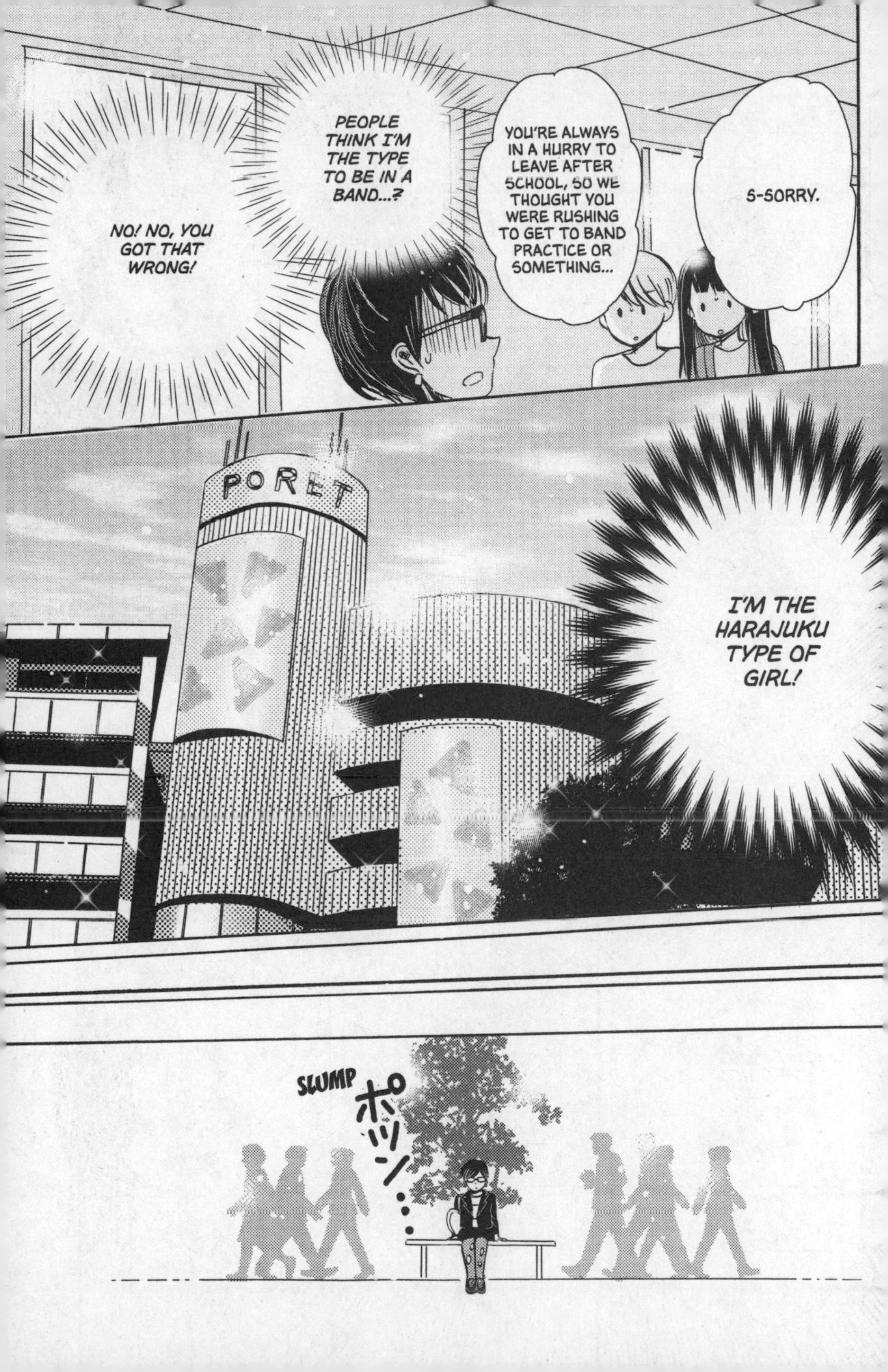
S-SORRY.
YOU'RE ALWAYS IN A HURRY TO LEAVE AFTER SCHOOL, SO WE THOUGHT YOU WERE RUSHING TO GET TO BAND PRACTICE OR SOMETHING...
PEOPLE THINK I'M THE TYPE TO BE IN A BAND...?
NO! NO, YOU GOT THAT WRONG!
I'M THE HARAJUKU TYPE OF GIRL!
PORET
SLUMP
ポツーン…

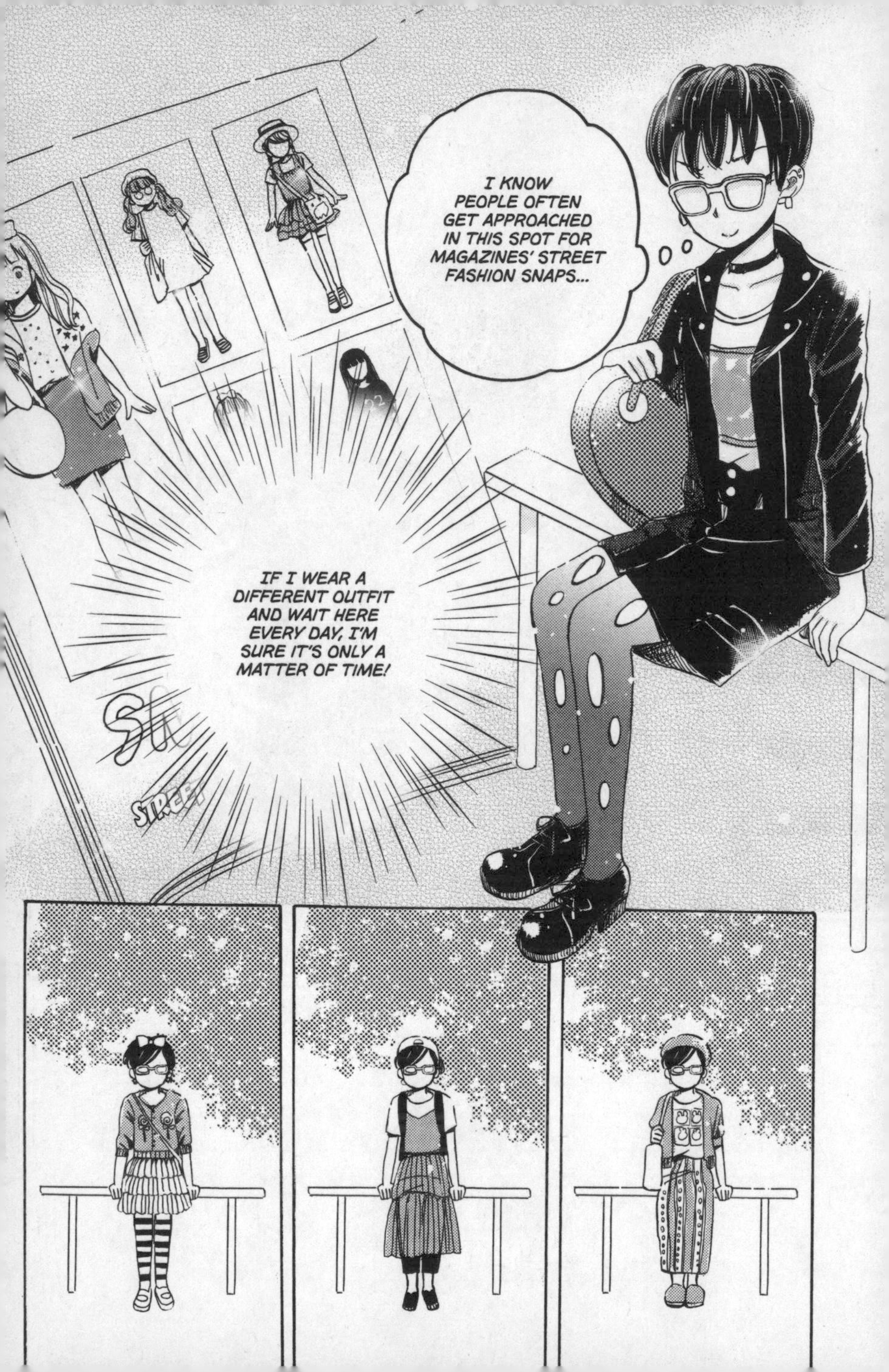
I KNOW PEOPLE OFTEN GET APPROACHED IN THIS SPOT FOR MAGAZINES' STREET FASHION SNAPS...
IF I WEAR A DIFFERENT OUTFIT AND WAIT HERE EVERY DAY, I'M SURE IT'S ONLY A MATTER OF TIME!

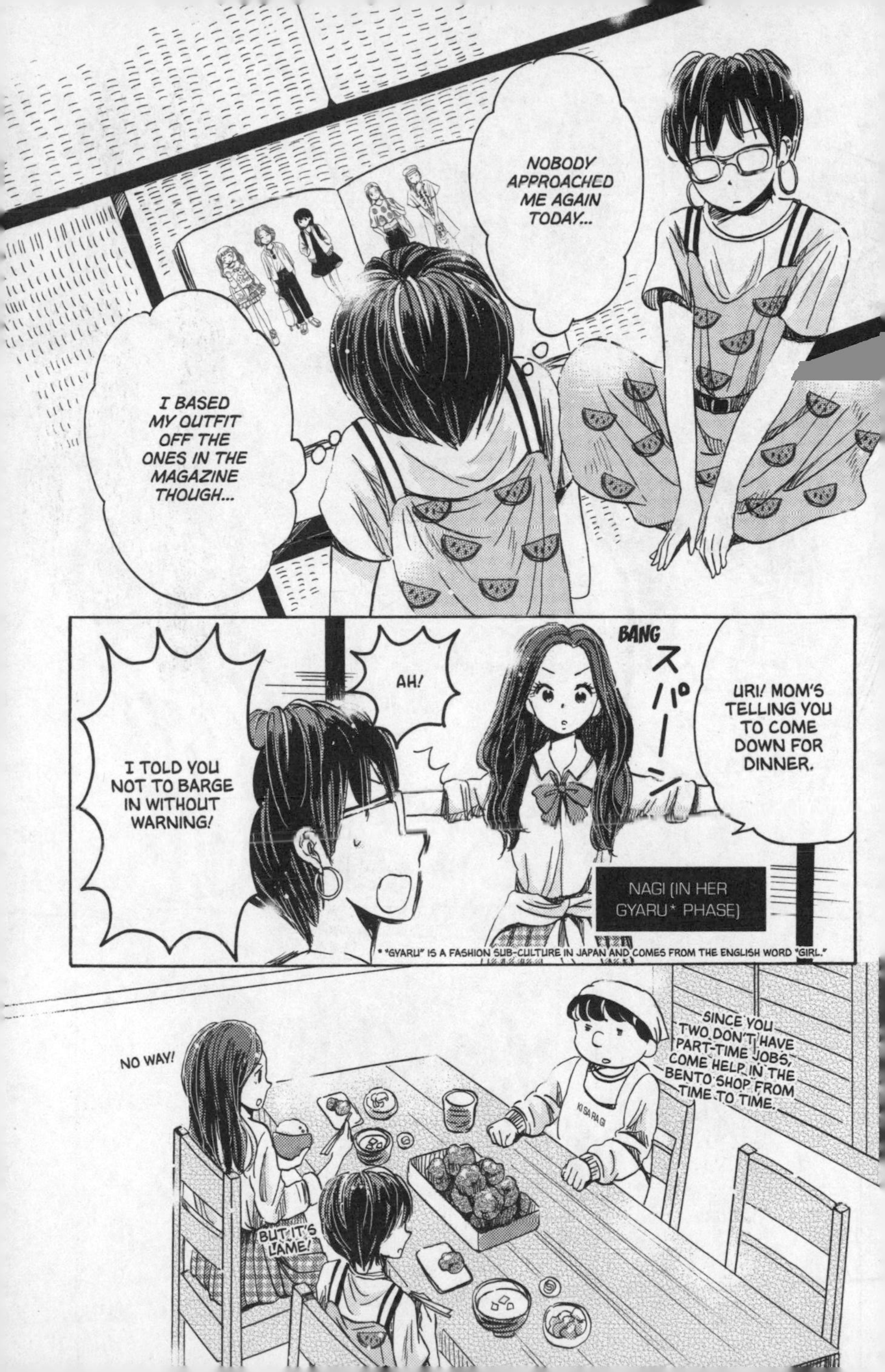
NOBODY APPROACHED ME AGAIN TODAY...
I BASED MY OUTFIT OFF THE ONES IN THE MAGAZINE THOUGH...
URI! MOM'S TELLING YOU TO COME DOWN FOR DINNER.
BANG
スパーン
NAGI (IN HER GYARU* PHASE)
AH!
I TOLD YOU NOT TO BARGE IN WITHOUT WARNING!
* "GYARU" IS A FASHION SUB-CULTURE IN JAPAN AND COMES FROM THE ENGLISH WORD "GIRL."
SINCE YOU TWO DON'T HAVE PART-TIME JOBS, COME HELP IN THE BENTO SHOP FROM TIME TO TIME.
KISARAGI
NO WAY!
BUT IT'S LAME!

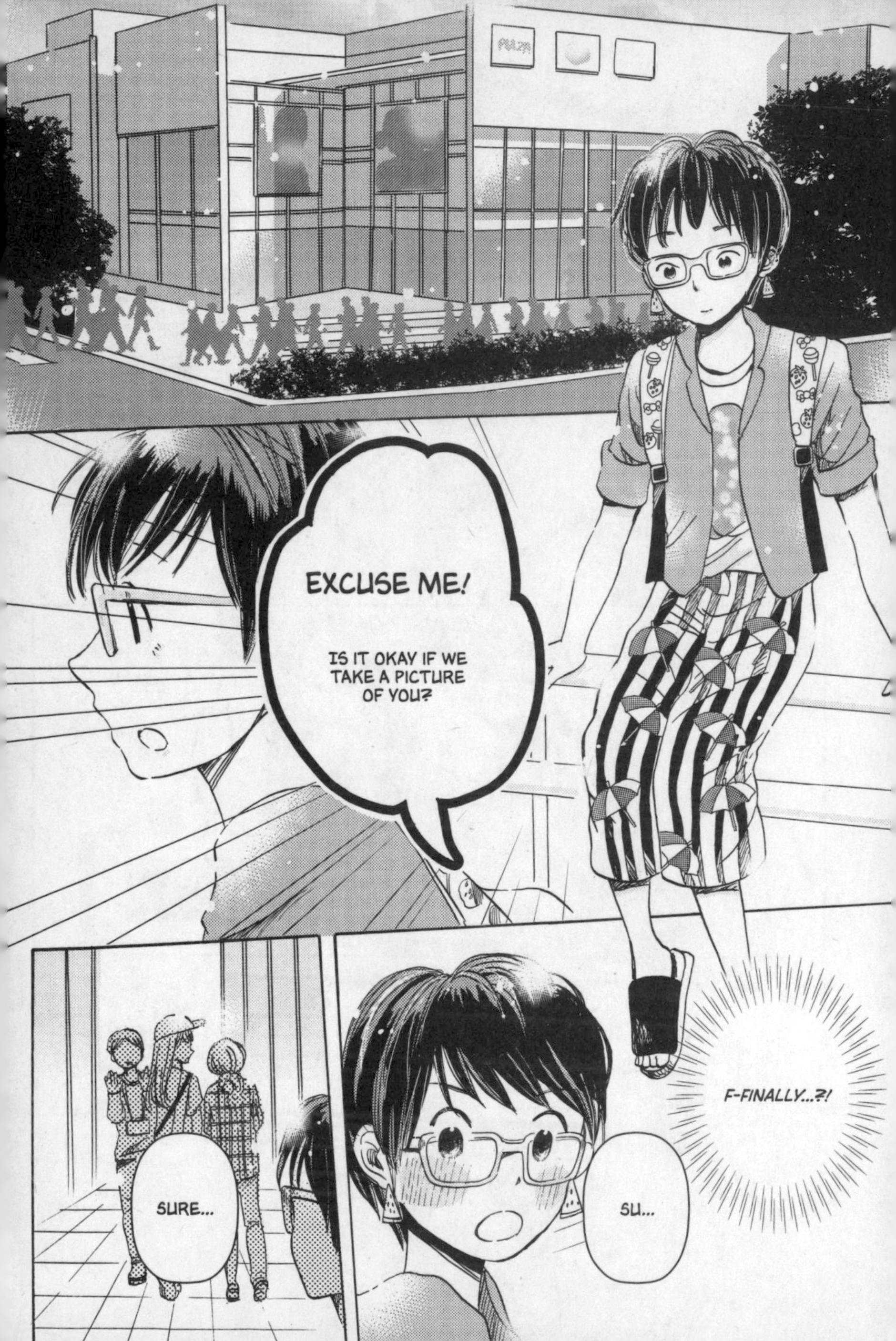
EXCUSE ME!
IS IT OKAY IF WE TAKE A PICTURE OF YOU?
F-FINALLY...?!
SU...
SURE...

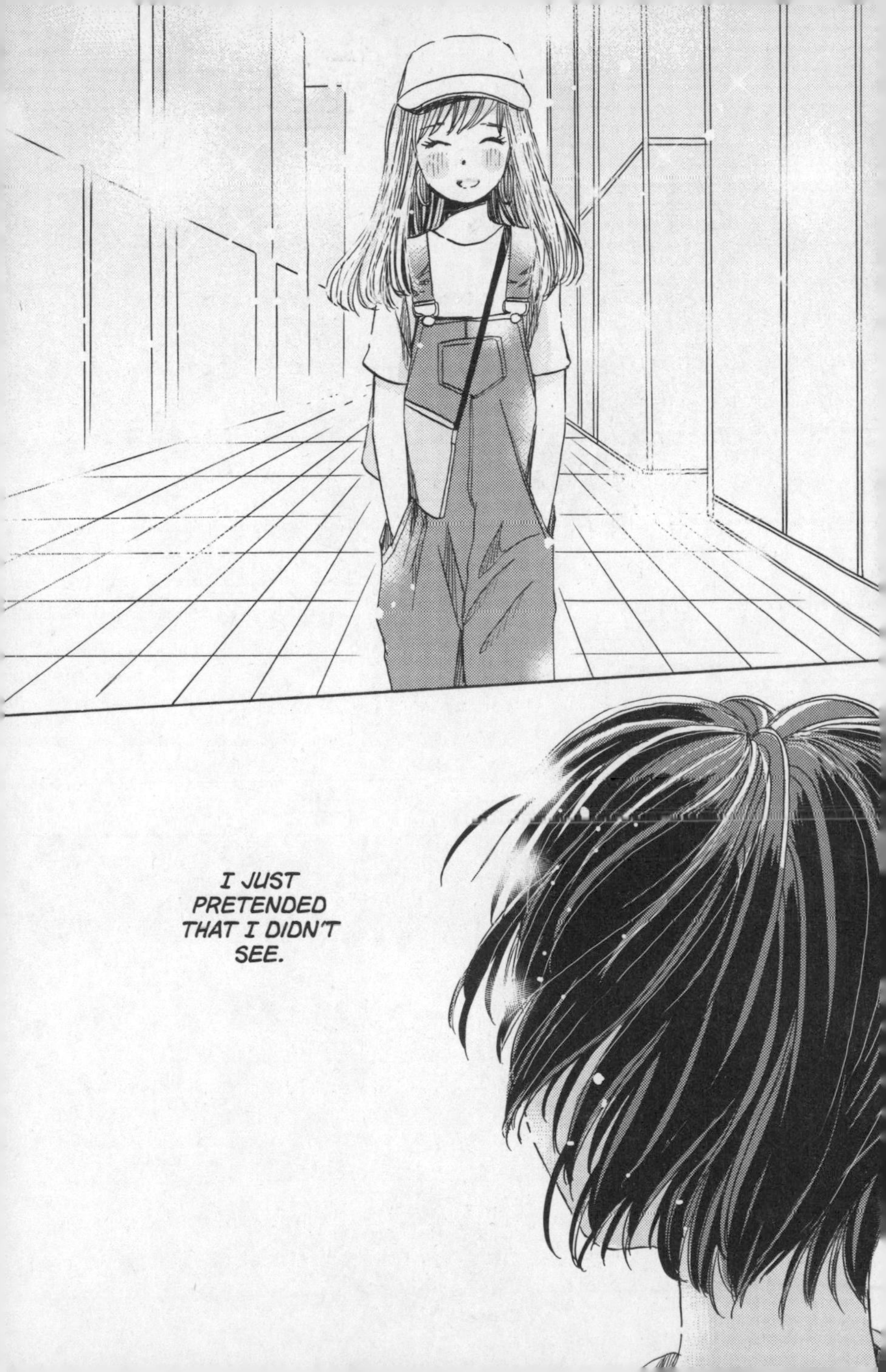
I JUST PRETENDED THAT I DIDN'T SEE.

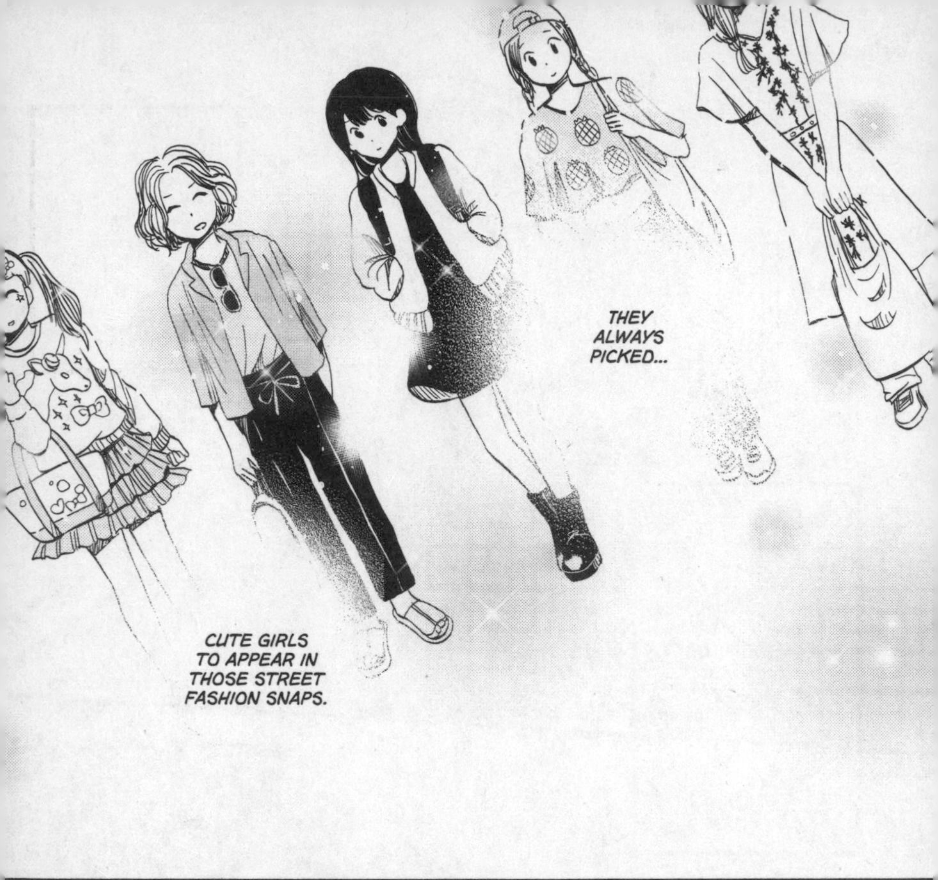
THEY ALWAYS PICKED...
CUTE GIRLS TO APPEAR IN THOSE STREET FASHION SNAPS.
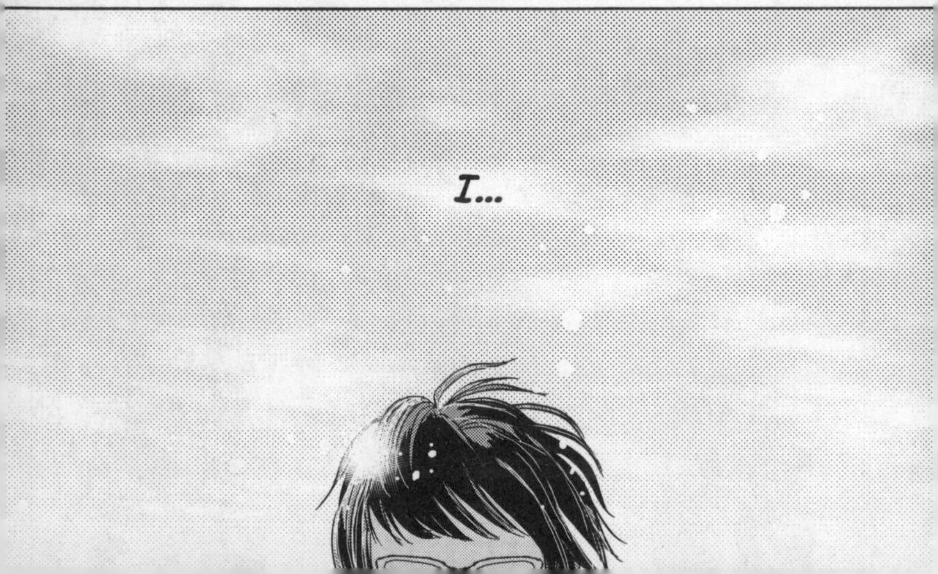
I...

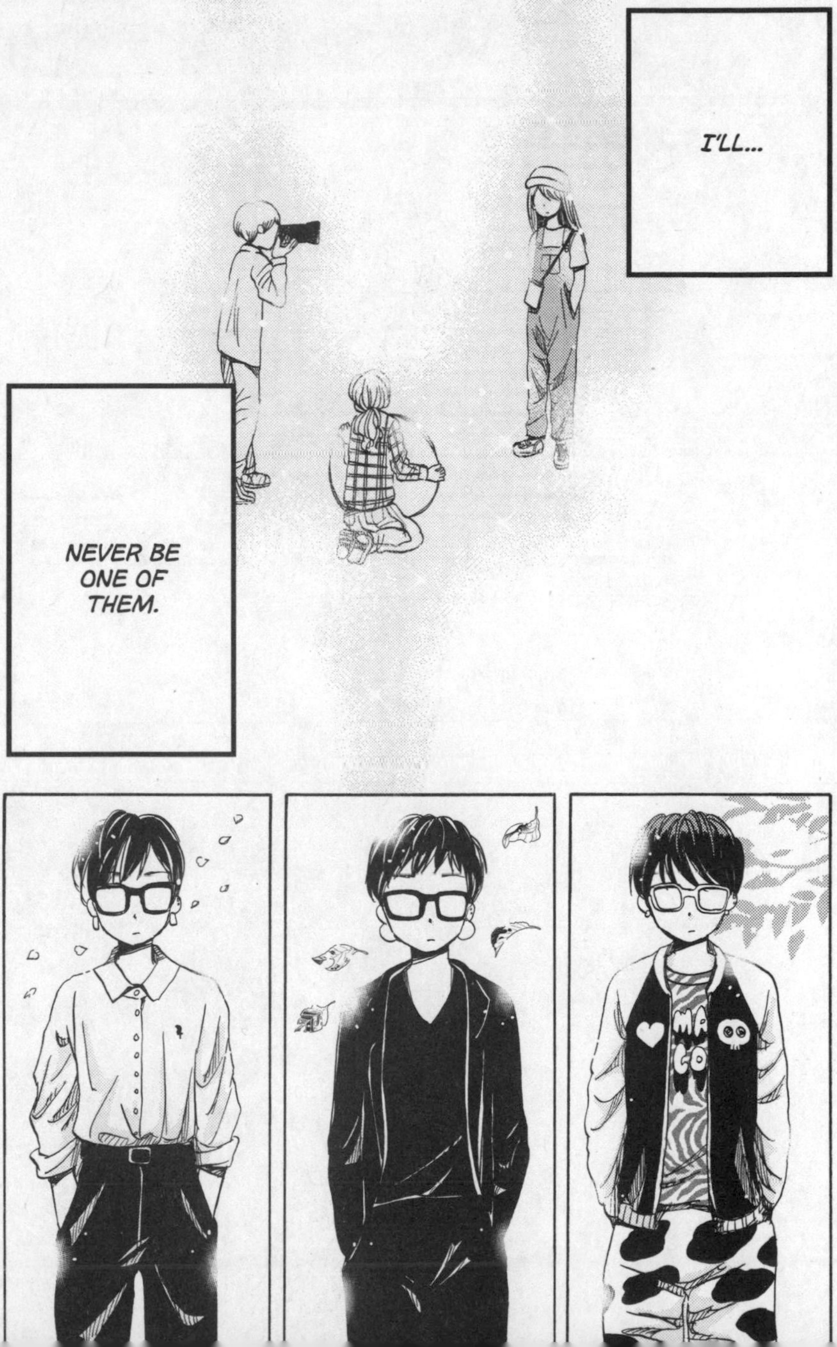
I'LL...
NEVER BE ONE OF THEM.

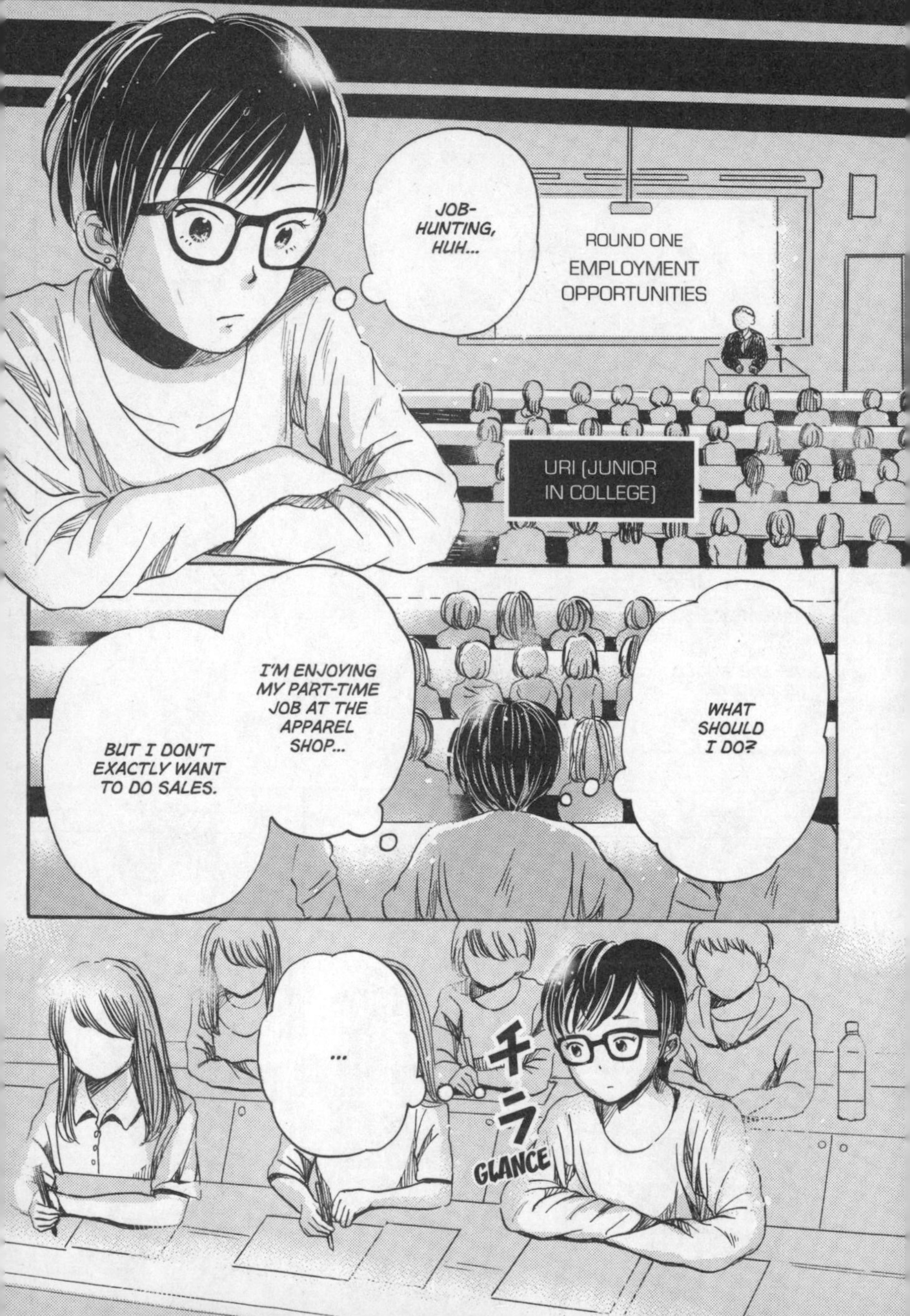
ROUND ONE
EMPLOYMENT OPPORTUNITIES
JOB-HUNTING, HUH...
URI (JUNIOR IN COLLEGE)
WHAT SHOULD I DO?
I'M ENJOYING MY PART-TIME JOB AT THE APPAREL SHOP...
BUT I DON'T EXACTLY WANT TO DO SALES.
チラ
GLANCE
...

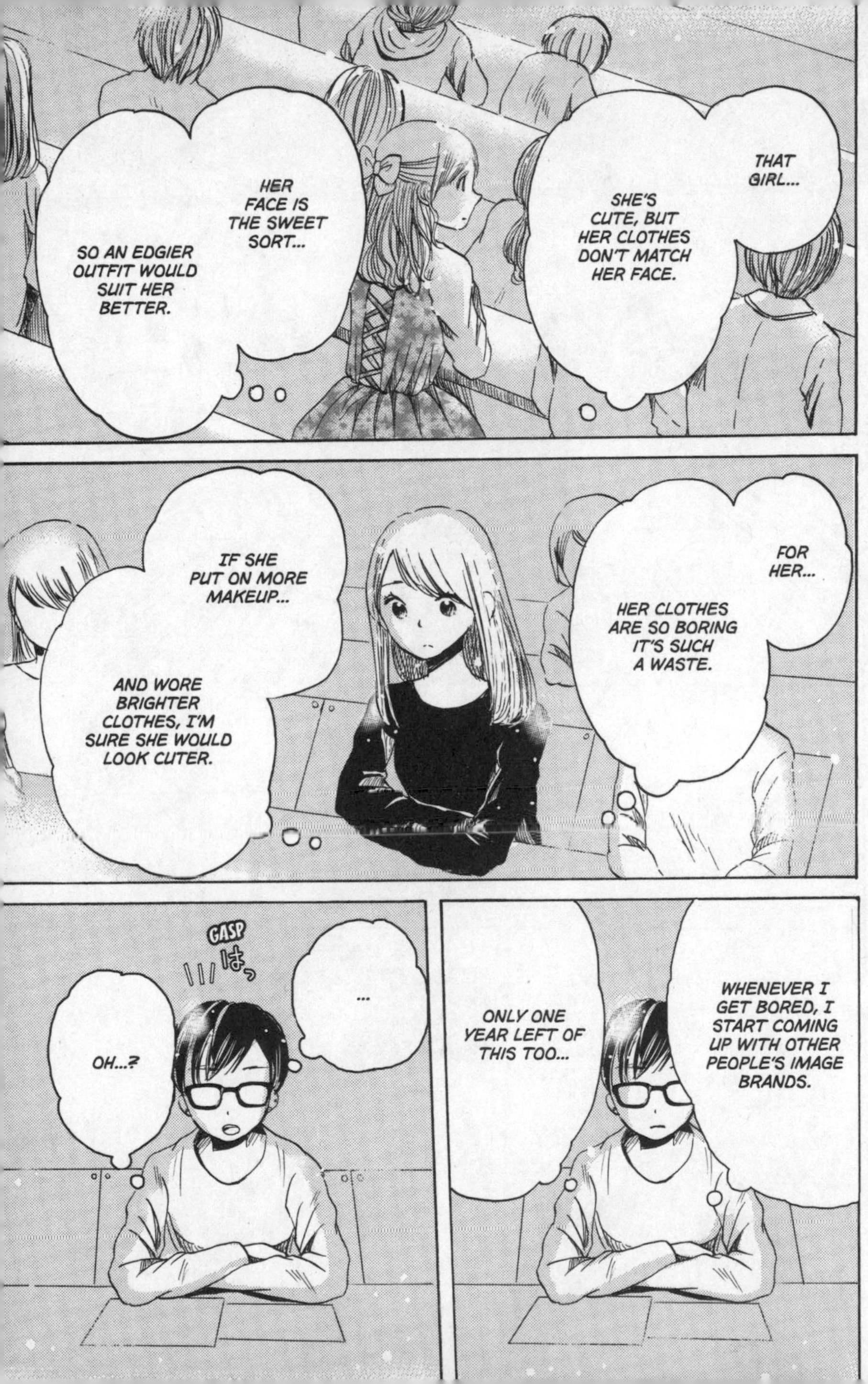
THAT GIRL...
SHE'S CUTE, BUT HER CLOTHES DON'T MATCH HER FACE.
HER FACE IS THE SWEET SORT...
SO AN EDGIER OUTFIT WOULD SUIT HER BETTER.
FOR HER...
HER CLOTHES ARE SO BORING IT'S SUCH A WASTE.
IF SHE PUT ON MORE MAKEUP...
AND WORE BRIGHTER CLOTHES, I'M SURE SHE WOULD LOOK CUTER.
WHENEVER I GET BORED, I START COMING UP WITH OTHER PEOPLE'S IMAGE BRANDS.
ONLY ONE YEAR LEFT OF THIS TOO...
...
GASP
はっ
OH...?

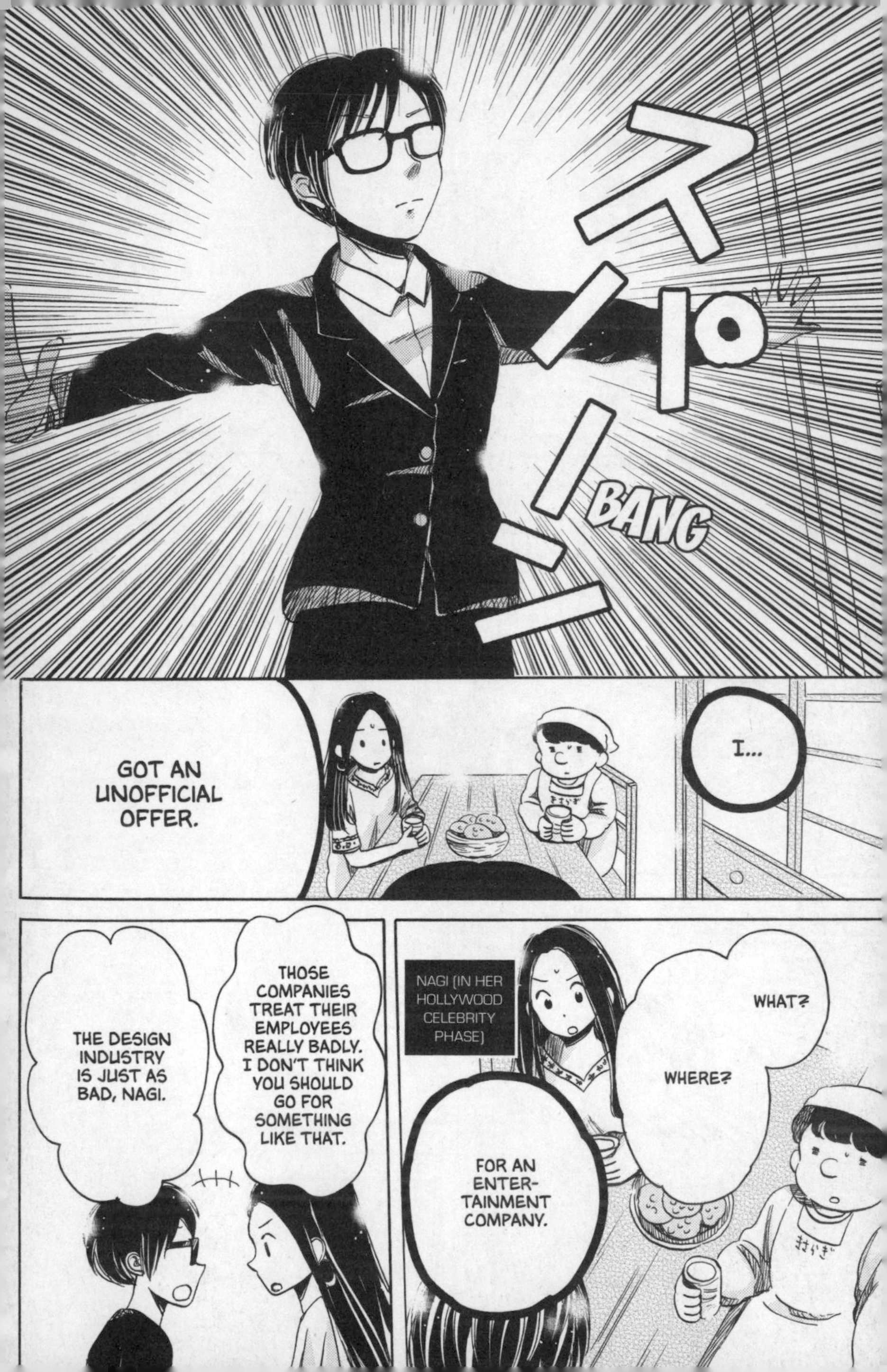
BANG
I...
GOT AN UNOFFICIAL OFFER.
WHAT?
WHERE?
NAGI (IN HER HOLLYWOOD CELEBRITY PHASE)
FOR AN ENTER-TAINMENT COMPANY.
THOSE COMPANIES TREAT THEIR EMPLOYEES REALLY BADLY. I DON'T THINK YOU SHOULD GO FOR SOMETHING LIKE THAT.
THE DESIGN INDUSTRY IS JUST AS BAD, NAGI.

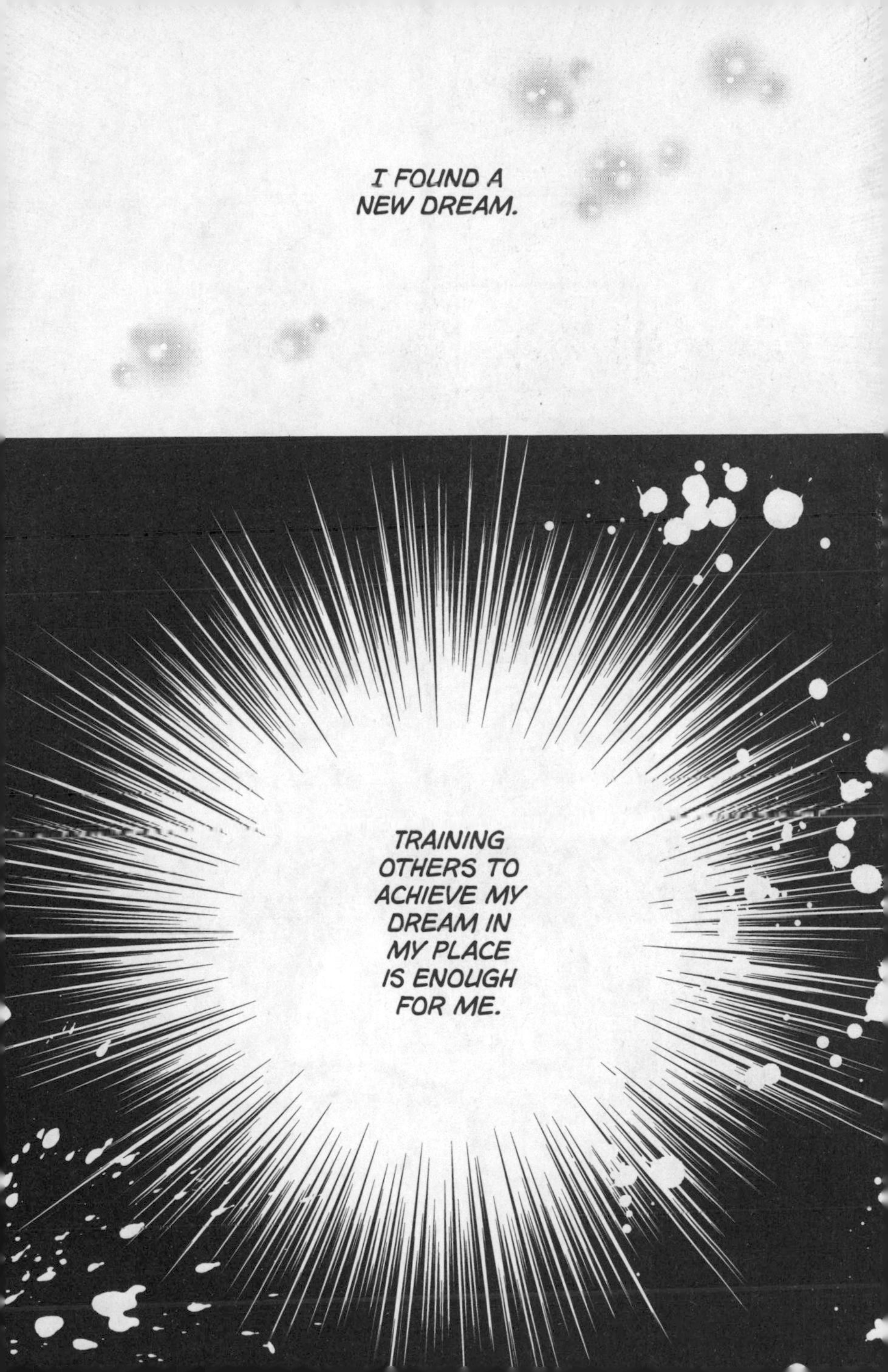
I FOUND A NEW DREAM.
TRAINING OTHERS TO ACHIEVE MY DREAM IN MY PLACE IS ENOUGH FOR ME.

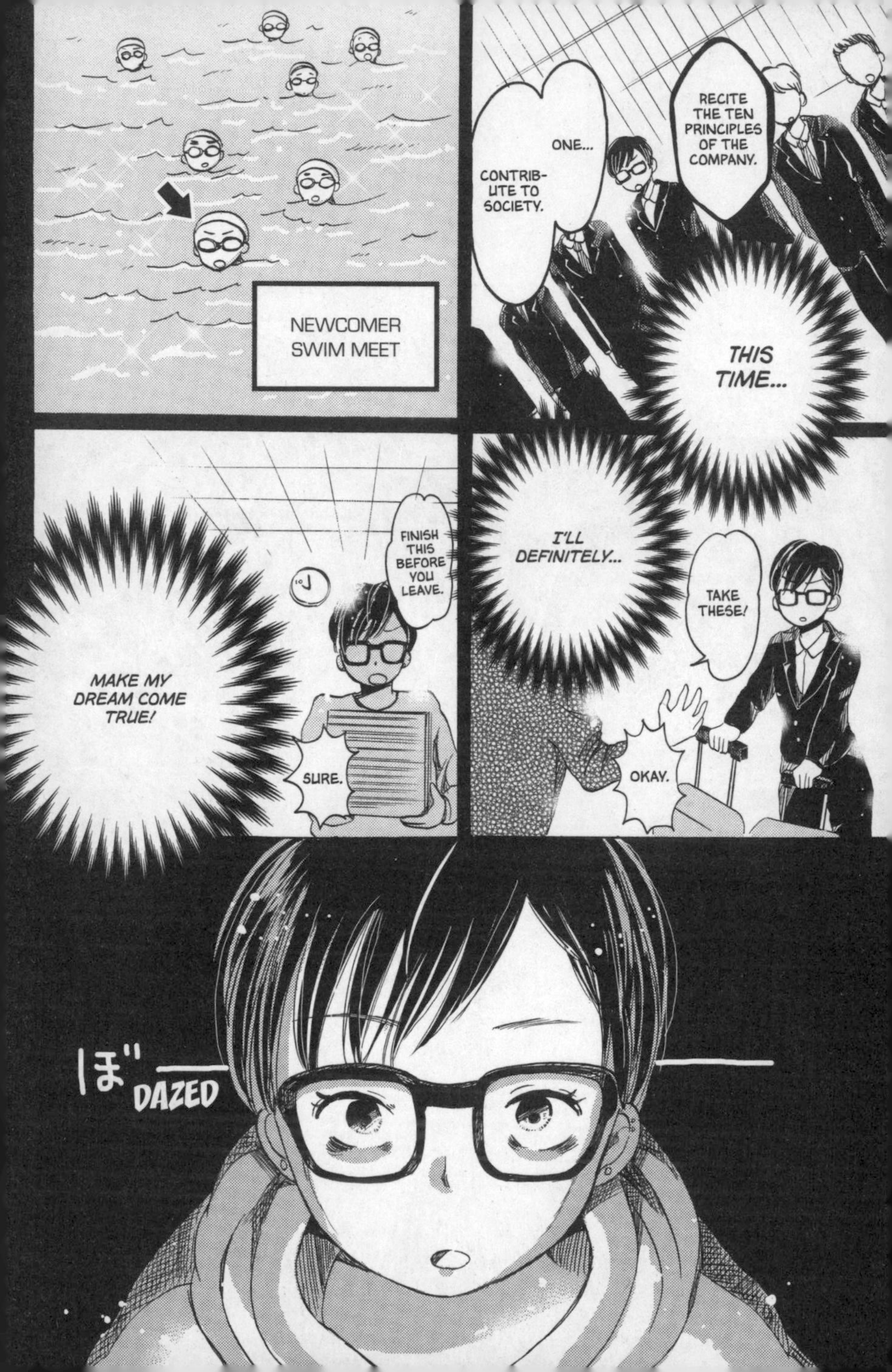
RECITE THE TEN PRINCIPLES OF THE COMPANY.
ONE...
CONTRIBUTE TO SOCIETY.
THIS TIME...
NEWCOMER SWIM MEET
TAKE THESE!
I'LL DEFINITELY...
OKAY.
FINISH THIS BEFORE YOU LEAVE.
SURE.
MAKE MY DREAM COME TRUE!
ぼ
DAZED

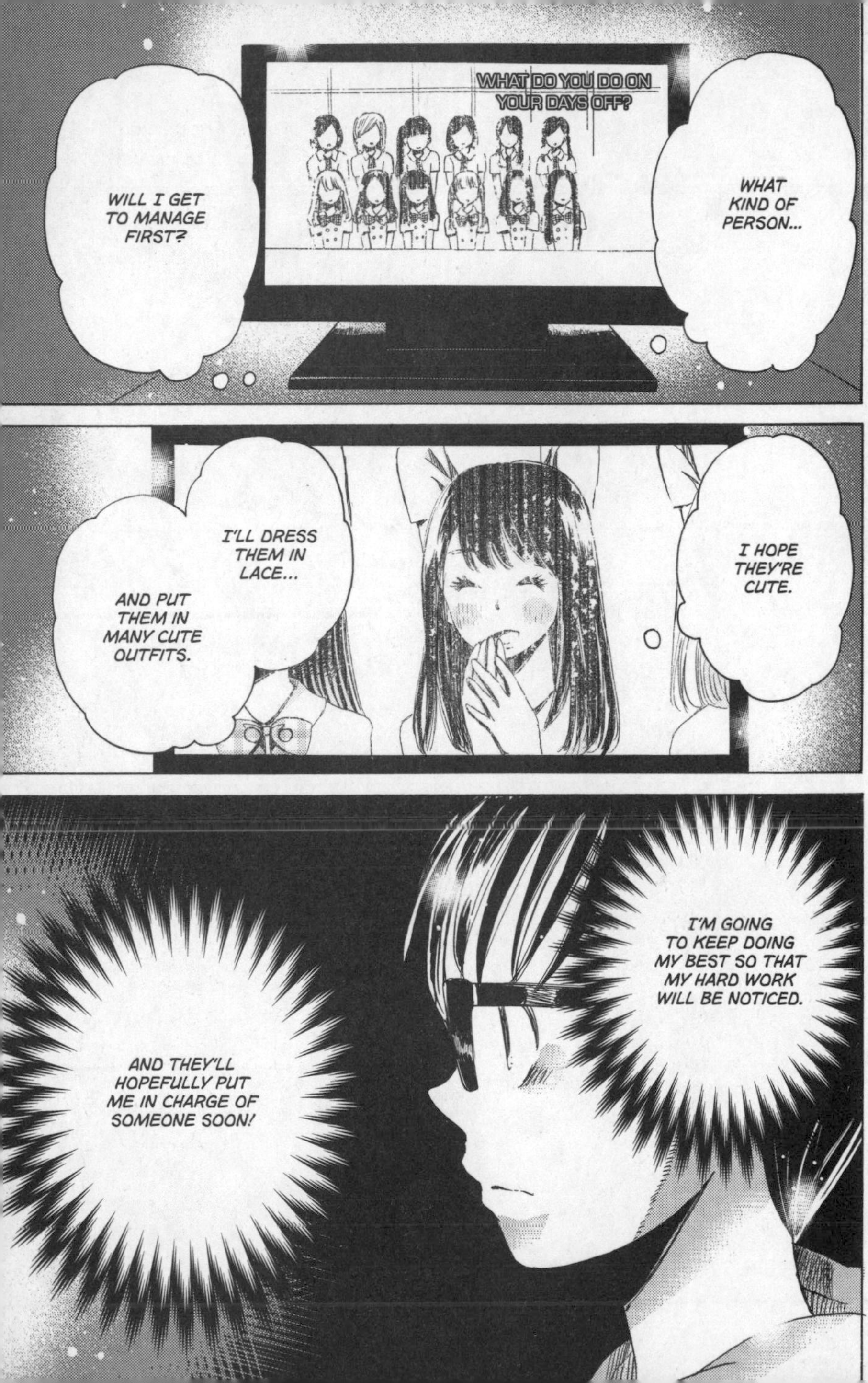
WHAT KIND OF PERSON...
WHAT DO YOU DO ON YOUR DAYS OFF?
WILL I GET TO MANAGE FIRST?
I HOPE THEY'RE CUTE.
I'LL DRESS THEM IN LACE...
AND PUT THEM IN MANY CUTE OUTFITS.
I'M GOING TO KEEP DOING MY BEST SO THAT MY HARD WORK WILL BE NOTICED.
AND THEY'LL HOPEFULLY PUT ME IN CHARGE OF SOMEONE SOON!

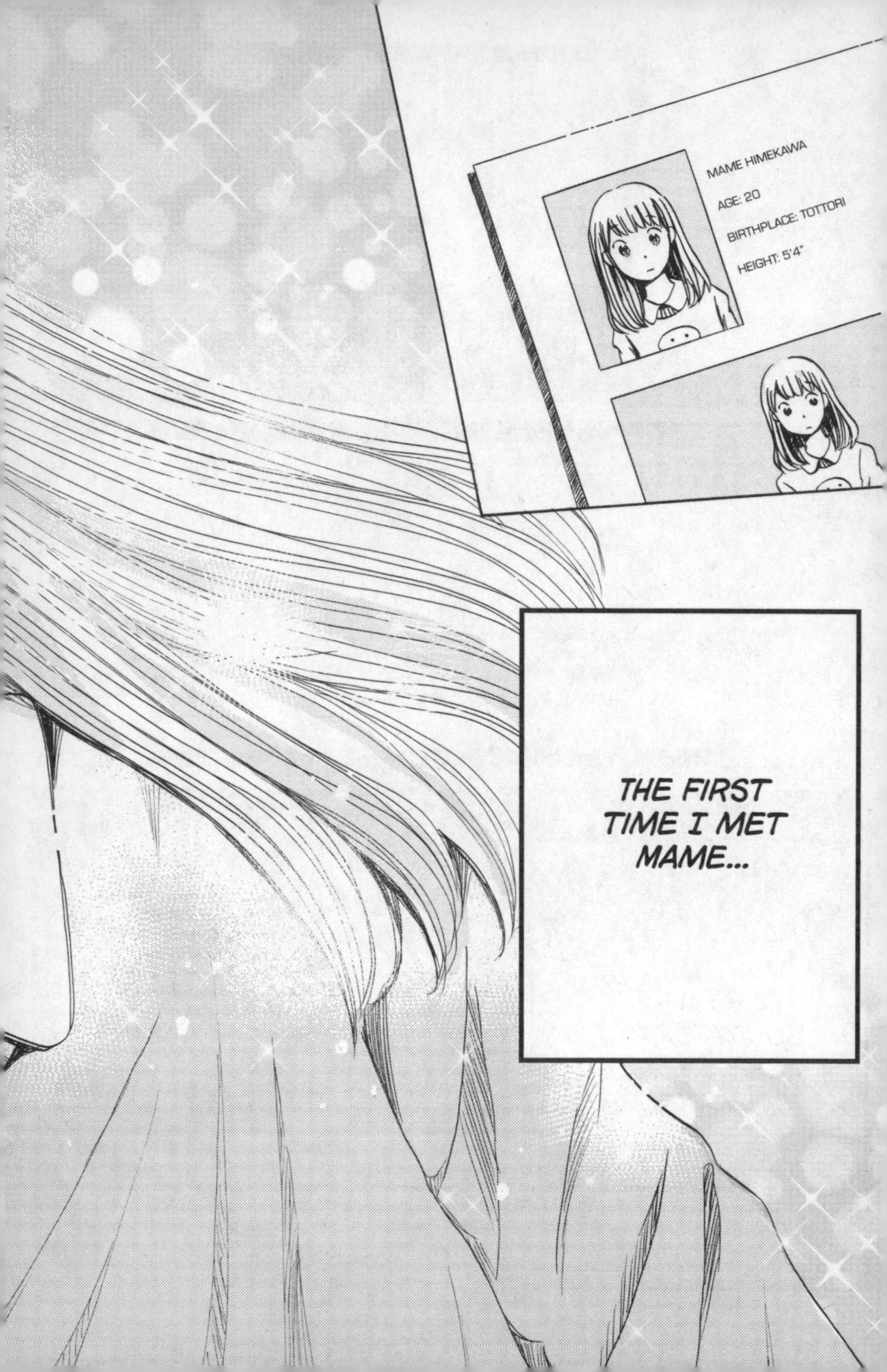
MAME HIMEKAWA
AGE: 20
BIRTHPLACE: TOTTORI
HEIGHT: 5'4"
THE FIRST TIME I MET MAME...

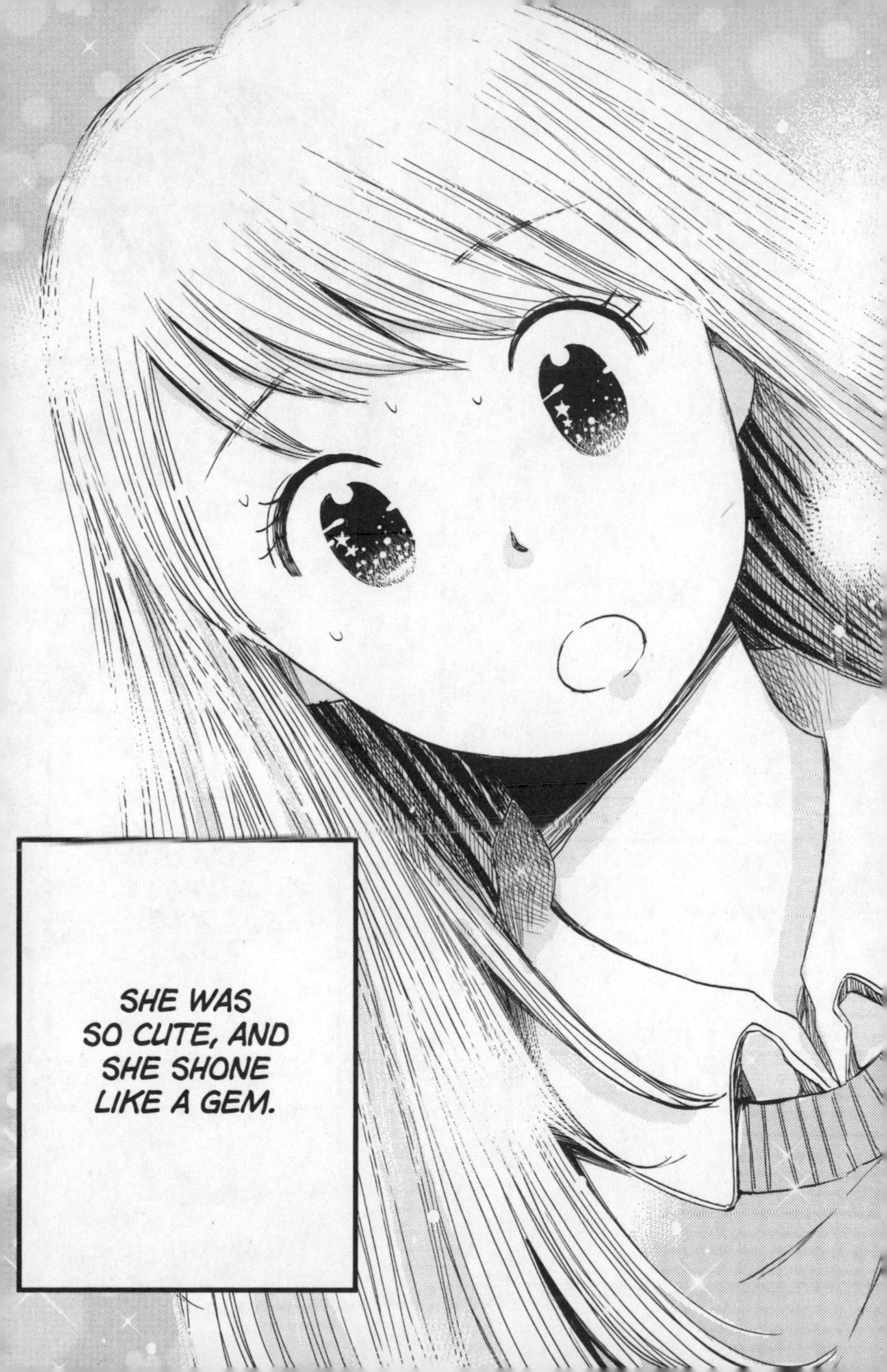
SHE WAS SO CUTE, AND SHE SHONE LIKE A GEM.

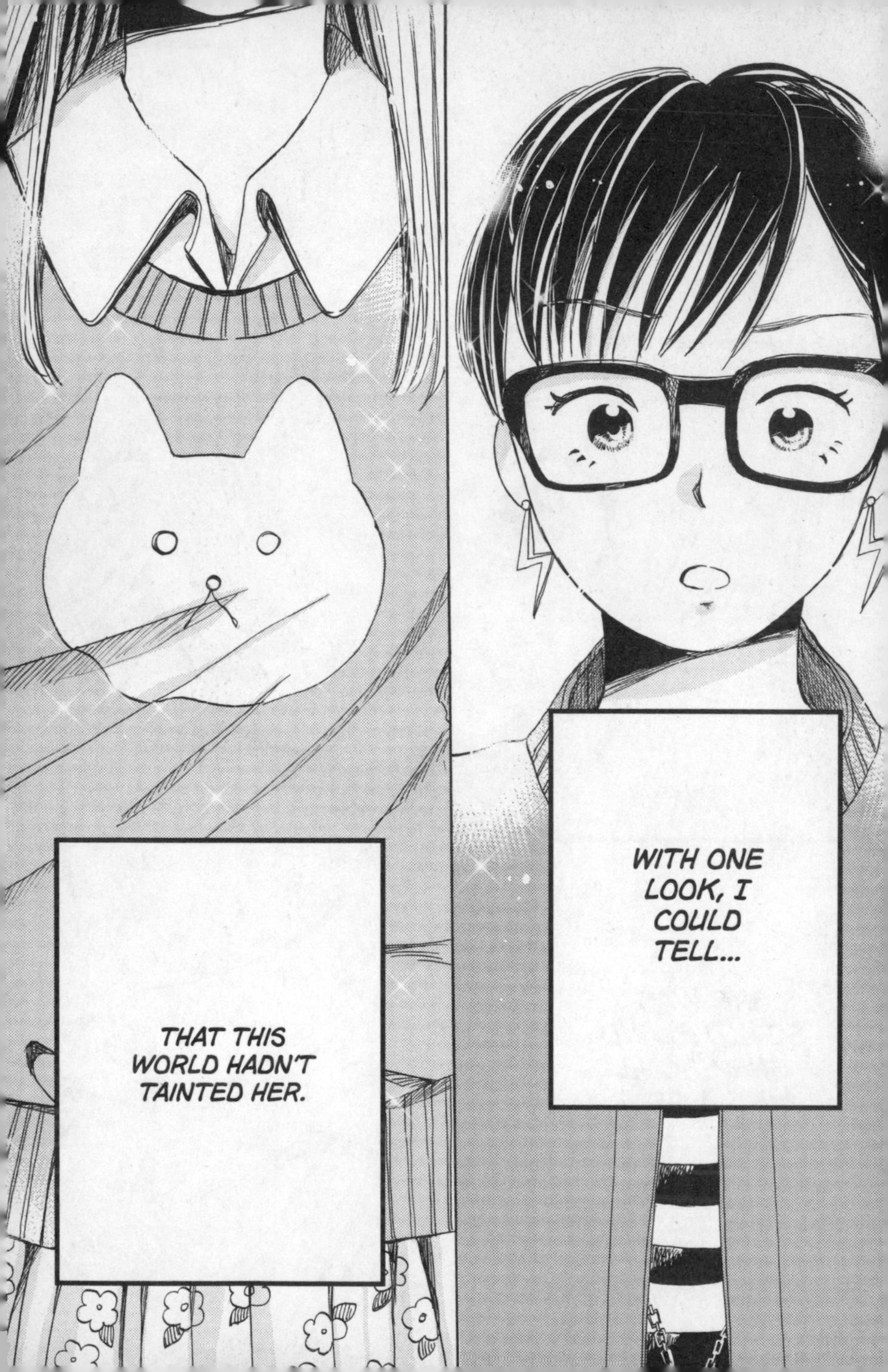
WITH ONE LOOK, I COULD TELL...
THAT THIS WORLD HADN'T TAINTED HER.

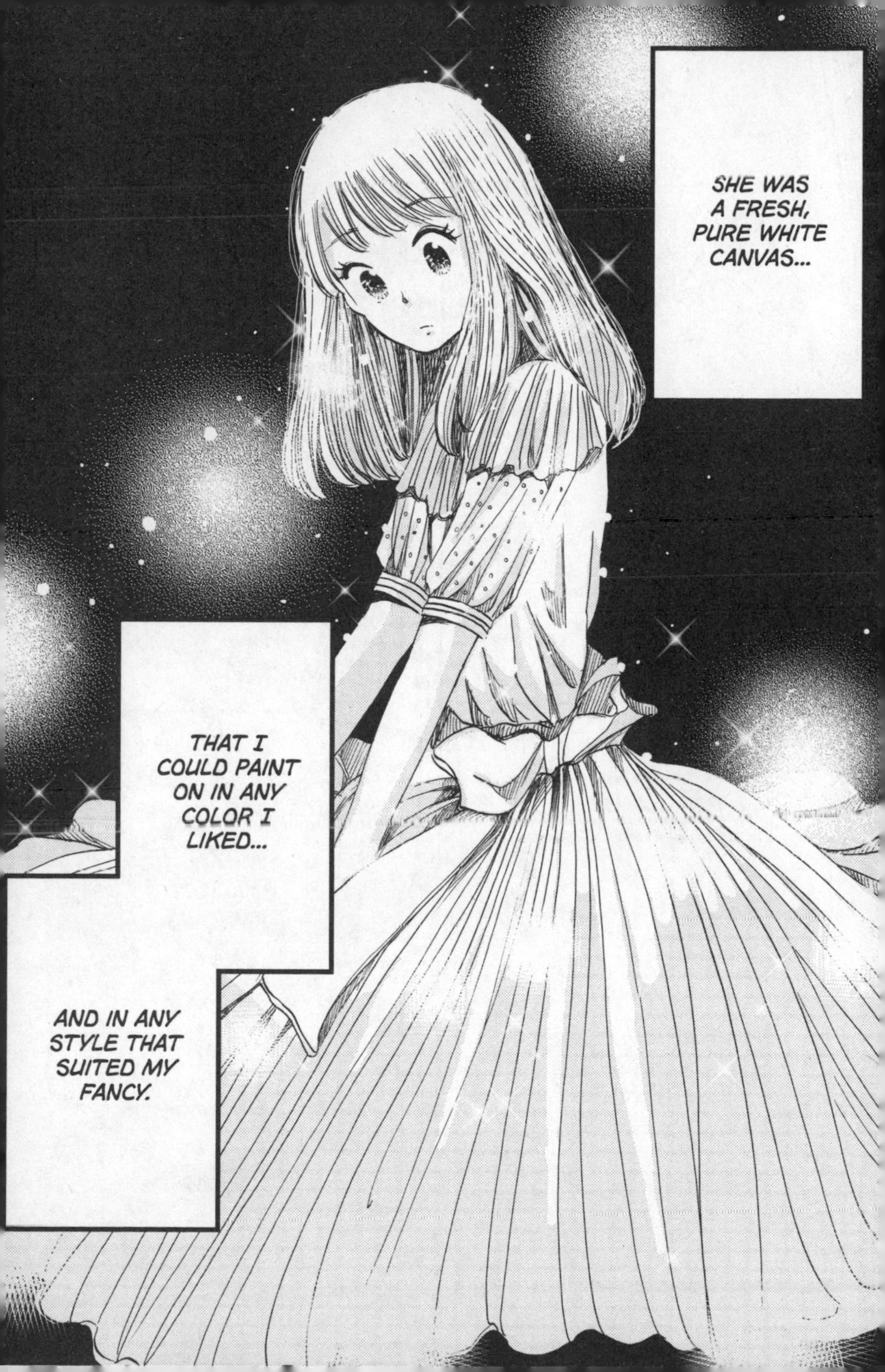
SHE WAS A FRESH, PURE WHITE CANVAS...
THAT I COULD PAINT ON IN ANY COLOR I LIKED...
AND IN ANY STYLE THAT SUITED MY FANCY.

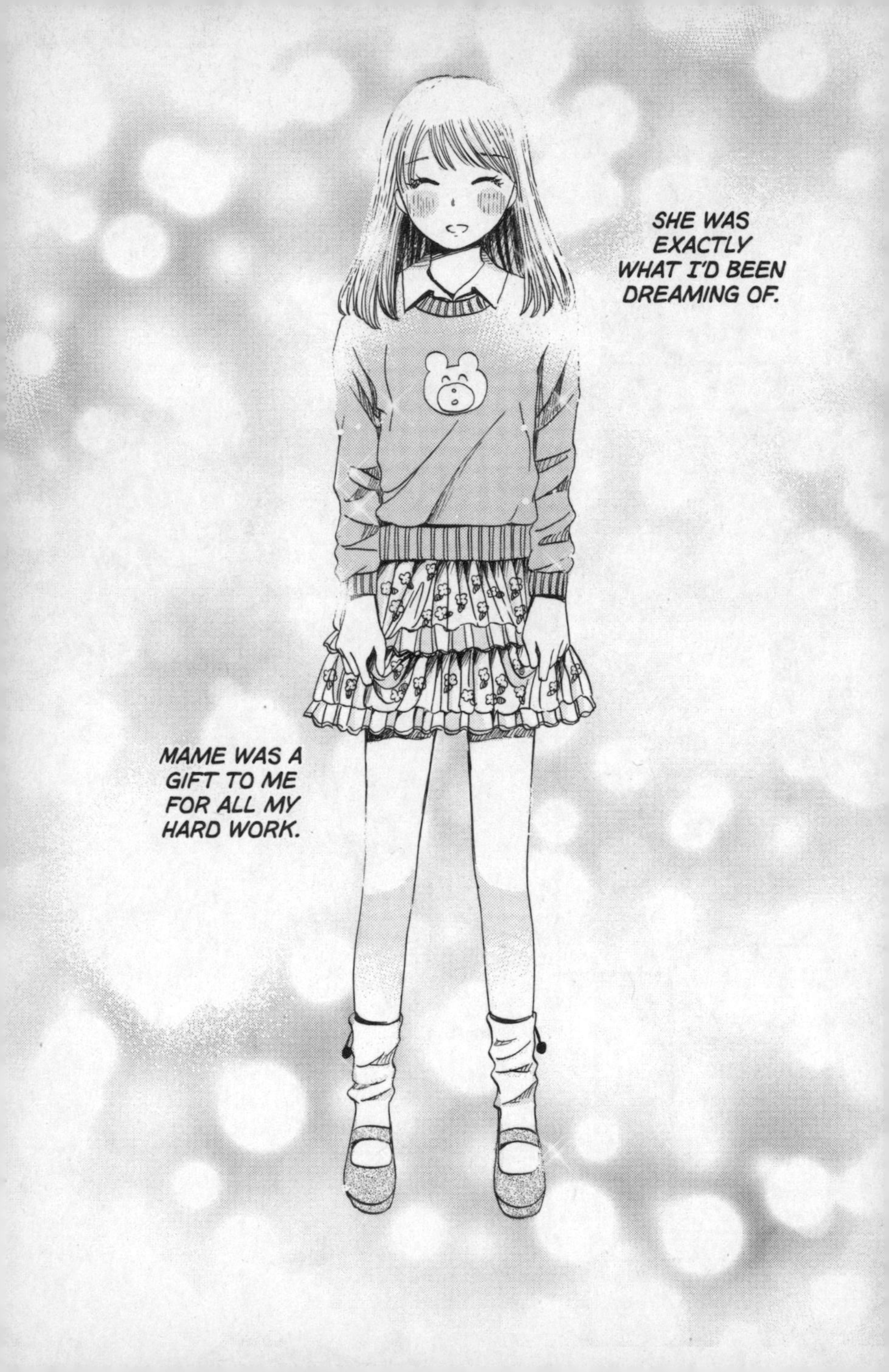
SHE WAS EXACTLY WHAT I'D BEEN DREAMING OF.
MAME WAS A GIFT TO ME FOR ALL MY HARD WORK.

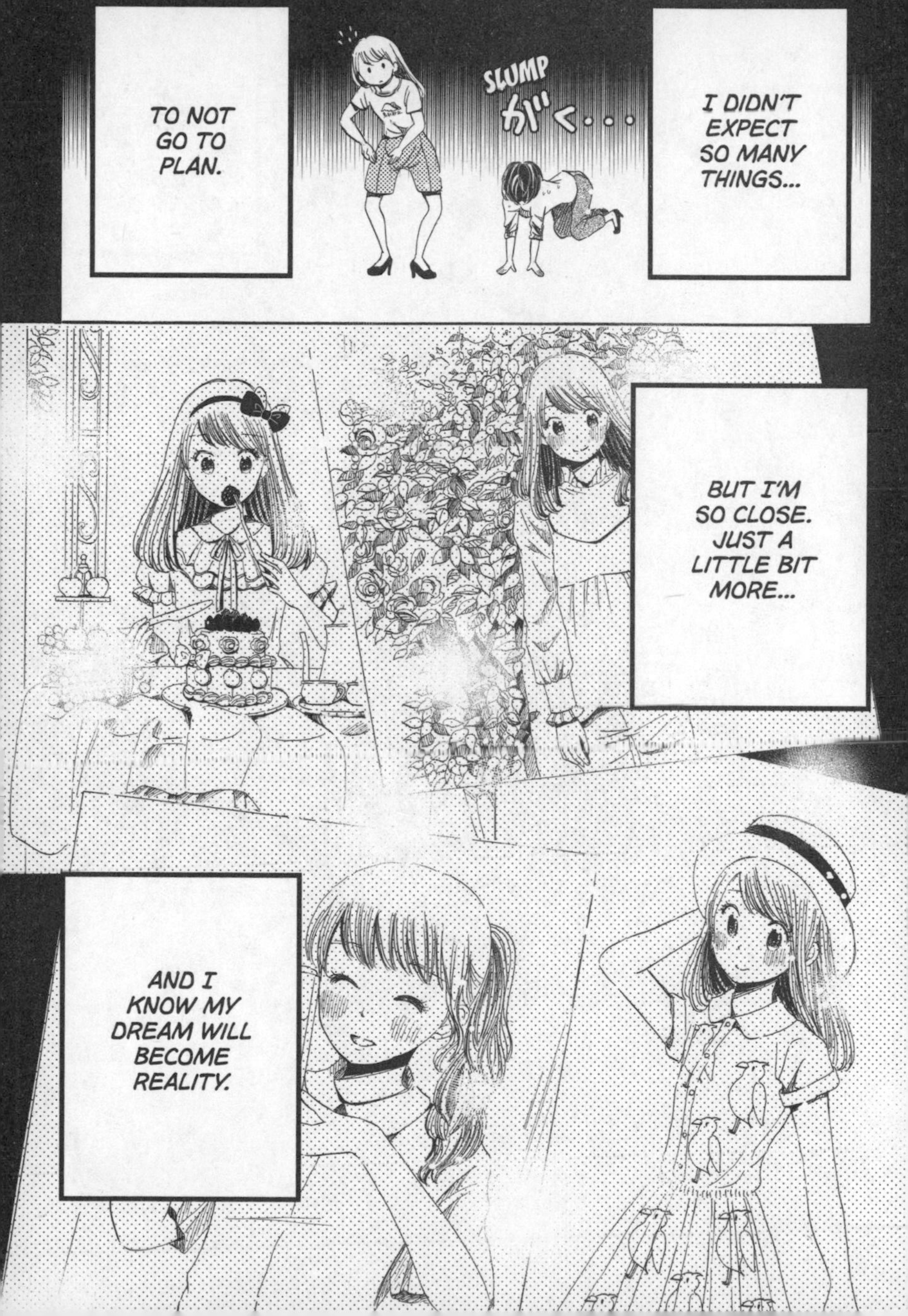
I DIDN'T EXPECT SO MANY THINGS...
SLUMP
がく...
TO NOT GO TO PLAN.
BUT I'M SO CLOSE. JUST A LITTLE BIT MORE...
AND I KNOW MY DREAM WILL BECOME REALITY.

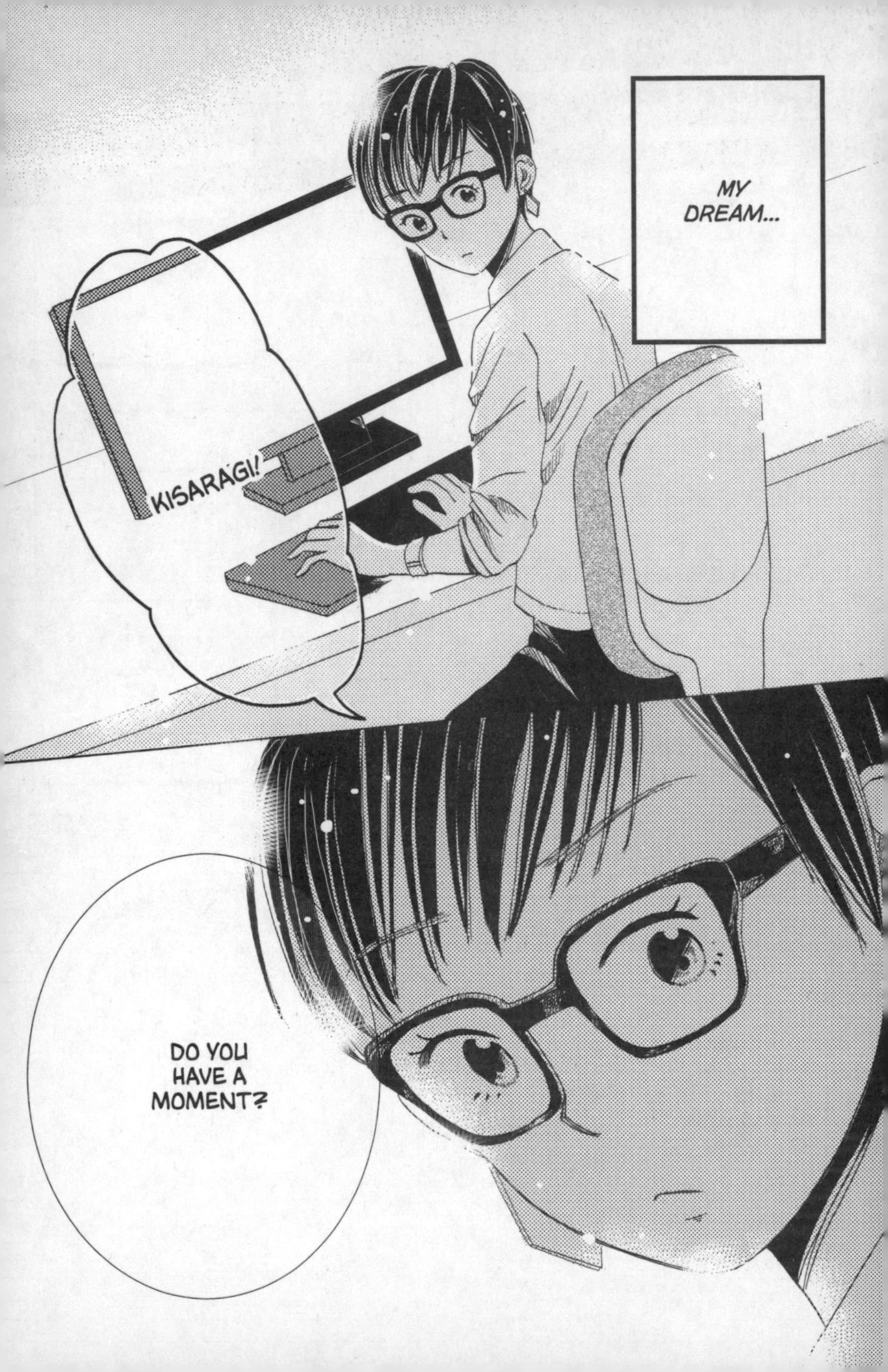
MY DREAM...
KISARAGI!
DO YOU HAVE A MOMENT?

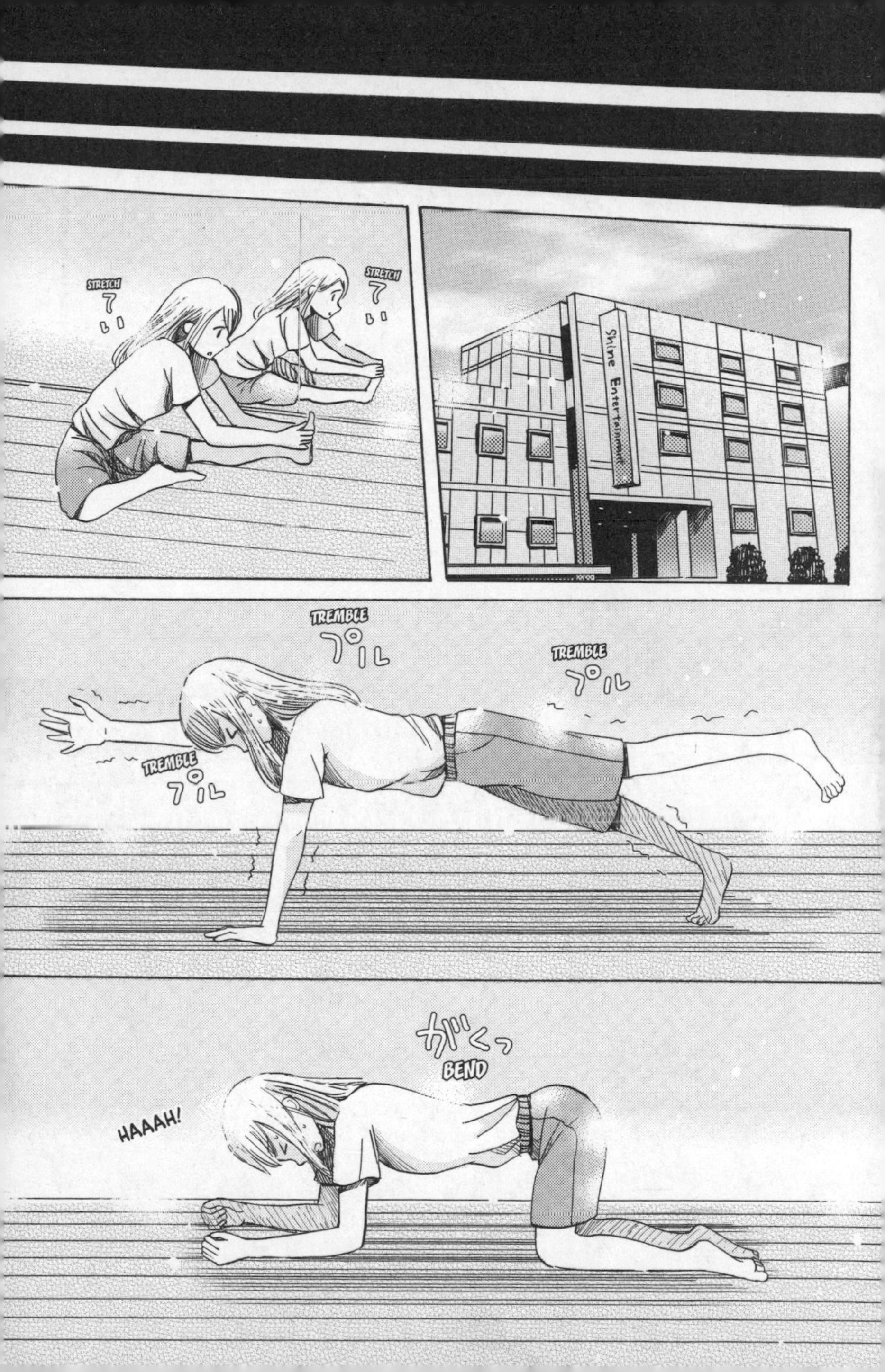
Shine Entertainment
STRETCH
STRETCH
TREMBLE
プル
TREMBLE
プル
TREMBLE
プル
がくっ
BEND
HAAAH!

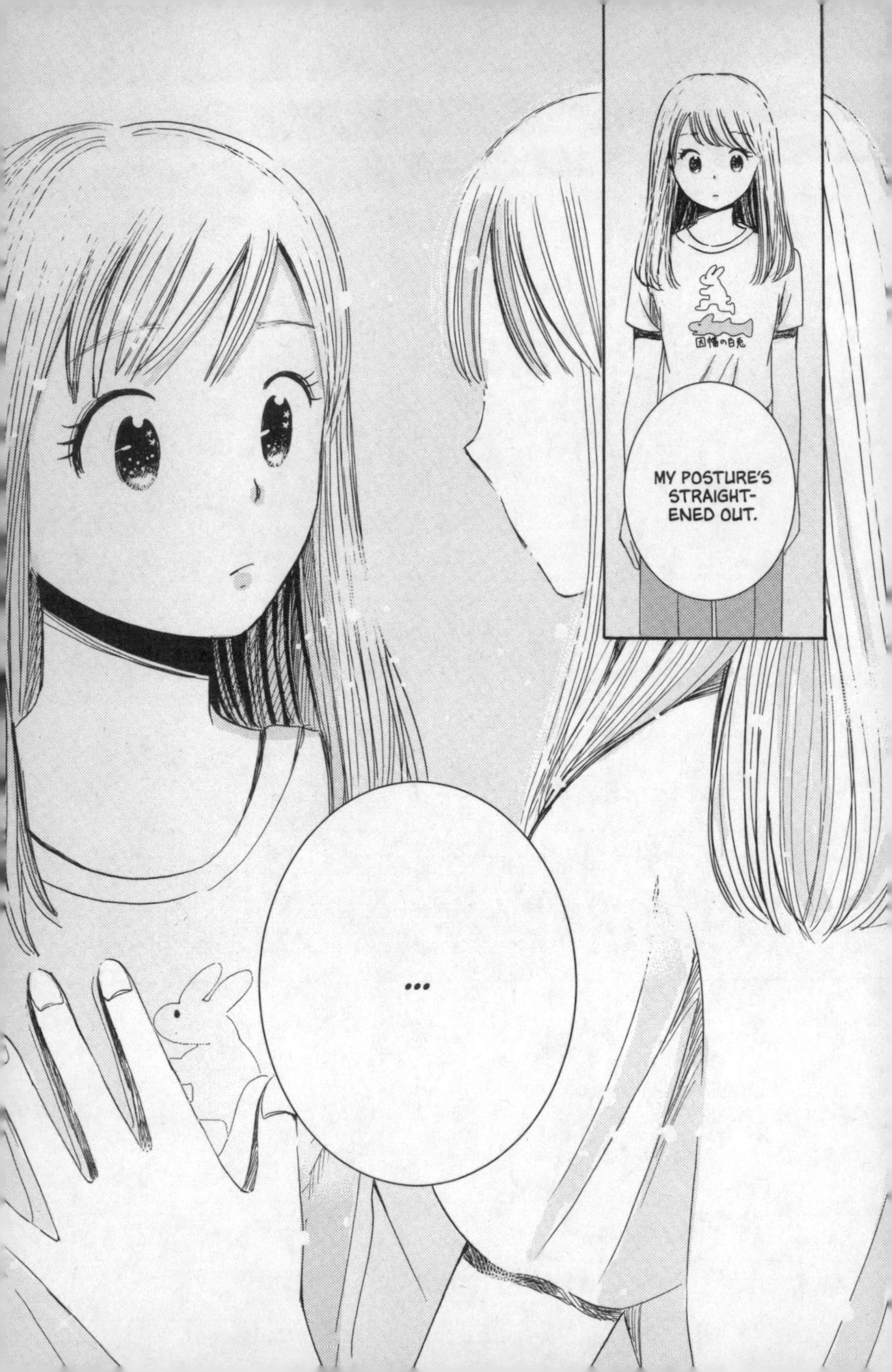
MY POSTURE'S STRAIGHT-ENED OUT.
...

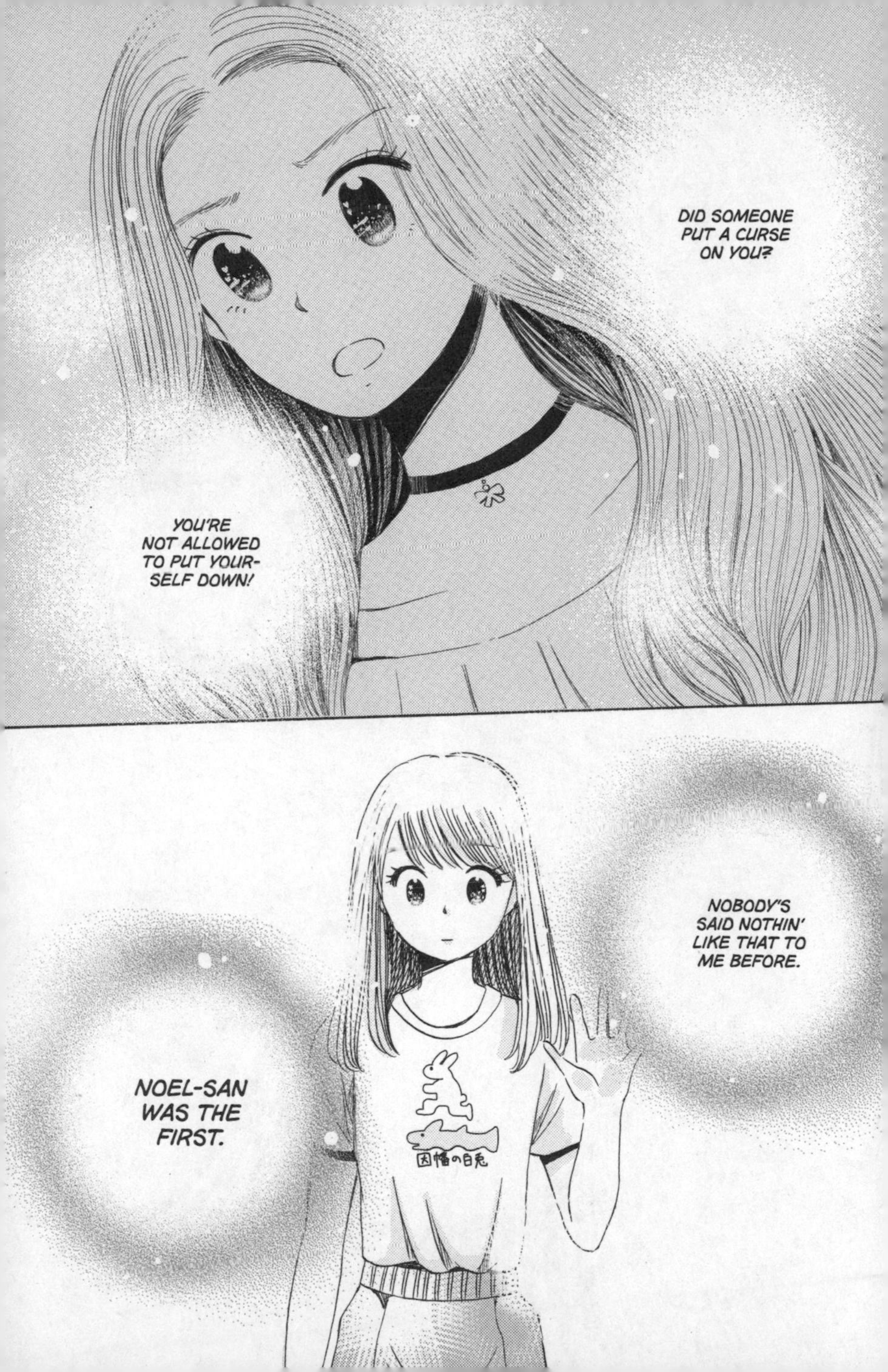
DID SOMEONE PUT A CURSE ON YOU?
YOU'RE NOT ALLOWED TO PUT YOUR-SELF DOWN!
NOBODY'S SAID NOTHIN' LIKE THAT TO ME BEFORE.
因幡の白兎
NOEL-SAN WAS THE FIRST.

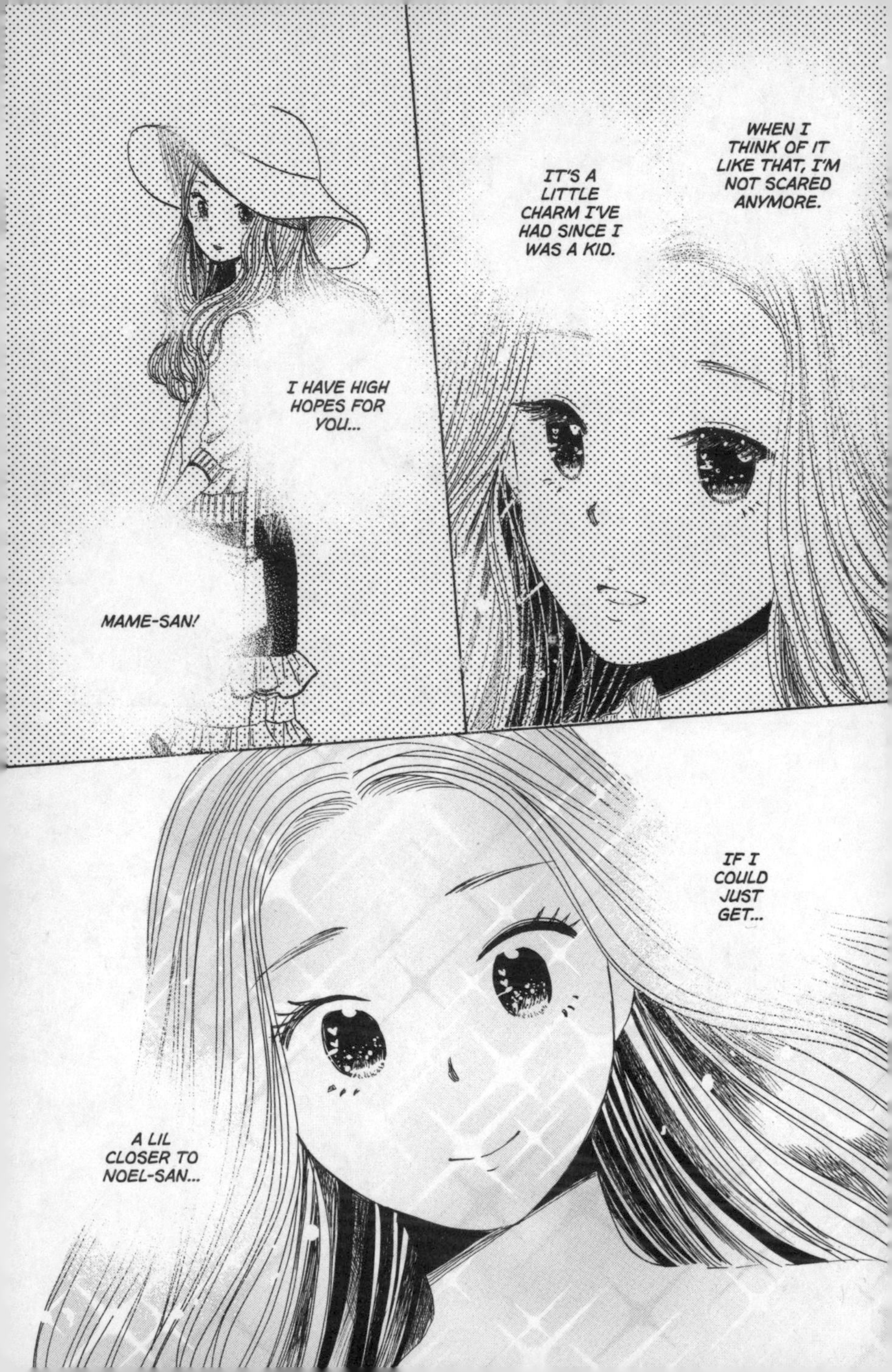
WHEN I THINK OF IT LIKE THAT, I'M NOT SCARED ANYMORE.
IT'S A LITTLE CHARM I'VE HAD SINCE I WAS A KID.
I HAVE HIGH HOPES FOR YOU...
MAME-SAN!
IF I COULD JUST GET...
A LIL CLOSER TO NOEL-SAN...

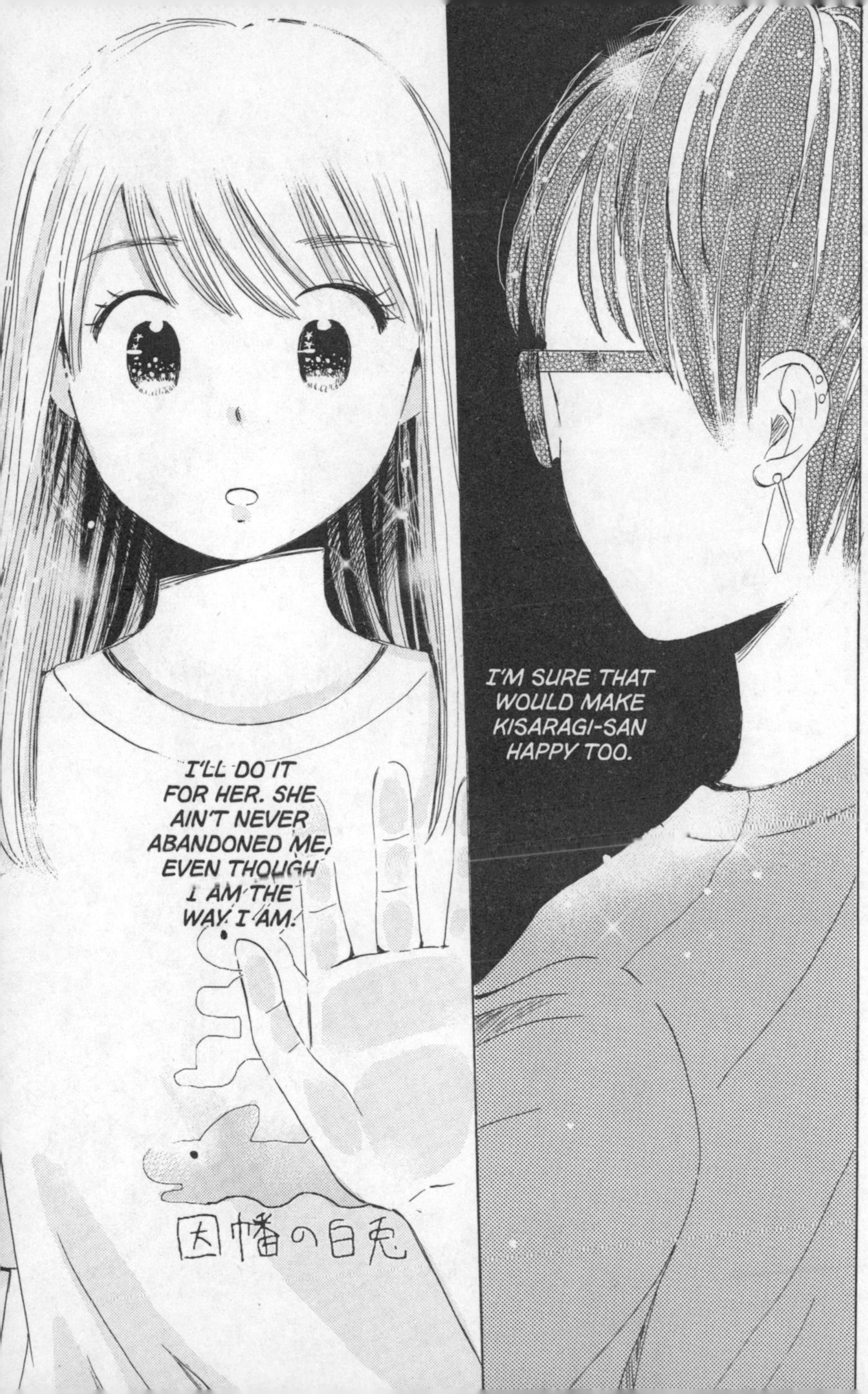
I'M SURE THAT WOULD MAKE KISARAGI-SAN HAPPY TOO.
I'LL DO IT FOR HER. SHE AIN'T NEVER ABANDONED ME, EVEN THOUGH I AM THE WAY I AM.
因幡の白兎

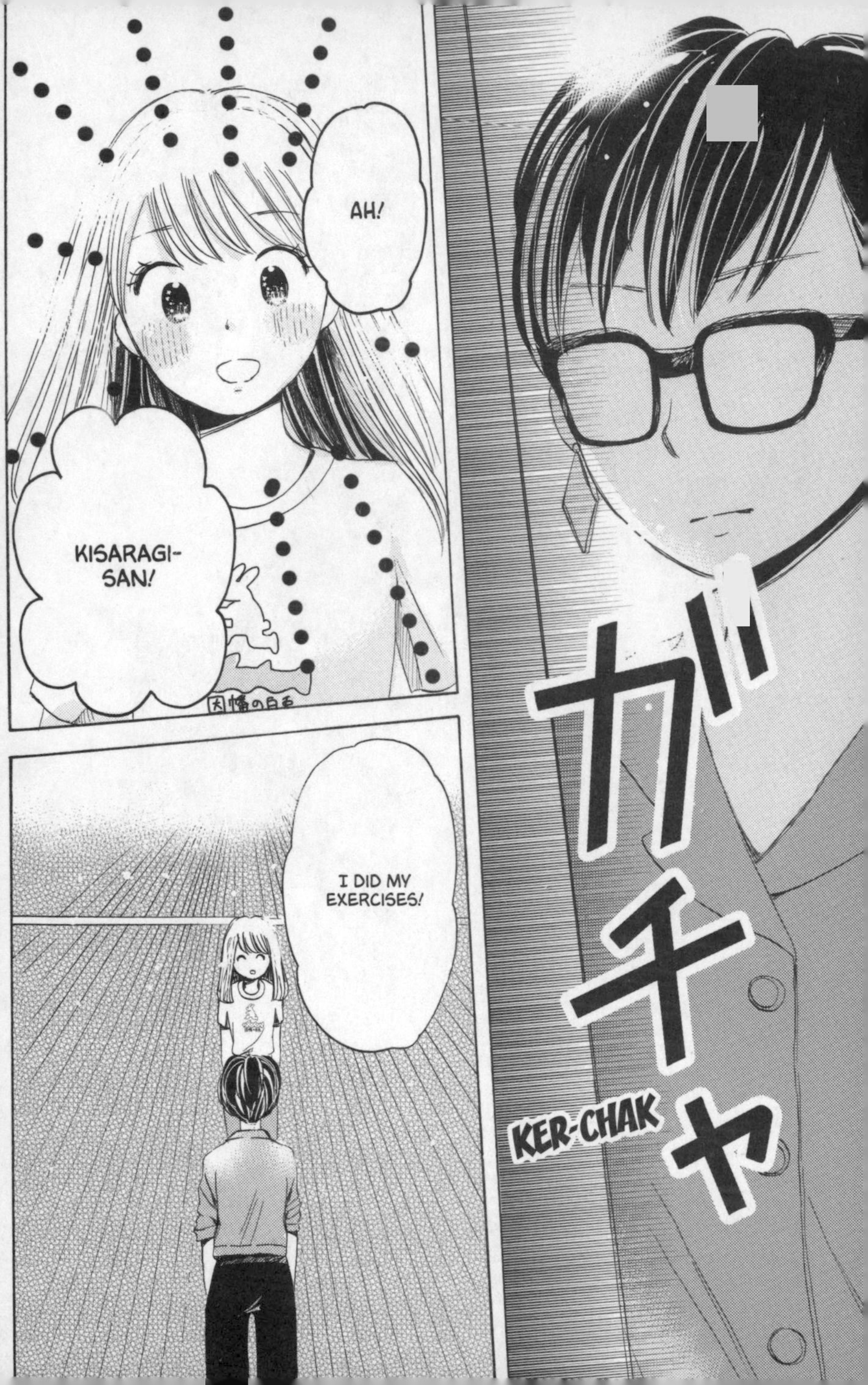
ガチャ
KER-CHAK
AH!
KISARAGI-SAN!
I DID MY EXERCISES!

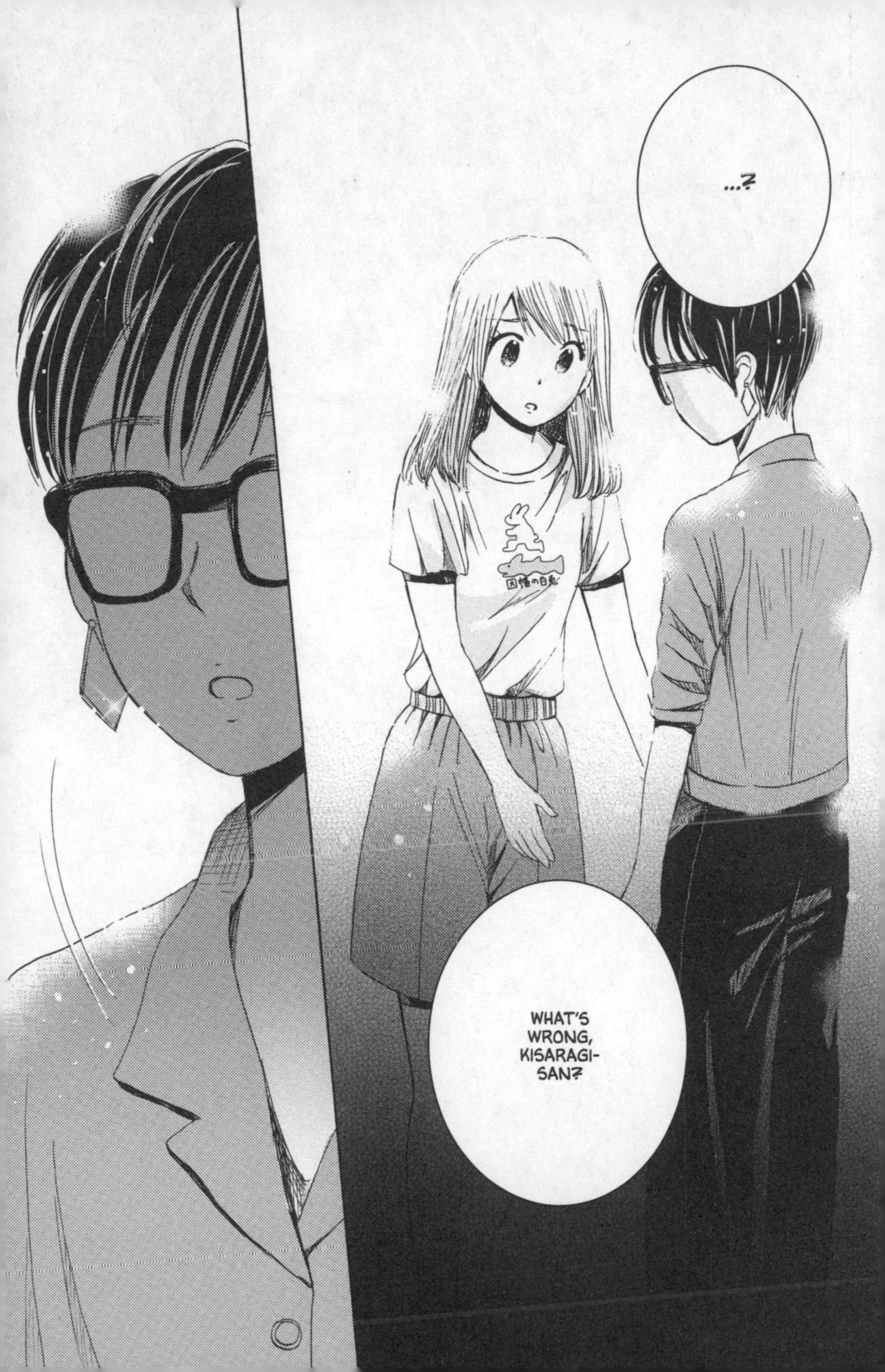
...?
WHAT'S WRONG, KISARAGI-SAN?

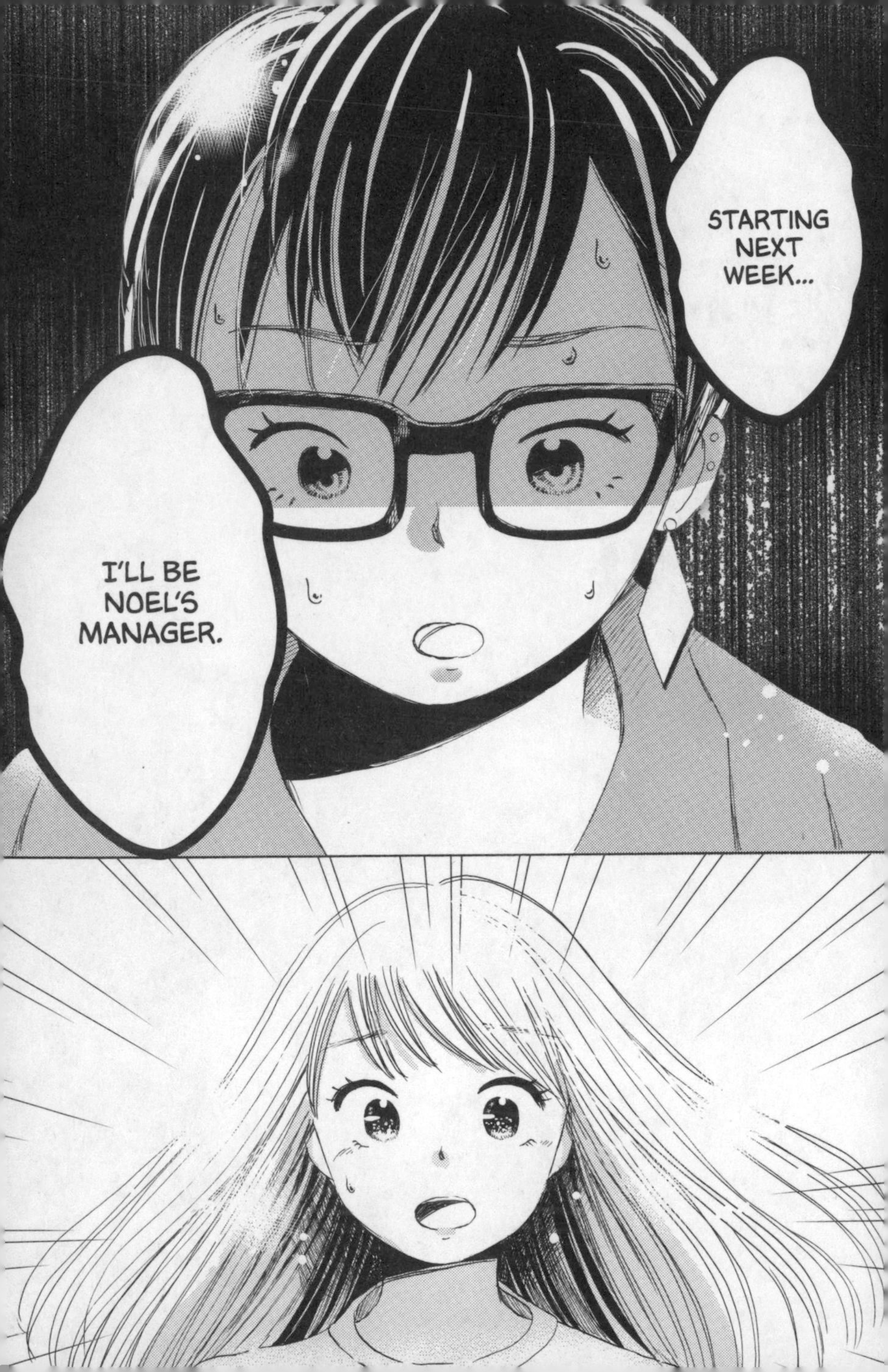
STARTING NEXT WEEK...
I'LL BE NOEL'S MANAGER.

MAME
coordinate

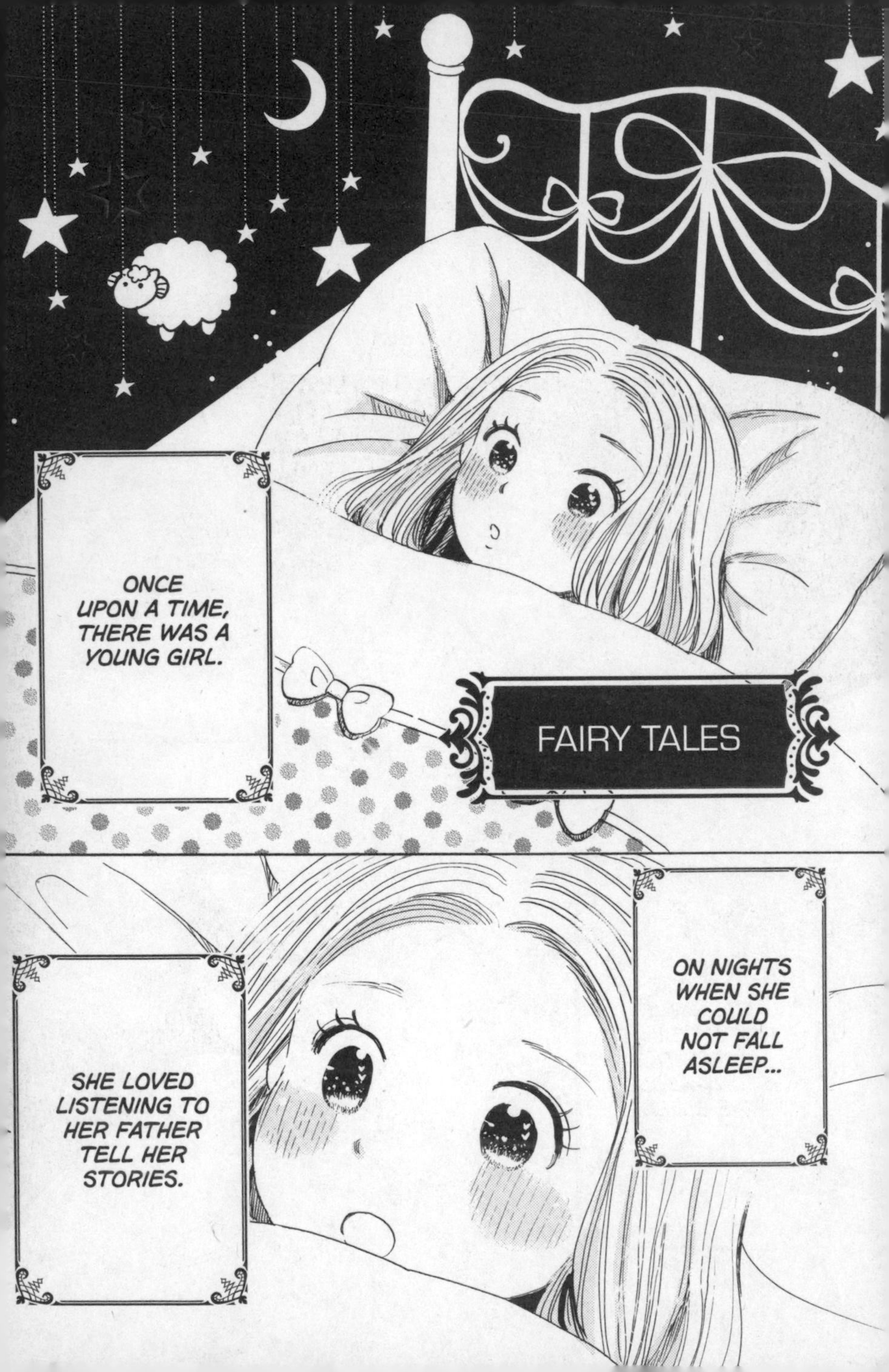
FAIRY TALES
ONCE UPON A TIME, THERE WAS A YOUNG GIRL.
ON NIGHTS WHEN SHE COULD NOT FALL ASLEEP...
SHE LOVED LISTENING TO HER FATHER TELL HER STORIES.

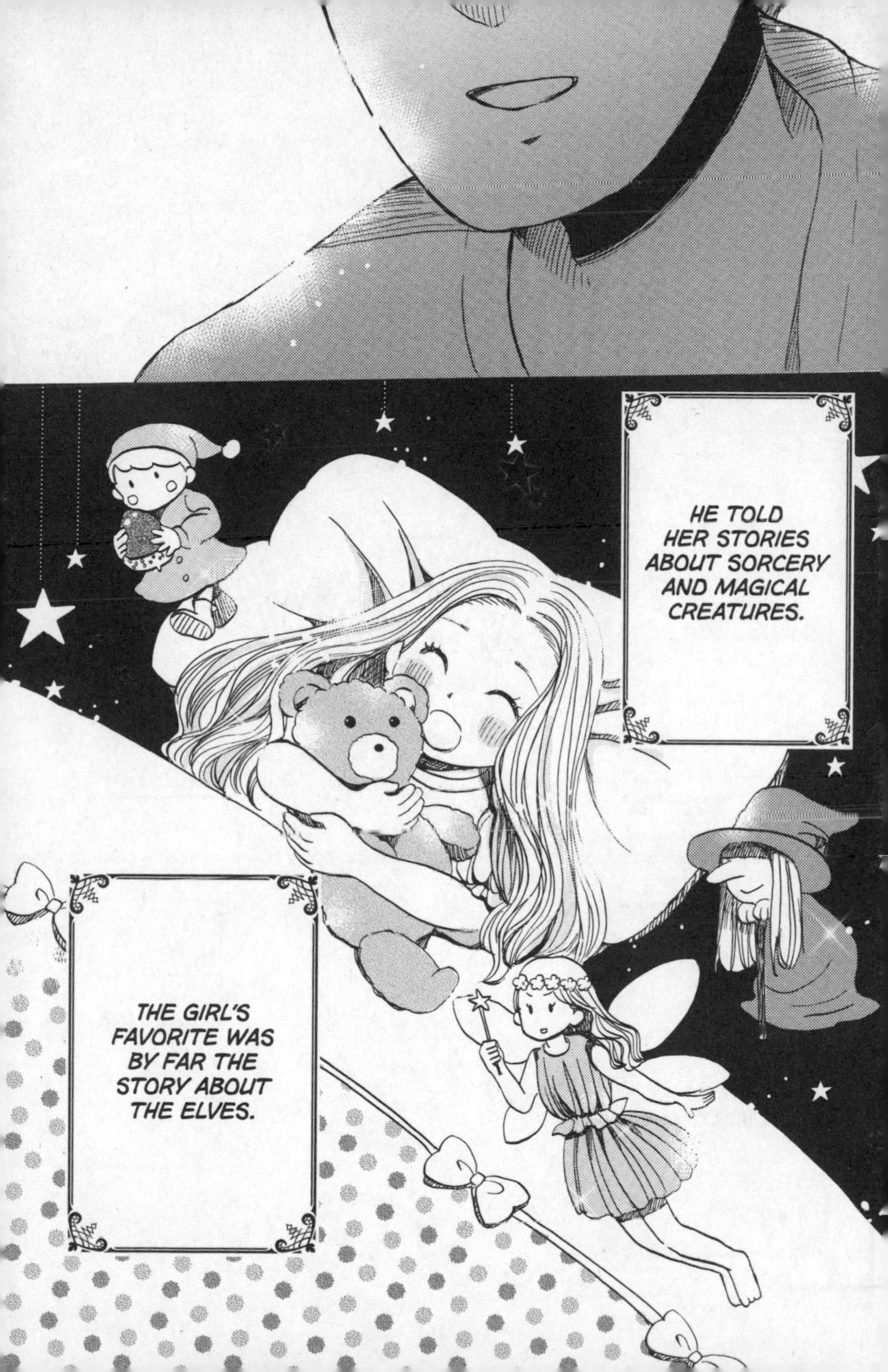
HE TOLD HER STORIES ABOUT SORCERY AND MAGICAL CREATURES.
THE GIRL'S FAVORITE WAS BY FAR THE STORY ABOUT THE ELVES.

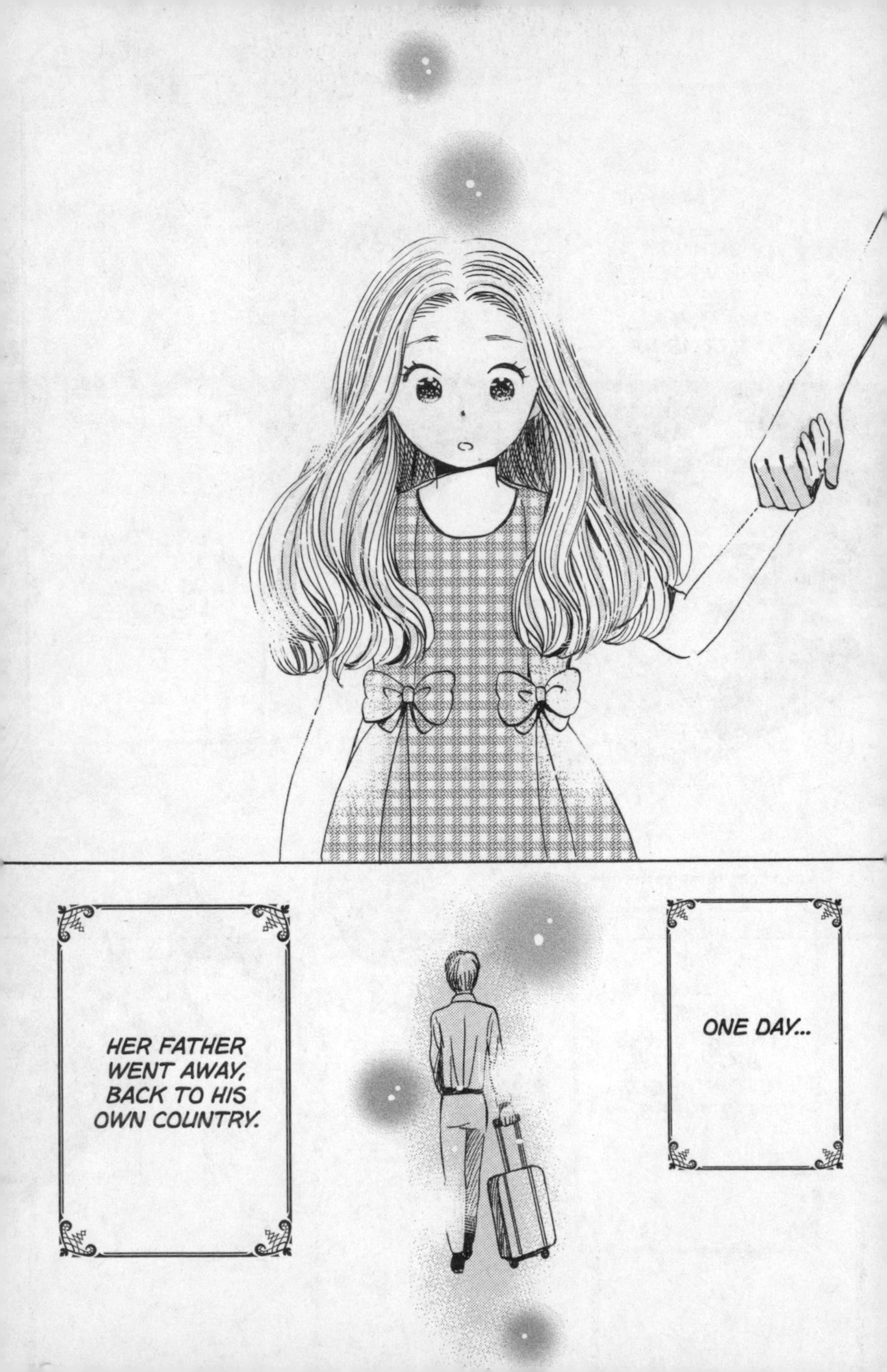
ONE DAY...
HER FATHER WENT AWAY, BACK TO HIS OWN COUNTRY.

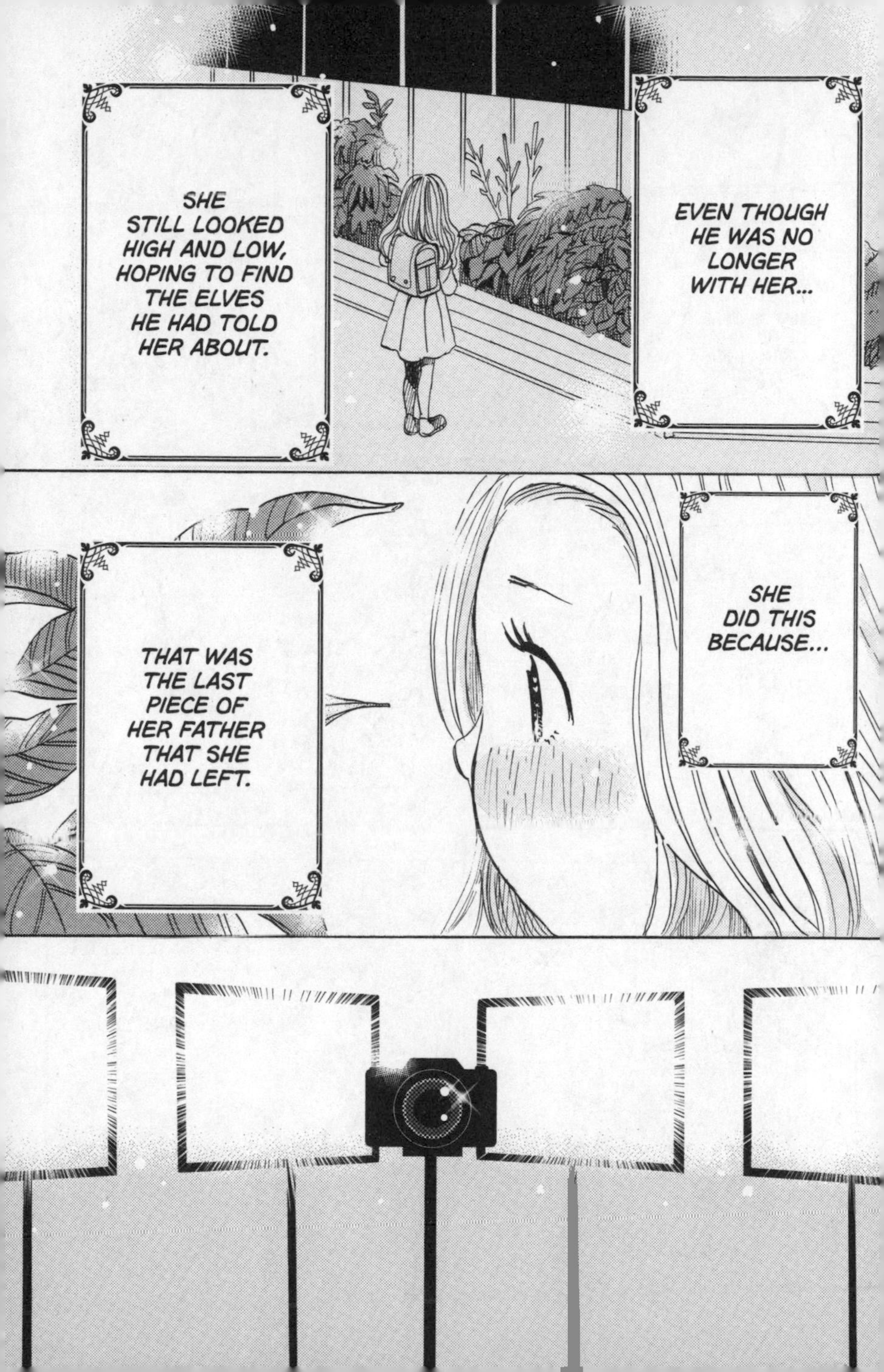
EVEN THOUGH HE WAS NO LONGER WITH HER...
SHE STILL LOOKED HIGH AND LOW, HOPING TO FIND THE ELVES HE HAD TOLD HER ABOUT.
SHE DID THIS BECAUSE...
THAT WAS THE LAST PIECE OF HER FATHER THAT SHE HAD LEFT.

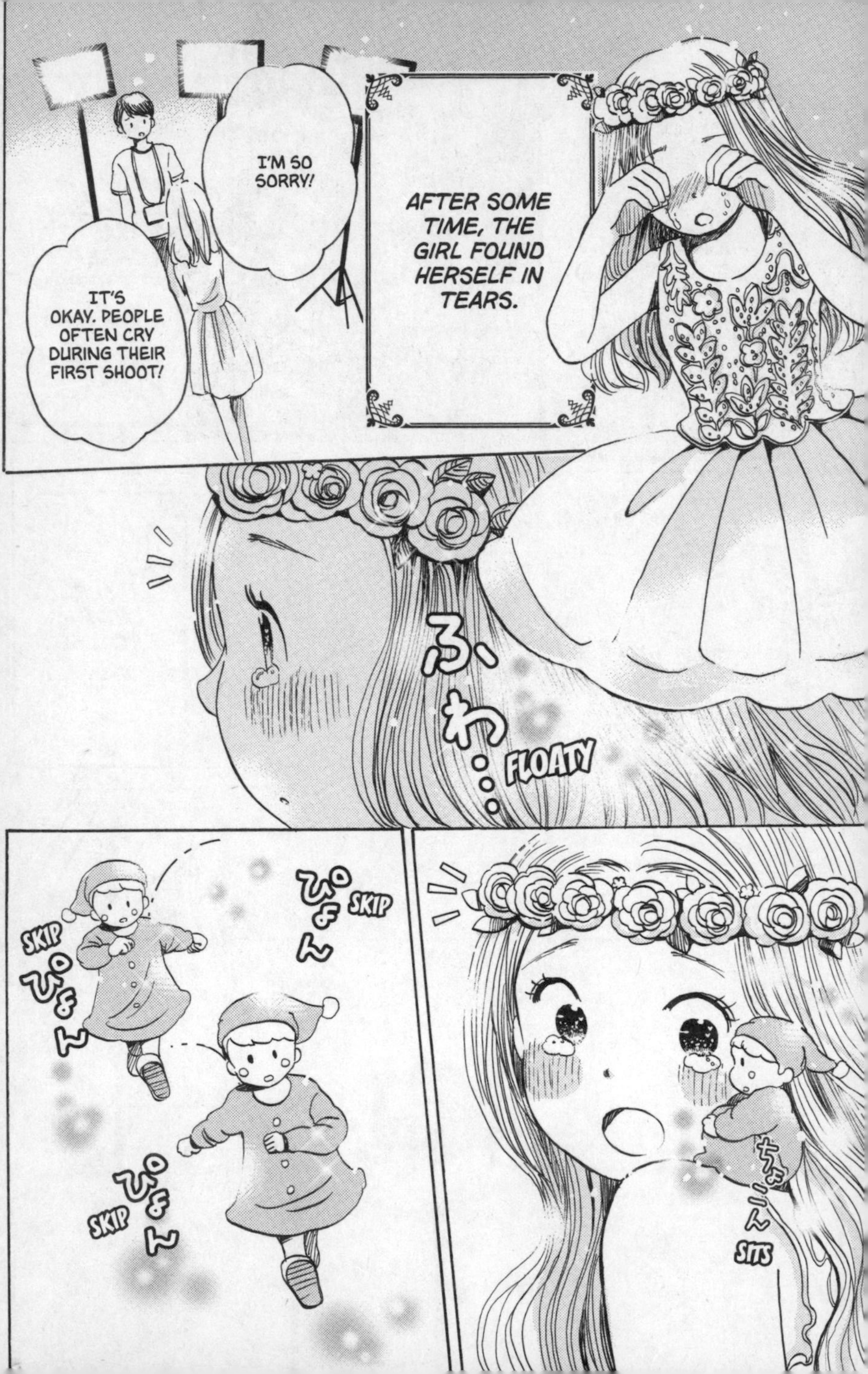
AFTER SOME TIME, THE GIRL FOUND HERSELF IN TEARS.
I'M SO SORRY!
IT'S OKAY. PEOPLE OFTEN CRY DURING THEIR FIRST SHOOT!
ふわ…
FLOATY
ちょこん
SITS
ぴょん
SKIP
ぴょん
SKIP
ぴょん
SKIP

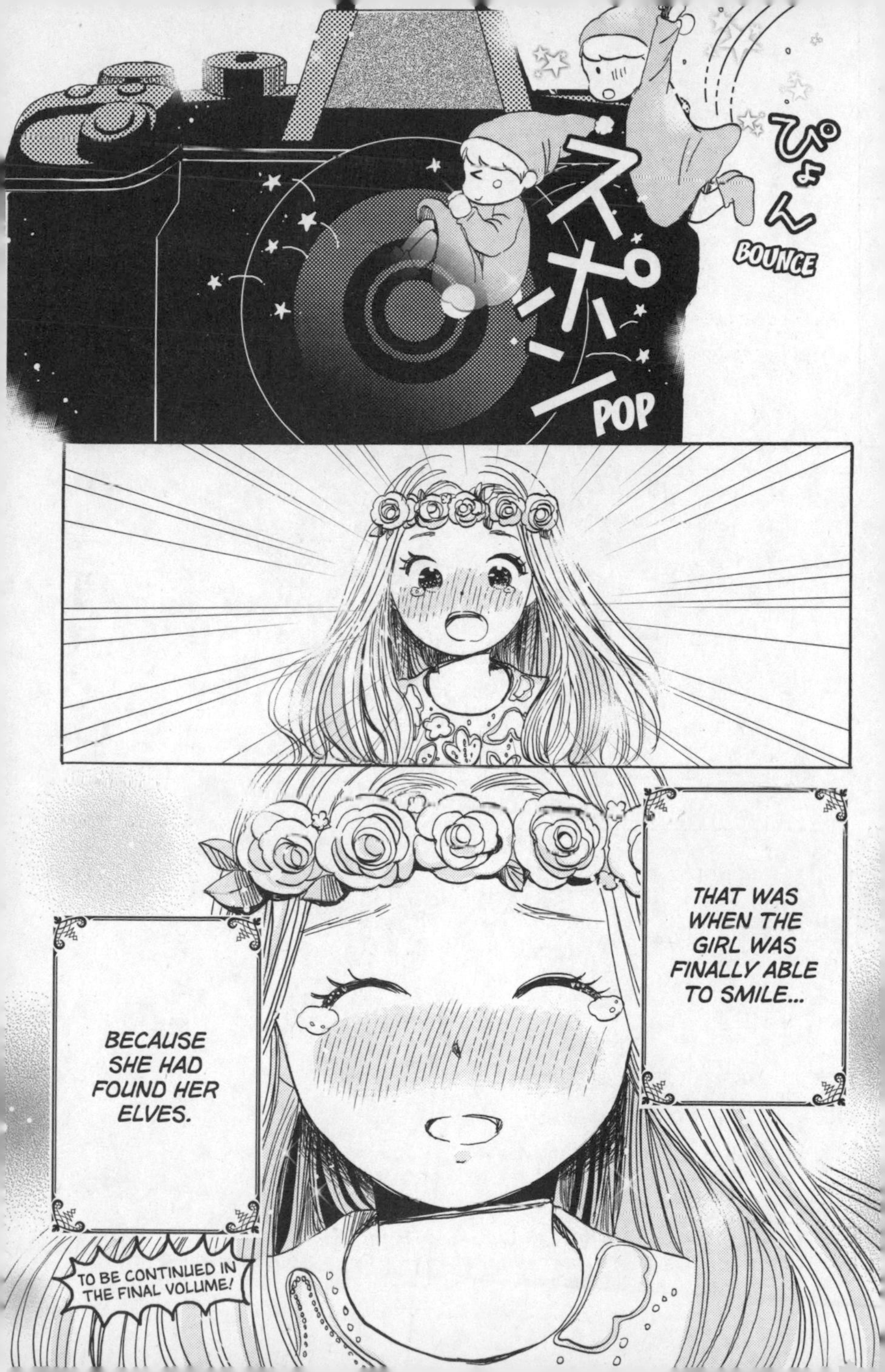
ぴょん
BOUNCE
スポーン
POP
THAT WAS WHEN THE GIRL WAS FINALLY ABLE TO SMILE...
BECAUSE SHE HAD FOUND HER ELVES.
TO BE CONTINUED IN THE FINAL VOLUME!

Haruki Niwa
Mai Mochizuki

Alice in Kyoto Forest

1

FANTASY

After being orphaned when she was very young, Alice has lived with her aunt for most of her childhood, but her uncle clearly doesn't want her around. At fifteen years old, Alice decides to return home to Kyoto and train as a maiko, an apprentice with the hopes of eventually becoming a full-fledged geisha.But when she arrives back to the city where she was born, she finds that Kyoto has changed quite a bit in the years since she left it. Almost as if it's a completely different world...

BIBI & MIYU, VOLUME 1

Hirara Natsume, Olivia Vieweg

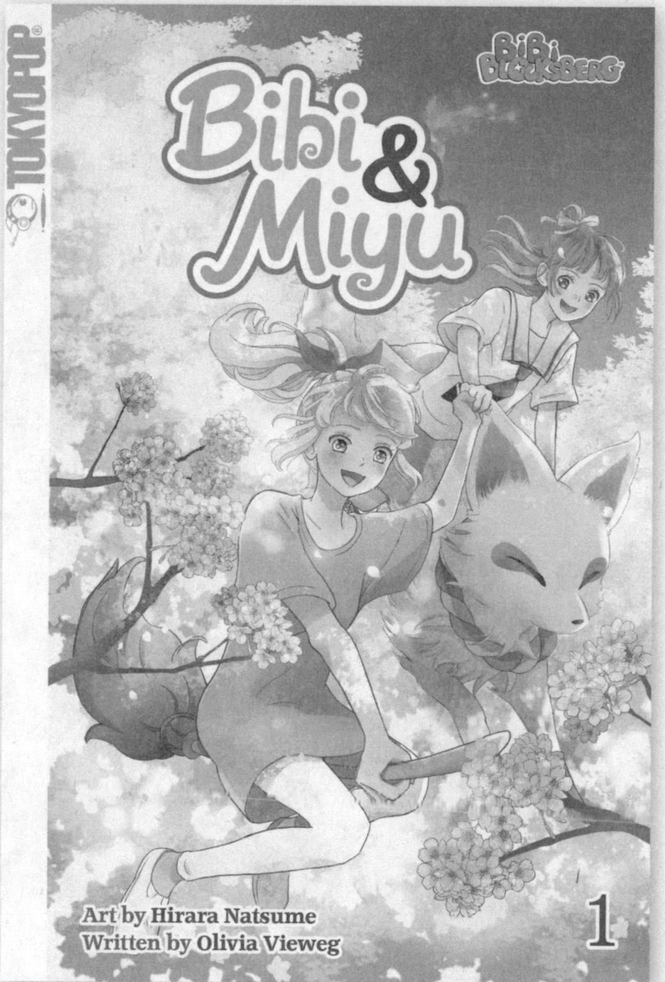
TOKYOPOP
Bibi Blocksberg
Bibi & Miyu
Art by Hirara Natsume
Written by Olivia Vieweg
1

FANTASY

TOKYOPOP

When a new student from Japan shows up at Bibi Blocksberg's school, she fits in immediately. But Bibi's suspicious; she knows Miyu's hiding something, and she's determined to find out what! Bibi's journey takes her all the way to Japan, and while learning about all the new rules and magic in this foreign land, she realizes that maybe she and Miyu can be friends after all!

LOVE-x-LOVE

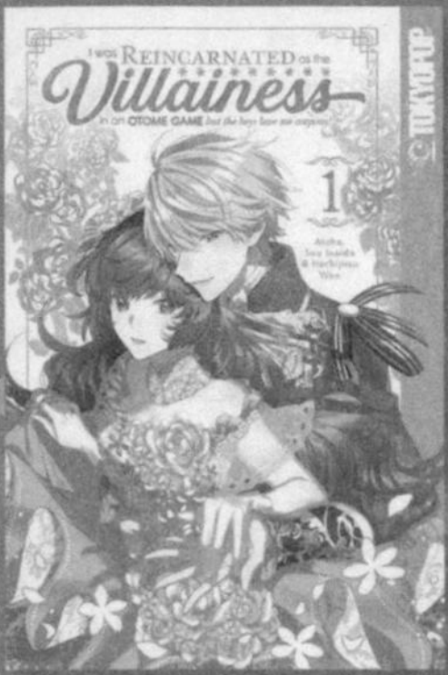

I was REINCARNATED as the
Villainess
in an OTOME GAME
1
TOKYOPOP

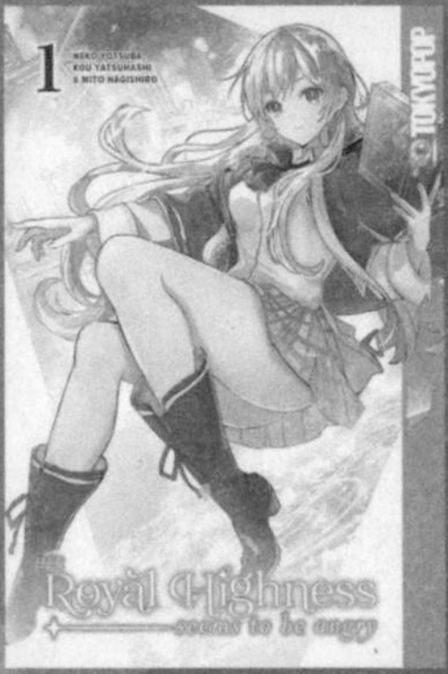

1
NEKO YOTSUBA
KOU YATSUHASHI
MITO NAGISHIRO
TOKYOPOP
Royal Highness
seems to be angry

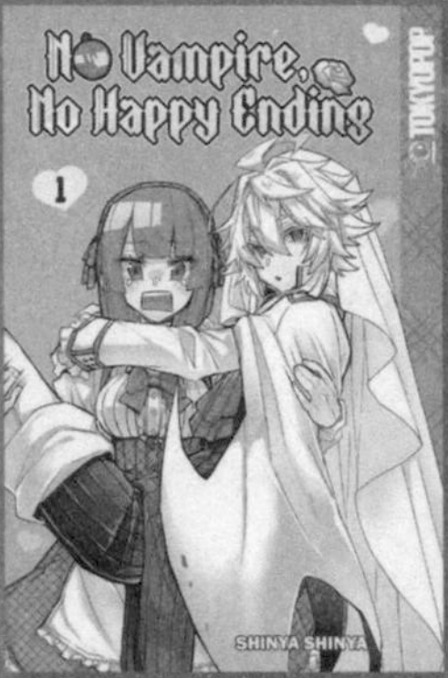

No Vampire, No Happy Ending
1
SHINYA SHINYA
TOKYOPOP

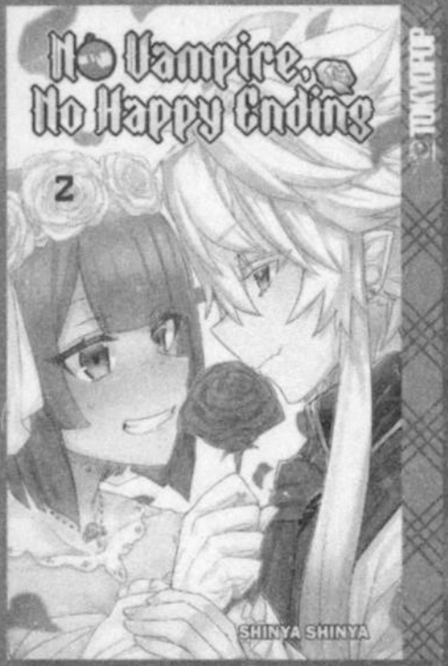

No Vampire, No Happy Ending
2
SHINYA SHINYA
TOKYOPOP

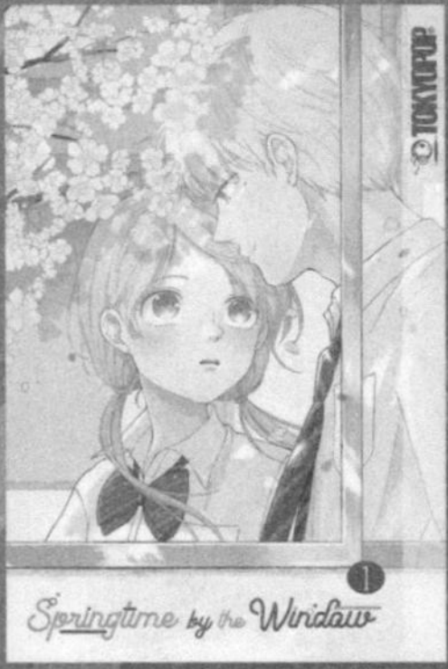

TOKYOPOP
1
Springtime by the Window

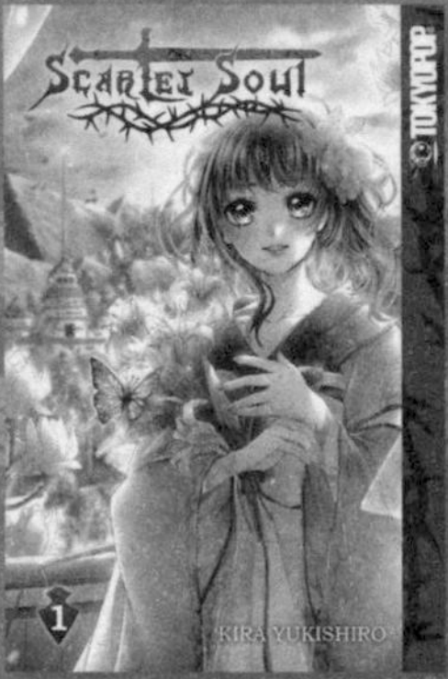

Scarlet Soul
TOKYOPOP
1
KIRA YUKISHIRO

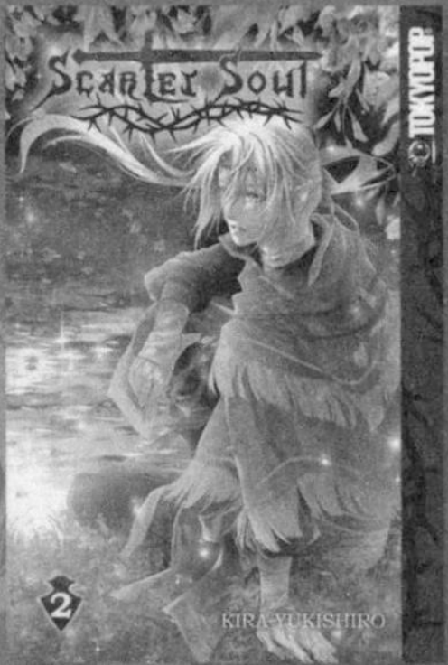

Scarlet Soul
TOKYOPOP
2
KIRA YUKISHIRO

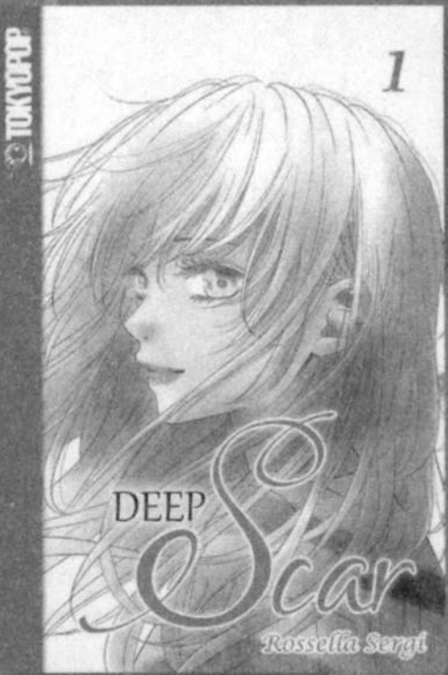

TOKYOPOP
1
DEEP Scar
Rossella Sergi

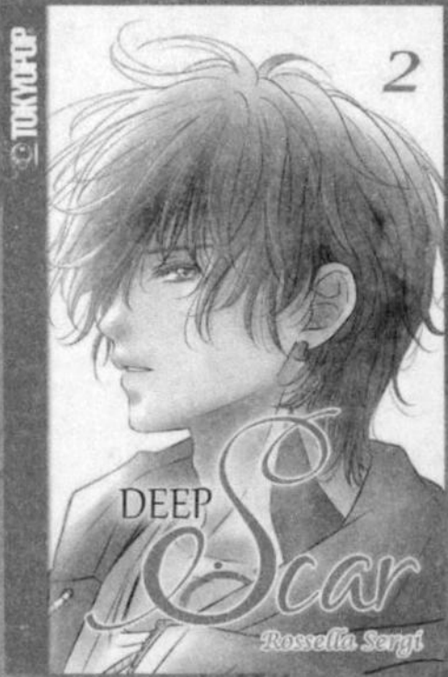

TOKYOPOP
2
DEEP Scar
Rossella Sergi

Check out *LOVExLOVE.info* for all kinds of romance!

LOVE x LOVE

TOKYOPOP believes all types of romances deserve to be celebrated. *LOVE x LOVE* was born from that idea and our commitment to representing a variety of stories and voices as diverse as our fans.

TOKYOPOP®

⚧LOVE-x-LOVE⚧

Arika is what you could charitably call a vampire "enthusiast." When she stumbles across the beautiful and mysterious vampire Divo however, her excitement quickly turns to disappointment as she discovers he's not exactly like the seductive, manipulative villains in her stories. His looks win first place, but his head's a space case. Armed with her extensive knowledge of vampire lore, Arika downgrades Divo to a beta vampire and begins their long, long… long journey to educate him in the ways of the undead.

SPRINGTIME BY THE WINDOW, VOLUME 1
Suzuyuki

♀LOVE-x-LOVE♂

Cool and collected second-year Yamada is in love with his childhood friend, Seno. His classmates Akama and Toda are also starting to think about romance, though neither of them realizes yet that they might actually feel the same way about each other...High school love in the spring of adolescence blooms with earnest, messy emotions.

DEEP SCAR, VOLUME 1

Rossella Sergi

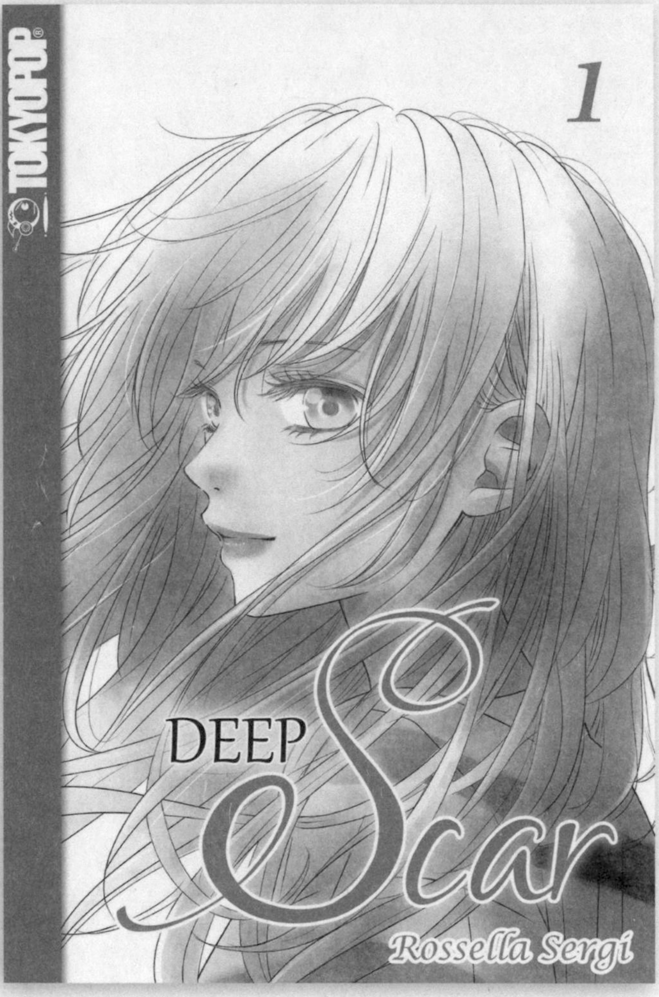
TOKYOPOP
1
DEEP Scar
Rossella Sergi

♀LOVE-x-LOVE♀

Sofia is a quiet, shy young woman who's never been away from home for long. When she moves to Turin for school, it's her first time away from her family and her boyfriend Luca. But her new roommate, Veronica, leads a life very different from hers: she prefers evenings in the company of beautiful boys! Meanwhile, Luca dreads the influence of Veronica and her entourage on Sofia, and especially the presence of the enigmatic Lorenzo, who seems to be a little too interested in his girlfriend...

SCARLET SOUL, VOLUME 1

Kira Yukishiro

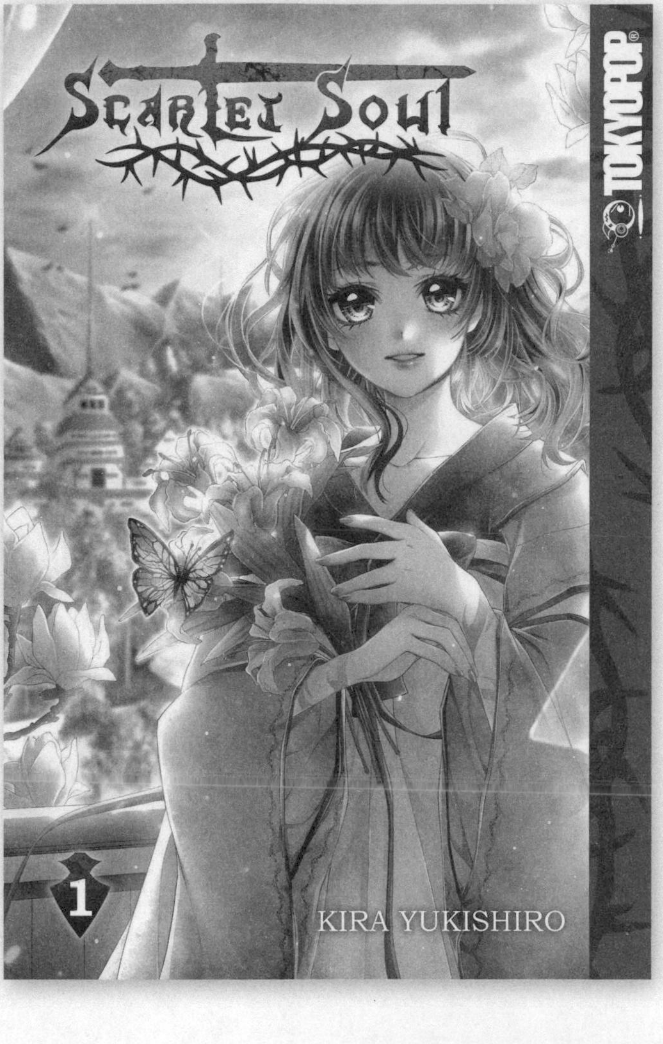

Scarlet Soul
TOKYOPOP
1
KIRA YUKISHIRO

LOVE-x-LOVE

TOKYOPOP

Long ago, Eron Shirano used the sacred Sword of a Hundred Souls to seal away the demon underworld Ruhmon. Since then, the Kingdom of Nohmur has enjoyed peace and prosperity with the aid of his descendants, the exorcist clan that protects the barrier. Until one day, for unknown reasons, demons begin slipping through once more... When Priestess Lys Shirano suddenly vanishes without a trace, it's up to her little sister Rin to take up the sword she left behind. Even though she's an outcast on friendly terms with the mysterious demon Aghyr, Rin sets out to find her missing sister... and try to restore balance to Nohmur before it's far too late.

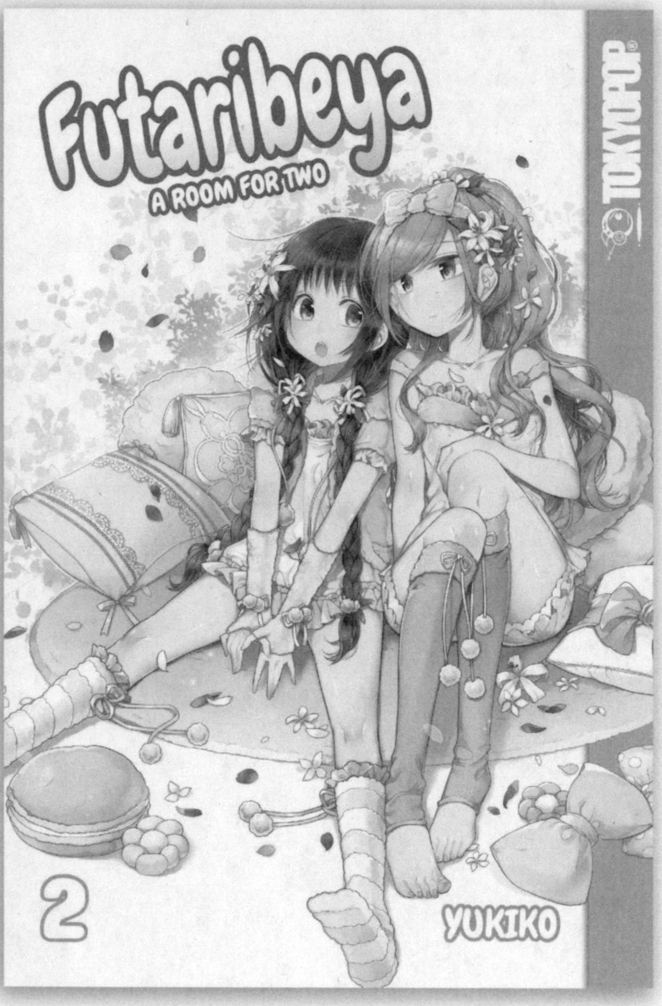
TOKYOPOP
Futaribeya
A ROOM FOR TWO
2
YUKIKO

FUTARIBEYA: A ROOM FOR TWO, VOL 2

Yukiko

♀LOVE-x-LOVE♀

In terms of personality, Sakurako Kawawa couldn't be more at odds with her lackadaisical new roommate, Kasumi Yamabuki. But even though hardworking, friendly Sakurako might get top scores in class and do most of the cooking at home while Kasumi is constantly nodding off or snacking, these two roommates actually get along so well, you'll rarely see one without the other at her side. Whether they're just walking arm-in-arm to class, watching the cherry trees blossom, or sharing cotton candy at the summer festival, Sakurako and Kasumi are always having fun together!

TOKYOPOP

FUTARIBEYA: A ROOM FOR TWO, VOL 3

Yukiko

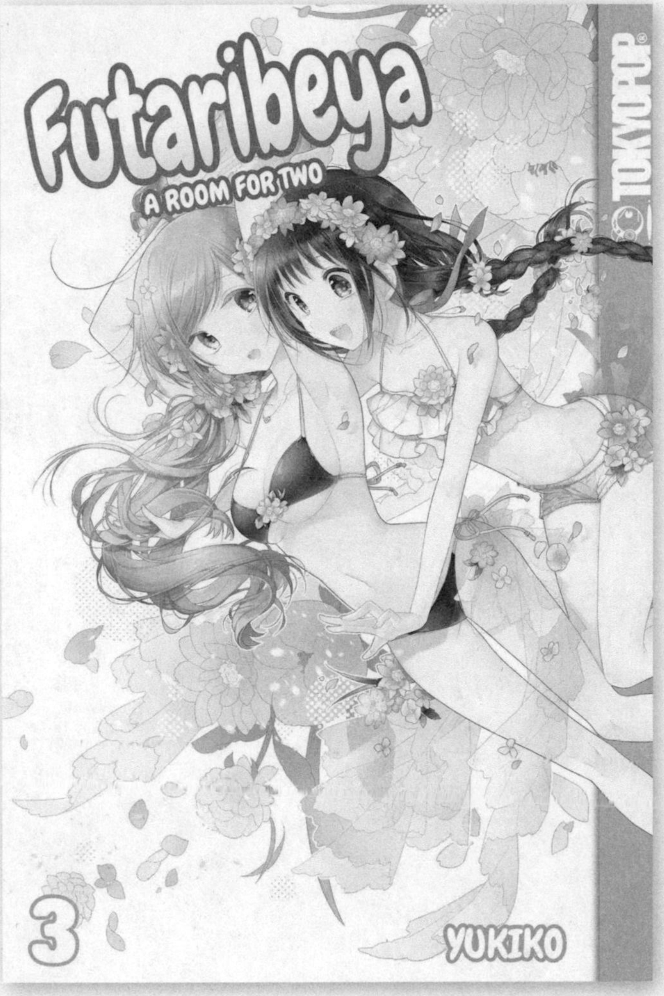
Futaribeya
A ROOM FOR TWO
TOKYOPOP
3
YUKIKO

♀LOVE-x-LOVE♀

Sakurako Kawawa settles into her new apartment with her lazy, easygoing, and stunningly beautiful roommate, Kasumi Yamabuki, who lives life at her own pace. This four-panel-style comic follows the everyday life of these two high school roommates as they go to class together, tackle the mundane necessities of laundry and grocery shopping for two, and learn more about one another in a cute and heartwarming series of short stories.

TOKYOPOP

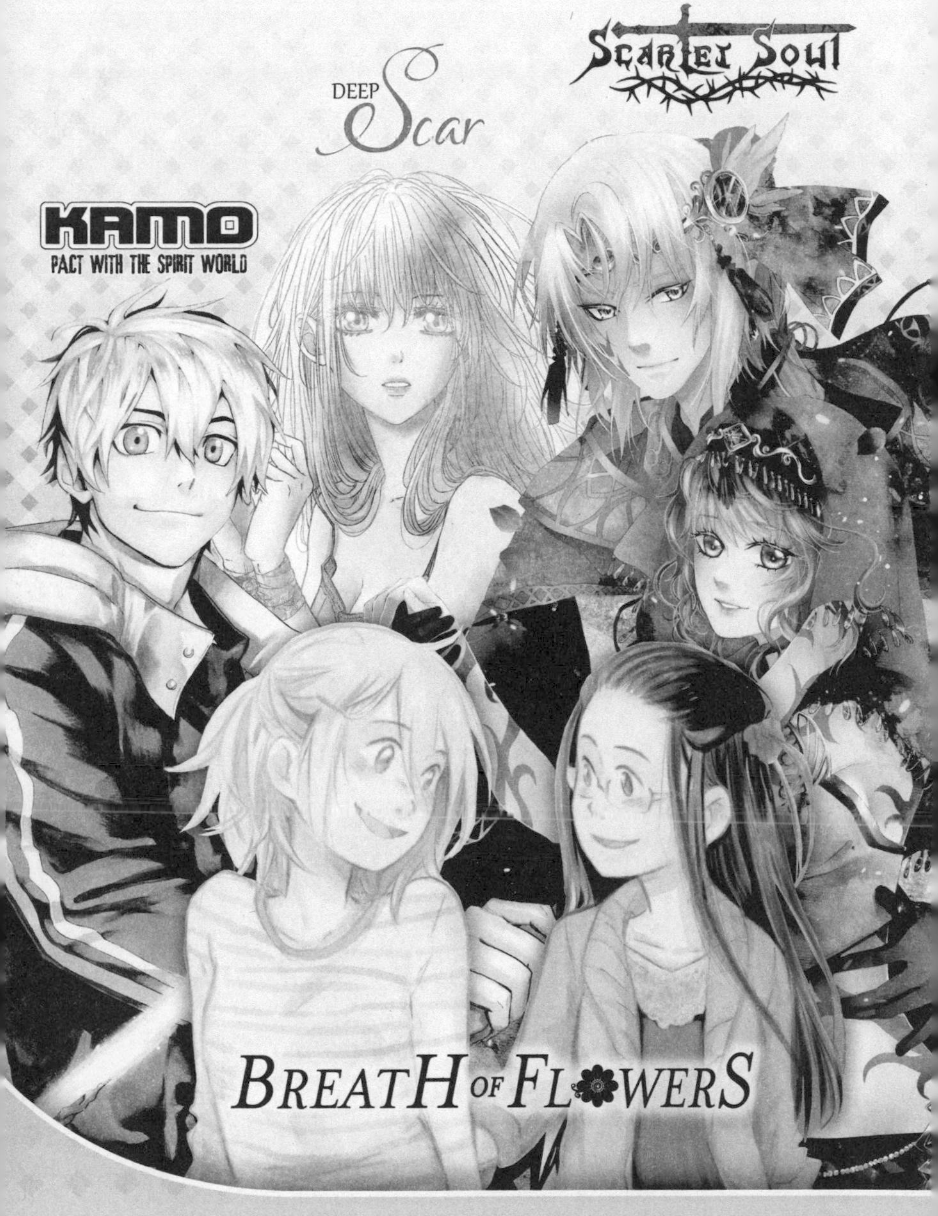
Scarlet Soul
DEEP Scar
KAMO
PACT WITH THE SPIRIT WORLD
BREATH OF FLOWERS

GOLDFISCH, VOLUME 1

Yaa, Nana

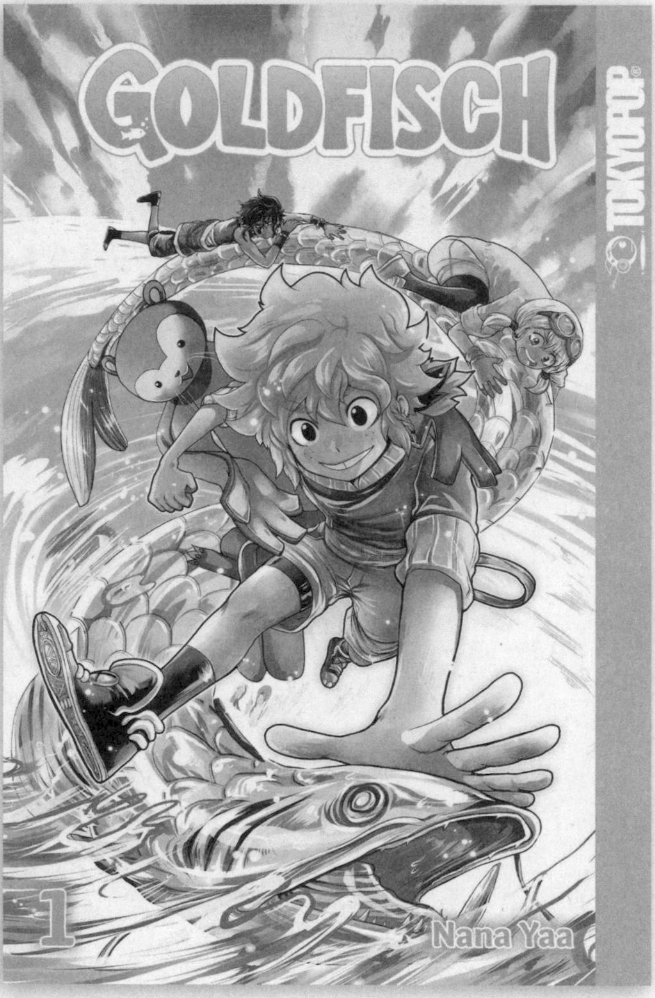
GOLDFISCH
TOKYOPOP
1
Nana Yaa

ADVENTURE

Say hi to Morrey Gibbs! A fisher-boy in a flooded world overrun with dangerous mutated animals known as "anomals," he's got his own problems to worry about. Namely, how everything he touches turns to gold! Sure it sounds great, but gold underpants aren't exactly stylish — or comfortable! Together with his otter buddy and new inventor friend Shelly, Morrey's on a quest to rid himself of his blessing-turned-curse and undo the tragedy it caused. That is of course, if they can dodge the treasure-hungry bounty hunters...

TOKYOPOP

KAMO: PACT WITH THE SPIRIT WORLD, VOLUME 1

Ban Zarbo

KAMO
PACT WITH THE SPIRIT WORLD
TOKYOPOP
1
Ban Zarbo

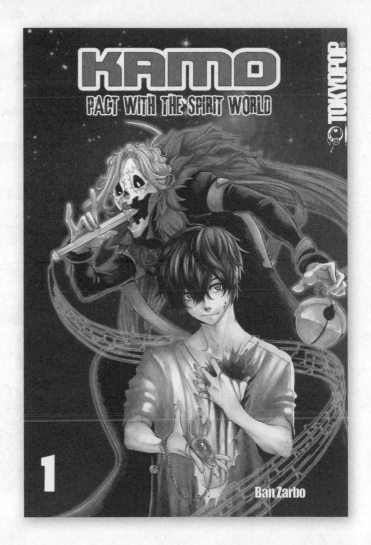

ACTION

Born with a failing heart, Kamo has fought death his whole life, but to no avail. As his body weakens and he readies to draw his final breath, he's visited by a powerful spirit named Crimson who offers him a deal: defeat and capture the souls of twelve spirits in exchange for a new heart. It seems too good to be true... and maybe it is. A pact with the spirit world... what could possibly go wrong?

TOKYOPOP

DEAR READERS,

Thank you for reading!

Have a question, suggestion, title recommendation, or just want to show some love? Visit us on social media, check out our website, or sign up to our newsletter for the latest release info and first dibs on exclusive sales and merchandise.

We appreciate your support, and can't wait to hear from you!

~ TOKYOPOP

@TOKYOPOP

We'd love to hear from you on our social media!

Scan code to visit
tokyopop.com/upcoming